Arbiter of Elegance

A BIOGRAPHY OF ROBERT ADAM

Arbiter of Elegance

A BIOGRAPHY OF ROBERT ADAM

Roderick Graham

BIRLINN

First published in 2009 by
Birlinn Limited
West Newington House
10 Newington Road
Edinburgh
EH9 1QS

www.birlinn.co.uk

ISBN13: 978 1 84158 802 5

British Library Cataloguing-in-Publication Data
A catalogue record for this book is available from the British Library.

Typeset by Iolaire Typesetting, Newtonmore
Printed and bound by MPG Books Ltd, Bodmin

Once again to
Fiona

Contents

ও৲

List of Illustrations

❧

William Adam by William Aikman (In a private collection)
Mary Adam by Allan Ramsay (Yale Center for British Art, Paul Mellon Collection)
John Adam by Francis Coates (In a private collection)
Robert Adam by George Willison (© National Portrait Gallery, London)
James Adam by Pompeo Batoni. (Baroness Knut-bone Collection)
Fort George. A model of military engineering.
Inverary Castle. A drawing by James Adam c1754. (Sir John Clerk Collection)
Dumfries House. Calm classicism.
Portrait of Charles, Lord Hope, and the Hon James Hope, with their bear leader. (Major P. T. Telfer Smollett Collection)
Caricature of Clérisseau by Pier Leone Ghezzi (© The Trustees of the British Museum).
View from Within the Rotunda of the Pantheon, by Clérisseau (*Clerk of Eldin Album*, RCAHMS © Sir Robert Maxwell Clerk, 11th Baronet of Penicuik)
View from Within the Rotunda of the Pantheon, by Robert Adam (*Clerk of Eldin Album*, RCAHMS © Sir Robert Maxwell Clerk, 11th Baronet of Penicuik)
Medallion of Robert Adam by Piranesi (*Campus Martius* by Piranesi, 1762)
Sketch for rebuilding Lisbon (Sir John Soane's Museum)
Design for a greenhouse for General Bland (Sir John Soane's Museum)
Detail of a Palace (Sir John Soane's Museum)
Kedleston House, South Front (The Courtauld Institute of Art, London)
Kedlston House, Saloon (The Courtauld Institute of Art, London)
Syon House, Entrance Hall (Collection of the Duke of Northumberland. Photograph by John Blakey)

ix

Syon House Ante Room (Collection of the Duke of Northumberland. Photograph by John Blakey)

Syon House Eating Room (Collection of the Duke of Northumberland. Photograph by John Blakey)

Syon House Drawing Room (Collection of the Duke of Northumberland. Photograph by John Blakey)

Syon House Long Gallery (Collection of the Duke of Northumberland. Photograph by John Blakey)

Croome Court Tapestry Room (National Trust)

Osterley Park Eating Room (The Courtauld Institute of Art, London)

Osterley Park Etruscan Dressing Room (National Trust)

Detail of a chimney piece, from *Diverse manieri d'adnoare I Cammini* by Piranesi Gianbatista, Rome 1749 (Trustees of the National Library of Scotland)

The Lanthorn of Demosthenes from *The Antiquities of Athens Measured and Delineated* by James Stuart (Trustees of the National Library of Scotland)

Frontispiece from *The Ruins of the Palace of Spalatro* by Robert and James Adam (Trustees of the National Library of Scotland)

'View of the Inside of the Temple of Jupiter', from *The Ruins of the Palace at Spalatro* (Trustees of the National Library of Scotland)

Carpet design for Mrs Montagu (Sir John Soane's Museum)

Ceiling Design for Mrs Montagu (Sir John Soane's Museum)

The Adelphi by Thomas Malton from *Picturesque Tour, 1796* (Trustees of the National Library of Scotland)

The Church at Mistley (Courtesy of *Country Life*)

Adam's sketch for the Bath House at Mistley (Courtesy of *Country Life*)

Register House, Edinburgh

Leith Street Elevation, Edinburgh. (Sir John Soane's Museum)

Robert Adam's idea for the South Bridge in Edinburgh, from *Architectural Heritage No XV* (Sir John Soane's Museum)

Edinburgh University Ground Story (Courtesy of *Country Life*)

Edinburgh University as built (Edinburgh University Library Centre for Research Collections)

Charlotte Square, Edinburgh. North side, Adam's 'Palace Front'

Charlotte Square, Edinburgh. West side, Reid's interruption

Culzean Castle

Culzean Castle, Oval Staircase (The Courtauld Institute of Art, London)

Introduction

❧

The eighteenth century has often been called 'the Age of Elegance' and no one person contributed more to its artistic eminence than Robert Adam.

During the eighteenth century, Scotland and England united their parliaments and endured two attempted rebellions by claimant dynasties. In Europe, Britain fought the wars of the Spanish and Austrian successions, the ridiculous War of Jenkin's Ear and the worldwide Seven Years War, thus establishing the foundations of the British Empire. For a moment these new foundations trembled slightly with the War of American Independence but by the end of the century, Britain was the most prosperous country in Europe and the most powerful in the world.

This prosperity was mainly enjoyed by the aristocracy whose role had become more decorative than militarily aggressive. With little further need for defensible living space, there was a greater desire for elegant town and country houses. There was a rising and wealthy middle class who wanted to spend their new-found wealth according to the latest standards of taste. They travelled continuously in Europe, in spite of 27 years of European wars, and, on the Grand Tour, embraced the tastes of classical Rome in literature and art.

The sectarian divisions of the previous century had coalesced into an uneasy peace inside the Church of England, and the European Enlightenment, with its roots in France, Holland and Scotland, abandoned blind acceptance of the past dogmas in favour of rational thought. However, the severe rationality of

Descartes was being softened by the humanistic scepticism of David Hume. This allowed emotion – or 'the passions' – to play a part in human activity, and left room for personal opinion.

This was especially true in making choices in matters of taste. Here the newly rich were often cast adrift on the dangerous seas of artistic fashion. Fortunately, however, there were guidebooks to this labyrinth of elegance and the newly prosperous could order their new homes 'off catalogue' by reference to a series of designs reaching back to the Roman architect Vitruvius in the first century AD. It was all too easy for the uninitiated merely to copy the classical past without innovation. Influencing noble minds whose taste had been formed on the Grand Tour and in the Classics schoolroom was a dangerous venture, undertaken only by the most confident.

Robert Adam literally went to the foundations of architecture, looking and commenting on nearly every building he saw from English Perpendicular to – in his four years in Europe – Renaissance and modern architecture. Above all, he studied and drew the ruins of classical Rome with a significant excursion to Split in Dalmatia. He could then not only offer his clients a catalogue of designs (although he did produce one), but also a sharply honed knowledge of the classical forms and a wealth of personal taste. He was also a thoroughly practical architect when it came to such mundane matters as central heating and plumbing, to the extent that, in his designs, central heating vents could be disguised as classical urns.

His researches led him to apply decorations using colours from Herculaneum and wall patterns from Etruria. In collaboration with Thomas Chippendale and Lancelot 'Capability' Brown he designed furniture for the interiors of his houses and gardens for the exteriors. Robert Adam felt that the completeness of a house evolved from a unity of design and, for all that he created very few buildings in their entirety, he designed every detail from keyhole covers to carpets. Door frames, mantelpieces, beds and, even on one occasion, a work bag for his patron's wife, all were given his total attention. For dining rooms – he called them 'eating rooms' – he favoured hard wall coverings, such as stucco, rather than damask, since it could more easily be cleaned and would not retain the smell of food. With his brother James he created a monumental urban housing development in the Adelphi – from the Greek ἀδελφοί, meaning brothers – although it brought him to the edge of bankruptcy. He designed theatres, greenhouses and castles, all of them innovative and individual.

Even today, in decorator's shops you may be guided to wallpapers and fabrics with 'Adam' colours and 'Adam' designs, many of which have no connection with his designs, but all cling to a name that, in terms of marketability, is still potent. His name has come down to us, not as the surname of an Edinburgh-schooled architect, but as an adjective in its own right. As a description of elegance, of the Enlightenment, of the best features of the eighteenth century, Robert Adam stands alone. He is the supreme arbiter of elegance.

A Note on Currency and Quotations

ॐ

In the eighteenth century the principal unit of British currency was the pound sterling (£). The pound was divided into 20 shillings (s) and a shilling into 12 pennies (pence d). Occasionally, guineas were used. One guinea was worth £1 1s. Also current was the pound Scots (£Sc) worth roughly a tenth of a pound sterling. The best guide to the contemporary values of these amounts can be calculated using www.measuringworth.com by Professors Lawrence H. Officer and Samuel H. Williamson. In 1750, a pound sterling was worth £138 in contemporary terms, but by 1790, probably as a result of the military adventures in the intervening years, had declined to being worth £93. There is, therefore, no simple multiplication factor which can accurately be used throughout. Multiplication by 100 gives no more than a very rough concept of eighteenth-century values.

In quoting from original sources I have made as few alterations as possible, only correcting errant spelling where it threatened to obscure meaning.

Acknowledgements

❧

I would like to thank Hugh Andrew, who, as managing director of Birlinn Ltd, encouraged me to write this book. Also at Birlinn the managing editor, Andrew Simmons, has steered me along the right path, while Seán Costello edited the text with sympathy and flair. Peter Burns tracked down the sometimes obscure pictures and drawings for the illustrations with stoical cheerfulness.

Needless to say library staffs are essential in the writing of such a book and I was made more than welcome by the issue staff at the National Archives of Scotland. The National Library of Scotland and Edinburgh University's new and elegant Centre for Research Collections provided eager and willing help. At one point in the National Library I was pursued out of the building by a member of the issue staff, who had traced a pamphlet we had both regarded as lost.

Also at the National Library, I was given encouragement from the beginning by Dr Iain Gordon Brown, Principal Curator of Manuscripts, who kindly loaned me many items from his own collection of Adam material.

Research on Robert Adam leads one inexorably to Sir John Soane's Museum in London's Lincoln Inn Fields and here I was given superb help by Stephen Astley, Curator of Drawings. I spent an amazing morning with him being shown the collection of several thousand drawings in the museum. He agreed to read the completed manuscript and then gave a considerable amount of time to making careful comments and corrections, while guiding me towards the most recent research. I am profoundly grateful.

The same corrective task was carried out by James Simpson and William Kay, both experts on the life and work of William Adam, who both deserve my thanks.

However, the first person to read the manuscript, as always, was my wife, Fiona, whose expert editing and critical acumen earned her my thanks and ill-tempered irritation in equal measure. I apologise for the paranoid irritation and reiterate the thanks.

Finally, and probably most importantly, on behalf of Birlinn Ltd and myself, I should like to thank Sir Robert M. Clerk Bt for allowing the publication of extracts from the Clerk of Penicuik papers which he has placed on deposit with the National Archives of Scotland, and without which I could not have written this book.

All of the above gave their help freely and unstintingly, but I take full responsibility for the use made of the material and any errors are mine.

CHAPTER ONE

Anarchy and Augustans

འ

At about half past eight o'clock on the morning of 8 September 1736 the eight-year-old Robert Adam walked the few hundred yards from his family's house to the street outside the High School of Edinburgh where he had been a pupil for two years. Every morning the boys would meet outside the school at the 'jube house' where they could buy 'jube', a species of tooth-rotting toffee, but on this morning the chatter was all about the events of the previous night when simmering discontent in the city had boiled over into a full-scale riot.

The cause of the discontent dated back to 14 April of that year when the public execution of a smuggler had taken place. Two men, Andrew Wilson and George Robertson, had been arrested for smuggling and for robbing the custom house where their confiscated goods were held; both were sentenced to hang. The new Custom Laws introduced by the prime minister Robert Walpole were, however, felt by many to be too severe, and the sentence was thus thought to be unjust. The men's attempt to escape from the Tolbooth jail had failed when Wilson, who was a burly man, became wedged in the window. Next day, they were taken to the High Kirk of St Giles for a church service before their execution, where Wilson, in an attempt to atone for his clumsiness, seized the guards, allowing Robertson to escape. The populace now felt that Wilson should be spared but he was duly taken to the Grassmarket and hanged. The attendant crowd soon turned into a mob and the commander of the Town Guard, one Captain John Porteous, panicked and ordered his troops to open fire, killing 6 citizens and wounding 20 others. His rashness had to be punished and he was arraigned for murder and confined in the Tolbooth. However, since Porteous was a close friend of General Wade, the commander of the regular troops in Scotland, he expected a more or less automatic pardon would be forthcoming on 8 September, the day fixed for his execution.

For weeks the city had been gripped with talk of nothing else, and the eight-year-old Robert had, far beyond his bedtime, often overheard his father's colleagues debate the justice of such a pardon. This debate came to an abrupt end on the night of 7 September when a mob of 4,000 people took the law into their own hands, swept up to the Tolbooth and broke into the jail. Porteous was carried down to the Grassmarket and a makeshift gallows was erected using a dyer's pole on the south side of the market. A shopkeeper found men searching her shop for a rope and 'the woman asked if it was to hang Porteous, and when they answered in the affirmative, she told them they were welcome to all she had of those articles. They coolly took off what they required, and laid a guinea on the counter as payment; ostentatious to mark that they "did all in honour".'[1] Porteous was duly hanged by this lynch mob. They may have felt themselves to be honourable, but they were not an efficient mob since Porteous was cut down and re-hanged three times before he died just before one o'clock on 8 September, the day officially fixed for his execution.

Robert, like his schoolfellows, had heard the clamour in the night and now the boys were gossiping like starlings as they filled in the background for themselves with the goriest details they could invent. These schoolboys were from prosperous families and even at their comparatively early age would be expected to have opinions of their own. Robert, like his companions, was dressed as a miniature adult, and was at that time of life which the eighteenth century found so inconvenient. As is evident from the portraiture of the period, childhood was a stage of life best ignored and passed through as quickly as possible. In the lower classes children were put to profitable work as soon as they were fit for labour, while children of Robert's class and age would dress as adults and be expected either to behave as grown-ups or to remain invisible.

The boys would be careful as to how they expressed themselves, since in conversation at the High School only southern English was allowed and *Decurios*, or prefects, were appointed to eavesdrop on their schoolfellows and report any lapses into Scots. A first offence was punished by a caning and a second was dealt with more severely by receiving a public flogging before the whole school. Conversation in Latin was strongly encouraged and senior boys would embarrass their junior fellows by addressing them in more or less fluent Latin. Indeed, in 1718 the school was called 'a club for the cultivation of Greek and Roman literature'.

The High School of Edinburgh had been founded in the Abbey of Holyroodhouse in 1127 and had had a vivid history, showing a penchant for independent action. In 1595, when the town council, which had taken over control of the school in 1519, refused to grant an already established holiday, the scholars barricaded themselves inside the building to begin the first 'sit-in' in history. The headmaster, Hercules Rollock, summoned the town council along with the Town Guard, and John MacMorran, a magistrate, called on the boys to surrender. The ringleader of the schoolboys, one William Sinclair, whose father was a secretary to the Privy Council, promptly shot MacMorran dead. The result of this was that the holiday was granted as a right in perpetuity, while the now hugely embarrassed town council investigated the matter of the murder. Given his father's position it is unsurprising that Sinclair walked free and the council minutes of the investigation are now 'lost'. The tradition of rowdiness continued and in 1716 disorder broke out again when the pupils broke every window in the school and in the nearby Lady Yester's church. The mob's action in hanging Porteous would have been seen in Edinburgh as part of a tradition of independently minded people deciding on right and wrong with little regard for the legal niceties.

The school had five masters under the headmaster, or rector, John Lees, who was authorised to charge four shillings a quarter from each boy in his class and one shilling from each pupil in the other classes in addition to his annual salary of £Sc33 6s 8d. Masters got a quarterly fee of 4s and classical masters got £20

3

annually. The school building, in Blackfriars Wynd, was only a two or three-minute walk from Robert Adam's home and was an example of the old traditions of Scots architecture, built on two storeys with crow-stepped gables and tower staircases enclosing four classrooms.

Robert's education had started in 1734 when he was six years old. He completed the exercises in Despouter's Latin grammar (published in 1530), and by the second year all classes were conducted in Latin. The boys were taught to read Virgil, Horace, Sallust and parts of Cicero, until their final year when they were taught by the rector himself, who read to them from Livy. There was also instruction in the Protestant religion and the boys were allowed to take breaks from Latin to march round the classrooms singing metrical psalms. By 1742, just in time for Robert, the school had purchased two terrestrial globes and, we presume, started to teach geography. So Robert, who was consistently first or second in his class, learned that the ideal world was that of Augustan Rome, with Cicero as the ideal of Roman virtue.

The contrast between the anarchic hurly-burly of eighteenth-century Edinburgh and the Augustan formality of Cicero's oratory stimulated Robert's spirit, giving him a love of contrasts and a certainty of personal style that served him faithfully throughout the rest of his life. Independent thought, as demonstrated by the Porteous mob, could be justified even within the boundaries of classical rigour, and Robert Adam would spend his career balancing the rigour of classicism with his own inventive and elegant flamboyance.

In his notes for a proposed biography, John Clerk of Eldin, Robert's brother-in-law, said flatteringly of him:

In every branch of learning Robert displayed the natural quickness of his parts, he was equally excellent and made rapid progress in the languages, in mathematics and in natural philosophy; but in his earlier years, and during an attentive application to these studies he gave proofs of the most decided predilection for those finer arts in which he afterwards so much

4

excelled. Architecture and landscape painting were his favourite amusements and very sedulously occupied his leisure hours. Besides the closest application to drawing and the other studies necessary to his profession, he has an excellent voice. Sung delightfully well, was of such a lively genius and spirit that from his youth and through the whole course of his life he was the darling and the admiration of the numerous men of the age resorting to his father's house.'[2]

Robert Adam's father was William Adam, whose family dated back to an ancestor who had accompanied Lord James Douglas on an expedition to Spain in 1330, while another forbear, John Adam, 'a man of spirit and fortitude', died at Flodden in 1513. His great-great-grandson Archibald married Mary Hay, daughter of a Montrose merchant and they bred a second son John, a stonemason who lived at Linktown of Abbotshall, a village to the south of Kirkcaldy on the Fife coast. There William Adam was born and baptised on 24 October 1689. Clerk of Eldin talks of his 'frugal ancestors' and describes William as 'an only son' but William's will tells a different story. In the will he acknowledged a debt of £33 9s to both Patrick Adam, merchant in Kingston, Jamaica, and to his niece Peggy Adam. Patrick Adam was William's first cousin. He died in 1747.

William possibly attended the local grammar school in Kirkcaldy, leaving in 1704 to become an apprenticed mason in the Guild of Hammermen in the town. Now aged 15, he served this apprenticeship as a draughtsman to architect William Bruce during the restoration of the Palace of Holyroodhouse. Bruce was a senior civil servant as well as an architect, but with noticeable Jacobite tendencies. As William Adam grew up he distanced himself from Bruce by supporting the Whig causes of Parliament and Protestantism. He was keen to call himself 'Architect' and to prefix his name with 'Mr', aspiring to the rank of gentleman. In this he was only partially successful and as late as 1850 William Henry Playfair declared that 'architecture is not a profession to be followed by gentlemen in this country'.

5

These attitudes caused William Adam no disquiet since for him business came before either the academic study of architecture or the acquisition of gentlemanly status.

William travelled in Europe – probably in 1714 – and on 8 May 1714 started the manufacture of Dutch pantiles in the Linktown Brickworks.[3] Brick was a comparatively recent building material and it is typical of a commercially-minded innovator like William Adam to make sure that he owned the means of production for the raw materials which would be used in the new fashion. William also brought back a model of a Dutch barley kiln. By 1716, he was 'master of the tile manufactory in the Links of Kirkaldy and of the barley manufactory at Bell's Mill [near the present Dean Bridge] in Edinburgh'[4].

His diversification brought him prosperity and he formed a partnership with William Robertson, a fellow entrepreneur. Robertson had lost the enormous sum of £1,000 in the disastrous Darien Scheme of 1689 but had recovered enough to buy a lease on the coalmines at nearby Abbotshall in Fife. The business arrangement was strengthened when, on 30 May 1716 William married Robertson's daughter, Mary, and their first child, a daughter, Janet, was baptised on 28 July 1717. William moved into his father-in-law's house of Gladney, in Linktown, a substantial two-storey house with Ionic pilasters and pedimented Dutch gables. He was now recognised by the town council as a 'measurer in Linktown'. Clerk of Eldin paid him the compliment of describing him as 'a man of distinguished genius, inventive enterprise and engaging address'[5]. The compliment, however, contains more than a hint of disapproval for a man who was in reality a building contractor and business entrepreneur.

At this time, the dividing line between contractor and architect was extremely blurred and William had already, in 1715, drawn up plans for the building of a house at Makerstoun in Roxburghshire. It has been described as 'British, yet recognisably Scots; serious yet never dull.'[6]

Sir John Clerk of Penicuik 'could not enough admire the enterprising temper of the proprietor who had at the time under his own care near to twenty general projects – Barley Mills, Timber Mills, Coal Works, Salt Pans, Marble Works, Highways, Farms-houses of his own a-building and houses belonging to others not a few.'[7]

William's career was flourishing and on 17 January 1721 he signed a contract to build additions to Hopetoun House. This great house had been commissioned by Lady Margaret Hope for her son Sir Charles. This family had come to Scotland when Jean de Hope arrived from France in 1547 as part of the train of the ill-starred Queen Madeleine: ill-starred, since she died within a month of her arrival. Jean, now renamed John Hope, set up business as a merchant in Edinburgh and his grandson was knighted as Sir John Hopetoun. Sir John's son, another John, saved the Duke of York, later James II, from drowning, although John himself was drowned in the effort. In gratitude, the king ennobled John's son, Charles, as the first Earl of Hopetoun.

The earl was a prime example of the emergent nobleman of the eighteenth century. No longer expected to fight for wealth, they could now display their love of culture by building their country houses. They would have done well to take heed of the advice of Sir Roger Pratt, who had built his own stately home at Coleshill in Wiltshire in the 1660s. Pratt was appointed commissioner for the rebuilding of London by Charles II and had travelled widely in Europe. He objected strongly to the model of one the proposed churches by 'Dr Renne'. The church was St Paul's Cathedral and thankfully Pratt's opinion was ignored. But for the aspiring nobleman his advice was sound: 'First resolve with yourself what house will be answerable to your purse and estate, and after you have pitched upon the number of rooms and the dimensions of each, and desire in some measure to make use of whatsoever you have either observed, or heard to be excellent elsewhere, then if you be not able to handsomely contrive it yourself, get some ingenious gentleman who has seen much of that kind abroad and been somewhat versed in the best authors of architecture: viz. Palladio, Scamozzi, Serlio, etc., to do it for you and to give you a design on paper.'[8]

While seeking an architect for his house, Hopetoun followed these precepts and took advice from the enthusiastic land improver Sir Thomas Hope, who had assumed the title of Lord Rankeillour, and from the clergyman draughtsman Alexander Edward. They settled on William Bruce, who was known as the 'Kit Wren of Scotland', despite the fact that he had never trained as an architect, although according to J.G. Dunbar, 'it seems likely that an inherent interest in the subject was developed both by theoretical studies and by travel.'[9] A perfect description of the dilettante practitioner. Sir John Summerson said of him, 'On the death in 1710, of Sir William Bruce, Scotland's last Court Architect, the architecture of the country was in a condition of remote provincialism from which it was not to emerge for half a century.'[10] As we shall see, this statement was not entirely true. Since Bruce had travelled to Holland and possibly to France, he was aware of the latest continental styles and could supply designs for the changing fashion in Scotland where the traditional fortified tower house was giving way to the elegant country house. An outstanding example of this is Bruce's own Kinross House, with its central hall facing west to the front drive and then east to a formal garden, with paths leading the eye to Loch Leven and the view of the ruined castle on its island.

These changes in fashion were first seen when the designs of Andrea Palladio were used as a basis for architectural design. These in turn prompted a return to the classical styles of Greece and Rome as described by Marcus Pollio Vitruvius, a Roman architect and military engineer who had served under the emperor Augustus and who had written *De Architectura Libri Decem* in about 27 AD. It was the only extant treatise on Roman architecture. Palladio, born Andrea di Pietro della Gondola in 1518 in Vicenza, was himself influenced not only by Vitruvius but also by the Bolognese architectural historian Sebastiano Serlio, who produced the first printed books of designs. It now became essential for all future architects to produce such books since they comprised a folio of designs from which clients could choose. The most influential of these practical books of designs was, without doubt, *I Quattro Libri dell'Architettura*, published in 1570 in Venice by Palladio.

Classical design was already appearing in Scotland. The architect James Smith was consulted by the Earl of Lothian in the 1690s because 'he really hath the best skill of them all'[11]. It seems that Smith had attended the Scots College in Rome in 1671–75 but 'became apostate', and returned to Scotland; 'seems' since James Smith was not an uncommon name in the period. But Smith did complete a large folio of drawings and many aspects of his buildings have roots in the designs of Andrea Palladio. These influences are echoed by Colen Campbell, born in Scotland in 1676, who may have known Smith and for whom the influence of Palladio was strong.

Palladio's influence throughout Britain was greatly advanced by Colen Campbell who, in 1712, was commissioned to build a house for Sir Richard Child at Wanstead in Essex. This he did totally according to Palladio's principles. In 1715, he published the *vade mecum* for early eighteenth-century architects, *Vitruvius Britannicus*. This was a record of the principal buildings of the era and included several, not always accurate, reproductions, of Palladio's *I Quatro Libri*. Some of these drawings show the influence of Smith. Campbell followed the success of the book with two more volumes and thereby laid down the strict rules for the newly fashionable classicism. It was a highly personal view of Palladio, who had himself given a personal view of Vitruvius and Serlio. So it was that the principles of ancient Roman architecture arrived in eighteenth century Britain severely filtered by contemporary architects. However, Alexander Pope was convinced that a door to classical architecture had been opened.

> Jones and Palladio to themselves restore
> And be whate're Vitruvius was before.[12]

Inigo Jones had travelled to Italy and possessed heavily annotated copies of Palladio's books. Although nearly 60 years his junior – Jones was born in 1573 – he became Palladio's most ardent disciple and the most fashionable architect in England. Jones also met Vicenzo Scamozzi, whose *Idea dell'Architettura universale* followed Palladian ideals, and who finished Palladio's Rotonda, a villa regarded as the classical ideal. However, 'The reformers of the age of the Enlightenment understood only the rationalist Palladio of the *Quatro Libri* and the drawings which had passed fortuitously into England, the most enthusiastic and influential of Palladian nations. They hardly knew him at first hand.'[13] For that they would have to visit Italy themselves.

There were many books by followers of Palladio already in existence as other European architects published their designs. One popular choice of patterns was *Manière de Bastir*, a book of designs by Le Muet, published in 1647. Later in the century the building of Heriot's Hospital in Edinburgh was started using a plan taken from Sebastiano Serlio's *Seventh Book of Architecture*. Internal features in the Edinburgh building came not only from a Farnese villa but also from the designs of Alexandro Francini. The hospital, now a school, boasts over 200 windows in which no single design is repeated.

At Hopetoun House Bruce created a mansion in the best modern style based on a Greek cross around an octagonal central staircase. By 1702, he had built two convex colonnades to connect the main house to the two service blocks. Bruce's love of practicality was reflected in the comparatively recent fashion of the rooms in the house having discrete functions such as dining, withdrawing and bedchambers. Bruce had seen the grandest expression of this when he visited Versailles, where Louis XIV's political principles of absolutism in politics were expressed in stone and glass. The main entrance to Hopetoun was a garden room giving on to a parterre with box hedges carved into crowns and Prince of Wales' feathers, thus linking house and garden in 'the combination of unity and grandeur'. Hopetoun House was Bruce's apotheosis.

Bruce may have introduced many architectural ideas, but he was a poor draughtsman and simply followed the drawings then available from Europe. Sir John Clerk of Penicuik said that Bruce was 'the chief introducer of Architecture in this country'. But Bruce was no innovator, but a walking catalogue of other men's tastes which he recommended to his clients; his draughtsmen and decorators then simply carried out their wishes. One of those draughtsmen was William Adam, his apprentice at Holyrood. In contrast to the sophisticated and well-connected Bruce, it has been said of William Adam, 'He was no patrician connoisseur but a builder with a little knowledge, and on the make.'[14]

Adam's opportunity for renown also came at Hopetoun House. Charles, the first Earl of Hopetoun, had married the sister of the Marquess of Annandale who was a classical enthusiast and a recent Grand Tourist to Italy. He had brought a collection of Roman marbles back from Italy, some of which were incorporated into the redesign of Hopetoun. Bruce's original building was classically correct for the period in which it was built, but fashion had moved forward with great speed and the earl, much influenced by his wife and his aesthetically minded brother-in-law, wanted to display the extent of his taste as well as his mastery of current fashions. In January 1721, he commissioned William Adam to replace one wing. Inevitably this plan grew to encompass a total remodelling of the house. Adam redesigned Bruce's frontage by adding Corinthian pilasters and making round-arched windows with grotesque heads on the keystones. He removed Bruce's colonnade and built another, this time concave and surmounted by a balustrade. There was to be a double curving stairway leading to a platform in front of the main entrance, but the construction of this feature, or perron, was abandoned in a later plan. Giant pilasters appeared at the angles. These were of the Corinthian order, but William's house at Gladney, which it is likely he himself designed, had very similar, if Ionic, giant pilasters. At Hopetoun he enclosed Bruce's entrance to make a garden room with spectacular vistas of the grounds but left the interiors of the western side of the house virtually as Bruce had created them. He did, however, install numerous marble fireplaces and chimney pieces. The effect is one of lavish splendour displayed in classical style, but, as with so many of William's buildings, it is heavy-handed and derivative. The earl, however, was delighted and he settled all of William's accounts without even checking the amounts.

Now established as Scotland's leading architect, Adam went on to renovate, or modernise, Floors Castle for the Duke of Roxburghe, Taymouth Castle for the Earl of Breadalbane, Redbraes Castle, the Drum and Arniston House. The 1720s was a boom time for architects and builders as periods of peace had allowed the aristocracy to visit Europe and experience the latest fashions there. The old traditions of Scots building were being swept away as solidity and defence were being replaced by elegance and decoration.

Thus the fashion of the time was dominated by the antique styles as determined by certain arbiters of taste. Of their work, Geoffrey Beard has said, 'In the construction of these buildings imagination was allowed little room'[15], and Sir John Summerson declared, 'With a fanaticism that at times verged on the ludicrous they adhered tenaciously to the holy script of Andrea Palladio'[16]. William Adam's library had books by Palladio, Vitruvius, (four copies) Serlio, and Scamozzi, the sixteenth-century town planner, 'all standard works for any serious architect'[17]. By 1726 he owned the first two volumes of Colen Campbell's *Vitruvius Britannicus* and the Earl of Stair became his patron. William Adam had arrived, not quite in polite society, but among the prosperous middle class. He had become the arbiter of architecture in Scotland.

'He had also become immensely rich since his work as a contractor continued to flourish in tandem with his work as an architect. By 1727, he owned the colliery and salt-works at Tranent and Cockenzie, all colliers, coal bearers, salters and servants [these men were, to all intents and purposes, serfs, and could be bought and sold as merchandise] gins wagons, tools and utensils.' There were timber yards at Leith and in 1728 he bought the glass works at Dirleton. 'To a large extent he appears to have dominated the Scottish construction industry and, like builders in all ages, he made a lot of money.'[18]

Adam did not, however, have his own way with all his clients and he was definitely overruled by Sir John Clerk of Penicuik. Clerk, the great-grandson of the poet William Drummond of Hawthornden, had set the fashion for things Italian and, as an arbiter of taste, was nicknamed 'the Lord Burlington of Scotland'. (Burlington, who published *Fabriche Antiche Designate da Andrea Palladio* in 1730, was the leading aesthete in England and the strongest proponent of Palladio's ideals as the finest achievement of architectural taste.) Born in 1676, Clerk was a baronet, an advocate and a member of the Westminster parliament who had travelled widely in Europe. He had studied at Leyden and on the Grand Tour had spent time in Rome to study music with Corelli. He was the owner of extensive coalmines as well as being an enthusiastic agricultural improver and this, combined with the colossal profit from his mines, made him one of the wealthiest men in Scotland. In 1723, he employed William Adam to build him a house at Mavisbank, a few miles south of Edinburgh. The relationship between client and architect was clearly spelled out by Clerk: 'In May 1723, I not only finished my designs for the house of Mavisbank under the correction of one Mr Adams . . .'[19] Adam was retained in an advisory capacity and supplied some of the craftsmen. (William, followed by his sons, paid little regard to the spelling of his name and 'Adams' was used indiscriminately and interchangeably with 'Adam'.)

William Adam descended on the site at Mavisbank with 23 masons and even at the completion of the building he had 11 men still on site. He did not, however, have his copy of Palladio's designs and had to borrow one from his patron. This was essential since the design for the roof was based on that of the Basilica in Vicenza and the outlying pavilions were copied from Palladio's Villa Barbaro. It was, therefore, a strictly Palladian structure. Clerk firmly believed that 'the ancient Greek and Roman structures, or the designs of them by Palladio and others, ought to be standards fit for the imitation of our modern architects'[20]. The house was a five-bay villa of two storeys surmounted by a pediment with sculptures and a domed roof. Adam wanted to add another storey but Clerk refused to accept this idea, and so this house remained looking like an elegant villa in the suburbs of imperial Rome. The antiquarian Roger Gale wrote to his brother-in-law William Stukeley that the house was 'in a true Palladio taste'[21]. Modern architectural historians have described it as 'arguably the most important single example of early eighteenth-century Scottish architecture'.[22]

Sir John and William disagreed over the internal decoration of the house, with Sir John wanting restraint and William eager to give free rein to Samuel Calderwood, his stucco artist. Stucco, in its purest form, is a fine plaster made from gypsum and powdered marble. It could be manufactured in an endless range of thicknesses, and is capable of being moulded into every kind of shape for application to walls, into cornices, or into ceiling decorations. At its thinnest it could serve as the final coat of plaster before painting or be used on exteriors to cover rough stone or brick. It was usually applied in three coats of increasing thinness ending with a final coat rich in lime and, for complete perfection, mixed with white Carrera marble. The mixture was then left to stand for up to three months. The acknowledged masters of this technique were Italian *stuccatori* but many British artisans became expert in its use. With much reluctance on the part of the trade guilds, 'by the mid eighteenth century foreign artists were frequently part of an English team of decorators'[23]. In the case of Mavisbank the opinions of Sir John prevailed and the interiors were plainer than most of William Adam's.

William visited London in March 1727 in the company of Sir John, who was buying marbles and pictures for Mavisbank, and there he met Lord Burlington. He studied the churches of St Mary-le-Strand and St Martin-in-the-Fields, both by fellow Scot James Gibbs, and visited Vanburgh's Blenheim Palace. Being the businessman that he was, he also started to raise subscriptions for a book of engravings of his own designs – or, rather, of the designs of others as interpreted by him – to be published as *Vitruvius Scoticus*.

William Adam's next move was obviously to profit from his reputation by operating his business from Scotland's capital city.

Edinburgh was, after all, where the bulk of his clients had their town houses and William already had a useful network of contacts in the city. On 21 February 1728 the town council of Edinburgh voted to admit William as a Burgess, 'gratis for services done to the good toune'[24]. This was essential to enable William to carry out his business.

In other words William's networking was proving its worth. His family was growing; he now had a son, John, born in 1721, and his wife Mary was four months pregnant. To allow her to avoid the extra disruption of packing and decoration he delayed his move to the capital during her lying-in and his second son, Robert, was born in Gladney House, Abbotshall, on 3 July 1728. He was baptised in the parish church of Abbotshall. Shortly afterwards William became a citizen of Edinburgh, where, in a wise piece of speculation, he had already bought an estate in North Merchiston, to the south of the capital. It would eventually be occupied by his son, John, and his family.

The eighteenth-century city of Edinburgh was an anthill of humanity crowding around the the principal thoroughfare, the High Street, which clung to the spine of rock running eastwards from the castle sitting on top of its cliffs, down to the Palace of Holyroodhouse. The palace was a mile away and situated in the open parkland at the foot of Arthur's Seat, a volcanic plug dating from the time before the dinosaurs. The city proper was still mediaeval in design and was bounded by the Flodden Wall, hastily erected in 1513, and now of no practical use except to define the limits of the city for the levying of tolls. In William Adam's time the massive toll gates at the Netherbow were still standing at the eastern end of the city, and were not pulled down until 1764. At the western entrance to the city, lying below the castle, was the West Port, which acted as access to the Grassmarket where incoming livestock could graze, for a fee, before sale. The Grassmarket was also the site of the gallows. At the eastern end of the Grassmarket one narrow curving street, the West Bow, led steeply up to join the High Street while the Cowgate ran out of the Grassmarket down-hill to the south of, and parallel to, the High Street. Like the ribs of a gigantic animal, vertiginous 'wynds' – narrow lanes roughly cobbled and perilous to all but locals – connected the Cowgate to the High Street at close intervals. 'So well accustomed are the Scotch to that position of the body required in descending these declivities, that I have seen a Scotch girl run down them in pattens.'[25] (Pattens were the wooden overshoes worn to raise one's clothing above the filth of the street.) Wynds also led northwards from the High Street to the Nor' Loch, on the edge of which were the fleshing houses and butcher's markets. Beyond the loch to the north rose a gentle hill on which were the Barefoot Parks, as yet largely unoccupied. Some of the first buildings to appear on these parks would be the work of Robert Adam.

Since none of the houses in the city had any kind of running water, except what was fetched manually from the various wells, all kinds of waste – human, vegetable, cooked and uncooked – was kept until ten in the evening, when to the beat of the city drum, all the waste was simply thrown out of the windows into the street below after a cry of 'Gardyloo!' – thought to be a corruption of the French *'gardez l'eau'*. According to David Hume 'a chamber pot is a very formidable weapon in Edinburgh.'[26] Occasionally passers-by, hearing the cry and, quite reasonably not wanting a baptism of filth, would respond hopefully with 'Haud yer hand!' Sometimes the plea would be effective. The stinking filth – the 'Flowers of Edinburgh' – lay until morning when it was partially swept away.

The houses themselves were particular to Edinburgh, since being built on the narrow spine of rock, they could not expand sideways, but instead rose seven to eight storeys high, forming what Benjamin Franklin called 'perpendicular streets' with the shopkeepers living above their premises on the first floors. The second and third floors – not too far to climb and far enough away from the smell of the street – were the prime positions, often inhabited by the nobility. The remaining floors – 'lands' – climbed in height while falling in price to the very attics where the poorest tenants lived. Not, however, the very poorest in Edinburgh, who simply found whatever shelter they could whenever they could. Since all these 'lands' shared a common staircase there was an informal democracy, as artisans passed high court judges and shopkeepers on the narrow, often damp and slippery, stairs. Some of these tenements were built of wood – a practice which was strictly forbidden – and fires were frequent. Even today the entrances to these properties have a dark and sinister appearance, often up narrow alleyways, or 'closes', but in the eighteenth century these entrances could lead to apartments of some luxury. Sir John Clerk had a tenement at the head of Blackfriars Wynd on the High Street consisting of an 'outer room', kitchen, dining room, bedroom and closet, as well as a drawing room on the third floor, two more bedrooms and another closet on the fourth floor and a cellar 'at the foot of the turnpike'. There were no rooms for servants and they slept wherever they could: the inside of a wardrobe was a favourite spot. These rooms were wainscoted with painted ceilings, and crystal sitting on mahogany tables glittered beside the silverware in the candlelight. Silver wall sconces reflected the velvets and silks of the inhabitants as the finest claret washed down venison ragout brought from the family estates and the conversations turned to politics and philosophy, although, later in the evening, as the French brandy appeared and the ladies retired, scandal and obscene verse might come to dominate the conversations.

There would be scandal enough available for gossip, since east of the Netherbow and beyond the Flodden Wall lay the downhill continuation of the High Street, now called the Canongate. This had been a separate borough, and was not incorporated into Edinburgh until 1636, with its own tolbooth, jail and two huge inns providing stabling for over 100 horses. But the Canongate had a mixed population and by 1769 it housed '2 dukes, 16 earls, 2 dowager countesses, 7 lords, 7 lords of session [law lords], 13 baronets, 4 commanders of forces, 4 men of eminence.'[27] It was also home to so many brothels of such variety that anyone suffering from venereal disease was said to be wearing 'Canongate breeches'. Here were the oyster taverns selling ale, porter and oysters to the poorest of the population.

Edinburgh was a city of huge contrasts, with a population of nearly 50,000 compared to London's 650,000; it had a Royal Palace but no monarch; a Parliament Hall but no parliament, but it was becoming a centre for intellectual debate like no other. The professors of the university met weekly in Ranken's Tavern in Hunter Square where they debated philosophy and politics while emptying claret bottles at a furious rate. In his *Traditions of Edinburgh*, Robert Chambers cites over 40 clubs of all sorts, from the pornographic Beggar's Benison to the Sweating, where members drank until midnight, then roamed the streets looking for – and usually finding – violence; from the Soaping Club where members composed extemporary obscene verse – James Boswell was a keen member – all the way to the Philosophical and the Select where Adam Smith and David Hume led debates on every subject under the sun. The Philosophical eventually became the Royal Society of Edinburgh. There were student debating clubs where the radical advocate Henry Home encouraged alcohol-fuelled discussions challenging even the very principles of the law.

The law courts, when in session, brought colour to the High Street as judges, in their scarlet gowns, walked from their homes to the court. Lord Monboddo would even brave the rain in his finery but would send his wig ahead of him in a sedan chair, wigs being expensive. The sedan chairmen were all Gaelic-speaking Highlanders and fiercely contested their right of way in their own tongue. By the Mercat Cross, where minor offenders were stood in the pillory or were nailed by their ears to a board, the 'cadies' would congregate. These were men of all work – messengers, porters, or deliverymen – and in spite of having disreputable appearances, were scrupulously honest. They were also a fount of gossip and knew the whereabouts of everyone in the city.

At 11.30 in the morning the bells of St Giles – the gill-bells – rang to remind the citizenry that it was time to have a gill of whatever was the liquor of their choice. For the poor it was time for porter or whisky while on the judge's bench a decanter of brandy would appear. In eighteenth-century Edinburgh the law was often administered through a haze of alcohol or throbbing hangovers. However, Mr Amyat, pharmacist to George II, declared that he could stand by Edinburgh's Mercat Cross and, in the space of a few minutes, shake 50 men of genius by the hand. The city of Robert Adam's youth was the birthplace of the Scottish Enlightenment

William Adam set up house at the foot of Niddry's Wynd, leading off the Cowgate. His tenement, comparable to Sir John Clerk's but with a fractionally less fashionable address, contained a dining room, drawing room, five bedrooms and closets, with a kitchen and pantry as well as two cellars and three attic rooms. There would be clients aplenty within easy walking distance and William could be part of the Edinburgh tradition of 'living above the shop'. Fashionable Edinburgh flocked to Niddry's Wynd in 1763 when Robert Mylne designed St Cecilia's Hall, Edinburgh's first concert hall, to stand at the junction of the wynd and the Cowgate.

Robert Adam's first memories were of Edinburgh and John Clerk of Eldin tells of his early precocity: 'He was, from his infancy, of a feeble constitution which frequently seems the attendant of genius and refined taste. It was early discerned that in him they were united, hardly could this infant's hand hold a pencil when he discovered by his childish production that in a riper season he would charm the world with those that flow from it.'[28] Clerk of Eldin became Robert's brother-in-law and a merchant in the Luckenboooths, a range of shops built along the north side of St Giles' Kirk in Edinburgh. Clerk became an expert on naval strategy.

William was soon appointed 'Clerk and Storekeeper of the Works in Scotland'. In 1730 he became 'Mason to the Board of Ordnance in North Britain'. These positions were highly lucrative and were no sinecures, since the mason was responsible for the maintenance of the Palace of Holyroodhouse and other royal buildings as well as being the contractor for all military building work carried out in Scotland.

The reason for this increased military presence would be found in a jittery London. In 1715, England had seen its eight-year-old partner in parliament convulsed by an attempt to restore the Stewart monarchy, an attempt which had come to an end at the battle of Sheriffmuir. Then in 1718 one Cardinal Alberoni hatched a plot of restoration, but his fleet got no further than Corunna when it was wrecked in a storm. However, the supporting force of 2 frigates and 307 Spanish infantry landed at Stornoway on the Isle of Lewis under the command of George Keith, Earl Marischal. They were unaware that, after the shipwrecks, the main force had abandoned the attempted restoration and the army was riven by internal disputes. When the tiny, squabbling, invasion force reached Glenshiel on 9 June they were easily routed and the thoroughly disheartened Spaniards were sent home, while the Scottish elements in the uprising went unpunished.

After the 1715 Rising, a Disarming Act had forbidden the Highlanders to carry weapons in public. This simply meant that the weapons were kept at home. A form of Highland militia, the Highland Companies, only had time to be renamed the Black Watch before it was temporarily disbanded in 1717. In 1722 the fanatically Tory Bishop of Rochester, Francis Atterbury, was involved in a restoration plot and there were rumours of a further landing in Scotland. The rumours were unfounded but the bishop was exiled for life. In London, parliament was now thoroughly alarmed – especially after the crash of the South Sea Bubble in 1720, when many fortunes had been lost and national confidence shaken. Not unnaturally, parliament wanted to know the true state of the Highlands. Lord Lovat, a Highland landowner sitting in the London parliament, duly obliged with a report declaring that blackmail was endemic, disturbances were increasing, that only the very few law-abiding Highlanders had disarmed and, finally, that Jacobite supporters everywhere were covertly gaining positions of authority. 'The use of arms in the Highlands will never be laid aside till, by degrees, they begin to find they have nothing to do with them.'[29] This was not the news that London had wanted to receive.

An ill-advised tax on malt of 3d a bushel in 1725 led to riots in Shawfield, Glasgow, with the militia being called out and shots being fired. The view from Westminster was that Scotland was destined to be a riotous partner in the new United Kingdom with the Highlands leading the lawlessness. To control this vast area there were four government garrisons: at Inverlochy above Loch Lomond, at Ruthven beside Kingussie, at Bernera on the West coast, and at Kilchumen on Loch Ness, with little in the way of a road network to connect them. Each fort held a permanent garrison of 30 Highlanders employed to act as guides to the regular troops, should they be deployed. The forts were as isolated as the American army forts in the Far West a century and a half later.

To improve the military presence London appointed General George Wade as commander-in-chief in Scotland in 1725. He arrived in time for the Shawfield riots and quickly realised that a firm hand was needed to bring Scotland under control. His priorities were the provision of good intelligence and speedy communications and, for the first, he established a network of paid informers – one of whom was the famous Rob Roy MacGregor – while for the second, he launched an extensive programme of road building. Inevitably, as Mason to the Board of Ordnance, this involved William Adam, and left us with one of Scotland's most elegant bridges. Featuring five arches and four obelisks, it spans the river Tay at Aberfeldy, 20 miles north-west of Perth. William was proud enough of the bridge to include an engraving of it in *Vitruvius Scoticus*. His firm was also employed as the contractor in rebuilding the forts at Fort William and Kilchumen, now renamed Fort Augustus.

These military contracts did mean that he was becoming more than just comfortably rich, and, still ambitious to be a gentleman, in 1731 he bought the estate of Blair Crambeth in Kinross for £Sc8,010 (£667 10s sterling). He set about building a modern extension and renovating the existing structures, mainly for the use of the factor and for occasional use by William. William described the existing estate as 'russet land' and built a long two-storey house on ground rising to the east where he finished the house with a square tower. His grandson, also William, raised a memorial stone in the garden telling that his grandfather 'began with a spirit of enterprise and with a forecast greatly in advance of that age to improve and plant this domain, then a wild and untended moor'.[30] William went on to buy the adjacent estates of Dowhill, Wood End and Ditch End. By 1747 his land extended over 3,000 acres. It included a profitable coalmine, beside which he built a village for the miners which he called Maryburgh as a tribute to his wife. His increasing prosperity now seemed un-stoppable.

This prosperity came at a price, since Robert can have seen very little of his father during his childhood except during his visits to the family home – visits which were becoming more and more infrequent since he was now spending more and more time on his various construction sites. The example of the ambitious professional man sacrificing family life for success in the world of business is familiar to us today. In a period without telephones or email it was imperative for the architect to be on site for as much of the building period as possible; so, during the 1730s, William Adam was seldom at home as he built a town hall in Dundee, the university library in Glasgow and a hospital in Aberdeen.

In 1735 he accepted, perhaps unwisely, a commission from William Duff, later Lord Braco, and Earl of Fife. As at Hopetoun there was an existing house at Banff which his lordship wanted to be renovated in the latest fashion. There were to be toilets for every bedroom, described on the plans as 'little stool rooms'. Since Duff House was only six years old and had been designed by James Gibbs, who was now at the height of his fame with St Martin-in-the-Fields and St Mary-le-Strand to his credit in London, and with his *Works in Architecture* regarded as the leading guide to fashion, Lord Braco would have been well advised to let well alone, but Adam, with Gibbs' drawings under his arm, set about bettering the master.

The house as redesigned by Adam is badly proportioned and John Fleming said of it, 'Combining the dour stolidity and solemnity of an ancient fortress with the fantasy of a baroque stage design, the vast pile rises out of the bleak northern landscape like some hirsute centurion; a local levy, of course, for its wild rugged grandeur is unmistakably Scottish.'[31] William applied almost every feature in his pattern book. There were Corinthian pilasters spanning two storeys; windows of all designs, round-headed with decorated keystones as well as square-headed with architraves; the second floor surmounted with a huge entablature enclosing armorial decorations with three statues on platforms; and finally, a balustrade with urns. At the main entrance William even managed to create a double stairway curving upwards onto a platform. A perron at last! The monstrous bulk of the house is emphasised, since the wings, which would have created some element of balance, were never built.

Braco hated the house, probably as a result of the bitter lawsuit, never lived in it and is said to have drawn down the blinds of his coach whenever he passed it. Unlike the Earl of Hopetoun, Braco took a keen interest in Adam's invoices, all of which he queried. A dispute about payment reached the Court of Session, and, although the court found in favour of Adam, Braco pursued him for redress up to his death.

William's business activities were by no means limited to architecture. He leased salt pans and coalmines at Cockenzie and, in 1738, he was awarded the contract to build the Edinburgh Royal Infirmary. Under the plans for the building in *Vitruvius Scoticus* its function is clearly set out. 'This hospital to be open to all curable distressed from whatever corner of the world they come without restriction'. It would be four storeys high, with a 200-foot frontage containing 12 cells for lunatics, all vaulted, on the ground floor, which also housed the offices and kitchens. There would be 216 beds with men and women in separate wards occupying bed spaces of 6 by 8 feet with a closet for each bed. The operating theatre was on the fourth floor with stone walls to 'prevent the noise occasioned by the performance of an operation'. Over the central stair was 'a pulley whereby patients may be hoisted to the wards to prevent 'the racking pain that might otherwise be occasioned in being carried up and down stairs'.[32]

The patients were presumably being hoisted before and after surgery performed without anaesthesia.

William had based his design for the infirmary on the current military plan for a barrack block and the charitable donors asked for something a little less severe. William consulted his pattern books and provided a portico with pilasters, a rusticated basement, and a vast pediment decorated with trophies, foliage, a crown, sword and sceptre, all topped off with a life-size statue of George II copied from the Antwerp sculptor Michael Rysbrack, who had also provided the models for some of the chimney pieces at Hopetoun House.

In 1739, William leased coalmines at Pinkie, to the east of Edinburgh, from the Marquess of Tweeddale, diverting water from the river Esk to provide the power for the pumps. The Marquess was warned by Thomas Hay, his factor, 'Your Lordship knows that Mr Adams is very sly and has abundance of smooth things to say and manages his point of view with prudence and address.'[33] Adam was also carrying out improvements at Yester, Tweeddale's house in Midlothian, showing a nice regard for the distinctions of class by including 'a house of office for servants, a lavatory for gentlemen, then a water closet with a marble seat for the Marquess himself'.[34]

By 1740, William Adam felt himself a significant enough part of the new architectural movement that he started using a seal bearing the head of Inigo Jones, based on a drawing by Van Dyck. According to John Clerk of Eldin, 'His fortune was very considerable from his various enterprises.'[35] His opinion of himself was strengthened even further in September 1740 when he returned to work at Holyroodhouse. This time his client was not the crown directly, but the premier nobleman in Scotland, the Duke of Hamilton. As hereditary keeper of the palace, the duke had a suite of rooms at his disposal and he decided to renovate them in the latest fashion.

Adam renewed three windows in the duchess's bedchamber, installed marble fireplaces, doubtlessly based on Rysbrack's designs and taken from his store of already carved stock, and replaced panelling, some with exotic and expensive mahogany. By December it was time for 'the stucco man Clayton' to start work, but unfortunately the winter was especially severe and his stucco was in danger of freezing before he could mould it into the desired shapes. His solution, which Adam had to accept, however reluctantly, was to light all the fires, import charcoal burners, and close all the windows. The atmosphere was stifling for the workmen, but Clayton could now be assured of a climate, however smoky and unhealthy, sympathetic to stucco. James Norrie, whom Adam had used at Hopetoun, was gilding the picture frames and would, in his own time, paint landscapes to occupy them. William Adam did not enjoy using a squadron of artisans in the confined space of a suite of rooms he had had no hand in designing, but he did assure the duke that he was using the best craftsmen – and craftswomen – that Edinburgh could supply. Mr and Mrs Shaw were upholsterers and Mr Broddie was the cabinetmaker providing chairs, settees, tables and mir-rors, as well as a magnificent state bed based on the design of one in use by the Duchess of Gordon. By the end of January 1741 the rooms were ready for the duke and duchess. The duke, delighted with the restoration, invited Adam to visit him in his new apartment and Adam, rather churlishly replied that while he would accept the invitation, 'Edinburgh is not the place I have most pleasure in and therefore it gets no more of my company than I can possibly keep from it.'[36]

William divided his time between Blair Adam and his various construction sites while his family remained in Edinburgh for much of the year. Mary looked after the now extensive family in Edinburgh (by 1743 there were ten of them), although John was now more and more often accompanying William on business, leaving Robert, James and William along with the six girls, Jenny (Janet), Elizabeth (Bess, or sometimes Betty), Margaret (Peggy), Mary, Susannah (Susan) and Helen (Nell).

In October the workaholic William was baffled by the rejec-tion of another profit-making scheme. 'I do not hear that the magistrates of Edinburgh or Glasgow had any view of setting the old project on foot for making a canal betwixt Clyde and Forth . . . I am satisfied that four hundred thousand pounds at the outside would effectuate the design.'[37] William had seen the canals between Ostend and Bruges and at Dunkirk and felt that a similar scheme in Scotland would be 'of great use to the trade from the West Indies to the Baltick [sic].' The letter recommends 'my son and myself', although it is, in fact, written by the 20-year-old John who is now very much part of the firm. He had not received the classical education of his younger brother, but, in William's eyes, had been destined for a career as an architect from birth. John had attended, not the High School in Edinburgh, but the grammar school in the village of Dalkeith some five miles distant which would provide sufficient education for a practical career as an architect and contractor.

Robert, however, was given an education suitable for a gentleman. He had attended the High School for nearly ten years and was now a fluent Latin speaker, so, in the autumn of 1743, aged fifteen, Robert signed the matriculation book at the 'Tounis College', now known as the University of Edinburgh. This had been in existence since 1583 under the direct control of the town council, but from 1703 to 1715 the principal had been the modernising William Carstares, whose far-reaching reforms were just coming to fruition as Robert arrived.

Carstares, like many of his compatriots, had received much of his education at Leyden in Holland and he had imported the Dutch systems of teaching. Previously the university had trained lawyers and clergymen, with divinity and moral philosophy accompanying law and jurisprudence as the chief subjects, while medicine was studied almost in a separate establishment. Under a system of 'regents' the students were taught throughout their time at university by the same professor, who was paid directly by the students when they graduated. Given the limited syllabus this was just possible and, unsurprisingly, there was a remarkably high pass rate. Carstares abolished this system, replacing the regents with professors in individual subjects, and introducing a wider range of subjects with the result that the richer families in

Scotland no longer felt the need to send their sons to Holland. There were inevitable complaints that some of the teaching was dull, with professors occasionally simply regurgitating the courses they had themselves attended in Leyden or Utrecht.

Teaching in Latin had meant that students from across Europe could attend Edinburgh, and an added attraction was that no religious declarations needed to be made by the students. In Oxford and Cambridge the students had to be communicants of the Church of England, but in Scotland the cosmopolitan atmosphere continued, even when teaching in English began. Another undoubted attraction for students in Edinburgh was that, being a non-collegiate university without strict rules concerning conduct, they could reside in the town and avail themselves of its pleasures. Some professors provided lodgings where students could 'benefit from . . . conversation which was easy and dignified'.[38] There were some lodgings in the college where shared beds for two were available at £2 per term or, if luxury could be afforded, then a single bed was £4. Poorer students shivered in attics living off oatmeal porridge. Robert was lucky to be able to stay in comfort at home in Niddry's Wynd.

Robert would have been obliged to study Greek, logic, metaphysics and natural philosophy, or physics in modern terms. He would also have had the choice of three elective subjects, one of which was certainly Colin McLaurin's course on the new philosophy of mathematics. McLaurin was appointed on the ringing recommendation of Sir Isaac Newton and the authorities gave him 'suitable encouragement to settle among us'. It is difficult for us to understand that the science of mathematics could be seen as dangerous in that it might challenge the church's precept that everything in the universe was created and controlled by an omnipotent God.

Robert also attended the lectures of Alexander Monro on anatomy. The Scots principle of a general education was upheld, with students often attending classes outside their prescribed curriculum simply because of the popularity of the professor. Monro's theatrical style earned him great fame and huge audiences. More academically conventional was John Stevenson, who taught logic: 'He had no pretensions to superiority in point of learning and genius, yet was the most popular of all the professors on account of his civility and even kindness to his students, and at the same time the most useful; for, being a man of sense and industry, he had made a judicious selection from the French and English critics, which he gave us at the hour of eight, when he read with us Aristotle's *Poetics*, and Longinus' *On the Sublime*. At eleven he read Heineccius' *Logic* and an abridgement of Locke's *Essay;* and in the afternoon at two – for such were the hours of attendance in those times – he read to us a compendious history of the ancient philosophers, and an account of their tenets.'[39]

Robert was in the thick of dangerous debate as students in their clubs argued about the new ideas circulating in Edinburgh. The most important of these were in David Hume's *Treatise of Human Nature*, published in 1739. Such a seemingly dangerous book, which discussed human behaviour and morals without ever mentioning God, would have been devoured by the students of the town. Robert would have absorbed Hume's pleas to maintain a balance between reason and the passions. Between the rigour of established rules and the uncontrolled emotions and instincts, using doubt and inquiry to find the perfect balance, man with his own tastes and intellect must wrench the reins of control from the dead hand of dogma. This was heady stuff compared with Cicero's rigorous grammar and the repressive teachings of the Kirk. In architectural terms Hume's thought could be interpreted as throwing out the pattern books of Palladio and Vitruvius in favour of establishing a personal style. In 1673 Claude Perrault had stated in his abridged edition of Vitruvius, *L'Abrégé de Vitruve*, 'It is absolutely necessary to be convinced that the taste one follows is better than any other'. The idea that each individual was responsible for his or her own beliefs and tastes was not only revolutionary, it was also very frightening. With no catechism or pattern book to rely on, clients and architects would be cast adrift without the compass of accepted fashion to guide them. Already the anarchy of personal taste was fomenting in Robert Adam's mind.

Meanwhile, he was receiving the traditional Scottish general education, with the combination of mathematics, logic and anatomy providing a strong basis for absorbing the principles of measurement and function, while Aristotle and Longinus laid down the classical ideas of taste and art. He was, perhaps unwittingly, focusing his studies on what he would need as a foundation for his future. Meanwhile, he was enjoying what he was learning at university to the point of repeating his lectures daily to his elder sister, Janet, who listened patiently to her brother's enthusiasm.

All this calm progress through life changed violently on 9 August 1745 when Charles Edward Stewart raised the banner of revolt at Glenfinnan. He had come to claim the crown of Britain for his father, the Old Pretender, now 57 years old, styling himself James VIII and III, although living in exile in Rome. Sufficient numbers of the Highland clansmen, still clinging to their old loyalties, rallied to his cause to make his task seem possible and the rebel army marched south towards Edinburgh. General John Cope moved north through the countryside to confront Charles, but Charles was marching south on Wade's efficient road network and the two forces passed each other without any contact. In fact, the unfortunate Cope had to divert to Aberdeen and take a ship south to Edinburgh, so that by September Charles was approaching the capital. The city was in a state of panic as the population expected a murdering horde of uncivilised savages to descend on them for rape, pillage and destruction. By and large Edinburghers knew nothing of the Gaelic-speaking Highlanders, except as the uncouth carriers of sedan chairs, and expected the worst. A popular cartoon showed wild and hairy Highlanders confronting an indoor lavatory with amazed bafflement. David Hume gave the Lowlander's view: 'The barbarous Highlander, living chiefly by pasturage, has leisure to cultivate the idea of military honour, and, hearing of naught else but the noble exploits of his tribe or clan he soon fancies that he himself is born a hero as well as a gentleman.'[40]

Behaving much less like a gentleman, William Adam, 'thought it prudent to retire from the metropolis' with his eldest son, John, who at the age of 24 was now very much part of William's business. This was a business William would not allow to be interrupted by a troublesome rebellion, and therefore, with no regard for their welfare, he left his wife and remaining children to the mercy of the presumably savage invaders. In Edinburgh, preparations were being made to defend the city and Robert's cousin, William Robertson, along with his friends Alexander Carlyle and John Home, had joined the College Company of the university as part of a hastily recruited resistance army to augment the few regular troops and the Town Guard. There were 126 of these mainly elderly, if not actually decrepit, men who, according to Home, shut their eyes before discharging their equally aged muskets. Adam's professor of mathematics, Colin McLaurin, was busy strengthening the city walls, 'endeavouring to make them more defensible and had even erected some small cannon near to Potterow Port'[41] and there is no doubt that his students were working alongside him. Robert was 17 years old and the excitement of defending his city against supposed barbarians must have been intense. Sadly, so great were McLaurin's exertions that he suffered a stroke and tragically became one of the very few casualties of the '45 in Edinburgh.

Robert saw the threat of what were, to his Whig-bred mind, the twin terrors of Catholicism and rule by absolute monarchy. He had been raised to embrace both Protestantism and Parliament and he regarded the Jacobite rising as the advent of chaos. This coming chaos could be averted by the rational application of military rules and order, but in the case of the defence of the city these traditional rules were being augmented by individual efforts. Robert learned that innovation could be applied to the universally accepted methods.

By 17 September 1745 the rebels were expected at the Colt Bridge, a mile to the east of Corstorphine, and two regiments of regular dragoons were encamped there. However, hearing of the advancing Jacobites, they retreated in terror along the Long

Dykes on the Barefoot Parks to the north of the Nor' Loch, leaving the city undefended and open. In fact, the expected pillage did not take place and Charles Edward peacefully occupied the Palace of Holyroodhouse, sleeping in the apartments which William Adam had renovated for the Duke of Hamilton. Alexander Carlyle himself made off to the east where he was confronted by two armed Highlanders. He said that he gave them a shilling and they went away happy and, later that day, an officer told him that the Highlanders would desert as soon as they had a full purse or a full belly. However, on 21 September, the Highlanders routed General Cope in a surprise attack at Prestonpans a few miles east of Edinburgh. On 1 November Charles left the capital, without ever attempting to take the castle. He invaded England with 6,500 men, but on 4 December turned back at Derby. On 16 April 1746 the exhausted remnant of his army met with the Duke of Cumberland outside Inverness on Culloden Moor. They were crushed with ruthless efficiency by the government forces of regular Lowland and English troops and the mad dream of the '45 was over.

The effect of the rising on Robert was to bring his university education to an end. Failure to complete a degree was not uncommon in the eighteenth century since employment as a lawyer, cleric, or civil servant depended more on personal networking or family connections followed by a period of apprenticeship. In 1745 only three students took the trouble to graduate.

At 18 years of age Robert would now be expected either to pursue a career of his own, or to join his brother John as an assistant to his father, but in 1746 'he was seized with a fever of so violent a nature that his life was despaired of and all the physicians who attended him, whom the extreme anxiety of his family had multiplied to the number of seven with two surgeons. He remained thirty days delirious when a crisis was perceived.'[42] He did, however, recover completely and became a junior member of William Adam & Sons.

For William Adam the 1740s was a time of continued prosperity. He leased the old leather market in Edinburgh which he used as a coal yard, and in 1743 he bought lofts and granaries in Leith, probably using them as warehouses for the prefabricated features, such as fireplaces and chimney pieces, which he would later install. To supply raw materials with greater ease and cheapness for his various projects, he leased stone quarries at Queensferry. In July 1743 the Duke of Argyll's agent, Archibald Campbell, suggested to the duke that his castle at Inveraray might be put into Adam's hands. 'If you have not already some other person in view, you know that Mr Adams [sic] the architect is considered as the best man we have in Scotland for carrying out so great a design.' Campbell also suggested that William's son, presumably John, might visit the site throughout the summer and William sent John to London for direct consultations with the duke and his architect Roger Morris. John was already aware that soon he would be taking over the firm from his father and used this trip to make sketches of various buildings which might provide useful material for future projects. The bulk of these are neo-Palladian, indicating that John was clearly intent on following in William's footsteps.

John obviously impressed the duke and Morris so that from 1746 onwards William Adam was engaged as Intendant General. That is to say he was the principal contractor for the enterprise, while Morris and the duke relayed their ideas northwards through Andrew Fletcher, who, as Lord Milton, was Lord Justice Clerk in Scotland. Morris and William themselves only once visited the site together in 1747 and chaos was the order of the day. William had recommended using Lowland workers but he was overruled and the bulk of the workforce was Highland and local. The historian Mary Cosh has concluded that 'on balance the local Highlanders were individualistic, undomesticated, unindustrious, Catholic and probably Crypto-Jacobite'.[43] The story of the building of Inveraray Castle was a farrago of theft, fraud and inefficiency. A further complication was that the design by Morris could best be described as 'pastiche Gothic' but William and John persevered, finally producing a building which is both extraordinary and aesthetically unsuccessful.

The state of military fortifications in the Highlands after the Jacobite defeat in 1746 was such that large-scale renovations and rebuilding had to be undertaken. During their retreat northwards, the Jacobite army had destroyed Fort Augustus when a lucky shell had struck the powder magazine. Fort William had withstood a siege until after Culloden, but the castle at Inverness had been demolished. The task of rebuilding was given to Major General William Skinner, military engineer for North Britain, who immediately faced the problem that the civic authorities in Inverness demanded compensation for the rebuilding of the castle. Skinner avoided this unnecessary expense by deciding to build an entirely new fort on a fresh site at Ardersier, a spit of land on the shores of the Moray Firth, dominating the approach to Inverness. It would be named Fort George.

William and John, now accompanied by the 18-year-old Robert, were appointed as contractors and plans were laid for total reconstruction in 1747. William's position as Master Mason to the Board of Ordnance meant that he travelled north to Inverness every year. 1748 was, however, to be the last year of William's life. He had become ill during the autumn of 1747 and more and more he had been passing responsibility to John. In September or October he fell ill. On 24 June 1748 he died, 'of suppression of urine – the last he passed was black like ink – he was affected with a swelling not only in his belly, but his right hand; when the swelling abated and not till then his head was affected [he] lost his senses and did not live many hours'. A modern diagnosis is that William died from acute glomerulonephritis, or Bright's Disease, aged 59. On 30 June the *Caledonian Mercury* reported:

On Friday last died Mr William Adam, Architect, generally lamented and deservedly so, not only by those who knew him, but by all who wish well to the public. His genius for architecture pushed him out of obscurity into a high degree of reputation. And his activity of spirit, not to be confined between narrow bands, diffused itself into many branches of business not more to his own benefit than that of his native country. As to the latter, 'tis fortunate he has left behind some promising young men to carry on what he has so happily begun. Their regard for so worthy a man, their parent, will be to them a more than ordinary incitement to tread in his steps for he was a good artist, but still a better man.[44]

He was buried in Greyfriars Churchyard in Edinburgh in a tomb reputedly designed by his sons, James and Robert. His collected designs and drawings, rather grandly entitled *Vitruvius Scoticus*, had been collected throughout his life but the finished volume of 150 engravings was not published until 1812. It contains drawings of all William's buildings as well as detailed plans for 'houses for gentlemen'.

William Adam's will was unsurprising in that he left his entire estate, including the 'tack of the mines at Pinkie' to his eldest son John. The 'tack' was the leasehold. Apart from the acknowledgement of his debts to his mysterious Jamaican relatives he had debts of £37 11s 4d to Lord Elphinstone and £57 9s 5½d to Colonel William Erskine and was owed £2,076 by Lord Braco – as a result of the long-standing dispute – while the Duke of Buccleuch owed William £2,339 12s 1d, and there was £2,087 7s 6d owing in unpaid rents. The total of £6,502 19s 7d – almost £400,000 in contemporary terms – is large; William was a wealthy man. He was no genius, but an ambitious and unoriginal businessman, raising one son, John, to follow him in business, while indulging his next son, Robert, with a classical education. His care for his family was, like his business enterprises, unimaginative and efficient. He left his family with what was probably his greatest achievement – a more than comfortable fortune.

CHAPTER TWO

The Search for Foundations

֍

At William's death his now extensive estate passed to John, who had already taken over many of the responsibilities of management. John immediately set about making a more just redistribution. 'John, as the eldest immediately assumed Robert as a partner in the architetion [sic] in which was included the Government employments.'[1] William's widow Mary continued to live in Niddry's Wynd and to care for the girls, as well as James, now aged 16, who was attending Edinburgh University and the youngest, William, who was only 10 years old.

Robert inherited Dowhill Castle from his father but the estate consisted only of two ruined towers in about 230 square yards of more or less useless ground. It did, however, provide the landowning qualification which would later allow Robert to stand for parliamentary election. With his share of the main legacy, combined with his income as a partner in the firm, Robert had no financial need to undertake any kind of career. Ten years earlier David Hume claimed that he could live the quiet life of a scholar in the country for £100 annually – a sum which was, at that time, beyond Hume's means. Robert Adam had no ambition for 'the quiet life of a scholar'. From childhood he had been surrounded by drawings and plans; during his father's visits to Edinburgh the talk had all been of architecture and at Blair Adam the library had been filled with books showing the grand buildings of antiquity. John had slipped easily into his father's role of contractor and architect, but Robert had the opportunity to step back and examine what the new firm of Adam brothers was doing.

Their work was largely repetitive and derivative of others'
designs. Even if a building was designed strictly according to
the drawings of Vitruvius, Robert was well placed to understand
the differences that could occur between the drawings and the
reality in stone. This reality could only be understood by examining the actual buildings, or at least the still extant ruins of the actual
buildings. With this knowledge a new vocabulary might be developed and personal taste could be brought to bear on new designs.

For the moment, however, Robert used his talents to assist
John in completing the work already contracted. This, of course,
meant the highly lucrative commission with the Ordnance Board
at Fort George, where Colonel William Skinner had already
agreed a plan with William at a very precisely estimated building
cost of £92,673 1s 1d. Needless to say, this figure bore little
relation to the final cost of over £200,000.

The fort was to be the very latest in military design, built to
withstand attacks either from sea or land. It would also provide
barracks for 1,600 men as well as detachments of artillery with
storehouses and a chapel. It was surrounded by a mighty wall
with bastions, semi-bastions, ravelins and sally ports. There was a
vast glacis facing the landward approach; this was an exposed
approach narrowing towards the gates, thus providing a killing
ground as the attackers were forced to advance without any
possibility of cover. There were casemates, underground rooms
in which the entire garrison could shelter from mortar attacks,
the mortar being the nearest equivalent of an aerial bombardment the technology of the times allowed. Skinner designed the
main gate to impress arrivals with contrasting bands of red and
yellow sandstone. Doric pilasters supported a heavy pediment
enclosing the royal arms. The officers' quarters were all fitted
with William Adam's trademark marble fireplaces and the
barrack rooms for the soldiers were at least proof against the
ferocious winds that swirl around the site. The fort is still in use
by the British army and has never been attacked. By the time it
was completed in 1769 the Jacobite threat was over and the fort
would never repel invading forces.

The architectural work was largely in the hands of Colonel Skinner, with the Adam brothers acting only as contractors for 'that stupendous work'. Robert's work as a junior partner in a firm dealing with no more than the logistics of the building would have been largely supervisory; since the designs for the fort were already settled, he simply oversaw a temporary site office where working drawings for the builders were made. With no practical experience he had no hand in controlling the 1,000 soldiers who were working as labourers, clearing ground and manhandling the quarried stone. It was, however, an excellent training ground for a man as yet untrained in any of the skills of architecture where he could see the organisational expertise of Colonel Skinner. To take one example: since the fort was built on a promontory of loose and unstable shingle, this had to be stabilised with heavy stone foundations, the result of very careful calculations and even more precisely judged placements. In 250 years there has been no subsidence.

Robert did regard the work as repetitive and the design of the fort to be unoriginal. It was based on the best ideas of the 17th-century French military architect Sébastien de Vauban and left little room for innovation. Robert's light-hearted attitude to his work did not always please Skinner and he did not always take kindly to Robert. Their relationship blew hot – 'we were cutting each other's throats' – and cold, 'we were kissing hands'. One can easily sympathise with Skinner having an apprentice who was already independently wealthy as a partner of the main contractors, and one who could come and go as he pleased.

Robert availed himself of the opportunity, during the winter of 1749 when building work was almost at a seasonal standstill, to leave for his first visit to London. He took with him his friend, John Home, now the minister of Athelstaneford. Home, born in 1722 and thus six years older than Robert, who had graduated from Edinburgh University in 1742. He had fought for the Government forces against the Jacobites at Falkirk in 1746, been taken prisoner and escaped. He joined the Kirk of Scotland as a minister, but spent much of his time socialising in Edinburgh.

Robert and he were firm friends. While John Adam was very much involved with the business of the firm and, eventually, with the affairs of his own family in Merchiston, Robert had already started to form the friendships which would last him for life. He was very much the social animal, enjoying gossip and intellectual debate, especially on all aspects of art, while John had inherited the more serious and business-orientated mindset of their father.

Of all Robert's friends, undoubtedly the greatest gossip was Alexander Carlyle, also born in 1722 and also a minister in the church. So imposing was his appearance that Walter Scott called him 'the grandest demigod I ever saw' and his friends promoted him to full godliness by nicknaming him 'Jupiter' Carlyle. A third friend was David Hume, wrongly regarded by much of Edinburgh society as a dangerous atheist. Alexander Carlyle tells of Mrs Adam meeting Hume.

> She said to her son, 'I shall be glad to see any of your companions to dinner, but I hope you will never bring the Atheist here to disturb my peace.' But Robert soon fell on a method to reconcile her to him, for he introduced him under another name, or concealed it carefully from her. When the company parted she said to her son, 'I must confess that you bring very agreeable companions about you, but the large jolly man who sat next me is the most agreeable of them all.' 'This was the very Atheist,' said he, 'mother, that you was so much afraid of.' 'Well,' said she, 'you may bring him here as much as you please, for he's the most innocent, agreeable, facetious man I ever met with.'[2]

In the company of John Home, Robert arrived in London to make an architectural tour and 'from a careful consideration of the best works in that country he first began to curb the exuberance of his fancy and to correct his father.'[3] In another draft the last phrase reads 'polish his taste' but both versions show the earnest hope that Robert will study and absorb the best principles of Palladianism. In fact he did nothing of the kind and his notebooks are full of crocketting and delicate Gothic tracery. Robert, who had never seen the Decorated or Perpendicular styles of English architecture, was expanding his vocabulary. There were no formal schools of architecture, or even of fine art, in Scotland and his predecessors had taught themselves by copying prevailing fashion. Their clients wanted whatever they heard was fashionable and they supplied it with very little personal intervention since insistence on an innovative style could brand them as avant-garde and, therefore, unemployable. Robert Adam was in the happy position of being financially independent and free to explore his own taste by experience. He bought himself paints and brushes for watercolours, draughts-man's and architect's tools, as well as some books on architecture, and a copy of Camden's *Britannia, A Chorographical Description of the most Flourishing Kingdoms of England, Scotland and Ireland.* First published in Latin in 1586, and reissued in 1610 in a much expanded English version by Philemon Holland, this was a description of Britain from a historical and geographical point of view. Robert was not 'polishing his taste' in a narrow sense but was broadening his horizons.

This brief excursion of discovery came to an end when Robert returned to Fort George, and in the spring of 1750 he was joined by his 19-year-old brother James, who was to have his first taste of work as an architect. James had been studying literature and belles-lettres at Edinburgh University, a subject which had only just entered the curriculum and which was still regarded as dangerously liberal. The situation of a younger son – James was not the youngest, the 13-year-old William, still at Dalkeith High School, held that unenviable position – was precarious. He was not expected to inherit much of the estate, so no practical education was needed. He might take up a profession, although he would lack the capital needed either to start on his own, or to buy himself into a partnership; or he might simply settle for a life as a dilettante. It seems that James had chosen this latter course and he did not take well to the discipline of life at Fort George. He did become a partner, although his architectural work is heavily derivative, but he proved himself as an able administrator and an occasional brake on Robert's enthusiasms, which frequently put the firm's finances in jeopardy.

As well as fulfilling its obligations to the Ordnance Board, the firm was carrying on as much other work as it could. Hopetoun House was still unfinished and the brothers were called in by John Hope, the second Earl, to complete the building. On the unfinished portico some of William's heavy-handed rustication, as well as his half-columns and entablature, were demolished while new work was put in place following William's style, but without his slavish adherence to existing designs. The two flanking service pavilions were built in the classical style but now with a lighter touch. The brothers then turned their attention to the interiors and stripped back the designs to give an overall impression of greater lightness and elegance. Some of Bruce's decoration was retained – the wainscot in the library is heavily carved and gilded in his style – but by removing some of William's decorations on the door cases they lightened the general effect. Stucco cornicing and ceiling decorations are floral with scrolling and an overall emphasis on delicacy. Furniture was made by James Cullen who also supplied 1,000 yards of red damask for £600 which was used as wall coverings. The decoration was not finished until 1758 but, already in 1752, the brothers 'did not despair of pleasing your Lordship as to the lightness of it.'[4]

The brothers undoubtedly had pleased the earl who played a key role in their first independent commission. This came from the Earl of Dumfries who had been in discussion with their father about building a house for him, although the negotiations had collapsed with William's death. The earl, unsure of the reputation of the two as-yet-untried architects, consulted Lord Hopetoun who recommended their engagement. The earl seems to have been a cautious man and detailed negotiations over cost went on for two years, so that the foundation stone was not laid until 18 June 1754 after a price of £7,971 9s 2d was agreed. Astonishingly, the final cost five years later, and including interior decoration, was £7,971 11s 2d! The two years of negotiation were well spent.

Robert, according to John Clerk, 'particularly supervised as a favourite of the earl'[5]. It was the first example of Robert's ability to become friends – and drinking companions – of the aristocracy, an ability which was crucial to his gaining commissions from them. It seems that the laying of the foundation stone on 18 June 1754 blended into a country house party at which he was welcome. *The Scots Magazine* reported, 'Tents were pitched for the reception of the company, who witnessed the foundation stone's being carried from the principal tent and laid attended by a band of music. The King, the Royal family, the Lord Chancellor and many other loyal healths were drunk . . . In the evening the trees were illuminated with lamps and the whole ceremony concluded with a ball.'[6] Only Robert's departure for Europe prevented his continuing as a regular guest at Dumfries.

The first example of an Adam design that the visitor meets at Dumfries House is an elegant bridge over the river Lugar with obelisks at the corners of the main arch. This bridge, built to a height which would accommodate the river in full flood, was the first identifiable work of John Adam. Some 20 years earlier, his father William had spanned the River Tay with four similar obelisks rising above the breakwaters and John's bridge is completely derivative of his father's style. John Adam would never display the originality of his younger brother and he was already becoming content to give Robert his head in matters of design as well as in social skills. Dumfries House is a very rare example of cooperation between the two eldest brothers.

The design of the house would have horrified William senior who had envisaged an uneasily proportioned three-storey building, so tall as to be almost square, topped with a fussy balustrade and urns. Twin curving stairways would lead to an elaborately pedimented front door. Robert's building has two storeys and nine bays with a broad flight of steps leading to a front door with a simple pediment. Another pediment surmounts the main frontage enclosing a coat of arms. There are no columns, no Corinthian pilasters and the two service pavilions are connected to the main house by short wings. It is, according to Fleming, 'as if the patron, in a fit of economy, had stripped his architects' design down to its bare bones'[7]. It may also be that the patron's parsimony was coinciding with Robert's wish to abandon the pattern books of the time in favour of new and, as yet un-discovered, designs and he was simply being artistically cautious.

The entrance hall was very plain, white with little decoration, since only the welcoming footmen would spend any time there and the contrast with the other rooms would be greater for the visiting guests. The internal decoration was carried out to Robert's designs and largely in his absence. He had already met William de la Cour and Isaac Ware, two outstanding stucco artists who were keen to abandon strict Palladianism in favour of 'judicious variety'; on ceilings and cornices Robert was all too keen to use his own ideas of foliage and garlands of fruit held by rococo masks. 'Exquisite patterns of crisply modelled foliage and flowers rippling out from the centres in concentric circles . . . as light as chiffon.'[8] Not all was entirely original since Robert connected the front and rear of the house with a gallery on the first floor. This gallery is lit by Venetian windows. These are sometimes known as a 'Serlianas', the style being illustrated in Sebastiano Serlio's *Architettura* of 1537; Robert simply inserted the design as shown in countless pattern books. What was original was that the front staircase is wooden while the rear one is stone. Carpeted stone would allow the servants to move around more quietly. Robert Adam was an architect of practical ideas, always considering function as well as style. He ordered quantities of material from the London suppliers he visited in 1754 which were delivered by 1756. On his return to London from Italy he continued to order goods, and in 1759 his first orders for furniture from Messrs Chippendale and Rannie were delivered to Dumfries House.

In many ways the work at Hopetoun and at Dumfries was a welcome relief from the day-to-day activities of the firm, which largely consisted of completing projects started by William and of attending to their contracts with the Ordnance. But, thanks to these projects, the brothers were now prosperous in their own right. John had married Jean Ramsay on 8 July 1750 and his son William, named, in the Scots tradition, after his grandfather, was born on 21 July in the next year. This little family moved into the house at Merchiston while Mary Adams continued to live in Niddry's Wynd with her daughters and her teenage son, William. When she could, Mary would visit the spa at Moffat in the Scottish Borders, a spa recommended, among others, by 'Dr John Clerk, the great practising physician', who 'had found Moffat waters agree with themselves and frequented it every season'.[9] Mary, now 53, was starting to suffer from the pains of arthritis and the waters combined with socialising and gentle exercise on the bowling greens gave her some relief.

On 7 July 1752 James wrote to his younger sister Margaret sending his regards to John's family – the Merchistonians – and hoping that sister Nelly's stomach was better.[10] Robert had clearly escaped temporarily from the fort: 'Where think you this wandering rogue Robert is got to, a visit to Moffat won't serve his turn but he must jaunt away to Carlisle also.' James does admit to guilt over having to call Robert back, but 'necessity has no law'. James knew very well that Robert had been accompanying his mother at Moffat for he is 'extremely pleased to hear that my mother continues to be tolerably well and walk about a good deal'.

Both Robert and James found the existence at Fort George irksome since James still hankered back to his days as a dandy in Edinburgh, and Robert's talents were creative rather than administrative. However militarily progressive the fort might become there would be no need for stucco swags or rococo patterning and the only decorative touches were the installation of their father's marble fireplaces in the officers' quarters. The social circle at Ardersier was small and limited to the officers and wives of the garrison, whose military gossip of promotions and postings was of no interest to the brothers.

Robert travelled up to the fort with Colonel Skinner and his wife in May 1753. Writing to his sister Jenny, he confirms that he finds the Skinners pleasant enough company and that they are all happily established in quarters at Ardersier, since none of them find Inverness attractive. 'I am a sort of favourite at present and am in a mood hospitable both with Skinner and Mr North. Since we arrived here all has been peaceable and he [Skinner] is well pleased with all that has been done hitherto. How long this may continue God knows. I think a week a great deal.' He is especially fond of the arrangements made by Mrs Skinner who 'esteems her belly her chief good' and has brought with them a 'good chef'.[11] However Robert's relationships with the Skinners were strained at best.

By July of 1753 the company was relaxed enough for Mrs Skinner to organise picnics and a boating trip. Unfortunately, the sloop that was to carry them had to stand offshore and they had to row out to it, only to find that it was now stuck firmly and would not float off until high tide. 'O! The uncertain fate of the Deep Seas! The too kind sloop had approached too near to the channely shore and there stuck fast. In vain were anchors fixed to haul her off. In vain the rigged sailors toiled to push her from the beach. The tide still ebbing left her parched sides and soon convinced us that it was to no purpose to think of proceeding on our expedition . . . Upon holding a council of war it was determined that we should not return home to be laughed at, wherefore we passed over on the ferry and went to walk about the town of Channery where we dined.' Robert was trying to make light of a wasted day but he still has the irritating tone of a young man sneering at the incompetence of his elders. The account of the trip is in a letter to Peggy, Robert's 22-year-old younger sister. Later in the letter is the first sign that Robert is capable of sly self-mockery. 'I have often remarked on your more than ordinary gravity in the midst of a Colonel frolic and rioting, not that I mean that as any imperfection, as I have often experienced the same insensibility to merriment when the joke did not hit my vein, and you know, I should be loath to condemn my own feeling.'[12]

The following year Robert was much happier working on Dumfries House, and it was while he was there that an invitation arrived which changed his future entirely. It came from the Honourable Charles Hope, the younger brother of the Earl of Hopetoun, and confirmed Charles Hope's intention to go to Italy. The letter 'proposed to him that Mr Robert Adam be his companion in the journey and advised Mr Adam not to delay any longer going to Italy to study the remains of antiquity.'[13] This was an opportunity Robert had always dreamt of and was now about to become reality.

Charles Hope wanted to visit his son, William, who was already in Italy, accompanied by his tutor. By inviting Robert to travel with him, Charles was following the convention of the Grand Tourist. Robert was financially capable of making such a journey himself, but to make it as the companion of an earl's brother was highly advantageous. Grand Tourists depended heavily on the introductions of friends, especially aristocratic friends, to arrange access to private collections and to the most reliable dealers, since shopping for art was a major part of the tour. If alone, Robert would be dealt with politely, but would be excluded from European society; Charles, as an aristocrat, would unlock all the doors Robert wanted.

Writing from Dumfries House on 11 August, Robert assured his mother that he was 'occupied with drinking and doing nothing' here with 'all the family in good health and top humour' since 'we are always merry and laughing'. Robert was in good standing with his aristocratic hosts, but although he was always to find himself accepted in their company he was not included in their circle. Notwithstanding the presence of Charles Hope, Robert, feeling it essential to carry letters of introduction to the influential aristocracy in Europe, approached Lord Dumfries. 'I often give hints about letters of recommendation but find that he does not choose to give any where Hope is to be the introducer, and I suppose he thinks them needless on that account. I told my Lord that I proposed writing [to] the Duchess of Gordon and ask her commands which he approves of greatly.'[14] The duchess never replied and Robert had to rely solely on Charles Hope for introductions.

He did set about making his status clear by commissioning James Norris to sketch him a coat of arms which he would have cut into a seal. Robert started to use this seal in November 1754 with its motto '*Qui vitam excoluere per artes*' – 'Those who have adorned life through art.'[15] It shows a Corinthian column flanked by primitive huts as described by Vitruvius. Thus Robert Adam, with his favourite column, has improved on the ancients and even on Vitruvius himself. It was a heavily laboured piece of self-congratulation and, according to Iain Gordon Brown, 'Robert's seal is a bogus piece of heraldry'.[16]

Five weeks later Robert was at Inveraray, where the Duke of Argyll settled his affairs with the Adam brothers. They agreed to receive £300 in final payment 'for all trouble at this place from the very beginning to this day'. Robert was, outwardly at least, on his usual good terms with his fellow guests. 'Miss Billy Fletcher [of Saltoun] told me today that her great taste was for painting, that she envied my happiness and wished she could accompany me.' Robert gave voice to his complex relationship with the aristocracy when he wrote that this wish was 'from the stinkingest of mortals' and therefore, he 'looked on it as no small compliment, till the next disdainful look . . . wiped entirely away all impression of it'. He despised their arrogance but was often required to ignore their attitude and bend his metaphorical knee. This comment is the equivalent of a rude gesture behind the lady's back. He also received a letter from Charles Hope urging haste 'from his dread of winter being too far spent before we get to Italy'.[17]

At no time does Robert comment on the effect his absence would have on the family firm. The journey could be expected to last for the best part of a year, if not for longer, and during this time he would contribute nothing to the firm's finances. John probably calculated that the widened horizons which Robert would bring back and the antique drawings he could add to the company's repertoire of designs might very well be worth more than the contribution he was making at this time. Robert, in his turn, pled that he was being constricted by carrying out other people's designs and needed to clear his mind of the past. This was the very embodiment of the new ideas of the Scottish Enlightenment put forward by his friends David Hume and Henry Home – now raised to the bench as Lord Kames – ideas which looked forward to the future rather than backwards to the orthodoxies of the past.

Robert spent no time dallying at Inveraray but returned to Edinburgh and prepared to set off for London. He was clearly in high spirits since 'Jupiter' Carlyle remembers seeing Robert, mounted on John Home's horse Piercy, galloping round and round Home's paddock like a madman. Robert afterwards bragged to Carlyle, probably falsely, that he had just been making love to Jenny, Carlyle's handsome maid, and had offered to take her to London with him. 'All his offers were rejected which put him in a flurry.'[18] The flurry died down, Jenny shook her head at the antics of young men, and along with James, who would accompany him part of the way, and their aged man-servant Donald, unfairly maligned as 'the King of Sleep', Robert set off for London on 3 October 1754.

Seven days later, on a foggy 10 October, the party arrived and Robert reported to Nelly, 'We met Adam Cleghorn and Watty Hamilton, Merchants on Change, dined in Dolly's, and found two bedrooms and two parlours with Mr Dollar, Wig Maker in Lancaster Court in the Strand opposite Rainbow Coffee House.' They had been warned that lodgings would be difficult to find in London but their final choice is interesting. In 1737, eight years previously, David Hume had lodged in Lancaster Court and had used the Rainbow Coffee House as his business address. It is more than likely that the Adam brothers had been provided with the address before they left Edinburgh. Next day, Robert wrote, 'Saw Gavin Hamilton the painter, I saw his pictures, I am to be with him again in order to get some advice about Italy as he has been so long there. We this day saw the Mansion House and Walbrook Church the first with detestation the last with doubly pleasure that I had before.' St Stephen's Walbrook was designed by Christopher Wren and completed in 1680 on a bold rectangular plan. A contemporary critic said that 'Italy itself can produce no modern building that can vie with this in taste or proportion,' and Robert enthusiastically agreed, already showing a taste for the avant-garde. But their tourist activities were limited by a letter from Charles Hope in Holland demanding an instant departure. Robert replied that they would meet him in Brussels in the first week of November. In St Paul's Cathedral the pair tried out the Whispering Gallery and James 'was more struck with that phenomenon than with the size or magnificence of the building'. Robert's designer's eye was caught by the shops in London. 'I see a thousand things every day that would answer charmingly for our habitation and that would tempt a saint. But as yet I am proof against purchasing for if I was once to begin I should not know where to stop.' He reported that James wanted his clothes made by 'a tailor of fashion' but still with an eye to business asked his sister to 'let Willie call at Alexander the painter and if he has got Rembrandt's head varnished it should be put in the frame by Robert Millar and replaced.'

The brothers visited Windsor briefly with Thomas Sandby who showed them his just completed landscape schemes in the Great Park and at Virginia Water. Sandby was draughtsman to the Duke of Cumberland, had accompanied the duke during the Culloden campaign and now was military draughtsman to the Board of Ordnance. He would have been well aware of the brothers' efforts at Fort George and their seeking him out demonstrates that the Jacobite Rebellion of 1745 was, for most Lowland Scots, a tiresome irrelevance and a matter best forgotten. On 28 October 1754 the brothers left Dover for Calais. Robert's Grand Tour had started.

The British, being an island race, have always had great curiosity about what lay beyond the sea – and, in particular, what lay beyond the English Channel. In the Middle Ages this interest was served by extensive voyages of pilgrimage, as personified by Chaucer's Wife of Bath. With the advent of the Reformation, Elizabeth I sent 'young men of promising hopes in foreign countries for the more complete polishing of their parts and studies'. Being a thrifty Tudor, she expected them to return with added skills which would bring financial benefit to England. Two hundred years later the situation had changed and the Grand Tourists of the eighteenth century had different motives. Their education was based entirely on the classics and now they could complete it by visiting the sites of classicism in Italy, and, if possible, in Greece. In France they would acquire the habits of polite society among the nobility – the habits of gourmandising, the style of dress, the skills of swordsmanship – and throughout the Tour they would see and learn to appreciate the fine arts. Dr Johnson said, 'A man who has not been in Italy, is always conscious of an inferiority, from his not having seen what it is expected a man should see. The grand object of travelling is to see the shores of the Mediterranean.'[19] Having journeyed south to Italy they would return through the German states to the Netherlands. Their fathers, who usually had paid for their trip, hoped to welcome back a cultured son with greater marriageable prospects and possibly a more modern view of farming, estate management, or even industry. The Tourist, usually accompanied by an older scholar, or 'bear leader', hoped to experience culture, provided it was entertaining and diverting, so that on his return he could pepper his speech with extravagant foreign phrases as well as amusing anecdotes from the exotic places he had visited. Also, there were the added temptations of foreign sex and the opportunities for gambling, more or less anonymously. However as the biographer and lecher, James Boswell, discovered to his chagrin, the opportunities for sexual dalliance with the upper classes were, in fact, merely limited to greater freedom of conversation and increased female empowerment. As at home, Boswell resorted to the local prostitutes and returned, as did many a Grand Tourist, with an empty purse and recurrent venereal disease. As his countryman Robert Burns put it, 'the consequential sorrows, love-gifts of Carnival signoras'.

Robert would be responsible for his own expenses and would not be paid, but he knew that Charles Hope's name would open doors for him. Neither of them was the innocent young nobleman of the typical Grand Tour but they were both aware that they were treading the unknown – and possibly dangerous – paths of a foreign country. Both might carry, either Sir Thomas Nugent's *The Grand Tour*, an exhaustive four-volume work, or else *The Gentleman's Pocket Companion for Travelling into Foreign Parts*, which had useful phrases in French, German and Italian. Most British Tourists spoke no foreign languages; when Dr Johnson visited Paris in 1775, rather than expose his deficiency in language to the French, he spoke only to scholars and *savants* in Latin. The Tourists also feared that familiar and, to them, essential goods would be unavailable, with the result that they carried a cornucopia of British goods with them, at least until they reached Florence where they would search out Molini's. 'Molini's, near the Royal Gallery, for James's powders, Reeve's colours, tea, sago, wax candles for coach lamps, paper, pens, pencils, ink, English books and excellent rum.'[20]

Before experiencing the dangers and delights of the continent, the first challenge the Grand Tourist had to face was the crossing of the English Channel. There were a number of crossing points from Harwich, London, Yarmouth, Brighton or Southampton, but by far the commonest was Dover, from where Robert and James Adam set sail. The sailing packets operated about three times a week, depending on weather and tides, offering a crossing for half a guinea for gentlemen and five shillings for servants. The reputation of the Channel was such that most travellers became nauseous before even boarding the ship but once out of the shelter of Dover harbour and into the grip of the ever restless Channel, seasickness was almost inevitable. The duration of this torment varied widely between the extremely fast crossing time of 2 hours and 40 minutes – a quick crossing by ship even today – to the miserable 14 hours experienced by the agriculturalist Arthur Young in 1787.

Frequently the packet boats arrived at Calais during low tide and, since there was no dredged deep harbour, the boats had to stand off shore. The seasickness may have stopped but often the travellers had to be rowed ashore by local Frenchmen who could demand up to another guinea as a fare for the final few yards. The exhausted passengers would now willingly pay anything to reach dry land. On landing they would meet the French customs officials and suffer the further indignity of having their portmanteaux searched. Then, at last, they could find an inn and think about their onward journeys.

These were journeys into a Europe which had only recently emerged from war. The mid eighteenth century marked the end of a political system stretching back to the days of Charlemagne, and a Europe finally dominated by the two great dynasties of the Bourbons and the Habsburgs. The Bourbon line had come to the throne of France to replace the Valois dynasty in the person of Henri de Navarre who, in 1589, succeeded Henri III, the last Valois king of France. Another Bourbon, Philip V, ruled Spain and had thrown the Austrians out of Naples, putting all Italy south of Naples under Bourbon control. Then, in 1740, the Habsburg Holy Roman Emperor, Charles VI, died without an heir and his daughter Maria Theresa became empress of Austria and the Netherlands. Sensing a possible weakness with a female inheritor, Frederick II of Prussia immediately seized Silesia, with its vastly rich mineral wealth, from Austria, while almost simultaneously France invaded Bohemia and occupied Prague. The only male Habsburg, Charles Albert of Bavaria, proclaimed himself Holy Roman Emperor and advanced on Vienna. Maria Theresa was encircled with only Hungary as an effective ally in central Europe. To everyone's surprise, possibly even her own, the tide then turned in Maria's favour; the French were driven back to Alsace-Lorraine, Charles Albert ceded the title of Holy Roman Emperor to Maria and Britain defeated Frederick at the battle of Dettingen in 1743. Frederick hastily concluded a treaty which let him keep Silesia – all he claimed to have wanted in the first place – and Europe drew a long breath.

A second bout of skirmishes led to the Peace of Aix-la-Chapelle in 1748, with the Duchy of Parma being ceded from Austria to Spain. In India, Britain had suffered some losses but, in Canada, had captured Louisburg and Cape Breton Island. The stage was being set, not for dynastic rivalries, but for wars of imperial conquest across the world. However, on 28 October, at the moment when Robert Adam landed in Europe there was peace.

The national boundaries of the countries through which he would pass en route for Rome were much as at the present time with the huge exception of Italy. In the north-east of the present-day country and under Bourbon rule were the provinces of Savoy and Piedmont, both of which lay beside the Republic of Genoa. South of Genoa were the Duchy of Modena, the Republic of Lucca and the Grand Duchy of Tuscany, while Rome and the centre of Italy was dominated by the Papal States. From there to the south was the Bourbon Kingdom of the Two Sicilies, centred on Naples. They were all fiercely independent and quick to rise to insult, especially at their customs posts where travellers could expect searches, confiscations and requests for extraordinary payments of duty.

Robert was thoroughly forewarned of some of the hazards awaiting him and, looking ahead to the fulfilment of one of the purposes of his voyage, he made arrangements for the easy passage of his artistic purchases through Calais' customs houses on their return to England. Meanwhile James wrote to Nelly reassuring her that neither he nor Robert had been sick (he had not 'thrown up his breakfast'), and that their crossing had been easy. The brothers made their way as rapidly as they could to Ostend, then by canal to Bruges and Brussels.

On arrival at Brussels the brothers met with Charles Hope who had been in the city for seven days and was already an habitué at the miniature court of Prince Charles of Lorraine. Hope immediately did what Robert had wished for and introduced them to the fashionable circles of Brussels society. Robert attended a dinner party with 'much discourse during our repast, without understanding one word that was said'. He went to a play experiencing 'the grief not to know one word of a million. We went to wait on Mr Dirole the English Resident, but the court was in mourning and without proper clothes we could not be received by him'. On the next day,

Going to the play, then to St Quistain's until midnight then to the masquerade, where we will probably stay until 3 in the morning. Every moment of our spare time is employed in seeing the churches, paintings, palaces and curiosities of this city among which the tapestries are remarkable. Jamie and I have each bought a suit of ruffles of the lace here, mine costs £6, Jamie's £4. I have also bought a full suit of laces for a lappet of ruffles, triple rowed, which I think are very handsome and hope you will like them if Jamie should get them safe conveyed to you. You can't buy anything for a lady under £10 to £12. We are to leave this [city] on Wednesday morning to go by Tournai.[21]

Robert was bubbling with the enthusiasm of a wealthy teenager over the fresh experiences available to him in Europe. The trio travelled on to Tournai where they met General Graeme of Bucklivie, now serving as Lieutenant General with the Dutch Brigade. They also met the Prince of Hesse-Philippsthal, who was in residence with his court in the garrison. 'I leave to Jamie to describe our reception which was the greatest of our lives, having dined, played cards and conversed with princes and princesses as if we had been dukes and earls.' General Graeme is described, with all the condescension of the young, as a 'hearty old cock' and Adam's lack of skill at cards is shown in another reminiscence: 'Played whist and I think I rather gained as lost tho' we played 3 hours'. The 26-year-old was not as sophisticated as he had hoped. Adam also visited the battlefield of Fontenay where the Allied armies had been defeated by the French under Prince Maurice de Saxe in May 1745. This defeat, combined with another at Lauffeld in the next year, raised the fear in Britain of a Catholic encirclement, a fear bolstered by the Jacobite rising, and thus the defeats in Europe had savage secondary effects in Scotland. The battlefield itself was of no interest to Robert.

On arrival in Lille they begged – and got – invitations to a reception which they attended in their riding clothes, having had no time to change. Robert described themselves as 'three

Englishmen'. 'Mr H's taste for company is as favourable as I could for my heart expect and he seems to make no scruple in letting me partake of everything with him without thinking my station or manners in any degree inferior to his own, except as to punctilios which no mortal can dispute and which I would be a fool to deny him. If I could play cards I could be of infinite service to him in this way. How I am to go through without them, Lord knows. I assure you I am quite nonplussed.' Robert's dread of social exclusion is extreme when he feels he will be excluded simply by his ignorance of the rules of card playing.

On Thursday, 5 November, Robert was disappointed with the masquerade, 'danced abominably, both minueto and country dances. In short we tired so much that Chas Hope and us [sic] retired to our rest half an hour after one in the morning. James bought a piece which is nearly 7 English yards for Jenny, and I bought another for Betty and Peggy. I fancy that next time you will have any letters from me will be from Paris where I expect to find a pacquet lying for me. These will be my entertainment when alone, as Jamie will, by the time we reach Paris, be almost at Rotterdam where he will get his intelligence.' Then, rather as though they were seeking the approval of an elder brother, both men showed Hope their ruffles. 'He likes one to dress well so much that I believe both for his honour and my own sake I shall be pretty extravagant at Paris. When I say I, I mean we, which saves long speeches from Jamie.'

In Lille James left Robert to return through Holland in a four-wheel chaise. 'He is also to go to Antwerp which I find I can't see until my return from Italy. It is now past the season of going over the Alps so my mother need not be anxious on that score; we must go to Antibes from that to Genoa by water, but we have not in all above 24 or 25 hours sailing, and that all along the coast of Italy.' In Lille Robert's head was now giddy with his unaccustomed whirl of aristocratic socialising. 'Mr Hope recollected the face of Count Lesley's brother who was in Scotland' and Robert met 'that old savage Lesley' now 'esteemed a great man at that place and was a Major in the French Service' whose wife was 'a young and beautiful lady who was in the most elegant dress, and who took her turn with the ladies at the harpsichord'.

Robert makes no comment on, nor seems to have visited, the Citadel at Lille. This was one of the largest forts in Europe, constructed by Sébastien Vauban a century previously and a Mecca for all who had an interest in military design. Robert's spell at Fort George belonged to a past under which the 26-year-old was keen to draw a line and military architecture no longer had any appeal for him.

A week later, on 12 November, Robert and Charles were in Paris. They had travelled by post-chaise – Charles had yet to keep his promise to buy a coach – which, while providing a degree of privacy, had the unfortunate effect of signalling to the population that the passengers were people of wealth. In September 1718, Lady Mary Wortley Montagu discovered that, 'when the post horses are changed the whole town comes out to beg, with such miserable starved faces, and thin, tattered clothes, they need no other eloquence to persuade [one of] the wretchedness of their condition.'[22]

Paris was an entirely different proposition to what Robert had already experienced on his tour, with a population in excess of 600,000 and elegant bridges linking the ancient heart of the city to the Right and Left Banks. The Île-de-la-Cité still housed the cathedral of Nôtre Dame but the seat of power had moved west to the palace of the Louvre. 'We are elegantly lodged at the Hôtel de Nôtre Dame – or Inn of the Virgin Mary – at the court end of the town.' Robert and Charles were in easy reach of the Rue St Honoré and the Place Louis-le-Grand – now called the Place Vendôme – where they could promenade and watch the ladies of fashion who had so appalled Lady Wortley Montagu: 'I have seen all the beauties, and such (I can't help making use of the coarse word) nauseous – [trollops] – so fantastically absurd in their dress! So monstrously unnatural in their paint! Their hair cut short and curled round their faces, loaded with powder that makes it look like white wool, and on their cheeks to their chins, unmercifully laid on, a shining red japan that glistens in a most flaming manner, that they seem to have no resemblance to human faces, and I am apt to believe took the first hint of their dress from a sheep newly raddled.'[23]

Such was the difference between fashion in Britain and Paris that in 1775 even Samuel Johnson had been inspired to make some changes in his appearance. Johnson, from a mixture of indifference and poverty, was celebrated as one of the untidiest and shabbiest men in London, but in Paris he acquired a new wardrobe topped off with 'a Paris-made wig of handsome construction'.[24]

Robert could not plead poverty and he was anything but indifferent to fashion. Having drawn money from Mr Selwin, his banker in Paris – 'a little sharp needle and pin man. We received more money than civility from that quarter' – Robert then attacked the Paris shops with all the vigour of a twenty-first-century fashionista. He invited his mother to picture his appearance,

a most Frenchified head of hair loaded with powder ornaments his top. A complete suit of cut velvet of two colours his body, which is set off by a white satin lining. White silk stockings and embroidered silk gushets his legs. Mariquin pumps with red heels his feet. Stone-buckles like diamonds shine in his knees and shoes. A gold handled sword, with white and gold handle knot, his side. Brussels lace his breast and hands, a solitaire ribband his neck and a smous hat his oxter. In the morning he honours his head with a large hat with a white feather, his side with a gold belt and hanger and in cold weather his whole body is wrapped in a white freeze cloak with black velvet neck and sleeves which is the mode amongst the seigneurs of this kingdom. In short was I to enumerate the collection of curiosities which at first adorned my body and made me laugh but now are as familiar to me as my garter I should both divert and surprise you. What I cut the best figure with is a white beaver cap which represents the crown of an old hat with two turn-ups, one before and one behind with a gold lace round the edge of it and a gold button on top. It is like to a cap worn by his

Grace of Argyll and is both warm and commodious for travelling for which purpose it was bought.

He laughed at how he would be received in his French finery, but since he and Hope found that they had the same taste they encouraged each other into dangerous extravagance.

They waited on the British Ambassador, Lord Albemarle, but missed him and left cards, only to have him call on them and miss them in his turn. They found the social life of Paris was less accessible than in the provincial circles in the north. Robert described his daily routine: 'We keep our coach and French valet, we breakfast at 8, go out by 9 in our machine, travel from one church to another with our books in our hands making such remarks as we think proper of buildings pictures and statues till half an hour past 2 when we come home to dinner. You may be sure we will be well disposed and wholesome. After dinner we dress which is scarce completed till our coachman tells us 'tis time to go to the opera, French or Italian Comedy which we never miss Sunday nor Saturday.' Since Robert could not yet speak French – he joked about this in a letter, calling it 'an unspeakable loss' – his theatre visits were entirely social. 'On Saturday we go to Versailles, Trianon and Marly. On Tuesday go to Lyons.' He was notably unimpressed with Versailles and Marly. 'I have seen massacre and destruction in every garden I have been in and a very small degree of perfection in any building.'

He did, however, receive useful introductions in Paris, especially one to François Louis Colins, 'painter to the king, a prodigious connoisseur in painting, a clever fellow, a *bon* companion', who showed him two private art collections and introduced him to Jacques-André Portail who, in turn gained him access to the royal collections. But Robert's main interest was in the classical buildings of Italy and both he and Charles were keen to depart for the south. He was somewhat dismissive as to what lay ahead. 'We will stay sometime at Aix where I cannot miss seeing much good company. In short, the south of France will consume as much time as the antiquities of Nîmes and adjacent places; Marseilles and Aix must be considered whilst I wait at some places of amusement. Tell Nelly I will not get my picture done until Italy. I shall remember you something of velvet in Genoa.' Not only has he transformed himself into a man of high fashion, he is now growing in personal confidence and the packet of letters is sealed with his Vitruvian seal.

Robert left Paris, and, having passed through Dijon, arrived in Lyons on 2 December where he spelt out his route to Elizabeth and her sisters. 'As you are become geographers, look at your map and follow my route. Leave Lyons on Sunday, see what is curious at Vienne, and stay at St Vallier all night, Monday we see Tain, Valence, Montelimar, Pierrelatte and lie at Pont St Esprit, where, as we are told, it is the most immense thing and the greatest curiosity.' He would then visit Nîmes and Montpellier. This was the traditional winter route to the coast, avoiding the Alps where the passes would now be closed. Even when they were open the Grand Tourist was often exposed to great peril as he had to be carried on the narrow paths by porters, and was exposed to even more risks than simply bandits. Horace Walpole's spaniel, Tory, was eaten by a wolf in the Mont Cenis pass.

Robert was delighted with Lyons. 'Lyons is one of the most romantic cities I ever beheld, situated on a neck of land between two rivers, the Saone and the Rhone, which join here and proceed down to the Mediterranean. Thus with these navigable rivers, the many public and spacious buildings, Gothic and modern, its romantic rocks, trees, bridges, and spires form a scene which would delight and charm one that has no taste for landscape'. He may have had no taste for landscape, but Lyons was the home of the finest weaving in France and the outcome was predictable. 'I am getting one of the genteelest and richest embroidered vests that I ever saw which will cost me at least £14 or £15 Sterling. But there was no help for it . . . At Genoa we both propose taking black velvet suits with which we can wear all our waistcoats by turn, and so will probably take for common forenoon dress uncut velvet suits.' He found it difficult to resist the shops with their 'curious and charming things' but was still determined to delay his major purchasing of antiquities until he reached Rome.

Robert and Charles visited the Roman theatre and pyramid in Vienne then travelled down the valley of the Rhône to see the 'great curiosity' at Pont St Esprit. This bridge was not, in fact, a Roman construction, but Robert found the aqueduct at Nîmes, the Pont du Gard, 'exceeding all description'. Charles Hope was more enthusiastic over Roman remains in France than Robert who, astonishingly, never mentioned the Roman theatre in Orange or the Maison Carrée in Nîmes. Since this building, a temple of Apollo, is the best preserved example of such a temple, it is astonishing that he gives no account of it in his letters home. These, however, are for his sisters and therefore contain as much gossip as he can muster, mixed with accounts of his extravagant shopping expeditions. Robert's contact with the female world was still confined to his sisters and the friends of his mother and he clearly felt that mere girls could not be expected to appreciate the intricacies of a Corinthian capital.

Having passed through the two principal cities in France, the companions were keen to reach Rome as soon as possible. But first Charles Hope wanted to make a detour to Montpellier and Robert wrote to Peggy on 2 December giving his revised itinerary. He decided that there was 'nothing at Avignon worth seeing, [so] we determined not to go there at all' and 'having only taken one glance at the antiquity of Nîmes, slept at that healthful town [Montpellier] then to Aix, to Toulon, to Antibes, then to Nice where Mrs Crawford and Peggy Forbes stay at present; and I am informed Colonel Crawford has made a trip from Gibraltar.' Colonel Crawford had been a friend of Robert's at Ardersier. In Montpellier he met Mr Marjoribanks, a banker and wine merchant, 'a Scotchman who, it is imagined had taken shelter here after the '45 to which he was a well-wisher. A Jacobite countryman to whom we had a letter of credit.' These letters of credit were as essential as the introductions, giving the travellers access to the private accounts of foreign residents, who would then be reimbursed by the Grand Tourists' British bankers. The Scots Grand Tourist was particularly well served in this respect since so many Scots, having fled after the '45, had found employment as mercenary soldiers across Europe. Hope got acquainted with 'a gentlemanly body, one Rouss, an apothecary who is intimate with all the grandees of this place and who has been intimate with the Marquis of Annandale when he was abroad.' The States General – the nearest thing the rigidly monarchical France had to a parliament – was meeting in Montpellier during their visit under the chairmanship of the Duc de Richelieu whom they met at his levée. 'The place is full of game, gaiety and madness at this time. We arrived when lodgings, vivres, and every necessity is triple priced.' Richelieu was the grand-nephew of the cardinal and the embodiment of vice and luxury. Immensely rich and a notorious seducer, he was thought to be the model for Valmont in Laclos' *Les Liaisons Dangereuses*. They met the Conte de Monçant, commandant of the town, and attended

a ball given once or twice a week by Madame Janestan to all the beau monde. Hope went in before me . . . no sooner were we entered [into] the ballroom but I found Mr Hope had been pressed to dance, but would not. I was immediately set on and immediately complied. I had Madame herself for a partner with whom I tripped my minuet. I was desired by her to take out the Intendant's [the local Governor] lady who is one of the greatest in the town, with her I danced my second, was much pressed to dance a country dance, but found them so difficult that I could not consent; but had great satisfaction on the inspection of the others who some of them performed wonders of grace and agility, and so different from ours that it could not miss giving high delight. Towards the end of the ball Madam Janestan insisted on my giving her another walk, which I again gratified her in. I after receiving a kind invitation from the Intendant's lady to dine or sup with her husband M. Saintepriest and her, and so excusing ourselves by our departure which was fixed for this day we took our leave and retired to the Duc de Richelieu's for supper where we had been invited and were honoured with his own table and among the ladies, whilst the nobility and many persons of distinction were at tables in other rooms. There was not above 30 at our table and there are near 300 people of one kind and another that sups or dines at the Duke's every day during the continuation of the States. After supper, which is the great meltith* in France, I was most superb in every aspect. The ladies withdrew about 11 and played out these hands at cards which supper interrupted, whilst the gentlemen betook themselves to gaming which was serious and would not perhaps finish until 4 or 5 in the morning. About 12 we returned home fully satisfied with our amusement and sorry that time forced us into retiring from acquaintance and company so high and agreeable, as I am considered upon furthering.

The industrious pair did manage to see two – presumably incomprehensible – plays and a concert before leaving Montpellier, reaching Aix-en-Provence on 21 December.

In Aix they were dined by one John Burgoyne who had eloped to France with the daughter of the Earl of Derby, and was already known as a dandy and man of fashion. His place in history lay ahead of him when as 'Gentleman Johnny' and a Major General he would surrender his army at Saratoga in 1777 and seal the fate of Britain's American colonies. Burgoyne made the inevitable introductions, one to the Duc de Villars, Governor of Provence, and with the same inevitability, the evening ended in gaming. Robert reported on a lady who, 'though not twenty-four, quits the field of battle with the wrinkles of fifty years, hollowed by her sour temper'. Robert was becoming bored with the vapid lives of the aristocrats whom he had set out to court and who would be essential to his architectural practice. Like many ambitious young men of his class he was an inveterate snob and

* 'Mealtime'. Archaic Scots usage.

realised that he was only just accepted as the friend of Lord Charles Hope. Therefore, if he made one false move he would, quite simply, be excluded from society; his inability to play cards, combined with his unwillingness to gamble had already isolated him as a member of a lower class. He was now starting to realise that the nobility were, to a large extent, his intellectual inferiors – a discovery he was careful to conceal. He was, however, happy enough to provide his sisters with grand names to bandy about in the snobbish society circles of Edinburgh.

On their next stage, bad horses forced them to return to Avignon where sightseeing around the entire town took them three hours. The present-day *Guide Michelin* recommends setting aside five hours for the palaces and churches alone, but Robert was too narrowly focused to be interested in mediaeval papal palaces. He was, however, entranced with the countryside. 'The verdure on the ground was as fine as in the Barefoot Parks in the spring.' He continues to assure his sister that en route for Italy 'we go in water so shallow that no pirate can come within reach of us' and 'they never come within 200 miles of where we sail. I will have very bad luck if in 20 or 30 hours we are not at Genoa.' He also has a letter to 'General Paterson at Nice who is commander of the Galleys who we are pretty sure will give us one to carry us to Genoa, in which case we shall have a fine cabin to eat, drink and sleep in with a fire which will prevent the only inconvenience I dreaded which was the cold of the sea air at this season.'

In Marseilles the couple dined at a *table d'hôte* – a comparatively cheap fixed-price restaurant – where, conspicuous as rich Grand Tourists, they were immediately importuned by a pleasant-mannered man who suggested that he send for some cards so that they could play 'as high as we pleased' for as long as they liked. Quite rightly, Robert judged him to be 'a light headed fellow and a sharper' in 'a town composed of gamesters or rather I should say sharpers' and they quickly left for Toulon on 26 December.

There they participated in more pleasant and uneventful

socialising, with Robert meeting Claude Vernet who had been living in Rome for 19 years. Claude-Joseph Vernet was a highly regarded exponent of sentimental Italian landscapes. Now Robert had 'a long walk and much discussion of painting' with him. This was much more to his taste than watching noblemen playing incomprehensible card games.

Then they left France, after a journey of two months, and arrived at Nice in Piedmont on 2 January 1755. Robert headed his letter, 'Nice in Italy'. While they poured with sweat in the sunshine of the Côte d'Azur, their chaise had to cross the river Var – 'as ugly a water as I ever saw' – but good care was taken of the Grand Tourists with 'four naked devils who stood on either side of the chaise and conducted it through the shallowest part'. On crossing the Var the pair entered the Kingdom of Sardinia, which had recently annexed the province from Savoy. In Nice, Hope had a letter of introduction to General Paterson, the commander of the province who had served 30 years in the King of Sardinia's army. With General Paterson they met another Grand Tourist, Kenneth Mackenzie, 'Lord Fortrose's son, a boy of 9 years', with a Dr Mackenzie as his bear-leader. Robert, still feeling his inadequacy with languages, somewhat bitterly reported of the boy, 'He speaks all languages with equal facility.' Robert and Hope rode on mule-back to the Villa Franca where they were lodging, but that night Hope went alone to the general's while Robert, rather priggishly, stayed at home writing to his mother. He found it was better than 'inspecting games I don't know and seeing a second time ladies who are ugly to perfection and the stupidest bitches I have ever met with.' This is yet another note of disillusion with the company he has been keeping. He did, however, meet a gentleman who was living in Rome who pointed out that as they would probably arrive in the city during Carnival 'when everything is dear and scarce', he would pre-book lodgings and servants for them. The gentleman in question was Peter Grant, an Abbé, one of the most influential foreigners in Rome, and with whom Robert would form a close friendship.

Arrangements were made for the voyage to Genoa, but not in the hoped-for galley.

> We have engaged our felucca* or vessel for going [to] Genoa . . . It is at present charming weather and if it continues we shall have a very pleasant sail and are assured we will not be above 24 hours on the water, and consequently but one night ashore on the way. We have provided ourselves with some charming wine, some cold roasted fowls and some bread for eatables and drinkables and in case our bedding should not be good for that night we sleep ashore, I bought a pair of excellent sheets at Lyons and have just now purchased a pair of charming blankets, while with the assistance of my surcoat, fur boots, we will bid defiance to the coldest air. Though unless we are very unlucky I am really of opinion there is neither danger nor inconveniency nor difficulty in it.

The fear of corsairs, or Barbary pirates, was very real. Heavily armed and expert seamen using fast ships from Algeria, Tunisia and Morocco, they were rightly feared throughout the Mediterranean, the West coast of Africa and northwards through the Bay of Biscay. The corsairs took Europeans prisoner before selling them as slaves to the rulers of the coastal cities of North Africa. The unfortunate captives were then put to brutal forced labour and heavily encouraged to write home for large ransoms to be paid. This was usually effective and the piracy ran as a smoothly organised business but, as Robert was advised, they seldom risked sailing too close to the shores of France and Italy.

During the first week of January 1755 Robert Adam and Charles Hope sailed for the Republic of Genoa.

---

* A felucca was a popular sailing craft in the Mediterranean with a crew of three and capable of carrying up to ten passengers. Feluccas had two 'lateen', or triangular sails on yard-arms at right angles to the masts. They are still in use today in Egypt and the Red Sea.

CHAPTER THREE

The Grand Tourist

꙾

The companions arrived safely in Genoa in January 1755 having avoided kidnap and shipwreck but were duly astonished at the changeability of the Mediterranean weather. Travellers were warned in their guide books that the air at Genoa was 'unwholesome and noxious to strangers' and Thomas Gray thought the city could 'make you sick of marble'. From having poured with sweat as they traversed the River Var they were now 'circumspect travellers and very careful of our persons until the weather improves', since it had rained and snowed since their arrival. 'We loved the conversing with Marquises and Counts who are our daily companions. In short we look upon the English consul here as a rank below. The locals think we are first rates who dare presume on such familiarities with the Balbis, the Rassos and other ancient families.'

Robert is slighting of the consul who 'deals a little in the merchant way, is a great attender of the opera, being mostly in company with a Genoese lady of whom he is much enamoured'. This rather nauseating sycophancy for people whom he often despised for their shallowness and devotion to mindless gaming can be explained by the fact that in a professional role Robert would, very soon, have to be able to pass among the aristocracy as a near equal. The reference to the consul dealing 'a little in the merchant way' is indicative of his disparaging attitude towards tradesmen and non-inherited wealth.

In Genoa this access to the great families meant the opportunity to have a private view of the frescoed and decorated Palazzo Balbi which had entranced Lady Mary Wortley

Montagu 40 years previously: 'The perfection of architecture and the utmost profusion of rich furniture is to be seen there disposed with most elegant taste and lavish magnificence . . . I was particularly pleased with a Lucretia in the house of Balbi. A Cleopatra by the same hand deserves to be mentioned, and I should say more of her if Lucretia had not first engaged my eyes.'¹ Robert was more attracted to the noble name of Balbi than to his collection but was delighted to have entry to the private boxes at the opera. The opera was, of course, much more of a social event than a musical one and visiting the boxes of society was an important part of the evening entertainment, where 'the ladies give you a little curtsey'. Robert in his letters is keen to show off his newly acquired knowledge of opera and praises the performances in Genoa, 'In which are both good singers and dancers, particularly one man called Rolfi, who in my opinion is the best I have ever heard.' Rolfi was a castrato and one can only wonder how many castrati Robert had previously heard. He asks his sister Jenny to get Nelly to enquire of Niccolò Pasquali, a minor composer and violin salesman who had arrived in Edinburgh in 1740, 'Perhaps Pasquali may know the touching air of the whole which begins *casa tu fosti e sei* in the opera *Sorestro* [sic] *Re d'Egitto* which has never failed to move me more than any thing I ever heard.' The opera is by Domenico Terradella – sometimes Domingo Terradellas –a Spanish composer who had died in Rome four years previously having had some slight success in London in 1746. Robert is pretending to be much more knowledgeable than he really is since he could never have heard the opera before. More realistically, he wrote of longing 'to be at Leghorn because I long to see your letters and surely they are there for me. I long to be at Rome for there we shall rest from our labours of travelling and begin those of taste and study.'

Unable, as always, to resist shopping, Robert sent home enough uncut velvet in grey, dark chestnut and light blue for three suits for 'Johnnie', some black for a cloak for his mother, and a 'bonny green' for his nephew 'wee Willy'. He ordered a pair of shoes and knee buckles for himself.

Robert and Charles set sail for Leghorn on 18 January but were detained by rough weather en route and stayed overnight at Sestri halfway between Genoa and Lerici. They then stayed at Lerici after 'rowing the whole way thanks to no wind and the sea as smooth as glass'. And on 'Monday morning driving on to rest overnight in Viareggio, then on Tuesday on fine roads through fine country, sometimes in the Duchy of Massa, sometimes in the Republic of Lucca and then in the Land of Tuscany that hitherto charmingest of country'. On Monday 21 January he reached Pisa and forebore a 'poetical rhapsody' on the beauties of the Arno since the weather has 'at present freezed up my lyric facultys'. He saw 'nothing but withered myrtle, frozen oranges and blasted evergreens'.

The party arrived in Pisa but since he was now within 15 miles of his letters, 'we hired a coach the next morning and left the hanging tower, the Cathedral and other curiosities to stand until our return.' He was delighted that he had news of home from his sisters but noted that 'Jamie, that worthless infidel has never wrote me'. In Leghorn it was so cold that there was skating on the canals between there and Pisa, 'a phenomenon never before known in this sultry soil'. They were accorded the usual round of hospitality by Mr Dicks, the English ambassador, and his wife, although when invited to dine with them the next day Robert hopes not to 'discover her a wolf in sheep's clothing . . . did not Shakespeare assure us that one may smile and smile and play the villain, alias a limmer?' 'Limmer' is a Scots term of abuse, often implying that a woman's morals are not above reproach: 'tart' or 'slapper' would be a modern equivalent. Robert was puzzled by the open cordiality of most women in Europe. On one hand he found the social flirting exciting, but on the other he had a very puritanical suspicion of it as being insincere and therefore to be condemned.

He attended a private concert with Nardini, 'a prodigious fine fiddle'. This was Pietro Nardini who would become director of music for the Duke of Tuscany and whose playing was greatly admired by Leopold Mozart, Wolfgang's father. More professionally he says, 'Tell Johnnie that I have been much on the observe with respect to concert rooms etc., but never have seen anything extraordinary in any shape as they perform mostly on the stage in playhouses, like the London oratories and the few concert halls are quite plain without any coving at all, which is certainly the right thing, as the cove forms echoes, reboundings and unjust sounds. Part cornices won't do, though I think the real ones [ought to have] no breakings of medallions, blocks, or even den[tils] which might in some degree hurt the sound. I shall not fail to enquire at Nardini concerning his opinion on the subject. I shall communicate intelligence as soon as [I] get any on this subject.' The modern science of acoustics was all but unknown in Robert's day but practice and experience had shown that from the Greek and Roman amphitheatres to the opera houses of the eighteenth century, a balance had to be struck between soft and hard furnishings, as the luxury of an interior could lead to poor sound transmission. Similarly, round or highly domed buildings, such as the Victorian Albert Hall, result in random reverberations. Robert here is putting function first, a concept which would have been foreign to his father.

Robert's sense of conversational isolation had been severe in France, where Hope could converse in French and Robert could not, but here, in Italy, he saw a chance to improve his position. 'He does not speak Italian so well as he did the French, and I will apply myself to the languages, whenever I get settled.' Before any settling could happen he had to return to Pisa where he found, 'the tower a horrible but most astonishing object. I studied its structure very minutely and jotted down my opinion of it.' Charles Hope was here able to achieve the purpose of his visit and meet up with his son. The reunion was the more pleasant since William Hope had taken a box at the opera for the season. Robert ignored whatever was being performed in favour of social anecdote. 'We soon cast our eyes towards a very pretty girl dressed in masquerade who went through the whole boxes in the house to pay her respects to the other company (a privilege all masks have). She sometimes pulled off the mask from her face and showed it superior in spirited expression, pleasing smiles, agreeable features to any I have seen whilst a prodigious delicate shape and thoroughbred manner made us cock our ears and make inquiry about her. We soon found her to be of no small rank being the nearest surviving relation of the Medici family. Her own name [was] Mary of Medici, but [she was] married to a gentleman of the customs of Pisa and now called Signora Gianni.' They met her again at the casino and Hope, who now spoke at least some Italian, was clearly stricken, visiting her in her box at the opera, handing her to her coach outside the casino, leaving the monoglot Robert standing apart. Robert wrote: 'Hope, who gibbers Italian, was soon in close conversation, whilst I stared and could say nothing. Think how I cursed Italian and all foreign languages!' Later they visited Signora Gianni in her box at the opera while Robert uttered not a word but moralised with some vehemence on the unfairness of languages. He did manage to share with Hope the privilege of handing her into her carriage and at a ball on the next night danced 'many minuets with her, as indeed I did with all the quality of Pisa – some dozens at least.'

By 30 January Robert and Charles had reached Florence. A huge Carnival was in full swing, with 'everyone from a marquis to a shoe-black traversing the streets from morning to night. Coaches are filled equally with princes and Killovy men,* Harlequin was the postilion and a devil the coachman while 3 or 4 monstrous figures loaded the back of the coach. I danced with all the greatest quality and with some of the greatest whores and with the handsomest of both kinds whenever I could get at them.' In his letter Robert asks, 'What way do you think I spent these three mornings? I wager you won't guess. Says one, seeing the Venus of Medici, seeing the antique statues and glorious pictures? No! Why, in short, skating on the ice. The Arno is frozen from one side to the other . . . We have scraped together 3 pairs of skates, on which Mr Hope and a very clever fellow, one Wilton, a statuary and your humble servant have crawled and straddled and paddled upon a dub.† without the walls of the

---

* I have been unable to trace this reference and presume it is an Adam family joke, referring to a group of workers Robert particularly disliked.
† Scots: pond or puddle.

town to the no small amazement of the bystanders who have uttered more Jesus Marias and other marks of astonishment than can be expressed.' Wilton was the sculptor Joseph Wilton now living in Florence and would prove a useful future contact for Robert. But Carnival came to an end, Lent began and Robert returned to his studies. 'Since I gave over the gaiety of this place which finished with the carnival . . . To feast on marble ladies, to dance attendance in the chamber of Venus and to trip a minuet with old Otho, old Cicero and those other Roman worthies whose very busts seem to drip contempt at my legerity.'

His 'legerity' did not prevent him from meeting, through the good offices of Wilton, one Charles-Louis Clérisseau. 'I have found a gentleman whom I am to carry to Rome with me who will put me on a method of improving myself more in drawing and architecture than ever I had any ideas of. I have got intelligence of some good drawings of antique things which I will buy.' Charles-Louis Clérisseau was born in 1721, the son of a 'perfumer of gloves' in Paris. He studied architecture at the Académie and, in 1749, took up a Prix de Rome to study under Gian Paolo Pannini, the French Academy in Rome's professor of perspective. A devout Roman Catholic and a brilliant and hard-working student, Clérisseau fell foul of the Academy authorities in a dispute over registration for Easter Communion. He refused to apologise publicly and a private apology to the principal of the Academy, Charles Natoire, only resulted in Natoire calling Clérisseau mentally unbalanced. Even allowing for his quarrelsome nature, he was a favourite among the visiting Englishmen in Rome, but in the spring of 1754 he left Rome for Florence.

The meeting of Robert Adam and Clérisseau was to change both their lives and Robert spelt out his future intentions in a long letter to William. Since William was the youngest brother and had little influence over the direction of the firm, Robert felt that he could be used as a sounding board for his personal thoughts. 'I have also got acquainted with one Clérisseau who draws in architecture delightfully in the free manner I wanted. I hope to reap some introduction from him. Chambers, whom Jamie knows of, owes all his hints and notions to this man with whom he has differed and to whom he has behaved ungratefully, this Wilton tells one.' Chambers was the 33-year-old architect William Chambers whose career would touch Robert's at many points. Born in Göteborg in Sweden, he had been educated in England, had served the Swedish East India Company in China and Bengal, and become seriously wealthy as a result. He returned to England briefly, publishing works on Chinese architecture and meeting Frederick and Augusta, Prince and Princess of Wales. He left England for Paris and Rome where he studied with Piranesi and was commissioned by several visiting noblemen to work on their English houses. He also designed the mausoleum of the Prince of Wales in 1752, although it was not built, and was appointed architectural tutor to the future George III. He left Rome in 1755 leaving an antagonised Clérisseau and a daunting reputation behind him.

Robert's meeting with Clérisseau made him realise that he faced several dilemmas. Firstly, his studies of the ancient masters must now take precedence over his socialising and he must look ahead to organising the pattern of his stay in Rome. There he could not exist simply as a rich tourist and dilettante sketcher but would have to put himself under Clérisseau's tuition. This he was happy to do, describing Clérisseau as, 'A Nathaniel in whom there is no guile,* yet there is the utmost knowledge of architecture, of perspective, and of design and colouring I ever saw or had any conception of. He raised my ideas. He created emulation and fire in my breast. I wished above all things to learn his manner, to have him with me at Rome, to study close with him and to purchase of his works. What I wished for I obtained. He took a liking to me. He engaged in doing what drawing I pleased. He engaged to go with me to Rome and if it suited my convenience would stay in the same house as me, would serve me as an antiquarian, would teach me perspective and drawing,

* An allusion to John 1: 43–51

71

would give me copies of all his studies of the antique basilicas and other ornaments. In short, he sets out the day after me to be at my command as soon as I arrived at Rome and I shall furnish him a chamber and pay his meltiths and think it is one of the luckiest circumstances [that] could have happened.'

Putting together his household, he next found Giovanni Batista Cipriani, a painter.

I got acquainted with Cipriani, the best natured lad in the world who draws in the most delightful manner imaginable in the style of all the great masters, engraves charmingly, and is exceptionally modest. From him I bought some academy figures, some heads, hands and feet which will do your business nicely. They are all done by himself and exquisitely drawn. Not contented with these advances in taste I hunted after drawings and pictures with design to see many but purchase few. And as to pictures I found them so exorbitant that there was no getting at them, but I have been the more extravagant in drawing of which I have made a noble purchase to the satisfaction of all the connoisseurs here. And I believe I may say they are as genuine and as neat an assortment as ever was bought and from the choice I was so lucky to make in which I stumbled upon the best thing. My reputation for taste in Michaelangelo, Guido, Raphael, Corregio, Jordano and Paul Veronese has risen greatly as I have a few of most of these great masters. And I have likewise a very good parcel of ornaments in architecture by Pietro de Cortona and Salviati which even Clérisseau hugs himself at the thought of having copies of. I cannot help telling you likewise of my having bought pictures of Lucca Jordano of small size but esteemed prodigious fine. And my whole purchases are reckoned extremely cheap which I fancy you will believe when I assure you it is not near £100.'

Robert was also aware that although he was independently wealthy, he was still a partner in the firm of Adam Brothers and therefore his exploration of classical architecture must have some practical results. He also excused his absence, which he could now see would be longer than originally planned, by the necessity to lay solid artistic foundations. 'You must conceive my ideas in time and with application would extend my taste for architecture, would like my manner of drawing become every day more free, more grand and more masterly. At London I first felt the change of taste grown on me from that I had contracted in Scotland, not greater was that change than is the present to that of the antique, the noble and stupendous. But here I play the touchstone, here I must suggest a difficulty of no small moment, as it is of the greatest consequence before one begins. And it is shortly this. Wilton, Clérisseau, and in short all my friends, tell me that, in order to do anything in Rome, I must first apply to drawing, I must walk much about and sketch after the antiques.'

Robert's second dilemma was that he realised that he could not continue with his social life amid the aristocracy and at the same time undertake close study. 'I must absolutely resolve to lay aside the fick-facks* of company. I am sufficiently sensible of the reasonableness of this advice. I am conscious that hitherto while I have dedicated my time to gay life I have done nothing else and I am conscious that if I attempt the same in Rome I must go through with it. If I lose Clérisseau, who will stay a month or two with me, I will lose my improvements in architecture entirely.' Time would tell how successful the gregarious Robert Adam would be at this self-discipline.

However, a third problem was that of his status. Robert could not continue at the elbow of Charles Hope at all times, and when Hope returned to Scotland he would have to rely on the introductions he had so far gained. Robert had experienced the deleterious effect of having the wrong introductions. He had brought a letter of introduction from George Mercer, a London builder, to Wilton, the sculptor, who was lodging in Florence with Horace Mann, the British Ambassador to the Tuscan court. Mann had done his duty and introduced Robert and Charles to the Governor of Florence as

* Scots: whims, trifles

well as inviting the pair to dinner. Robert seemed pleased enough with the dinner party but received no other invitations from the ultra-snobbish Mann. Mann had regarded Wilton as no higher than a servant, and since Robert had consorted with him as a fellow aesthete, he had placed himself on the same level. The door to Florentine society slammed shut. 'On the other hand, if I am known in Rome to be an architect, if I am seen drawing or with a pencil in my hand, I cannot enter into genteel company who will not admit an artist, or if they do admit him, will very probably rub affronts upon him in order to prevent his appearing at their card-playings, balls, and concerts. If I am not at first introduced by Hope to Cardinal Albani and the other great people to whom he has letters, I never again can have that opportunity. If I am introduced at first by him, I lose the most precious time which is that [when] Clérisseau stays with one.' Robert then put his problem plainly.

So that the difficulty is, shall I lose Hope, my introduction to the great, or shall I lose Clérisseau and my taste for the grand. Mr Wilton, who interests himself much in my affairs, and to whom I have communicated my difficulty, says that he would advise me to give up thought of the great ones entirely as there are not one of a hundred that are in Rome that ever see them, so that I would be no worse than them. But as the only way to indulge both a little he proposes the following expedient. When you go to Rome, says he, you may be introduced to Albani, etc., and as soon as you have got your introductions over, you may leave Rome and go for eight or ten days to Naples. Return incognito from Naples to Rome and live private, indulging amongst your acquaintances pursuing your studies and improving. And in this way you will find much more satisfaction than from having paid twenty visits to the same Duchess or Countess and will have more to boast of when you get home.

And he added that before leaving Rome, 'you would incline again to appear in public you may do it, posing for a great connoisseur and a gentleman of fortune passionately fond of architecture and the fine arts who had retired to Rome on purpose to study them a little. This is all feasible and sensible, but I doubt the practicality of the execution, though the plan is well laid out.'

Robert obviously wanted to keep both balls in the air for as long as possible, but he has clearly realised that he must at some point make the step from wealthy Grand Tourist to scholarly researcher. But it is a step which he only wanted to have to take in extremis. 'In short I hope to have my ideas greatly enlarged and my taste formed on the solid foundation of genuine antiquity. I already feel a passion for sculpture and painting which I was before ignorant of, and I am convinced that my conceptions of architecture will become much more noble than I could have attained had I remained in Britain. Now and then I launch out into the fine world and again I retire among my fellow connoisseurs and virtuosi. In one hour I dote upon my Marquis Corsi, next you see me amongst a heap of portafolios [sic] surrounded by Clerisianos, Ritters and Chiprianos. Thus I pass my time.'

He ended the letter asking that James's opinion be sought. He also begs him not to put 'architect' on the back of the letters. He should be addressed as 'Robt Adam, Esq. or Mon.r. Robert Adam, Gentilhomme Anglais'. As was common amongst Scots at the time, he felt no shame in being addressed as 'English', Scotland being officially 'North Britain'. Robert spoke in the Lowland Scots dialect and wrote in Southern English with, as we have seen, occasional Scots words. The urge for Scotsmen to speak Southern English or 'Anglice' did not gather speed until 1761 when Thomas Sheridan, an Irishman, gave a series of lectures on English speech in Edinburgh, starting a decline from which the Scots dialect has only recently begun to recover. Sir John Summerson identified the multiple strains in Adam's character. 'He is at once the climbing bourgeois, the arrogant patrician, and the dedicated artist and in all three characters madly ambitious – lovable only in his profound loyalty to his own kith and kin.'[2]

Finally Robert heard from Rome that Abbé Grant had arranged lodgings, a coach and servants for him. He looked forward to 'a life less sedentary', although his life in carnival Florence can hardly have been described as sedentary. Writing to his sisters, he expresses doubts that his letters from Rome will be inspired with the spirit of eloquence. 'Lord knows that was never my gift and I doubt it is too late to acquire it. But if plain Brosy Hall* erudition and Cowgate style will suffice to describe my thoughts of that so much renowned place you may chance to have a sketch of it.' He warns Elizabeth that his trip will cost twice as much as he had intended, 'as I am determined not to pinch in any way as it is but once in a lifetime and therefore ought to be honoured a little.' He assures her that he has not forgotten them all and still holds Blair Adam in his imagination. 'I often look out to the deer park, survey its winding paths'. In his mind's eye, he sees her in her pantry, 'I think it is quite cured of damps' and asks for the Lord's blessing on all his family. In these letters there is just a hint of his apprehension at the step he is about to take.

On 19 February, the day before his departure, he wrote to James, 'I sought out virtuous draughtsmen. I enquired out drawings, prints and heard likewise of some pictures that are to be sold. I saw and liked and contracted an intimacy and friendship with Wilton the sculptor who is sensible, civil and good hearted'.

In a final round of Florentine shopping Robert bought three volumes of Tuscan house designs which he found 'far from disagreeable' and copied down some operatic airs for Helen. He also sent the family four Parmesan cheeses, one for his London agents, Innes and Clerk and one for Colonel Skinner in Inverness. He hinted that a whole cheese might go to Lord Dumfries. He apologised for not having bought silks in Florence but assured his sisters that he had heard that Naples might be the place. His journeying was now at an end and the pair of travellers could leave for Rome, the Eternal City and the fount of classicism. Robert was on the brink of what he hoped would be the discovery of the true essence of architecture.

'There was a time when, after a long day's drive the *vetturino*

---

* Brose was a cheap but nourishing soup, so Brosy Hall was a place for the unpretentious commoner.

would look round and exclaim *"Ecco Roma!"* The vast *campagna* stretched for miles around and in the distance, at the focus of all the converging lines of broken aqueducts, there was a huddle of roofs and a bubble-like dome, the cupola of St Peter's.'[3] And so it was for Robert and Charles on 24 February as their coach approached the Eternal City after four days on the road from Florence. The first sight of the Piazza del Popolo may have disappointed some travellers: 'A man on his first arrival at Rome is not much fired with its appearance. The narrowness of the streets, the thinness of the inhabitants, the prodigious quantity of monks and beggars, give but a gloomy aspect to this renowned city.'[4] However, Lady Mary Wortley Montagu felt that, 'Whatever notions I had of the magnificence of Rome I can assure you that it has surpassed all my ideas of it.'[5] In the eighteenth century Rome's magnificence was limited to the Vatican and the classical ruins, with a permanent population of barely 150,000, mainly clustered around St Peter's on the north bank of the Tiber. Here the principal employer in the city was the Church, causing the population to swell or shrink according to the occurrence of religious festivals. On the other bank were the principal classical ruins with a few of the houses of aristocratic families inside extensive gardens, where the Grand Tourists found properties to rent, with the British contingent tending to settle themselves in the vicinity of the Spanish Steps. For the most part the ruins were unfrequented except by shepherds with their flocks. In Piranesi's etching of the site, the Baths of Caracalla were surrounded by fields of cabbages. This somewhat melancholy grandeur was one of the many reasons leading to plentiful 'ruins' being constructed in English deer parks.

Robert was laid low with migraine on arrival but by 1 March he managed to write to his mother and assure her that 'all reports of Alps and pirates and other terrifications are all exaggerated'. The rain and his headache had prevented any sightseeing, although he took a 'vomit and physic with no effect', after which he was bled and was cured. During his confinement he was visited by Abbé Grant who, while ensuring that the domestic arrangements he had made were all satisfactory, sat with Robert in the evenings and read to him. 'He is a friendly, obliging and sensible creature,' Robert wrote. Peter Grant, the son of John Grant of Blairfindy, was a Gaelic speaker who had been ordained at the Scots College in Rome in 1735. He acted as a guide and facilitator for most British visitors to Rome regardless of their religious persuasion, earning him the nickname of '*L'Introduttore*'. He had known William Adam, Robert's father, when William was working for Lord Braco. Abbé Grant is 'as good a Jacobite and as good a Catholic, as true a friend, as worthy a man, as e'er a Christian in Europe. He is constantly with me, for four or five hours a day'. Physically, Grant was of substantial build and Robert occasionally referred to him as the 'Abbé Grande'. Robert was probably unaware that, with James Stewart, the Old Pretender and self-styled James III still keeping his court in Rome, the British government kept a close watch on people such as the Abbé, as well as those visitors whom the Jacobite exiles befriended.

No suspicion can have been aroused by Robert's first visit on his recovery – to his fellow Edinburgher, Allan Ramsay. Ramsay was 42 years old, with his success as a portrait painter was still ahead of him,but he was now living in Rome with his 'wife and sister who are well and hearty, [but] she is almost at the down-lying'. Ramsay was living on the Viminale hill on the edge of the city with a 'view of the most remarkable places in ancient Rome. But what chiefly recommends the situation to me is its distance from the Piazza di Spagna by which I am able to seclude myself a good deal from the English travellers without falling out with any of them, and to preserve the greater part of my time for painting, drawing and reading, which were I living in the neighbourhood would be altogether spent in dinners, suppers and jaunts.'[6]

Robert continued to his mother, 'We are situated on the banks of the Tiber and from our windows we have a most charming prospect of St Peter's, the castle of St Angelo and the hills fields and woods in the country. And we are on the very spot, formerly called the Campus Martius, or the field of Mars . . . it is the fashionable, the Westminster end of the town'. Here Robert makes parallels with London as if he were a regular inhabitant and seems to wish to appear to be as familiar with it as with his native Edinburgh. His mother would have smiled at his growing ambition to be regarded as a cosmopolitan.

Old Rome and its ruins are inhabited only by people who love retirement, cheap palaces and study, here Ramsay has retired, here are amphitheatres, triumphal arches, fragments of temples and other antiquities so grand, so noble and awful that it fills the mind with a reverential fear and respect. What pleased me most of all was the Pantheon, of which the greatness and simplicity of parts fills the mind with extensive thoughts, stamps upon you the solemn, the grave, the majestic and seems to prevent all those ideas of gaiety or frolic which all our modern buildings admit of and inspire. St Peter's is a very noble building and is not admired without justice. The proportions are so well affixed to particular parts and to the whole that, though a monstrous building, it has a very opposite air neither being heavy nor huge in appearance.

As usual, for the classicist, the Renaissance, however splendid, is felt to be inferior to the grandeur or nobility of the antique. Robert's reverence for the Pantheon, for example, would influence many of his future designs

The old temptations of living the glamorous life are still with him but he says he will consult with the Abbé as to whether he should 'dip into company'. Hope, who is clearly dipping extensively into company, is seldom at home except when the couple dine with guests. Robert's establishment now includes Clérisseau who is quartered in the next room 'where is very convenient, as we can sit and draw in one another's rooms or amuse ourselves as most agreeable to us'. Robert has also acquired an Italian servant, Antonio, who addresses him as 'most illustrious' or '*illustrissimo*' and has his valet de chamber, Donald, to attend on him. Donald, no longer nicknamed 'King of Sleep', is praised by Robert for doing 'very well' in his new environment. There is also a coachman and his equipage, so Robert Adam is settled into Rome in as gentlemanly a style as can be arranged and is ready seriously to set about his Grand Tourism.

'I have not as yet seen any of the great ones of this place, only Cardinal York in his coach coming from St Peter's.' This was Henry Benedict Maria Clement Stewart, Duke of York and younger brother of Bonnie Prince Charlie. Not only was he a cardinal and a duke but he was also Bishop of Frascati. The cardinal was one of the sights of Rome and tourists could see him daily saying mass in a side chapel of St Peter's.

Robert tells his mother that he is learning Italian and finds foreign languages a curse, but necessary. However, Robert did speak fluent Latin so he was not entirely without a means of communication. The monuments and 'curiosities' of Rome were liberally captioned in Latin, albeit epigraphic Latin, with all the abbreviations used in carved inscriptions, but with imagination and ingenuity he was able to read these inscriptions.

His first entry to Rome was not the Piazza del Popolo but the end of the Flaminian Way – Via Flaminia – a road trodden by the very writers he had struggled over in the cold classrooms of Edinburgh's High School. On every side he was seeing classical history made stone, the tombs of Hadrian and Augustus, the Temples of Vesta and Claudius, the Column of Trajan and the ruins of the Forum. At the edge of the Forum was a small undecorated brick building measuring about 70 feet by 100 under a shallow pedimented roof with dentillated eaves. This was the Curia Julia, which for most of the Roman Empire's duration housed the Senate. Its power extended from Poland to Portugal and from Carlisle to the Caspian and yet it was much smaller than Edinburgh's now empty Parliament House. The building was erected in 29 BC by Octavius, who was to become the Emperor Augustus. He said of Rome, 'I inherited it brick and left it marble' and it is likely that the senate building had been clad in the finest stucco, with a high proportion of powdered marble. It would have glittered in the Roman sun. If, as he thought, Adam was returning to the first principles of architecture, then this was an outstanding example.

To be the man I may be, much is to be done and I don't exaggerate when I assure you as yet, with all I have seen, studied, and done hitherto, [I] think myself a mere beginner, and what's more I hope to make of being here [more] than any body would imagine. Chambers, who has been here six years, is as superior to me as I am to Deacon Mark*, for greatness of thought and nobility of invention, drawing and ornamenting. But, damn my blood, but I will have a fair try for it and expect to do as much in six months as he has done in as many years. But then it will require study and attention with application. But as this study, attention and application is of the most pleasant and wholesome sort, walking 4 or 5 miles every day through glorious antiquities, pleasant gardens, with fellow students and my instructor Clérisseau who reveres me as a sovereign monarch and prides himself on having such a scholar, I shall have infinite pleasure in my operations. I must write Johnnie and Jamie later and tell them how I am getting models made of all the antique ornaments, of friezes, cornices, vases etc., all in plaster which I am to send to Scotland. How I am employing painters, drawers etc., to do all the fountains, the buildings, the statues and all the things that are for use for drawing after and for giving hints to the imaginations of we modern divils [sic]. How I am buying up all the books of Architecture of altars, chapels, churches, views of Piranesi and of all the gates, windows, doors and ornaments that can be of service to us. In short, how I intend myself to send home a collection of drawings of Clérisseau's, my own, our myrmidons, which never was seen or heard of either in England or Scotland before.'

He wants the 'Gentlemen's' opinion of whether he should buy up a parcel of fragments of antiquity although he is afraid the freight charges could 'come very high'.

In short I am antique mad or what they would call in Scotland an Antick. But antique here, antique there, I hope to be capable to invent a great thing; if I should never be

---

* The deacons were the officials of the Guild of Hammermen, to which the brothers were obliged to belong. Robert had a low regard for 'deacons'.

able to execute one, and that's my ambition. Rome is the most glorious place in the Universal World, a grandeur, a tranquillity reigns in it, everywhere noble and striking remains of antiquity appear in it, which are so many that one who has spent a dozen years in seeing is still surprised with something new, the hills it stands on gives you every-where elevated prospects of town and country, the town rich with domes, spires and lofty buildings ancient and modern. The country near Rome, uneven, hilly, woody and adorned with villages and churches, so that had one their friends, nothing could persuade one to quit it for any other part I ever saw. In fact, for a man of taste, the day is too short.

The day was not too short for Robert's inevitable socialising and he dined with the Duke of Bridgewater who was visiting Rome with his bear-leader Robert Wood, the author of *The Ruins of Palmyra*. The duke had been a reluctant Grand Tourist. After a dismal childhood under a grim stepfather he journeyed first to France, where he had a scandalous affair with a French actress and disgraced himself by drinking to excess even by the standards of the eighteenth century. He did, however become fascinated by the Languedoc Canal and studied the science of canal building at the academy in Lyons. While in Italy with the long-suffering Wood he bought a considerable collection of art and antiquities but never unpacked them on his return, being more interested in coalmines and canal building. Like the eager puppy that he was, Robert asked Wood for his advice as to socialising in Rome. Wood replied, 'It will rather be a loss to you as an advantage, as you don't know the language, and as it will surely consume your time in some degree, as it will draw you into gaming, which you don't know and must lose at, and as I don't think it will be of the least service to you with your own countrymen who will rather regard you more as a gentleman who will despise these things and applies to study.' Wood, perhaps rendered cynical by his experiences with the drunken duke, clearly felt that any overt enthusiasm for aesthetics would render Adam *persona non grata* and advised him to concentrate on his study privately. However, Wood said that he could introduce Robert to the Duchess of Borghese where 'you will be extremely welcome'. 'But he says again that there are some of our own countrymen here who would be the readiest of any to put you out, as they did to a gentleman of above £5,000 a year, because his father, who was dead, had been a brewer in London.'

Robert still could not shake off his ambition to be a man about town, to 'dip a little into Italian company', and to this end he approached the ever reliable Abbé Grant. He advised him to wait and see if Hope would introduce him, but felt that socialising once or twice a week should not harm his studies too much since, anyway, 'the conversations and card-playing did not begin until 7 at night'. However, with the relationship between Adam and Hope now cooling rapidly, Robert reported, 'This he was so far from offering or doing that he shunned it, declined it, and showed that he did not want I should go anywhere alongst with him'. Grant advised him to encourage 'genteel though not noble conversations' until his Italian was better. Robert admitted that these rebuffs had one positive effect. 'Another good of this affair is that had Hope behaved with any tolerable civility like a companion or friend, I should have had regret at parting with him, whereas now I shall be infinitely happier without than with him, as I have here the good Abbé Grant and Clérisseau who would go through fire and water for me and the other is a vain, affected, childish coxcomb. He has bought about 20 things for his fingers within three days. This truth must be out. It lay long dormant and I wish to God it may come safe to hand that you may read and burn.' Robert also complained that, although Hope and he shared their lodgings and their costs, Hope issued invitations to his friends to dine with them solely in his own name so that the return invitations were to Hope alone. This example of aristocratic selfishness came as a surprise to Robert who had been optimistically presuming that he and Hope were now becoming able to behave as equals. In truth, Robert's continued close attachment was an embarrassment to Hope. During their time in France, Robert had been an entertaining enough companion, although the excursion to Montpellier had been Hope's idea and had never been discussed with Robert. Now Hope wanted to spend time with his social equals and Robert Adam, who had been an employee of his brother's, could not be regarded as one of these equals. But Adam was neither exactly a servant nor a bear-leader and therefore could not simply be dismissed. Hope simply ignored the dilemma and ignored Robert, thus, by his rules of behaviour, avoiding blame.

After a month in Rome Robert, in chatty mood, wrote to Helen on 22 March 1755, noting that he had heard that his brother John had had a daughter to be called Mary after their mother. This is followed by more news from Rome. 'Next week commences the Holy Week, so famous for the music of the *Miserere* which is sung three times that week and draws such crowds from all corners to hear it.' The *Miserere* was the choral setting of a psalm by Gregorio Allegri sung only by the choristers of the Sistine Chapel and closely guarded against copying. Fourteen years later, to the benefit of the wider world, Mozart, at the age of fourteen, transcribed the entire piece from memory after hearing it a single time. 'After the Holy Week, the strangers file off, many go to Naples, many to Venice and many return to England and some stay in Rome of which I am one. For this reason to be so comfortable as possible I wanted to secure myself a good house and a convenient one which should be cool in the summer, and contain the following chambers. A good bedchamber for myself and a little one for my friend Clérisseau, a hall in which to have 2 or 3 tables for draughtsmen and other myrmidons of art whom we employ, a good dining room, and a chamber for King Donald, with a kitchen if necessary. Such a house I found, with excellent rooms, well furnished and cool, situated on the top of a rising ground with a prospect both of the country and the whole city of Rome.' Robert's decision to set up accommodation for himself caused an acrimonious break with Hope and Robert became open in his hostility, 'I never had any affection for the man'.

The house was one of the most attractive of those available to visitors, standing on high ground near the Villa di Malta and the Piazza di Spagna. From these headquarters overlooking Rome he could sally forth for study or for shopping. 'I have already picked up some antique vases, antique altars and some lion's heads which tho' John, James, and John McGowan might well be ravished with, would be thought dirty scabbed stones by the females of our society.' Robert was pleased that Hope was jealous of them and, for the moment all seemed to be going well.

Needless to say, Rome and the expatriate community were hotbeds of rumour, political as well as social, and with the route to Italy passing through France, and the route home passing through Austria and Silesia, international politics were of vital interest. Britain's king was also Elector of Hanover and a natural ally of Frederick the Great who was now feeling his ambitions threatened by Britain's old enemy France. The results of the War of the Austrian Succession were, at best, inconclusive and the likelihood of France making further incursions into Eastern Europe and the Netherlands was high. Britain was already in conflict with France in Canada, India and the West Indies, so the possibility of war was always present. Robert, however, was optimistic and wrote to calm fears at home. 'As to the war with France, I believe *we* will have none. I can have a pass which will carry me the same as if there was peace, so that your friends have told you the truth.' He was wrong about the war but the freedom of travel he felt assured of was not unusual. If you managed to avoid contact with any of the armies and could reassure people that you were not a spy then travel was not greatly affected and it seemed extremely unlikely that any hostilities would prevent Robert from planning a journey to Naples.

His companions were Clérisseau, Grant and Abbé Stonor, the English Catholic agent and friend of Grant. After '5 days journeying in a *voiturine chaise* over Appian Ways and Classical plains' the quartet entered the twin Kingdoms of Naples and Sicily which were under Habsburg rule. While Rome was the home of the papacy and the centre for Grand Tourists seeking the classical ruins, Naples was a thriving and crowded Mediterranean city, the second largest city in Europe at the time. 'The suburbs contained above 3 thousand people who danced along the road to music of all different kinds in the most antique and Bacchanalian manner I ever saw, whilst others were assembled in gardens at the doors of their houses in drinking, eating and gaming. These multitudes of men women and children, their gay dresses and active spirit formed a most delightful scene. The infinite number of chaises also astonished me, all ranks of people use these light chairs drawn by a single horse which with difficulty holds two people and is driven by a man who stands on a board behind and with a long whip makes these little machines go like the wind.' In a later letter Robert calls these light chairs '*calèches*'. 'The town is a perfect beehive swarming with coaches, chariots, chaises and people and, though very large, every street is in confusion from morning to night.' Obviously some of the antagonism Robert had felt towards Hope in Rome was fading since, 'After dining with my old fellow traveller Hope, upon particular invitation, I am returned to the inn where all my company are fled to see catacombs and other curiosities, which charity has made me put off to the Lord's day, in order to employ the night in remembering my Scottish friends'. In other words, he was doing this duty by writing letters, in this case to Margaret on 8 April.

> Since I came here we have been every day busied with seeing curiosities and really they are of a very extraordinary kind, abstracting from the additional merit they acquire from their antiquity and the mention made of them in Classical writers. In one day's jaunt we visited the ancient town of Puteoli, now called Pozzuoli, the Infernal Lake, the Grotto of the Sybille, the Temple of Apollo. From that we went to the ancient Baia where Nero had a palace, the ruins of which are yet conspicuous. The consequence this town was of may be judged by the many ruins of temples which are yet to be seen such as the temples of Diana, Mercury and Venus of which my friend Clérisseau and I took sketches to enable our friends to partake of our pleasures.

Robert, of course, also had professional reasons for sketching the ruins. 'The many places underground, with curious remains of stucco ornaments, mosaic paving, etc., I have not time to describe as they deserve. So I shall only add that the Elysian Fields, the River Sticks [sic] all answer to Virgil's description as to situation but gain much from him with respect to their beauty. We closed the day with the Solfatara Hill and Grotto del Cane. The first being a Vesuvius burnt to ashes and only flaming in 2 or 3 places, and the last a small cave from the ground of which there issues a sulphurous flame which at once destroys any animal who is forced into it.' They witnessed a local man attempting to suffocate 'a very strong cur' which collapsed in the fumes before they pulled the unfortunate animal to fresh air and recovery but Robert makes no mention of the reaction either of the canicide or of his victim. 'The Grotto de Pausilippe, which is a road cut by the Romans for near a mile under ground is another of the many thousand convincing proofs of their grandeur.'

The opportunity for the classically trained Robert to see the actuality of what had previously been merely a grammatical and literary exercise turned him into an enthusiastic tourist. He was bubbling over with joy when he continued,

Yesterday morning we went to Portici, the town situated on the famous Herculaneum. With great pleasure and with much astonishment we viewed the many curious things that have been dug out of it, consisting of statues, busts, fresco paintings, books, bread, fruits, all sorts of instruments from a mattock to the most curious chirurgical probe. We traversed an amphitheatre with the light of torches, and pursued the tracks of palaces, their porticos and doors, division walls and mosaic pavements. We saw earthen vases and marble pavements just discovered while we were on the spot, and were shown some feet of tables in marble which were dug out the day before we were there. Upon the whole the subterranious [sic] town once filled with temples, columns and palaces and other ornaments of good taste is now exactly like a coalmine worked by galley slaves who fill up the waste rooms they leave behind them according as they are obliged to go a-dipping or strikeways. I soon perceived that the vulgar notion of its being swallowed up by an earthquake was false, but it was still worse, it was quite overcome by a flood of liquid stone from Mount Vesuvius which runs out upon an eruption, is called lava, and when cool is as hard and black as our whinstone, of this you find a solid body of 50 or 60 foot upon many places which had come down with such force from the hill and will overturn all houses and everything else it met with . . . I am afraid they will never be able to make anything of the books they have found, they are so black and rotten that they are no sooner touched than they fall to ashes. A priest has invented a machine by which he separates the leaves by degrees and has made out a few pages wrote [sic] in Greek by one Bion in defence of the Epicurean philosophy and another treatise against music, the author not known. The other rolls of books they have not yet been able to unfold and I'm afraid they never will.

The twin towns of Pompeii and Herculaneum had been popular holiday resorts for wealthy Romans until, in 29 BC, Vesuvius erupted and both towns were buried in the superheated pyroclastic flow. They remained lost until 1599 but major excavations did not begin until 1738 at Herculaneum and 1748 at Pompeii so the digging teams of the archaeologists – Robert's 'galley-slaves' – were still uncovering the ruins. It seems likely that the work at Pompeii was still so little advanced that it was not thought to be worth visiting.

Nothing daunted, Robert continued sightseeing. 'This morning we paid our devotions to the tomb of Virgil situated on the side of a most delightful hill near Naples. It is now almost quite ruinous and is only beautiful from its antiquity which induced me to make several sketches of it.' Robert intended to visit Caserta where Carlos III, the King of Naples, is building a palace 'of immense size'. 'I also intend seeing an ancient town of Cuma 6 or 7 miles from this town where there are many temples and other curiosities.' He did admit that he preferred the society in Rome but Abbé Grant and he dined out at a General's 'conversation' where there were 'pretty girls and civil people'.

Robert's socialising in the south of Italy was limited but thanks to Clérisseau and his own efforts he had now amassed a considerable portfolio of sketches of ruins and, from Herculaneum, wall decorations, domestic interiors and details. From time to time, inevitably, he met Charles Hope at the ancient sites and he managed to maintain a strictly formal friendship, but his interest was now in the whirlwind of sightseeing and sketching. This whirlwind was suddenly calmed by a letter from James suggesting that Robert should not return to Scotland but should remain in London and establish a practice there on his own account.

This suggestion brought about a lengthy self-appraisal by Robert. The proposal 'affected me much and afforded much matter for ruminating inwardly'. So that the subject would not cause any distress to the female members of his family, he addressed his reply to Adam Fairholme, an Edinburgh banker and friend of the brothers, knowing that Fairholme would pass it on to James. He would regard the opinions of his brothers and friends as having 'infinite sway over me' and, should the project go ahead it would 'prove both agreeable to my taste and flattering to my ambition.' But Robert, knowing he was without any reputation in England and that he had little experience of major projects, started, in the typically Scots way, of addressing the negative aspects of the scheme. 'Chambers is a mortal check to these views in several ways. All the English who have travelled for these five years are much prepossessed in his favours and imagine him a prodigy for genius, for sense and for good taste. My own opinion is that he in great measure deserves this encomium though his taste is more architectonic than picturesque. As for grounds and gardens Boucher can't be more Gothic.' François Boucher was the 'painter who best embodies the frivolity and superficiality of French life in the middle of the 18th century'. Boucher objected to nature on the grounds that it was 'too green and badly lit.'[7] However, Robert thought that Chamber's

> taste for basrelievos, ornaments and decorations of buildings he both knows well and draws exquisitely. His sense is middling, his appearance is genteel and his person good which are most material circumstances. He despises others as much as he admires his own talents, which he shows with slow and dignified airs, conveying an idea of great wisdom, which is no less useful that all his other endowments and I find sways much with every Englishman, nay, he is in so great esteem, so intimate and in such friendship with most of the English that have been in Rome that they are determined to support him to the utmost of their power, amongst whom are Tylney, Huntingdon and others of great consequence and even reckoned of great taste. Was I conscious to myself of having superior genius of drawing as well of being as well provided in good hints for designing and as many grand designs finished, finely drawn and coloured as he has to show away with it would be a different thing. But that can only come with time and time alone can determine whether I am meet enough to cope with such a rival and if I find that I can make the improvement that I require, then I can with more certainty trust to English employment and I can advise you from time to time if I have any prospect of arriving at a state much superior to what I ever thought of before I was in Rome and which, at this moment I am quite ignorant of.

Having described the principal drawback Robert felt that perhaps he might improve sufficiently during his stay in Italy. This hope made him examine how his household might be established in London. Now he is moving from impossibility to practicality. 'I know the situation of our family. Either my mother stays with you in Scotland or she must do what is almost impracticable and stay with me in London . . . If she does not, [then] 1 or 2 of my sisters keep house with me, my mother and the rest stay with you. Willie, I doubt not, will settle in London, as you see Scotland is but a narrow place, besides that, whoever he goes partner with can play their cards better with a London partner than without. If this conjecture, founded on pervious conversations should happen, you find it shall recur to you to be the sole guardian to so good [and] so charming a family.' Robert wondered if James might consider a move south, leaving John to run the Scottish practice, which could be workable if he avoided troublesome contracts and stuck to earning 'money by advantageous contracts'. 'I imagine that my mother would have great objections to leaving Scotland at her time of life which she must of necessity do were both of us to leave it and settle in London.' Robert is now thinking aloud and this letter was clearly written without any revision as he returns to his objections that London is expensive and he remembers that Chambers is not the only architect returned from Italy to work in the capital. There was also Matthew Brettingham although his 'genius is much inferior to his fortune'. Finally Robert proposes 'still to continue as a triumvirate co-partnery wherever settled, by which means the first outfitting would not be so heavy on the beginner, who could have it in his power to repay his partners in his prosperity, which is a parallel case with the bankers.' Robert has now almost completely talked himself round while admitting that there are problems but, 'All these I can overcome if thought requisite, and if I find I can do my friends and myself honour by my genius, which I assure you I find more diminutive since I came abroad than I had before any conception of.' In Italy, Chambers has 'played the rake and brought a girl with him to Rome whom he married after having a child with her. She is no doubt a check to his ambitions.'

Robert ends this letter on the positive note that 'If there is war, which is undoubted, the forts in Scotland will undoubtedly go the better for it and if Fort William succeeds Fort George it will at least be a good stroke for the Scots Master Builders'. In less than ten days he had completely reversed his views on the possibility of war. He was now determined that his future was to be in London, but like many Scots before him and even more after him, he was very properly apprehensive at the prospect.

Two days later Robert wrote to his mother that he had

received a letter from James but made no mention of the proposed move to London. He had visited the opera 'with some very pretty music' and arranged to have it copied for his sister Helen. 'I have also purchased 3 very handsome snuff-boxes of yellow and black tortoiseshell studded with gold and with gold hinges one of which I intend you for a tobacco box. I will take the first opportunity of sending 2 of them home that you may have the pleasure of reviewing the folly of your son every morning and every night when you take of your plug. And that Jen may regale her nose with another pinch more each hour to show her present the oftener.' It is not surprising that his sister was an avid snuff-taker but the picture of the bourgeois Mary Adams chewing tobacco twice daily is more shocking to twenty-first century ears. Robert bought his first summer suit, 'a red camlet coat, waist-coat, and britches with a slight gold lace and a red Persian lining'. 'Camlet' was, in fact, angora wool and, although lightweight, would not have been of the coolest. He did plan to have 'another suit of genteel silk to be purchased at Rome', although he would delay buying silks for his relatives until he returned to Florence.

The unaccustomed heat of south Italy was affecting both Robert and Clérisseau. 'This place is the hottest I ever was in, Clérisseau and I went to take the air at 9 at night and though we scarce went a hundred steps in an hour we were both in a drip of sweat and this moment it falls from my fingers and does so from morning to night as you sit in the room with windows and doors wide to the wall.' Robert assures his mother that he will be frugal, his coach costing about 4s 6d per day including coach-men, the *valet de place*, or servant for going errands and [standing] behind the coach whom we will pay at the rate of a shilling a day, for which he feeds, clothes and provides himself in everything. In short, I imagine for 12 shillings, one day with another, we shall defray our whole expenses of eating, drinking and equipage which, Lord knows, is not dear. My old friend Hope has been jaunting about with several other English people who are at Naples. They have been out 3 days and at some of the islands. He proposed going to Sicily but I find that scheme is broke up, so that I suppose he will soon return to Rome in order to get to Venice for the Ascension which is about the middle of May. We are excellent friends and never meet without shaking hands most cordially with other expressions of love and esteem. The truth is that I believe the only chance we had to keep in friendship was by parting.'

The 'islands' visited by Hope were Capri, then famous as the site of Tiberius's villa with its sinister reputation as a place of unspeakable Roman orgies, and the volcanic Ischia. The 'Ascension' in Venice was the spectacular ceremony held on Ascension Day – Thursday in the sixth week after Easter Sunday – when the Doge sailed out aboard a spectacular barge to throw a gold ring into the Adriatic, thus sealing Venice's marriage to the sea. Robert, however, returned to Rome by way of Old Capua to see 'that place so destructive to Hannibal's troops by their voluptuousness and idleness. There are only some remains of antiquity to be seen now, we go by a famous and beautiful mountain called Mount Cassino and they tell me through a most glorious country. If this war breaks out I'm afraid it will prevent the regularity of our correspondence which you see is already sufficiently uncertain.' After the battle of Cannae in 216 BC, Rome seemed to be at Hannibal's mercy, especially when the city of Capua joined his campaign, but Hannibal hesitated to undertake a siege of Rome and remained in Capua, seduced by 'voluptuousness and idleness'. The campaign faltered and five years later he returned to Carthage. This would have been of tremendous interest to the classicist Adam, unlike the Abbey of Monte Cassino founded by St Benedict in 529 AD as the mother church of the Benedictine order. St Benedict had replaced a temple of Apollo with a cathedral dedicated to John the Baptist, but for Robert this repository of sixth-century manuscripts was merely a 'beautiful mountain'. The abbey was destroyed in 1944 during one of the bitterest battles of the Second World War and has since been rebuilt.

By the start of May 1755 Robert had completed his first excursion, parted, more or less amicably, with Charles Hope, and was settling into his new apartments in the Casa Guarnieri. He was about to become 'Bob the Roman.'

CHAPTER FOUR

Bob the Roman

Robert was now established in Rome. With the slight disquiet of possible loneliness which always troubles expatriates he wrote to his sister Janet on 3 May 1755, reviewing his life. He had been offered introductions, presumably by the indefatigable Abbé Grant, to all the great houses but had rejected them since his lack of fluent Italian made his feelings of insecurity grow. However he had seen the Duke of Bridgewater and Robert Wood, his neighbours on the floor below, and been visited by Lord and Lady Kilmorly who 'caressed me as if I had been her own son'. In his letters Robert, who never married, was always keen to point out how popular he was with the ladies. Lady Charlotte Burgoyne, 'my old friend' – they had met in Aix in December, less than four months previously – 'could not put up' with his red suit but he was sure that his 'new silk suit which is almost completed will please her'. Anyway, he reassured himself, the English leave Rome in the summer, and 'the thought of misspending so much time to no purpose amongst a most stupid, ridiculous set of people and gamesters, where you must play or be reckoned a scrub, was my great stop. I go to creditable houses, genteel people, and have all freedom, we have sometimes dancing, often concerts and gaming for a trifle, so that to exchange that freedom for formality, that ease for constraint, I thought as yet absolutely needless and as I have it my power to go when I please, my not going for some time gives me no concern. When I am thinking of leaving Rome I shall think of the Borghese, the Gabrielli, the Viani, and the Cheroffini, but at present I shall think of bas relieves [sic] and antique architecture only.' It is more likely that he was here re-confirming his ambitions to himself rather than giving information to his sister, who would have shaken her head at his repeated declarations of his intent to concentrate on his studies.

Robert Adam was by no means the first aesthete to undertake the Herculean task of studying and recording the antiquities of Rome. On 1 August 1514, Pope Leo X appointed Raphael d'Urbino as *Maestro della Fabrica* with a similar task. Raphael was also empowered to prosecute any vandals or thieves, a task he undertook with some efficiency. As to his documentation of the ruins, 'Raphael's method of architectural rendering . . . proceeded from ground plan to elevation [and] comes straight from Vitruvius's classification of ichnographia, orthographia and scenographia.'[1] Raphael delivered a *Memorandum* to Leo and after his death in 1520 the work was carried on by Flavio Calvo who, in April 1527, wrote a *Similacrum* of what had been achieved. This was destroyed by the troops of Francis I and in Robert Adam's day there was no recognised map or description of ancient Rome.

Robert was still getting used to living in a city so different from anything he had previously experienced. Hot weather he had endured before but it had been a passing phenomenon, whereas here it was the norm. He noted that there were now very few people in Rome as 'they are all gone to Frascati and Tivoli, to the *villagiatura* when they will stay for a month and then, if the heat come on, they will return to town which is reckoned much [more] wholesome than the country, though both are as hot as hell, but if any one person is coolly lodged in Rome it is me'. Although, 'The sun chases me from room to room. At midday a dog can hardly endure the sun so that morning and evening are the only hours for recreation.' Coming from Scotland, where the climate was to be avoided if at all possible, he is astonished at the extent to which life in Rome, as in Naples, is very much lived in the streets. Butchers and cobblers ply their trades in the open air, during festivals around St Peter's there are sail cloths stretched over streets to provide shade, and, 'I have not had a hat on my head these 5 weeks. They hang up as useless machines whilst a silk whirligeck* adorns my left oxter'. Although it is still only May, the harvest is coming on. Robert was baffled by the various fruit harvests which took place in what he thought of as late spring and for all that he regarded himself as a sophisticated European, his attitudes were still those of a Lowland Scot.

Inevitably the Scots aesthetes in Rome clung to each other, and Robert's close circle included Grant, Wood and the Elliotts, a Scots couple, to whom he had been introduced by Lady Charlotte Burgoyne. Robert took an instant liking to Mrs Elliott and an almost equally instant dislike to Mr Elliott: 'The orders of knight-hood, stars, garters and ribbons are his constant talk . . . Madam is a good-natured, clever little woman [who] sometimes laughs and sometimes blushes at the foolish remarks of her beloved who, in the midst of the most interesting story, interrupts the teller and demands if the person spoke of has or ever wore the King's order, if there was a nobleman in the family, if it is ancient and a hundred such nothings'. Although the Ramsays had now moved out of Rome completely for cooler weather in Tivoli, some 25 kilometres distant, Robert occasionally journeyed out to them as Allan Ramsay was painting his portrait. Of this he says. 'Ramsay has done it, as I found he was more to be trusted in the portrait way than the history painters here who very often paint shocking bad portraits. It is near finished and [I] am assured by everybody [that it] is a striking likeness. For my own part, I don't think it half handsome, but he promises to clear its completion with a last sitting.' Robert regarded Ramsay, who preferred home and work to the social whirl of Rome, as his inferior, and evidently took delight in taunting him with stories of his social and other triumphs. However he was careful never to provoke 'Old Mumpty' too far.[2]

The group often met in the city for supper and, 'extremely good iced creams and iced strawberries.' After supper Ramsay and his party

> went home but Elliot, Grant and me took a most agreeable walk up the Trinita del Monte where assemble every night all the best people of Rome, cardinals, princes and monsignors. There they walk in disguise with *robes de chambres*, and other

* A loose cravat, used as a handkerchief for wiping away perspiration; 'oxter' is Scots for armpit.

light dresses of calicos . . . with each his lady in his hand who may be either wife, relation or mistress. On this hill some 5 or 6 different companies of singers some good, and some indifferent, there in concert give you the airs of the times and render the world the more cheerful and agreeable. I am here like the king of artists, and have flocks of them daily about me who come to pay court to me. They are highly honoured when I give them or their wives or their daughters a whirl in my coach, which, provided they are handsome I never fail to do.

Robert was still just managing to bestride the two worlds of student and dilettante and, probably thanks to Grant, he was finally introduced to Cardinal Albani. Alessandro Albani was the nephew of Pope Clement XI and one of the most influential men in Rome. He owned a vast collection of antiquities which he intended to be housed in the Villa Albani, a mansion he was creating especially for their display. He was the absolute arbiter of classical taste in Rome and a word from him could open many doors for Robert. The meeting seemed to go well, 'as I had several favours to ask of him for allowance to mould in some churches and draw in some places. In consequence of this introduction I went to the Cheroffini's conversation the same night where he always goes and which is the first quality visit I have paid. My reception was extremely good and every Tuesday night I will renew it as there are concerts of music, genteel company and the daughters [are] fine girls'. The Contessa Cheroffini was the cardinal's mistress and held her salon in the Palazzo Frascara. In spite of his intentions to the contrary, Robert now socialised nearly every night since 'I now begin to speak a kind of broken Italian . . . Such is my stupidity I know nothing of any game so that whilst others are playing I knife with the girls in broken Italian.'

'The forenoon I devote to study and drawing, after dinner I ride out to places and draw on the spot and after returning home I pay some English visits till 9 o'clock and from that I go among my Italians where I stay until 11 or 12 and then home to bed . . . The ladies are so partial as think me amongst the best minuet dancers of any Englishman they ever saw in Italy.' He was still keen to meet the Duchess of Borghese 'as I cannot show my face anywhere until I speak of the Borghesi as I would of Mrs Jap'. This was a typical ambition of the Grand Tourist as the duchess was as much one of the sights of Rome as was St Peter's.

Robert continued to count Grant as a friend. 'We never think of religion and so never talk of it . . . though Catholic and Jacobite, his greatest friends are Church of England Whigs because he says they deserve his regard the most'. His relationship with Clérisseau was also one of firm friendship. 'Clérisseau was given an offer by Wood to go to Sicily but he told them he would not leave me unless I turned him out a doors.' 'But, says he 'If you [Robert] will go to Egypt, Greece or Sicily I will set out with you tomorrow morning.' He is the best natured fellow and the cleverest body I ever saw with an unalterable turn for friendships, despises all mercenary views and only desires to live quietly and happily with a real friend which with the pursuit of his studies and the Catholic religion are all his desires.'

Robert had arranged lodgings for Hope to return to in Rome and claimed that he remained friends with him, but, in fact, his relations with Hope were now woefully cynical. He wrote, 'Thus I adopt it as a maxim that to appear in friendship to outward appearance with one you have no regard for, you must see them as little as possible and have few or no transactions at all, what you have must be conducted in the ceremonious style with a thousand French, false and deceitful compliments. But upon the whole, this affair is as happily ended as could be wished by all parties'. Even allowing for the hypocritically elaborate formal manners of the eighteenth century, Robert's adherence to this principle cannot but leave an unpleasant taste in the mouth.

Robert's wit could be playful and even self-deprecating but he could dip his pen in acid when he wrote about those he came to dislike even at long distance. When he was given news that Colonel Skinner, whom he disliked, and Mrs Skinner, whom he had no reason to dislike, had become the parents of a son, he wrote, 'Young Skinner I regret, if he dies he may improve (with

God's grace) in the next world which he never would in this. As witness that genius his daddy and that harlot his mother who both strove to produce one that should partake, if not exceed them in their weakness and Killovy* manners and God has blessed their endeavours with ample success'. Like his precepts on treating failed friendships this is unpleasant and unnecessarily rude, especially since he had previously enjoyed the company of Mrs Skinner on picnics.

Robert is affectionately witty when he gets news that John has fathered another daughter, advising him to try for a son and 'no more daughters as they are a burthen on a Presbyterian stipend' and he was sympathetic when, on 7 June, he responded to William's news that there had been a disastrous fire in Edinburgh. None of the family was hurt since his mother was in Kirkliston, a village a few miles west of Edinburgh, and sister Helen was 'on the road', returning from Moffat. Robert thought the fire gave the opportunity for rebuilding 'rather better than before and will afford [a] place for a fine open entry to all the houses in the land from the Cowgate and might be made very grand'. This became a very real ambition he sought unsuccessfully to achieve some 30 years later.

Robert still felt that he should contribute to the ongoing work of the partnership in Scotland and he sent Lord Hopetoun a sketch for a chimney 'but it is done in a hurry so that it cannot be expected to be great things'. His heart and mind was now in Rome.

I have not as yet attempted designing anything, in the way of composing anything in the grand style, as I am applying to those things from which I shall be able to make such compositions, viz., to figures, to ornaments, and to perspective. When I have studied them some time I will then put them in different forms, so as to be simple and great. For I consider beginning compositions just now as one would do as a painter who had never learned to draw hands or head or feet or eyes and yet would attempt to draw the Laocoön or to compose a

* See footnote p. 69

99

history painting. I am just now making an exact plan of a
church which is built upon the old foundations of Diocletian's
Baths and filled up by an Italian architect, one Vanvitelli, but
I think it may be greatly helped and will make a noble design,
so that sooner or later I will make a new design for it with all
the alterations in the antique style.

Laocoön was a Trojan priest who warned against accepting the
Greek horse whereupon he and his two sons were crushed to death
by pythons for their presumption. The second-century BC marble
group of the event was much copied and drawing it was a favourite
exercise for student artists. Luigi Vantivelli was Carlos III's
architect for the Palace of Caserta of 'immense size', and had
altered the church of Santa Maria degli Angeli which Michelan-
gelo had built in the ruins of the Baths of Diocletian. Robert was
now becoming easily conversant with the models of antiquity.

By mid June, his routine of study had become established. It
would have been possible for Robert to enrol at either the French
academy or at Rome's own Accademia di San Luca. However,
Clérisseau's conflicts with the former rendered that impossible
and by attending the latter as an individual Robert would have
declared himself an artisan, thus destroying the flimsy disguise of
gentleman dilettante. The social distinctions of this most snobbish of centuries were intricate, and Robert's place in the social
hierarchy ill-defined.

In the meantime, Clérisseau was teaching him perspective,
using a method devised by the Caracci family at their Bologna
academy, combined with the theories of Charles Lebrun, a stern
adherent of classicism. Lebrun had published a *Méthode pour
apprendre à dessiner les passions* in which he proposed that art,
springing from the emotions, could be controlled by the laws
of reason. This was a neo-Enlightenment view. Arguing for the
reverse, David Hume had claimed that 'reason is, and ought to
be, the slave of the passions'. Hume was arguing for a state of
balance 'between the unreasoning brute and the unfeeling logic
of the "control freak".'[3] Having raised the subject in this way

Lebrun had brought the arguments of the philosophers into the realm of the aesthetes, and Robert became a brilliant example of how Hume's plea for balance could be achieved in stone. In his work he showed how the rigid rules of the past might be adapted to accept the introduction of individual inspiration. His designs were rooted in the classicism he was seeing in Rome, but his method of application of the ancient models was shocking to the traditionalists such as Chambers.

As early as 1663, people who were 'free from superstition or prejudice' were called 'enlightened', and in 1690 John Locke's *Essay concerning Human Understanding* brought a new light to the process of thought itself. This was following the European paths where Enlightenment ideas had swept away many of the rigid precepts which had dominated philosophy since the Reformation. In 1696 Pierre Bayle's *Dictionnaire historique et critique* combined with the writings of René Descartes to lay the foundations of scepticism. This meant that everything from the past had to be re-examined and, in many cases, cast away and replaced. In 1707 Handel composed an oratorio, performed in London in 1757, *Il Trionfo del Tempo e del Disinganno – The Triumph of Time and Enlightenment* – in which beauty and passion are reformed by reason. In architecture this reforming movement meant that the classical bases, as laid down by Vitruvius and Palladio, had to be abandoned as slavish models and the individual imagination of the artist had to take precedence. It also meant that taste could not be governed by rules but had to be developed through study and experience. Only then could a personal vocabulary of architecture be developed. This was a challenging concept to strictly classical devotees like Chambers, but Robert filed these precepts quietly away for future use.

His establishment now ran to six draughtsmen and a young French painter, Laurent Pécheux, had joined the household. Although Pécheux was an academician of St Luke's he undertook Robert as a private pupil to teach him the classical French styles including Lebrun's theories. Robert also had been recommended by Clérrisseau to employ Jean-Baptiste Lallemand as a tutor for landscape painting, although 'Lallemand's association was a shadowy one which Adam was typically keen to keep that way,'[4] and Robert Adam was now the sole pupil in his own personal university of artistic theory.

'My time is chiefly employed now in drawing and copying feet and hands and noses and lugs which I am convinced is so absolutely requisite that nothing shall prevent me pursuing that study for some time without which an artist cannot ornament a building, draw a basrelievo or a statue. Here Chambers excelled and by that means a design in itself neither immensely ingenious nor surprising appear excessively so, and with the Lord's will, Monsr. Pécheux's advice and my own application a few hours every day, I hope to outdo that formidable rival. I suppose this hint will be sufficient to put John and James in mind of their duties'. When Robert laid down this challenge he was tacitly accepting James's suggestion that he return, not to Edinburgh, but to London, although still very much as a partner in the Edinburgh firm. 'I am just now getting a complete set of studies done for me by Pécheux which are charming and when I have done with them will put them in a book for the use of the Brotherhood. My drawing of the Laocoön is finished and reckoned prodigious fine. Clérisseau has lately finished two of his views of Architecture for me which for composition, grandness of style and execution exceed anything I have seen. He gives me great hopes I may acquire his manner but it will require much practice and study.'

Now Robert met the person who was destined to become the third of his close Roman colleagues. Giovanni Battista Piranesi was a 35-year-old Venetian etcher and aesthete who vehemently championed Roman architecture over its Greek counterparts. In 1745 he published his *Vedute*, a collection of etchings of ancient Rome. This was the essential purchase for a Grand Tourist and did much to romanticise ancient Rome, a copy even ending up in Abbotsford, the Gothic country mansion of Sir Walter Scott.

Piranesi, who is I think the most extraordinary fellow I ever saw is become immensely intimate with me and as he imagined at first that I was like the other English who had a love for antiques without knowledge . . . Upon seeing some of my sketches and drawings [he] was so highly delighted that he almost ran quite distracted and says that I have more genius for the true noble architecture than any Englishman that was ever in Italy. In short he threatens dedicating his next plan of ancient Rome to me but of this I have no certainty, and he swears whenever he can find opportunity he will thrust me into all his prints as a gentleman possessed of that love, that taste and that genius for ancient architecture who admired such things that he got modellers to copy them in order to instil that taste into the minds of his countrymen. When I told him that I had two brothers as fond and as capable as myself he begged his humble compliments to them and said he hoped that people would yet travel from Italy to see our works, for his own part he now reckoned he had real friends, having real lovers of true architecture in Scotland.

It would take a man of strong character and self-restraint to resist such fulsome flattery and Robert Adam was not such a man.

Piranesi was born in Venice in 1720 and had settled in Rome in 1745 where he made etchings which were sold to Grand Tourists, rather in the manner of today's picture postcards. He was heavily built with close-cropped hair and a commanding stare. Given his reputation for violence – he had frequent loud quarrels with Angelica Pasquini, his young wife and mother of his eight children – he was not accepted by the artistic establishment in Rome. He annoyed them by taking up lodgings in the same street as the Accademia di San Luca and 'instead of anthologising the decorous elements of Roman antiquity which best illustrate the strict canon of ordered architecture, laid down by Vitruvius and codified by Palladio, Piranesi went out of his way to select the unusual and bizarre.'[5] He also showed a great enthusiasm for the company of the students, encouraging them to seek out new ideas. Piranesi had been involved in a bitter dispute with the Irish peer James Caulfield, Earl of Charlemont to whom he had dedicated a book of etchings, the *Antichità Romane*, clearly expecting a financial return from the earl. While in Rome, Charlemont had also met Chambers and had employed him as architect for his estates in Ireland. On leaving the city Charlemont travelled to Turin, and when the *Antichità Romane* was published, Charlemont refused to pay, leaving the short-tempered Piranesi in a justified fury.

'He was an anglophile, financially grasping, quick-tempered, intensely proud of the status conferred on him by his work on the antiquities, boldly assured of the Horatian immortality secured by his monumental labours.'[6] He dressed eccentrically, with a vast hat, its wide brim pulled down over his neck, and a short *camisole de chasse*, or smock, looking dangerously uncivilised. Among the classical ruins the trio of Piranesi, Clérisseau and Robert Adam, sketching away as hard as they could, became a familiar sight. 'Piranesi is always brisk; always allegro', Robert noted, as the two men fed each other's enthusiasms. 'Before his arrival in Rome and his encounter with Piranesi Adam was already excited by antiquity and grandeur. Piranesi heightened this excitement but he did not create it.'[7]

Hovering above them was not only the burning Roman sun, but the terrifying possibility that true classical architecture was not, in fact, Roman, but Greek and that the Romans had been mere copyists. Greece was not an obligatory part of the Grand Tour and, being under Ottoman occupation, was difficult to reach, with permissions, or *firmans*, often obtained with expensive difficulty from local warlords, being necessary every step of the way. Neither did it offer the aristocratic hospitality so essential to the Grand Tourist. Unlike Italian, the language of the Renaissance, modern Greek was hardly spoken outside the country and ancient Greek was not so commonly taught as Latin. The very word 'Greek' had come to include any art east of Italy, including even Byzantine, and the entire subject was one which the aesthetes of the eighteenth century felt was best ignored, with some significant exceptions. Foremost among these exceptional aesthetes was Comte Claude-Phillipe de Tubières Caylus who, while supporting the idea of a return to classicism, had produced a considered history of ancient art in his *Recueil d'Antiquities Égyptiennes, Étrusques, Grecques, Romaines et Gauloises* published in Paris in 1752. In this massive, seven-volume work, he declared that Roman taste was flabby and coarse and that almost all the works of architecture with any elegance owed their inspiration to the Greeks, who had been copied by the Etruscans, only to be copied in their turn by the Romans.

This storm in the aesthetic firmament was bad enough, but in Rome itself, and working under the patronage of Robert's new-found friend the Cardinal Albani, was another champion of Greek art. This was Johann Joachim Winkelmann, a German scholar now employed as the cardinal's librarian. His contribution was a book called G*edanken über die Nachahmung der griechischen Werke in der Malerei und Bildauerkunst,* or *Thoughts on Copies of Greek Painting and Sculpture* in which he saw the foundation of all European art in Greek culture. A contemporary commentator has pointed out that much of Wincklemann's argument is based on his fervent adoration of Greek statues of male nudes, but his book, combined with that of Caylus, sowed the seed of suspicion that Vitruvius had created nothing and that Palladio merely copied what was in itself already a derivative art. Indeed, some people went so far as to believe that Greek Doric was derived from ancient Egyptian styles.

From Robert's point of view, 'Palladio he considered rather *vieux jeu*, and, as for contemporary Roman architects – he averted his eyes lest his taste be "spoilt and depraved" by their excesses. From Clérisseau he learnt the doctrines of neo-classicism, the new rationalist and archaeological attitude expounded by French and German theorists, notably Winckelmann . . . the whole movement was crystallised in the Parnassus ceiling by Raphael Mengs, the friend of Robert's other teacher Laurent Pécheux.'[8] This ceiling was in the Villa Albani and used classical themes but distorted in perspective so that they appeared to be seen at eye-level. This was a break with slavish copying of styles and techniques, but Mengs, whose frescoes executed for Charles III in Madrid used revolutionary foreshortening techniques, never received the recognition he deserved. His life was tragically cut short in 1779 when he died from a chill caught while copying decorations in an excavation under the Villa Negroni. He was an important technical innovator and provided a useful building block in the construction of Robert's personal style.

The debate, like so many similar disputes, was generating more heat than light and Piranesi, in a boiling rage, replied in 1760 with *Della Magnificenza ed Architettura de' Romani* in which he defended the Roman style although, being the short-tempered man he was, his argument descends into a confused cacophony of vituperation. He did, however, expose the futility of the argument and laid down what might well be taken as the artistic manifesto of Robert Adam: 'An artist who would do himself honour and acquire a name, must not content himself with copying faithfully the ancients, but, studying their works he ought to show himself of an inventive and, I had almost said, of a creating genius, and by prudently copying the Grecian, the Tuscan, and the Egyptian together, he ought to open himself a road to the finding out of new ornaments and new manners.'[9] Adam followed these precepts enthusiastically. The friendship between the two men was strengthened by mutual admiration, and Adam used much of Piranesi's *Diverse Maniere d'adornare i Cammini*, published in 1769, as a basis for some of his own decorative styles.

Back in Scotland Allan Ramsay joined the debate with a *Dialogue on Taste*. This short work is in the popular eighteenth-century form of a dramatised conversation, in this case among Colonel Freeman, Lord and Lady Modish and Lady Harriot. After discussing the merits of champagne as opposed to canary wine, the discussion turns to why one lady should be thought more beautiful than another. The free-thinking colonel then argues that since both of these are matters of personal taste and 'taste is no more than the analysis of certain things which custom has rendered agreeable', then taste in architecture is 'one of those tastes which custom, a second nature, has bestowed upon us; and is so much mere taste that it can never, with any propriety, become a matter of dispute or comparison'. He argues that an adherence to the rules means that 'an artist may, by a Palladian receipt alone, without any taste, form a very elegant Corinthian pillar' and that 'an admiration to a degree of bigotry seized the Roman artists and connoisseurs, and put an effectual stop to any further change of improvement in architecture. Their sole study was to imitate the Grecian buildings . . . there is nothing which can be imagined to give it a total overthrow, unless Europe should become a conquest of the Chinese.'[10] Five years later, no less an architect than William Chambers did, for a moment allow a 'Chinese conquest' when he built the 50-metre tall Pagoda in Kew Gardens, London. Chambers was, however, a firm supporter of the Romanists. 'They might with equal success oppose a Hottentot and a baboon to the Apollo and Gladiator as set up the Grecian architect against the Roman.' Nothing would shake Chambers from his dedication to the excellence of taste as laid down by Palladio and his mind was firmly closed to any diversion from his designs.

Robert would find it difficult to outshine Chambers's list of clients, but the way could be opened for architectural innovation and enlightenment. Robert listened to the arguments and read the various books and pamphlets but he was unconcerned as to which school of architecture he would follow. He was intent on learning as much as he could from as wide a variety of sources as he could find and then choosing whatever designs would fire his considerable imagination. He then could form his own style according to whatever was most suitable for what he was being asked to build. He could thus have a continuity of design in every building but each building would stand alone as unique.

By 4 June 1755 Robert was more than halfway convinced that he would establish himself in London and that the principal obstacle to his metropolitan success was Chambers. Once again he argues the case to James while commiserating with him for suffering under Skinner at Fort George with the 'flashes furies and madnesses of the most ridiculous of mortals . . . all which, I suppose, you allow to blow over, make the penny and laugh at the difficulties'. Robert excuses himself by saying that he had only planned a career in Scotland 'a narrow country where the very name of a traveller acquires respect and veneration to no great genius' but now he realises that he must delve further. 'These considerations made me determine to go to the bottom of things, to outdo Chambers in figures in bas relievos and in ornaments, which with any tolerable degree of taste so as to apply them properly make a building appear as different as night from day.' His drawing was improving: 'My instructor gives me great encouragement and assures me that in 3 or 4 months I shall do infinitely better than Chambers ever did or ever will do, thus you see, Jamie, that obstacle is not insurmountable. I find my ideas of architecture are a good deal enlarged and my principles of the grand more fixed than ever they were before'.

Clérisseau was perhaps aware that his eagle chick of a pupil was impatient to soar above everyone, and urged caution. Robert paid no heed to the Greek versus Roman dispute and, as far as he was concerned, he would incorporate the best from any source into a new vocabulary of his own. In the same way that David Hume had used scepticism to clear the way for a new humanism, Robert was examining everything he could find and retaining only what fitted his newly nascent tastes. This pleased Piranesi so much that he decided not to dedicate his plan of ancient Rome to a cardinal – presumably Cardinal Albani – but to Robert, with the title of 'friend and architect and delectantissimo nell'artichità'. Piranesi, with the typical instinct of the freelance, sent his fulsome regards to James and John who are assured by their brother that he will return the compliment 'in the best Italian I can muster up on the occasion'.

Robert has thought about Piranesi's dedication and can find no harm in it, writing that 'it cannot fail to have good effects in making me the object of everyone's attention as one so beloved and prized by Piranesi . . . It will however cost me some sous in purchasing 80 or 100 copies of it which I propose sending to England and Scotland to be resold . . . He has told me that whatever I want of him he will do for me with pleasure . . . There are many people here and in different countries would have given him a present of £50 or £150 for such a dedication.'

Robert was very keen to establish himself as an artist as well as a gentleman; the two positions were mutually exclusive in some eyes, and he found it difficult riding both horses. 'There is a danger that one's friends may look on one as a patron. Much in this way am I at present with respect to the artists and fellow students in Rome who view in such a way my house, my coach, my number of purchases in pictures, drawings and other virtuosi that they fear me as the populace do the pope; but envy me as many do your wealthy cardinals. Piranesi's dedication will give a finishing blow to their already despairing situations.' The fact that the dedication would come in a separate volume to that already dedicated to Charlemont would not 'detract from the honour of the intention'.

Robert's active mind never missed a commercial opportunity and he told James he had another scheme 'no less conducive to raising one's name and character'. This was to reprint *Les Édifices Antiques de Rome*, a book published in 1682 by Antoine-Baruty Desgodetz with revisions and corrections made by Robert. He would print Desgodetz's original drawings with his own corrections delineated in red and with, 'A smart preface, a clever print of the author's head, an allegorical print in the way of Palladio and some remarks added to those of Desgodetz in different characters, [it] could not fail to be of great authority and introduce me into England with an uncommon splendour.' This scheme would have shown the world at large that Robert Adam was a more accurate architect and surveyor than any of his predecessors, as well as being a man who had studied every building in ancient Rome.

But, as so often during Robert's Grand Tour, he found a diversion, and on 5 July he wrote to his sister Margaret with a description of one of Rome's great spectacles. 'The fireworks at St Peter's were impressive as were the displays at Castel St Angelo. The grandest part of the operation they call the Girandola being thousands of rockets which are sent up at one time when they spread out like a wheat sheaf in the air, each of which gives a crack and sends out a dozen burning balls like stars which fall gently down wards till they die out . . . and appeared to me the most romantic and picturesque sight I have ever seen.' Robert's later designs of multi-branched candlesticks and wall sconces have taken the name of 'girandoles'. 'The fireworks ended at the Farnese palace where the Duke of Bridgewater had taken windows and invited the English ladies to see them, I as conductor of them in my coach was always present where we had a good supper and were merry. Later the duke promised to take £50 worth of Clérisseau's drawings and £60 worth from my other French friend who teaches me drawing of figures.'

The prospect of the London practice was now firmly in Robert's head and on 12 July he sought Helen's opinion. As a joke he asked her if a letter he had sent through her to Lord Hopetoun, was 'wrote in a right strain, if it was becoming the dignity of an architect who expects to despise Inigo Jones as he did Deacon Jamieson, to regard Palladio as Deacon Butler and Chambers as an inferior genius'. Presumably having made Helen smile at his denigration of great and small – even unknown – architects he moved into more direct personal reflection. 'I often think it is a pity that such a genius should be thrown away upon Scotland where scarce will ever happen an opportunity of putting one noble thought in execution. It would be a more extensive scheme for me to settle a family also in England and let the Adams be the sovereign architects of the United Kingdom.' Now the subject is out in the open and he can move from theory to reality. 'Would you have any objection to a London life, Nell, to your coach and livery servants, to the best of company and the most exquisite diversions? We must carry our mother with us and some reliable housekeeper such as Margaret Annan. To you who are settled in Scotland, the going to London seems a mighty matter, to me who views you within 2½ days posting, you don't seem so far as from my house to Frascati where I can go and return the same day. Comparisons diminish the vastness of all things, those who make the Levant voyage, who travel to Syria, to Egypt and Greece, think themselves at home when they get to Rome. Even those whose utmost distance Rome is, think Paris at home, a Scotsman at Paris thinks London is but a step from Edinburgh, and how much more then must that distance appear trivial to so extensive traveller as I am.'

Having planted the thought in Helen's brain of a move to London, he then moved swiftly on to tell her how he coped with the unaccustomed heat. 'My night dress is a green silk short coat and waistcoat without linings with a pair of thin silk britches and in that way, with my stockings ungartered, I go up and down the house from 7 in the morning till after dinner. Then I make my expedition in the coach where I ride, walk and visit till 11 or 12 at night. Thus the world wags.'

His world wagged quite comfortably around the salon system of different hostesses holding *conversazioni* on set days, a system he felt would do well in Scotland. Robert – who now called himself 'Bob the Roman' – was well on the way toward the arrogant snobbery which was an inevitable by-product of the Grand Tour. The food was superior and although Clérisseau observed the Catholic fasts, Robert observed that 'with me it is always *gras*'. He ate 'desserts of prodigous fine peaches, apricocks, charming figues, delicious green almonds, pears, salads and parmesan cheese' and he wished Scotland could have these fruits. However, 'even at 1 at night and lightly dressed' he was sweating, although he was now getting used to the heat, but never ventured out until after sunset at 6 or 7 at night. Of his neighbours, 'the Duke of Bridgewater is now at Naples where he went some days ago in the midst of the Mal Aria or bad air between Rome and that place', while 'the Ramsays are thinking of moving into town as no visiting is possible until 7 or 8.'

'There is to be an inundation in the Piazza Navona 2 foot deep in which all the coaches of Rome drive up and down for 2 hours whilst the whole windows are filled with spectators. The greatness of the place, the numbers of people and the parade of machines shall induce me to paddle in it amongst others for no other reason but to be like neighbours.' 'We are soon to have more fireworks for the coronation day of his Holiness known in our country by the heretical name of the whore of Babylon. Though his conduct

is not of that kind but is as wise and sagacious old bod as I ever
saw.' Since this Pope was Clement XIII, and he was not crowned
until 6 July 1758, Robert is crying up the splendours of Rome
beyond strict fact. As to being sagacious, Clement XIII is
remembered for, among other things, equipping all the male
nudes in the Vatican Museum with fig leaves.

On 3 September Charles Hope left Rome for Viterbo and
Florence. Before his departure Robert dined with Hope who told
him that his brother 'would not be for me returning to Scotland
as he would be afraid of my finding fault with everything about
Hopetoun House and with my dictatorial authority making him
do a thousand things that he would wish to avoid.' Robert

> told him that was very possible and that I had already
> thought of [a] scheme for his library which would make it
> one of the finest things in the world. I explained my scheme
> to him and he agreed it would, but said I must make his
> brother think it was his own contrivance. I objected to that
> but told him I was sure he would not do it for though he
> thought it right he would reason until himself and every-
> body tired of it, and in that way would parry it off. He
> agreed that would certainly be the case and thus our
> discourse on that subject finished . . . Notwithstanding all
> that has passed I was sorry to part with him as we had
> always workings together and one must be entirely devoid of
> feelings who does not contract some sort of friendly sensa-
> tions from much intercourse, though not of the purest
> affection, my sense of injuries vanished insensibly and I
> own I felt at leaving him.

However Robert also regretted that Hope had, 'cost me near three
hundred pounds to attend that snaking bougre who wormed me
out of all he could without allowing me the least honour or credit
by it, called for <u>his</u> coach, called for <u>his</u> servant, paid <u>his</u> house, all
before my face.' As Robert's father had found with Lord Braco,
relationships with the aristocracy, could, on occasions, be difficult

Next to leave Rome was Robert's young neighbour, the Duke of Bridgewater, who departed suddenly when he heard that a member of parliament was being sent to Westminster 'in his interest' but without his approval. Hope had been envious of Robert's friendship with Bridgewater. 'But Bridgewater is a man who hates horse racing and gaming as he hates to die, and who loves a shilling more than his lordship. In short if he wants more proofs that I am in no danger of offending, I can produce his own signed order telling he will be much obliged to me to purchase for him such things . . . He has left orders for above a thousand pounds with his antiquarian who is to do nothing without my consent and approbation . . . We parted exceedingly good friends a proof of which was his leaving me four and five dozen of exceedingly good claret with a promise of doing everything for me he possibly could whenever it lay in his power.' The duke was accompanied home by Wood, another member of Robert's expatriate circle, and Robert felt Wood a great loss for his knowledge and joviality. 'Though he was free and easy himself in company, I never could bring myself to be so with him as his superiority in every way rather struck me with awe, than infected me with ease . . . He went so far as to plan schemes for my succeeding in England in case I should be advised to attempt to try my fortune in that country and, having some notion that the Duke of Bridgewater would build a magnificent house, said that he could secure me in having that as a piece on my return which would at once set me above all opposition.' This would also set Robert on the same path as Chambers.

Robert tried, as best as he could at a thousand miles distant, to monitor the situation in London. When he heard that he had been asked after by Lord Home at Fort George he was greatly cheered. John and James had designed a house for Lord Home at Paxton near Berwick-upon-Tweed in Robert's absence and since Lord Home was a close friend of the Duke of Argyll he hoped that Argyll was still looking kindly on the brothers. Although the duke was known to favour Roger Morris as an architect in London and the brothers had worked well with Morris when building Inveraray Castle, Robert felt that Morris was a rival he could easily outshine and keep the ducal favour. However, 'Chambers is a more formidable foe, and being already sometime in England is no doubt establishing himself in business whither my coming sometime after may change the vogue.'

With the emptying of Rome Robert was feeling occasionally disenchanted with the more obviously repellent members of the population and in a foul temper he called for a return of gladiatorial sport so that 'hundreds ought to be butchered every day, and fewer villains would be left'. It is the remark of a man who, in hot weather, has just been jostled and abused in a busy street.

Meanwhile the threat of war was becoming more real. 'If this war is in earnest there is nothing to be done at home. The architects may go to bed and sleep till peace [be] made, or they may travel to divert themselves.' Robert dreaded the French impounding all his purchases and thought it better to let them all lie at Leghorn until peace returned. John had told him how pleased Hopetoun was with the chimney he had sent 'which shows how much a trifle from Italy will impose, even on a sensible man'. Tongue in cheek, Robert offered to propose that Hopetoun should pull down his house and start again 'so that I may [have] the satisfaction to try my genius on a new one . . . I have bespoke for him six of the prettiest tables I ever saw, which are making here, and if they escape the French and get safe to the Firth of Forth I hope will give him much content'. By mid August all the British members of parliament had left Rome and Robert made arrangements to have his mail redirected through Germany.

With now almost none of his acquaintances left in the city, Robert decided on a short architectural tour of Italy and wrote to James with his proposed itinerary. He was planning to travel north east and to visit 'Caprarola, Narni, Termi, Foligni and Spoleto. Betwixt which two places is a temple which you will see in Palladio with immense long stairs that go up sideways rather like a ladder than a stair with a small portico you enter by, I daresay you will know it by this description'. He then intended to pass over the spine of Italy and go to Rimini and Ravenna on the Adriatic coast, but would not continue north for the hundred or so kilometres to Venice, which he intended to visit later. He would then 'tack about and return coasting it all the way back' as far as Ancona before turning inland for Loreto and Foligni and then back to Rome. He would not stay in Rome but would 'go directly to Albano, Genzano, Ariccia, Palestrino and Marino, famous for the summer seats of Pope and Pretender as well as many good paintings in the churches . . . There, having many acquaintances, English and Italian, all gay with music, dancing, card-playing, I shall spend the last eight or ten days of my journey agreeably and come into Rome with fresh spirits for my studies.' Clérisseau and he were to ride in a post-chaise with Donald on horseback. 'He [Donald] can now make out enough Italian of the clept kind as not only prevents himself from starving but to provide us sumptuously. And what more could a man wish?'

Robert also asked James to find him a copy of Lord Burlington's book of the baths of Diocletian and Caracalla. These were a selection of Palladio's drawings which Burlington published as *Fabbriche Antiche* in 1730. Robert's interest in books of drawings was growing: 'I have lately purchased some good pictures in the landscape and architecture way which I think I have bought at such rates that I could sell at double the money in England . . . Ramsay is of the same opinion and approves much of my buying them.'

Now Robert's problem was how to acquire the chaise for himself and Clérisseau to ride in, a problem quickly solved. 'A young English gentleman who had fallen in love with an Italian lady here, had, about a month ago, bought a very handsome little chariot which he had new painted, gilt and in tip-top order with his arms and other marks of chivalry. This exploit having run out his fortune and stopped his credit, his friends thought it proper to call him home in a hurry and in a hurry he went away. Hearing that this machine was made for posting and that by removing the fore-wheels and the forepart of the carriage it, Skinner-like, served as a most admirable post-chaise, I went, saw it and bought it. It is one of the handsomest little chariots I ever saw, painted green and gold, well lined and as good as new for which I paid 35 pounds sterling nearly. It will serve me this jaunt, it will serve me all the winter and spring in Rome and then will be proper for pursuing my course through Italy, Germany and France and after all will sell for something considerable. If I fix in London I must have immediately one of the handsomest chariots and prettiest pair of horses I can afford as I imagine there is no way to get the better of these fellows than by throwing them onto despair at first sight.' This is pure bravado: Robert was dreading the various commitments he would have to make in London which must make or break his career.

From 24 September to 12 October 1755, Robert wrote, 'we have driven post from one town to another staying half a day at any of these places where we found game. And going to the place directly so that we have brought home with us a portfolio loaded with triumphal arches, ancient bridges and other views of whatever appeared curious and worth drawing.' Having made these drawings Robert felt no need to describe his feelings about the buildings he saw. In Ravenna he saw the flowering of late Roman and early Byzantine architecture covered in the finest mosaic work in existence but he makes no mention of it and only a few sketches of it survive. In these we can see that Clérisseau's influence was taking effect and Robert's eye for detail and perspective had improved by leaps and bounds.

On returning to Rome he told Jenny in a chatty letter that in a few days he intended to go to Albano where Grant and most of his acquaintances were and where he was getting the tables for Lord Hopetoun valued and insured for onward despatch. Most importantly for the ever-snobbish Robert, he had met Lord Huntingdon with whom he had dined in Florence but who had now arrived in Rome. Robert and Clérisseau were invited to dine with him again.

On 19 October, Robert wrote to James confirming his intention to settle in London. He also presumed that both James and John intended to visit Italy. John had wanted to travel first but now preferred to wait for two years until Robert had established himself in London. It is also possible that John was essential to the continued military contracts and, quite reasonably, also wanted to postpone leaving his new family. Blithely ignoring all this, Robert thought the idea of delay was unsatisfactory. For John to spend two years in Rome unsupervised, he wrote, would be 'to little purpose. Without Clérisseau I should have spent several years without making the progress I have done in one fourth of the time. The reason's evident, the Italians have at present no manner of taste, all they do being more French than anything else. Piranesi, who may be said alone to breathe the ancient air, is of such disposition as bars all instruction.'

Robert, as often happened when he tired of a friendship, was becoming weary of Piranesi's '*sempre allegro*'. Also, by the time John was due to arrive Clérisseau would have returned to Paris and there would be no one left in Rome to teach him. At no point in Robert's proposal does he take any account of the fact that John had married over five years previously and was the father of William, aged four and a half, and the infant Mary. Robert's first thoughts were always for the firm and for the advantage of the practice. Family matters were, for him, largely a subject of gossip with his sisters, and more of a recreation than a serious concern.

James, however, being younger and unmarried, was a different matter. 'But what if you boldly set out in a week or fortnight after the receipt of this letter?' Robert would then be able to integrate James into his household and tutoring system and his education could be completed in a twelvemonth, whereas John, tutorless and coming later, would have to start from scratch. 'You are just now of a right age, and every day's delay is losing time and of dangerous consequences as you suck in prejudices which with pain you will quit.' He quoted the case of a 'young Swiss' who had known Clérisseau in Florence 'but as Clérisseau nor I liked his disposition we resolved to have nothing to do with him'. The unfortunate student then went to the French academy and was 'herded with the young Italians' producing nothing but 'childish fancies'. Robert felt sure that Skinner could cope at Fort William even if that meant hiring another architect. 'Christie [presumably the clerk of works] must stand the charge and some dozens of wine must appease his angry spirit.' Robert was so sure that this plan would be accepted that he ended the letter by telling James where to buy clothes on the journey.

He repeated the scheme in another letter but sent both to John McGowan, the family's Edinburgh lawyer, for onward transmission. Indeed, James might even persuade 'that harpy MacGowan', to accompany him, but apart from discussing the plan with Lord Hopetoun he should be careful as to how he approached his elder brother, John. Robert simply concluded that John must simply do what he thought best.

Elizabeth sent him the sad news that Sir John Clerk of Penicuik had died aged 79. He responded: 'It's a pity the bod defuncked before he saw some of my antique collection of curiosities. I'm sure it would have revived the soul of him for half a dozen years longer.' In high spirits he gossiped on, 'Lord Brudenell is to have the lodgings under me . . . His Gouvernour is a sensible man, himself a naught . . . I have this day a letter from my old friend Carlo Hope whose deaf son and doited* Gouvernour are now in Rome.'

Helen wrote to tell him that James had joined the Speaking Club. This was one of the large number of clubs which had sprung up in Edinburgh as part of the new expansion of curiosity brought about by the Scottish Enlightenment, but Helen may also have been hinting that James was establishing himself in Edinburgh society. Robert dismissed the news petulantly. 'In Edinburgh club rage reigns like the disease among the horned cattle in England or horned husbands in Italy.'

On another subject, he wrote to his sisters, 'I thought you would have had my pretty phiz before this time but that wight Allan Ramsay puts off so abominably that I have no longer patience with him'. Robert had asked Laurent Pécheux to 'do a head and shoulder secretly and in a fortnight hence it will be completely done. As soon as it is done I will send it to London in order to be transmitted to you.' Elizabeth was to keep the picture secret, so as not to upset Ramsay. 'It will break us entirely who at present live

* Scots: deranged

like the babes in the wood and dwell in unity.' He was, however, delighted with the result and he told Peggy, 'Pécheux's portrait really makes as pretty a haunty* picture as I have seen and is worth a thousand Ramsays. But all this is *entre nous.*'

Disaster had nearly struck Robert when coming home from his '*villigiatura* at Albano'. He wrote: 'I had stole out of the chaise my writing case with all my papers even from my leaving England to this day which misfortune I would not write you of till I could at the same time inform you of its being again found, the thief thereof on a reward of a guinea or thereabouts being published and pasted on kirk doors and corners of streets brought it back and received his money. Donald my honest friend having put it on the seat of the chaise brought up the great trunk to the house during which operation said writing case was taken away at my own stair foot and a-missing for more than ten days'. He lost no money and boasted that he never gambled, but what little money he had, 'I spend on pictures and drawings and I believe will be master of a very pretty collection well chosen and cheap, in so much that I am fully convinced on selling one half of my pictures at London, I shall have the other half for nothing.'

Robert's scheme for James to join him in Rome received a setback when he read James's response to it. On 17 November James had written that he was 'puzzled and perplexed' by the offer and, contrary to Robert's wishes, had immediately consulted John, who, 'with the utmost ease consented to allow me to follow my inclinations'. James's objections started with the strictly practical: he had no command of the language and the season was so advanced that the daylight available for travel was strictly limited. 'I must have even hurried through Paris and, if war should break out, with the uncertainty of ever seeing it again.' Then James pointed out the difficulty of leaving the Adam family for at least a year. With John looking after his wife and children at Merchiston, and William only 17 years old, James was now the mainstay of life for his mother and sisters. Although James

* Scots: handsome

admired Robert's lavish lifestyle in Rome, he knew that financially he could never aspire to it. 'The study of economy is what of all things I should hate to mix with my other studies.' James's final objection was that if he travelled now and then established himself in England on his return, he would 'entirely debar Johnnie from travelling' since he would then be the only representative of the family in Scotland. On the other hand, if James joined Robert and then returned to Scotland, allowing John to travel, and then on John's return, if James in turn joined Robert in London it would have been some years since he had visited Europe. 'I should lose to you and myself the advantage of a fresh Italian reputation.' He accepted that to study under Clérisseau in Italy would be advantageous but if that could not be arranged, 'I can only trust to my good fortune.' James ended with, 'We have all along been very little accustomed to make acknowledgements to one another for favours received. I may say our friendship and gratitude have been on a deeper fixed and a better footing and I have no intention to change our ordinary way but leave it entirely to the warmness of your own heart to inform you what I must feel when I see you so much interested in scheming out my future improvement and happiness. My dearest Bob, unchangeably yours. JA.'

Robert was shocked that any scheme of his should not meet with instant approval but by 27 December he claimed to be mollified. 'In a few days I composed my mind and now am myself again.' He reassured James that seeing Paris is 'not worth a farthing' but he continued to hope: 'I am still of the opinion that either John or you should come this spring to this town.' As if his plan might now be acceptable, he continues to give instructions to bring 'a gross of lead pencils' and 'accoutrements for drawing'. He warns James that Clérisseau will have gone by the time of his arrival but Pécheux will still be available as a tutor; and although he is not an architect, it is 'better some fish than no fish'. However Robert knew that he was writing to no purpose and that he would have to continue his studies in Italy alone.

CHAPTER FIVE

Spalatro

❧

As 1755 ended Robert was established as one of the leading
connoisseurs in Rome with his own entourage of artistic tutors
and researchers. He maintained sufficient show to be accepted on
the borders of society and to be seen as suitable company for
gentlemen. He told his sister Jenny that there were only three
salons favoured by the English which he avoided: the Princess
Borghese's, and those of the Venetian and French ambassadors.
As Europe drifted towards war the French ambassador would
soon be *persona non grata* for the English, but Robert was assiduous
in clinging to his local aristocratic circle.

> I have seen Cardinal Albani and I am turned very thick as
> he has discovered my hidden talents for the hidden treasures
> of antiquity. He has given me allowance to mould several
> things from his originals, shakes me by the fist like an honest
> good one and slaps my shoulder. In short *son éminence* and me
> are as grit as dogs' heads, and with all the English my fame
> is great. I am told I shall be the restorer of ancient grandeur
> and a mover of the taste from Italy to England. It is all a
> puff, by God, and not a syllable of truth in it. But as falsities
> gain the English more than truths, in God's Holy name let
> them swallow the Gilded Pill and open their purses liberally
> to reimburse a poor Scotch man, who, if he has not got
> much skill has at least spent much money attempting it.

By contemporary standards it is all too easy to characterise
Robert Adam as a hypocritical snob with a sycophantic adoration of aristocracy. But his chosen career was to be an architect,

whether for the domestic pleasure of the aristocracy or for the public buildings erected under their political patronage. Today contracts are awarded after competitive bidding by those firms which are invited to tender. In Robert's day such invitations depended on the whim of an often none-too-bright aristocrat and, while Robert had a reputation in Scotland with the Duke of Argyll and the Earl of Hopetoun, in London he had none. Learning as much as he could from the examples of classical architecture and developing his own vocabulary from what he saw and drew was all very well, but with no opportunity to practise what he knew all his efforts were worthless. The opportunity to mingle with the people he earnestly prayed would be his future patrons was invaluable and Robert was determined to make the best use of it. Being well aware that his father had grown rich without gaining any position in society made him more conscious of the hill of prejudice he had to climb.

To this end Robert was dining with Sir William Stanhope when the ever present Abbé Grant assured him that this acquaintance would lead to an introduction to the fourth Earl of Chesterfield, Stanhope's brother. 'This [Stanhope] is the man I want as a patron and I intend to gain his favour as far as civility, and any trifling favours I can do for him, will have effect. He says that my Lord Leicester is the Burlington of the time; that his condemnation or approbation is sufficient either to raise a man in my way or else to knock him in the head.' The fragility of a patron's favour could not be expressed more clearly. Stanhope also advised Robert to shun surveying of proposed buildings. Architects who did their own surveying charged five per cent of the total cost which the nobility objected to paying. Apart from a natural dislike for paying for anything as intangible as an estimate of what the eventual building would cost, experience had taught them that such estimates were usually wildly inaccurate and far too low. (In 2005 a contemporary architect stated that if clients were given a true estimate of the final cost of a building, nothing would ever be built.) Stanhope's advice was for Robert to confine himself purely to designing buildings. Another factor mitigating against survey work was that such dealings with the price of stone and timber could lead to Robert being seen as a tradesman, which would make him totally unacceptable as company for a gentleman. However, Robert's wooing of Stanhope proceeded well but with more 'honour than profit, which is but an unlucky circumstance'.

Much more to his satisfaction, he told Helen that, 'My portrait by Pécheux is finished and just now on the chimneypiece before me, it is as resembling as it is possible to paint to resemble nature and vastly well painted. It shall be sent to you as soon as any occasion of a ship casts up, and hope in due time you will have it in Scotland.'

In the same letter he wrote: 'The news of the earthquake in Lisbon is very terrible and I dare say both Scotch and English have lost many friends in that destruction.' This earthquake, on 1 November 1755, had its epicentre in the Atlantic some 200 miles south-west of Lisbon but the effect on the city was savage. In 3½ minutes 80 per cent of Lisbon's buildings were destroyed as a 5-metre-wide fissure cut through the city centre. Up to 90,000 people were killed as the surviving population rushed to the harbour, now filled with stranded shipwrecks, and where, 40 minutes after the first shock, three enormous tsunamis engulfed the survivors of the ruined city. What was not covered by the incoming waves caught fire and the destruction was almost total. The north coast of Africa suffered severe flooding and there were unusually high tides along the south coast of England. Voltaire wrote of the event in *Candide*, its arbitrariness causing him to reconsider the divine purpose in creation. Rousseau took it as a proof that the development of cities was contrary to true civilisation and Immanuel Kant set about a scientific examination of its causes. It would even touch the life of Robert Adam in April 1756.

For the moment he concentrated on the latest arrivals in Rome. There were 'shoals of English' and two Scotsmen of his acquaintance. 'There are two sons of Deacon Mylne in Rome at present studying architecture, one of them had studied in France and has accordingly that abominable taste in perfection. The other who came straight from Scotland has made great progress and begins to draw extremely well so that if he goes on he may become better than any of those beggarly fellows who torment our native city, for which reason, to keep all superiority in our hands it will be absolutely necessary that the family of Adam all see foreign parts without which that Mylne may turn to our disadvantage, as I assure you he promises well and having it to say he was abroad so long may have sway with many of our Scotch Dons for whom, as he is poor, he will work much cheaper than we can do'. The Mylnes, he noted, 'have neither money nor education to make themselves known to strangers.'

For his part, Robert Mylne wrote of Robert, 'I assure you that as an architect, he makes no more figure than we do'[1], but socially Mylne had a different view. 'He makes a great figure here, keeping a coach and footmen.'[2] Mylne would, in any case, be inclined to treat Robert as his superior since, when Mylne had attended the High School in Edinburgh, he was a first-year pupil when Robert was a distant god in his final year. Such distinctions of rank can stay with a person for life. Mylne had travelled with his brother William, not as Grand Tourists but as students with an allowance of £30 a year and they fully intended to study as hard as they could. 'Unless a man settles for some years under a master he cannot attain to any degree of merit.'[3] Robert Mylne studied at the Accademia di San Luca in Rome, gaining the gold medal, but most of his work in Britain – the original Blackfriars Bridge in London – has now been demolished. Ironically, Mylne won the competition to design the bridge in preference to a design by Robert Adam.

Robert now told his mother that he had abandoned his scheme for James to join him in Rome. 'I don't expect to see one or other of my brothers in Rome, for I know John will never get the Government business left in a time of war, where his office demands his presence, and at the same time his constant expectation and earnest desire to set out will prevent Jamie who might easily have returned before Johnnie will get away.' He did find it difficult to accept that his idea had been rejected and a faint hope still lingered since neither brother had 'wrote me their final determination . . . But surely this summer I must beat a march and spend some time at Venice and Vicenza, and from that through Germany into Holland.'

Knowing that his mother would want gossip of Scots ladies in Rome, Robert obliged with a sketch of poor Mrs Ramsay. 'She is of a good family, her being wife to an artist prevents her being admitted into any company, so that if she had not by great good luck encountered Mrs Elliott here, who is a spirited lively body, she must have been extremely dull, not to say miserable, as Allan is a capput*, tyrannical body in his own house. Besides that, there can be nothing more mortifying than for a lady who is respected in her own country to be utterly debarred the company of genteel people in others.' Mary may then have shaken her head despairingly at Robert's lengthy and discursive description of the Roman carnival which had exhausted him by being even more extravagant than that in Florence.

By 20 March 1756 Robert's plans had become firmer. 'I have persuaded the faithful Clérisseau to stay with me this summer in Rome for 4 months longer. Though he is waited impatiently for at Paris and his whole friends enraged at his not returning home and though I have no less than half a dozen people working for me I believe I shall not be able to accomplish what I want to have done. But all I can say is that I shall lose not time as Mr Ramsay and Mr Elliott's families continue in Rome till September next, their company and our constant traffic together makes it much more agreeable.' He had to take account of the effects of war on his journey home. Technically there was no official declaration of war between Britain and France; Europe was quiet, if tense, as Maria Theresa looked over her shoulder at Frederick the Great in Prussia and Louis XV rattled French sabres. In India Clive had taken Arcot from the French and the two sides were readying themselves for further conflict. On the other side of the Atlantic skirmishing between the two nations extended northwards from the West

* Scots: quarrelsome, short-tempered

Indies to the shores of Cape Breton in Canada. By the time Robert would be travelling war of some kind seemed inevitable and thus his choice would be made for him: 'If a regular war [occurs] I shall be determined as to my return through France or Germany'.

In the meantime his life in Rome continued with the occasional break into hooliganism. He spent a quiet suppertime with the Ramsays, then met some gallants on his way home, got very drunk with them and pursued one of their number to his home where he indulged in an orgy of window breaking. He wrote jokingly to Edinburgh asking whom William had got pregnant and hoped that he and James were employing their leisure hours producing children. 'I shall need a good many lads to draw for me in England and surely architect's bastards are the best of all for that purpose as they will have the genius of kind. I hope Margaret Annan's belly will be up in a few months that by the time she becomes housekeeper in London she may be ready to beget one that partakes of the Italian air and genius.' There is a growing loneliness in his letters at this time, however. As he was cut off from his family and the gossip of Edinburgh, Robert tried to chatter in his letters and what would have been gentle humour in conversation becomes more and more forced and heavy. He told his sisters that every time he dined with the Ramsays and the Elliotts they toasted all his absent siblings. Given the number of healths to be drunk – four sisters and three brothers, to say nothing of his mother and nephew – the evenings must have had a convivial start.

When Carnival ended he was happy that he hadn't caught a cold and reported that 'I exhibited in [the] character of Signor Pulcinello*, most notably'. He even deceived Grant and Sir William Stanhope. He described a procession in the Corso on the last day with 'several cars draped up, one full of Bacchante, all draped with habits covered with vine leaves and bunches of grapes, each holding a bough in his hand. Festoons of grapes formed a canopy over them and upon the top of all was a Silenus

* 'Punch' in English. Usually in a white cloak, a black mask and a long hooked nose.

bestriding a hogshead crowned with vines and two Bacchante supporting him. They eat and drink away very merrily and had music along with them. There being at least 25 people in the car, drawn by six horses each with a little Bacchante on his back. After it turned night each of these people held a wax taper in his hand which made a very fine illumination. It was draped up in an amphitheatrical manner and I'm convinced the Silenus was 20 feet from the ground.'

He and Clérisseau went for an eight-mile walk the next day to clear their heads. He assured Janet, 'In short, my dear lady, this is the most intoxicating country in the world.' Once again he determines to go out drawing every day, 'until dinner time, ordering the coach to the place where we are to be in order to bring us home to eat and drink like Turks'.

Peggy was now learning French so Robert wrote half a letter in French for her. But his professional fears were, for a moment, lessened. 'I hear from England that Chambers is not doing great things. I may hope to come in for a share of the pock pudding with the rest.' He wants James to trim up draughtsmen 'as I will draw them off by shipping to the capital as they will be both cheaper and more tractable than your English sons of bitches.' He went on: 'I should like to have a set of the best plans in Scotland, such as Braco's house, Yester, Dumfries, etc., which with changing and shifting about gives one hints to compose other things.'

Robert was still taking measurements for his revision of Desgodetz and producing drawings under the eagle eye of Clérisseau when the idea for yet another project occurred to him. He had written to James concerning an application he had made earlier to be the architect for the rebuilding of Lisbon and he hoped for the endorsement of Lord Hopetoun and Sir William Stanhope. Allan Ramsay had written to the Duke of Argyll 'vastly strongly in my favour' but Robert wanted to delay the duke's endorsement in case it should antagonise Lord Hopetoun. He presumed that Sir William would write to Lord Huntingdon. For a 28-year-old student who had never designed even a single house, except as part of a collaboration, to imagine that he would be granted an entire city to design and that he would have the talent to carry out the task leaves one gasping in astonishment at Robert's ambition and optimism. His optimism was more than a little tempered by realism when he described his 'private incitements to a scheme which there is a thousand chances to one will never take place.' But he dreamed of the increase of reputation, even of being ennobled by the King of Portugal. On his return he would 'beat down at once the pride of presuming Chambers or any other who may at the present vie with a young inexperienced stripling . . . If God brings about this desired event, surely that earthquake was a heavenly judgement intended for my behalf. . . Laugh at me as much as you will, I daresay you think I am crazy to look so high, but I assure you, I am much in credit even in this country'.

Summing up the characters of his hoped-for supporters he revised his view of Sir William as being more, 'weak than sensible, fickle than steady and proud than humble with all these imperfections on his head he has nevertheless been my friend and perhaps may continue so'. On Portugal, 'he said he would befriend me by giving me such letters as he thought might be of use and added that Lord Huntingdon should bestir himself in it'. But Robert again wanted to delay until he got an answer from Lord Hopetoun, a tactic endorsed by 'the corpulent Abbé'. He realised that his scheme was causing some anxiety in Edinburgh and apologised to his mother on 19 June: 'You can't imagine how vex'd I was to find that my project of Lisbon, which I always considered as a desperate one, joked about it as such, never imagining it could or would take place, had made such [an] impression upon our family, or given you one moment's uneasiness. I am sure that if you reflected seriously on the lordly terms I asked them to grant me, and at the same time the only terms I would receive or accept of, you may see that it would be absolutely impossible to obtain them. Besides you may be assured that had not you and the rest of the family approved of my arduous scheme you had only to say the word to make me for ever forsake it.' But Hopetoun's response was unhelpful. He would go no further than to recommend Robert to Mr Hay, the British Consul in Lisbon, and Robert felt that he could well have done that himself. But he had thought, talked and dreamt of nothing else for some days and the scheme had broken the monotony of study and drawing.

Robert was meanwhile working out his already well-formed plans for London. He told James that he would regret not seeing him in Rome and, somewhat disingenuously, wondered why their elder brother should delay coming to Rome. 'My opinion is that he never will and in that resolution I leave him and go to plan our schemes. Clérisseau and I being together will continue so, on the road homeward as long as we can, at Venice and Vicenza, at Pola in Istria and at many other places which will consume the next spring to the best of purposes. If I return through Germany he will continue to go with me perhaps into Holland from which I come to England and send him to Paris.' But Robert had discovered that Clérisseau's ambition was merely a salary of £150 or £200 a year.

It occurred to me that supposing we travelling brothers should fix that upon him and keep him a purpose for travelling till such time until we were well established in England when I would bring him over and give him the inspection of our Drawing Office and to put things in perspective and make views of all the principal places in England, get him to oversee anything one intends to publish which would I imagine, make him quite happy. And would be much for our advantage. The Travelling Scheme, you see, keeps him distant some years, so that he can neither interfere nor eclipse the first flash of character and, after that is over, he comes secretly like a thief in the night and no one regards him. Tho' a Frenchman he has no *allegria* in company nor no thoughts of *éclat* or ambition. Thus, though sensible of his own merit (which is infinite) yet he may be managed like a lap dog. Allow him to cross himself, eat fish on meagre days and hear mass on Sundays and say prayers morning and evening which may be called the Compendiary of the Whole Duty of Catholic man. He neither desires nor aims at more.

Robert's arrangements for Clérisseau may seem peremptory and almost callous, but he knew that Clérisseau wanted to continue in his employment and he was, after all, a servant to be employed at his master's whim.

Robert also employed 'a young lad from Liège' whom he intended to bring to England as overseer of the line drawers. This was Laurent-Benoît Dewez an 'honest and laborious' drawer of plans. He told James that he had found another draughtsman, Agostino Brunias, for ornaments and landscape figures. They only spoke French or Italian so there was little chance of their being 'soon debauched by evil communication which is no small advantage'. Robert proposed that when he returned to London, James should visit him so that he could see what gaps needed to be filled in the collections he had made but, typically, he doubted that there were any gaps. 'In short I have left you Rome to view as a gentleman would do for his pleasure.' This meant that James would have time to visit Calabria, Sicily and Greece. James would visit where Demosthenes harangued and where Pericles counselled. 'I never go near the Capitol or near the Forum Romanum where harangued Cicero, Caesar, the Consuls, the Tribunes, the Triumvirs but I am struck with a respectful horror mixed with pity. The total extinction of all that's great and virtuous, nothing but depravity of sentiment, lowness of manners and mercenary aims reigning in their head.'

Robert returned in his letter to his personal arrangements for London: 'I must have house and furniture and servants and chariot and the Lord knows what all. Two of our families must move to London and will with judgement and economy aid me in domestic determination.' He confessed that he had no head for figures but, 'if Willie was to be with us in London he would do the business of overseeing and directing our books to a nicety'. However even the genius and caution of Willie would never achieve that 'nicety'. Robert was aware that while he spent time in Rome, hopefully preparing himself to be the leading architect in Britain, he was not earning the partnership any money, while his share still accrued to him. He had, therefore, a nagging conscience which he had to calm by making arrangements for the future which would be of advantage to the brotherhood, either by encouraging them to the same indulgence which had been accorded him, or by making concrete arrangements for the proposed London establishment. His plans for the rebuilding of Lisbon also fall under this category in that, had the commission been granted to him, he would, at a stroke, have solved all his problems. He would have earned a staggering fee for the partnership, he would have been involved in what he most wanted – innovative architecture – and he would have become instantly famous. The plans he sketched for Lisbon were entirely speculative and bore no relationship to the situation of the city surrounded by a giant semicircular escarpment, but Robert knew it was only a dream.

Meanwhile there was gossip to impart to Edinburgh. He had written to Wood to keep his name before the Duke of Bridgewater to be ready for his arrival in London early next summer. He also had a commission to find a picture for Lord Hopetoun and was having the inevitable difficulties with size, subject and price range. He had extended his search to Florence but although there were some good pictures there, they all had naked figures in them. Robert commented that 'his lordship may well know that without nakedness no pictures can be found. Italian painters are given to nakedness as the sparks to fly upwards.' Clearly, his lordship, unlike his contemporaries, was averse to depictions of naked flesh on the walls of Hopetoun House.

Robert had yet to receive a firm commitment from John as to the establishment of a London practice and he was afraid that such an arrangement might cause the partnership agreement to founder, which would deprive him of an income on his arrival in London. Therefore he wrote to Helen hoping that it might continue for a year after his arrival, arguing that 'a poor devil deprived of a sure income with nothing but 3 or 4,000 pounds of his own in capital will be sadly put to it'. He begged Helen to clarify the situation. 'As money shall never be the cause of any difference between the co-partners, so that all I ask is that after conversing seriously on these affairs Jamie will inform me of the whole matter and of John's thoughts of it and I shall regulate my conscience and bring myself to agree and fall in it with it accordingly.' It is interesting that Robert was always cautious about challenging his elder brother John over financial matters. However, in spite of these worries, he proposed taking a box at both opera houses for the coming season.

Writing to James on 11 September Robert revealed that he had given up the plan to revise Desgodetz since, 'It retarded more material studies such as that of Adrian's Villa and the baths of Caracalla and Diocletian which are in a very prosperous way and I dare say will please you and take with the public. I am to show the baths in their present ruinous condition and from that to make other designs of them as they were when entire and in their glory'. His book would improve on Palladio and 'though I say that should not, will be a most glorious work to which your Palmyras and Balbecks are less than nothing and vanity.' He notes that when Palladio saw the ruins when they were in better condition. He had made other drawings based on those by Pirro Ligorio, Alessandro Algardi and Nicola Salvi.

It was at this time that a plan began to take shape in Robert's head. Burlington was justly praised for his *Fabriche Antiche*, as was Wood for his books *The Ruins of Palmyra* and *The Ruins of Baalbec*. Colen Campbell had risen to fame as the author of *Vitruvius Brittanicus*, so why should not Robert Adam produce a similar volume? His work at the baths of Diocletian led him to think of that emperor's vast palace at Spalatro* on the Dalmatian coast and easily reachable by boat from Venice. If he travelled with his entourage of draughtsmen as well as the faithful Clérisseau, then he could produce a work to rival Burlington and Wood and make a tangible contribution to the profitability of the partnership.

While still considering the proposed London practice he sketched out the personnel he had in mind. 'I think I now have as good as agreed with my two lads who work for me here to

* Now renamed Split in Croatia

accompany me to England.' They were his 'Liègeois', Laurent-Benôit Dewez and Agostino Brunias. Dewez, who had studied under Vanvitelli in Naples, was his 'plan man and line drawer of an active, undaunted and bustling spirit, but hitherto much attached, honest and laborious,' while Brunias was

> bred a painter, I have converted into an architect. He has done all my ornaments and all my figures vastly well. Besides these two I have an Italian lad who does all the drudgery business of putting things in proportion from sketches. But him I hold in no esteem but as a daily I have at 1 shilling a day. Clérisseau and I are in the direction of these youths and by means of their industry and my pay we get more time to think and to apply to sketches of taste and invention which otherwise I could not do . . . I have, besides these three another beagle who is the most worthless young dog I ever knew, but draws ornaments to perfection. He it is I am to set about copying over all the things I have in a little book, that when you are here you may see what I have and if there is any other thing that you would wish to have done, and he is one of your men at 1 shilling a day These things no doubt cost me a great deal of money. But what can I do? Without them boys I could absolutely do nothing, but work like a slave to little purpose.

These arrangements seemed modest enough, but Robert was worried about his financial state on arrival in London, stating that 'for as sanguine as all my Edinburgh friends are in imagining that I am to make millions in money, I own I think these hopes most absolutely chimerical.' He did not now intend to bring Clérisseau to London, since that could allow Chambers to spread the rumour that all the ideas coming from the Adam brothers were in fact the sole creation of the Frenchman.

Back in Scotland John wrote to Mrs Adam endorsing Robert's plan and pointing out that Chambers (now often called Chalmers by the brothers) had been traversing Scotland in the manner of one unconcerned with business, thus showing that he could not yet be in high demand in England. 'A book of Chinese affairs he is publishing cannot raise his reputation high among the truly learned in Architecture.' Then on 18 September Robert sent a letter to Lord Hopetoun setting out his plans. But he first sent it, unsealed to Helen. 'If any words should be changed they may be, then sealed and sent to him.'

By 2 October Robert met Allan Ramsay, now apparently recovered from the fever he had suffered at Viterbo. Robert however thought that he looked 'like a man going into a consumption'. He hinted to Ramsay that 'the bargain twixt we brothers was that whoever settled in England should be excluded from the co-partnery in Scotland'. Ramsay thought that this condition was unfair and that there should be at least a year or two 'for trial'. Robert told him he had asked for one year only. In the meantime, a Mr Stephens left Rome for England carrying endorsements of Robert's abilities to his previous ac-quaintance the Duke of Bridgewater. He was managing, just, to keep all his balls in the air.

Robert's feelings of isolation from his Edinburgh friends were calmed when he heard that there was a chance that Adam Ferguson might join him in Vicenza. Ferguson was an old school and university friend, 'a brilliant, quick-tempered Highlander, the future Professor of Philosophy at Edinburgh'[4] and had served as chaplain to the Black Watch. He corresponded with Robert, asking to be addressed 'without any clerical titles, for I am a downright layman',[5] and gave him advice on possible return routes. Robert did receive a letter from Adam Fairholme, the influential Edinburgh banker, introducing him to Mr Smith, the British Consul at Venice, 'but it so badly written as to be useless'. He now wanted more introductions 'in a genteel train' for Holland and 'any of those towns in Germany where they may be useful' although he was not going to Vienna, Dresden or Berlin. Following the Grand Tourist's always reliable precept that no one could have too many letters of introduction, he wrote to Charles Hope for a letter of introduction to John Murray, the British Resident at Venice.

Then, by way of tidying up his remaining business in Italy, he wrote with supreme confidence, 'I intend to be made Professor of Architecture, Painting and Sculpture in the Academy of St Luke in Rome, the ceremony of which and getting out my diploma will cost me 25 guineas at least, but is extremely honourable and showy in all books or things you may publish. I shall obtain this easily and grandly. I will solicit my good friend the Cardinal Albani to ask it in person though I could obtain it without his means but like to do it grandly as otherways. I hope also to be made member of the academy of Florence on passing through that city which Sir Horace* will push with pleasure. At Bologna I shall be received Fellow of the Institute of that city, also coveted by all the great men of the arts, and these three with what additional titles I may acquire in England will be very sufficient to show the person that has been honoured with all of them was not altogether without merit in his profession.' These purchased distinctions, Robert felt, were 'fully as desirable as being member of the Select Society in Edinburgh'.

Lord Hopetoun approved his staying on longer than he had planned, which delighted Robert as he would have more time in Dalmatia and Pola in Istria. 'If you know with what a sad heart I return without seeing Greece, especially to be on the very coast of it. I shall, like Johnnie, still live in hope to see Athens and Sparta and look wistfully on Egypt and the Holy Land.' Robert was not only regretful at this missed opportunity, but also worried that some of his hoped-for commissions in England might not come to fruition. 'I am somewhat uneasy at Bridgewater's silence, but hope, without cause. I doubt not but Mr Wood will say something soon in case the duke does not. But if they should all dance reels on one another's heads I can't return to England this season.' He was greatly cheered that Chambers appeared not to be at work in England. Then, in a brief flash of determination, he wondered if James knew 'how much I despise our famous Inigo, he would be astonished and that even Palladio was much

---

* He had already met Sir Horace Mann, British Minister to the Tuscan Court, on his journey south.

to be criticised, he would marvel. But this we keep quiet and endeavour to follow their footsteps in what is praiseworthy and revile their failings.'

On 13 November he discussed with Peggy the idea of having Willie with him as a clerk in London. On the whole he found the idea acceptable, 'If he is intelligent, modest, and given to application and not to foppery' – this from a man who had written to his sister Elizabeth on 30 October to discuss buying a white suit with gold buttons! Jamie could quickly train him up and James might also consider,

> That one should have a set of designs drawn out applicable to gardening. With ruins, temples, cascades and groups of trees is surely right in order to show the connoisseur and people either of taste or pretenders to it . . . In short to sum up the whole the more you can keep people from seeing, the more their imaginations have occasion to work, so that at Paris the same stratagem is practised with unfailing success. Show none but people of true taste and leave them to praise you and be shy in showing to the ignorant rabble . . . If ever I should have the fortune to execute a dozen of temples and lay out a set of gardens which are approved of and admired by the world, then is the true time to publish them, dedicating each plate to the proprietor of the different places which will both be pleasing to them, honourable and profitable to me.

This burst of energy – largely consisting of plans for other people to carry out – reached a climax on 30 November, St Andrew's night, when he attended a celebratory dinner with Lords Elgin and Rosebery in 'a sea of liquor'. Clérisseau had to put him to bed since Donald, a below-stairs celebrant, was too drunk. The resultant penitence led him to make arrangements for his other servants and he advised James that either he or John could take over his *valet de chambre* and cook. He was, Robert assured James, the best cook in Rome – after three previous sackings. James could simply send a boy by sea while he travelled overland and the boy would be cared for by the Abbé Grant until he arrived.

On the days leading up to Christmas Day Robert had a serious falling-out with Allan Ramsay who had received a letter from David Hume. Hume had heard of Ramsay's bad health from John McGowan, the Edinburgh antiquary, who, in turn, had heard of it through Robert's letters to his family. The irascible Ramsay was afraid that his enemies were 'spreading reports of his death, and thereby hurting his business on his return home'. But by Christmas the two men were reconciled.

Turning back to business and money he proudly announced, 'I have made a purchase of a St Catherine by Guido Reni, finely painted and well preserved and I think is a capital piece. And now that it is in my possession value it at a great price, at least 200 guineas, though I had it for much less money, not having cost me 20'. McGowan was to be told of the purchase but not of the price, since such intelligence could affect the picture's resale value. 'It would have been a fine picture for my Lord Hopetoun had it been of sufficient size.'

Now we get a hint of pleasures to come. 'Some morning soon I am promised a visit from Miss Molyneux and Miss Bury who come to breakfast with me in order to see my Baths and other drawings of virtu.' Miss Molyneux was Diana Molyneux, the 39-year-old daughter of Sir Francis Molyneux travelling with her sister Mrs Bury and her brother-in-law. Robert had met the pair in Naples and had initially found Miss Molyneux proud, affected and immensely coquettish, but on this occasion he was immediately taken with her and enthusiastically attended supper at the Bury's house. 'I was very merry t'other night at the Bury's where a gentleman whom Miss Molyneux had accepted some time ago as her nominal husband, i.e. her partner for the evening, was discarded in a public company and I was accepted of in his place, and triumphed over the poor gentleman. The lady likewise discarded me half an hour after our marriage to the no small entertainment of the company who in their turns crowed over my

miserable blushes.' When the Misses Molyneux and Bury re-
called with the Abbé Grant for breakfast,

'Lord bless me,' says Miss Molyneux, 'Is it possible that that
gay cheerful and frolicksome Mr Adams that we see in our
house, is the same studious laborious and enterprising Mr
Adams that one sees him at his own. I'm surprised how you
can laugh, how you can joke or be merry when you have such
a crowd of objects to distract your imagination and employ
your thoughts. The twentieth part would turn my brain.' In
short they said more than this sheet would contain and
expressed their praises so genteelly that a man less susceptible
of flattery must have been highly pleased. They likewise were
immensely satisfied with my good Frenchman's operations
and bespoke two drawings of him, which Molyneux presents
to a count at Naples in return for some presents she had got
from him. Never were people happier than we all were with
another and ever since I have been more like a brother in their
house than a Scots Architect and have received such distinguished marks of their regard before all company that a baron
invited me to dinner as Miss Molyneux's particular friend for
whom he has no ordinary regard, and I thanked that lady for
so good a dinner, as I told her the respect shown me by M le
Baron was entirely on her account. Indeed I must say for her
that I never saw so agreeable a woman, or so accomplished
with an inexhaustible fund of good sense, a most pleasing
address, and most engaging manner. If my heart was not as
hard as iron, I would most undoubtedly be over head and
ears and desperately in love, but, thank God, my plan and
elevations of baths and virtu have a surprising effect to keep
down that passion. Besides that, I am not so vain to think that
a lady with 900 pounds a year portion, who has refused the
best noblemen in England to attend a sick sister, would ever
think of so poor a devil and that's another check to ardent
love. Yet I must acknowledge that did I give way to my
inclinations I should be intoxicated.

He had read the ladies two poems and they were 'prodigiously pleased'. 'Miss Molyneux I take to be a very good judge, she has read an infinite deal and writes as genteely as anyone can do. Talks and writes Italian and French as well as any lady of these nations. All the times I have heard her, never can find her fail in one word, and what's more surprising was equally master or mistress of them before she left England merely from her study and application.'

The year 1757 started with a surprise when Robert received a letter from Chambers, now back in England. It was a scrupulously polite letter asking Robert to send him two drawings by Laurent Pécheux but it triggered Robert's paranoia and he became convinced that Chambers was maintaining a network of spies in Rome to evaluate the work of other artists. This was a complete misconception since Chambers felt, with some justification, that he was too well established to be threatened by anyone.

Although Robert's time was heavily occupied with masquerading, plays and operas, Miss Molyneux, 'whom by this time is to write to her relative the Duchess of Norfolk about me,' was still very much in his thoughts and he intended to correspond with her even after her return to London. She 'writes with the greatest ease and fluency that any man is capable of'. There is a nicety of manners in this since the relationships and ease of acquaintance which were found to be acceptable during the Grand Tour were not always so welcome on return to Britain. Robert was aware that he was still only on the edge of society.

He continued to buy works of art, either for his own satisfaction or for resale on his return. 'I have lately made some great purchase of some noble pictures of the great masters. I have never yet been so lucky as to get one for Lord Hopetoun, but perhaps may meet with one before I leave Rome though the time is now drawing wondrous near.' Robert had exhausted what might be construed as commercially useful studies in Rome and was now being accepted, not as an aesthetic visitor and socially excellent company, but as a member of that *demi-monde* of the expatriate resident. It was time to move on.

When a man can no longer make the same figure in the same town, it is surely much more advisable to live like a scrub in any other. I am sorry to think of leaving this place where I have lived so happily, with many agreeable and good friends, unmolested by Kirk or State and respected by all good people and hated and envied by the wicked and villainous only. Master of myself with a proper application and amusement and a constant improvement in my own business in the most elegant and lordly way. Would anything but want of money oblige a man to forsake this ease and peace and tranquillity of mind to rush into a bustling world, to struggle with boisterous lords, to wade among scrawls and accounts and be liable to the capricious temper of every rich and senseless squire and lord, or proud and overbearing noble? But there is no remedy and therefore the only way is to make it as easy as possible and struggle by every method to make one soon rich and struggle boldly to arrive at independence.

The advent of spring brought with it what anyone else might have passed off as a head-cold, but for Robert merits three sides of paper in a minute description of his – quite normal – symptoms. Robert had what might, with charity, be called, the marks of a thoroughgoing hypochondriac. Back in January he had lecherously and probably drunkenly attempted to pursue his host's landlady's daughter armed only with a candle. Inevitably he ended up falling over a trunk and barking his shins. No less an eminent doctor than the Young Pretender's own physician, Dr Murray, was summoned and rest was advised, but when Robert developed headaches sterner methods were undertaken. Dr Irwin, an old friend and another Scot – no Italian doctors were consulted – administered poultices and doses of salt and wormwood, until the doctor could announce, 'Ye hae nae mair fever than I have and a guid glass of claret will cure you quite'. It would probably have done the trick at the outset. In this case Robert recovered from what was no more than a spring cold.

At the end of March 1757 Miss Molyneux left Rome for Naples. 'She is perfection and so devoted to her sick sister, when Mrs Bury is in distress, Miss Molyneux is miserable, nay, I believe suffers more than Mrs Bury herself . . . She has all along denied the best matches England can afford, denies herself every pleasure of life to sit constantly with her sister's side and declares she will never leave her, either till she recovers or dies.' In fact, Diana Molyneux died a spinster.

Gavin Hamilton, whom Robert had met in London, had returned to Rome and they dined together in March at Hamilton's villa on the Janiculum with marvellous views of Rome and the surrounding hills. They spoke of the arts and sciences, of Greece and the Greek Islands, 'which, if I had the cash, I would go and see with pleasure'. Robert dreamt openly of meeting John at Vicenza, setting sail from Venice for a cruise around the islands ending in Athens. He would take Clérisseau and two draughtsmen and in '3 months time return laden with laurel'. This dinner was, in fact, the first of many marking his farewell to Rome. Meanwhile he made transport arrangements for his now considerable collection of art.

On 19 March 1757 he wrote to his agents: 'I expect in 3 weeks hence to leave Rome, a very severe cold and rheumatism has retarded my affairs.' He gave detailed instructions for a letter to be sent to his mother and a 'large Packet for my Lord Hopetoun'.[6] He made banking arrangements and gave addresses for Venice and Vicenza. He also wrote to John, 'I hope to leave Rome in a fortnight hence, having all my boxes in order and ready to send off but am determined to let them rather remain a year at Civita Vecchia rather than risk them at present hoping this summer may do much to bring in a peace, provided no more Byngs command our navies.* As to all my valuable things these come in my trunk which is of a most enormous magnitude a purpose to contain all my drawings sketches and studies, books necessary on the road with all my habiliments and utensils of war.

* In July 1756 Admiral Byng had failed to recapture Minorca and was shot for his incompetence.

It is the astonishment and admiration of all who see it and cost me 7 good zecchinis which is 3 guineas and a half.' It was now Holy Week when all business in Rome ceased, which held up the awarding of his diploma, although, the cardinals 'are lazy enough without so good an excuse'. Piranesi showed Robert his dedications in the forthcoming book and the name of Adam appeared satisfactorily eminent with all his diplomas: ' "To Robert Adam, Britain, Patron of Architecture, this plate of Campus Martius is dedicated by John Battista Piranesi." Then on a frieze above is a medal, where fame points to a piece of architecture and leans on my shoulder in the attitude of going to proclaim my praises. Round the medal is this description; Robert Adam Architect, Member of the Academy of St Luke in Rome and of Florence and of the Institute of Bologna – all in Latin.'

He then begged news from Edinburgh and London: 'I shall be glad to know the fate of *Douglas* at Covent Garden House.' This was the play *Douglas* by John Home, based on the ballad of Gil Morrice and whose title role had been turned down by David Garrick. It was, however, successfully performed in Edinburgh on 14 December 1756, causing a member of the audience, probably apocryphally, to shout out, 'Whaur's your Willie Shakespeare noo?' The play was revived in London by John Rich at Covent Garden in March 1757 with enough success to warrant the great Garrick commissioning Home's later work. Robert also wanted to see his cousin William Robertson's *History of Scotland*, but since this would not be published until 1759, what he received – and admired – was an early proof copy.

As to his own work, Robert wrote that: 'My Baths are all now completed and to be sure it has cost me a deal of trouble and plague and now I must begin to write the description of it being determined like Scotch heros to become the author who attacks Vitruvius, Palladio and all those blackguards of ancient and modern Architecture sword in hand.' Robert had amassed, if only theoretically, his views on the architecture as expressed by the authors of copy books and their followers. 'In the nearly four years he was in Italy 1754–8, Robert Adam came to realise that the Romans had invested their buildings and interiors with a freedom of execution denied them by precise theorists and producers of books on antiquity in later years. Their freedom, reticulation expression of taste, and movement he carefully abstracted. Then he intensified and altered it as he thought expedient and used it with flair, skill and originality.'[7]

He had heightened his 'wise appearance by taking a wig which gives me at lest ten years more to that old phiz I had before. The reasons were too strong for this change to be rejected. The principals was the time spent daily in dressing my hair [was] a fatigue and lots of time I could no longer put up with and which I am sure would have been impracticable in England should I ever become man of consequence.'

Robert Adam left Rome at the beginning of May 1757 with Clérisseau, his two draughtsmen and the much maligned Donald. Allan Ramsay followed in a hired chaise with his family. Robert and his entourage stayed overnight at Viterbo and then continued to view Etruscan sites at Ferento, arriving in Florence behind Ramsay and his wife, sister-in-law and children. Here Robert was received by Horace Mann whom he had met on his journey south when he was merely the bear-leader for Charles Hope. Now, however, 'All the virtuosi of Florence have been crowding to see me, and I am received member and I have got all my diplomas both of Rome, Florence and Bologna.' Robert's spirits were also raised even higher by receiving a letter from Miss Molyneux in Naples, describing her fairly comfortable circumstances – a little far from the sea – and recommending that he read *Della Antichità di Saloni vicino a Spalatro, composto del' Autore della Comp'n di Giesui.*[8] Robert had clearly told Miss Molyneux of his plan to publish a book of drawings of Diocletian's palace. The letter is a normal, friendly one but Robert, with hopeful misinterpretation, told his sister Janet that the letter was not to be taken as a declaration of love and that he only wanted her good wishes and recommendations. Having been fêted by Horace Mann, who invited him to his box at the theatre, and having had dinner invitations extended to him, Robert reflected: 'How Hope prevented me doing myself the least honour last time we dwelt in this blessed city together is inconceivable and had that stink of quality continued to haunt me at Rome, I had never risen in the esteem or good graces of any lady . . . But catch me now under the claws of any great man if you can, I'd be damned first. They pilfer your cash, they make use of you as a servant and they thief-like strip you of your honour'.

Robert Adam was not the first tourist to suffer from master-piece fatigue and he was certainly not the last: 'At Bologna so numberless are the pictures of Guerino, of Guido, of Domeni-chino, and of the 3 Caraccis, Hannibale, Augustino and Ludo-vico that I swear my brain was confused and my body fatigued to death with them so that I was glad to get out from amongst them and to have some respite from my labours and rest to my understanding.'

Robert did, however meet Conte Francesco Algarotti, one of the most celebrated aesthetes in Italy. The count met with Robert and admired his drawings – 'I had emptied my trunk a-purpose to satisfy his curiosity' – and then gave Robert letters of introduction to a 'great virtuoso and man of taste at Venice'.

And with that he diverted to Padua, thus making his entrance into the Most Serene Republic of Venice, of which Padua was a part. In the city there was 'a very fine opera' which would be attended by Murray and Smith, respectively the British Minister and Consul at Venice. He was well received by them but the opera was not outstanding. Robert also demonstrated his single-ness of purpose in his account of sightseeing in Padua. He visited the Basilica of St Antony and gave scornful descriptions of the display of relics of the saint, who was patron of 'ostlers, postilions and low people'. Confining his interests to the classics, he completely ignored the statue of General Gattamelata by Donatello outside the basilica, the Salone of the Palazzo della Ragione with the largest unsupported roof span in Europe, to say nothing of Giotto's frescoes in the Scrovegni Chapel, thought to be the first example of the use of perspective in art. 'The Paduan nobility is very stand-offish,' he noted, and so Robert left the city to travel past Palladio's villas beside the River Brenta and to arrive in Venice early in July. 'These regions of water, gondolas and voluptuousness,' the Most Serene Republic was at its hottest and smelliest and Robert sharply left the city to meet Smith at his country house with his wife, the minister Murray's sister, 'a beauteous virgin of forty'. There he admired 'as pretty a collection of pictures as I have seen, not large pictures, but small ones of great masters, and very finely preserved.' Smith also arranged to get Robert his permits from the Republic for digging at Spalatro as well as letters for governors and others. By happy coincidence 'my old friend General Graeme' was to be there at the same time. He had met General Graeme in Tournai in early November 1754 and called him 'a hearty old cock'. General Graeme was now commander-in-chief of the Venetian land forces and, since his power extended to Spalatro where he would be reviewing his troops, he would be of great use. 'I daresay he will desire me to live with him and eat every day at his table.' It seemed to Robert that it was, 'as if God was always puzzling his old noddle as to how to oblige me . . . I have today hired my boat, we coast it all the way and lie ashore every night . . . In the mean time laying up stores of wine, bread, tea, sugar, tongues, hams and other necessaries for gentlemen voyagers and expect to have a very pleasant trip of it.' Spalatro, on the Dalmatian coast, was still technically part of Venice which had, in the Middle Ages, controlled the entire coastline. Robert would have to avoid the Istrian peninsula and the port of Trieste since they had had been taken from Venice by Austria with whom Britain was at war, but entry to Spalatro was still controlled from Venice itself, although the hinterland of Dalmatia was under threat from the Ottoman Empire.

Robert was also indulging in casual sightseeing, 'a pretty slothful way of doing business . . . visiting here being performed on the broad of your back . . . stretched out at full length in a gondola . . . in full dress'. He did little socialising since 'the whole English either herd together or converse with dancing or singing girls who are very numerous and very handsome and very wicked.' Of his quartet, poor Brunias had never left Rome or seen the sea before and was already seasick, while Donald 'is groaning in secret at his decanting prospect'. Robert thought him the most useless and lazy creature on earth.

On 22 July 1757, Robert had his first sight of Spalatro which was 'not only picturesque but magnificent' and he immediately met his old friend General Graeme who in turn introduced him to Count Antonio Marcovitch, the second in command to the governor. The governor himself, otherwise the *Proveditore Generale*, was dealing with unrest in the interior. The town was dominated by the ruins of the palace of Diocletian – ruins since the palace had been used as a quarry for dressed stone in the building of the town. Diocletian was born in 246 AD a native of Dalmatia and the son of slaves, and was raised to the throne in 284 at the age of 38. He divided the empire peacefully, sharing power with Maximian, who ruled the eastern empire while Diocletian held the western empire. Then, in 305 AD, aged 59, he abdicated to live in retirement in his palace at Salona, the Latin name for Spalatro. 'He was distinguished as a statesman rather than as a warrior, nor did either of those princes employ force, whenever their purpose could be effected by policy. The victory of Diocletian was remarkable for its singular mildness.'[9] Maximian begged him to return to rule but Diocletian is reputed to have said that if he could show Maximian the cabbages he had planted with his own hand at Salona, he should no longer be urged to relinquish the enjoyment of happiness for the pursuit of power.

His palace for retirement was quadrangular with two sides of 600 feet and two of 700 containing a basilica, baths, and state apartments approached through a peristylum with granite columns. The emperor's apartments were bounded by a 500-feet long portico, 'which must have formed a very noble and delightful walk'. In spite of the ravages of time and the depredations of the locals – Diocletian's mausoleum had become the cathedral of Spalatro – the building was still hugely impressive and Robert was determined that his book of plates would outstrip Wood's *Ruins of Palmyra*. On 1 November he told James that his quartet had arrived in Spalatro on 22 July and had left on 28 August. He pointed out that Wood was just 15 days at Palmyra with one assistant – 'judge then the accuracy of such a work!'

Since there was so much over-building and conversion of use inside the palace, a considerable amount of excavation was needed to establish the exact limits of the Roman foundations. This led the local administration to assume that Robert was preparing plans of the fortifications and to demand that all excavations cease. Since, needless to say, the permits from Consul Smith had not yet arrived, Robert had no option but to comply. He and his team now worked within the walls of the palace until a limited permit came from the *Proveditore Generale*. Smith's permit never arrived. On 6 August Robert wrote from Spalatro to Jamie: 'I have met with many stoppages in my operations here by means of a wrongheaded governor, but General Graeme took my part with great warmth of heart and I hope now all difficulties are removed and that 8 or 10 days or at most a fortnight I shall be ready to depart for Venice with all my operations in my pocket.' The people he found

vastly polite, everything vastly cheap, a most wholesome air and glorious situation. Beef sells at one halfpenny a pound and fowls at 2½d each and a hare for 3 pence and indeed all vegetables are cheap in proportion so that for £50 sterling per annum 10 people may live like princes. It will cost me nevertheless some cash as I have had to hire some furniture from the Jews, to furnish my house, which was nothing but bare walls as there are no inns, nor furnished lodgings to be had here for love nor money. We have a company of comedians from Venice and have a play every evening. They are a strolling party and though not exquisite in their kind, yet it is a great amusement in the evenings – I have a box at my command every night which I use as my own. I dine with the General almost every day . . . We hear there are a set of singers coming soon with dancers to Spalatro so we shall have an opera.

Again Robert goes on to give a report on the female inhabitants. 'The ladies here are generally very handsome with fine complexions and dress well.'

Robert had already decided which aspects of the ruins were to be drawn, and Clérisseau made the original sketches to be copied by Brunias or Dewez. These copies were not only made *in situ* for the sake of accuracy, but also to ensure that the original sketch did not contain any unintentional errors. The pace of work was frantic, with Robert aware of the size of the task and the limited time available.

With his task completed in five weeks, Robert returned to Vicenza where he was unimpressed with the architecture of Palladio – the 'so much adored master' – much preferring the work of Michele Sanmichele, Palladio's forerunner as the leading architect in the Veneto. Since Sanmichele's work is grimly militaristic, it seems likely that Robert was simply refusing to accept the fashionable view. He wrote to Elizabeth of his plans for Clérisseau. 'I dare not speak to him on the subject, he would, if he thought he had to wait a year longer, renounce altogether and settle himself in Paris. As to bringing him to London or Scotland [this] would spoil him entirely, for once let a Frenchman get amongst people who flatter or praise them they become good for nothing.' He also feared that if people saw Clérisseau's work it 'would detract from my reputation'. Since Robert was now making arrangements independently of John's opinion he closed the letter, ineffectually as it turned out, 'Burn this cover because John should not see it.' Clérisseau accepted Robert's plan and agreed to remain in Venice and to 'wait my brother's joining him according to *parole d'honneur* given by me'. Clérisseau would now set in motion the engraving of the Spalatro plates until he was joined by either John or James, while Robert set about his return to Britain.

He faced the problem of safe passage across Europe; since it was rumoured that Britain was on the brink of a naval bombardment of Trieste, all travel permits had been suspended. But Murray reported to William Pitt from Venice that 'Mr Adam, an

English architect, by means of a little bribery and a promise of secrecy, procured one . . . though I really believe he is the very person that has occasioned all this expense and alarm at Trieste . . . and it was given out that he was employed by the English Ministry to sound the coast and to take a draught of* the fortification.'[10]

After braving the Alpine roads – roads which occasionally had sections missing – Robert arrived in Augsburg, writing to Elizabeth on 17 August 1757, 'I am in this half-Catholic half-Protestant town of Augsburg with my two myrmidons and Donald, King of Sleep.' From here he would go to Frankfurt – a five-day journey – before continuing either by post-chaise or by boat down the Rhine. The language problem could be overcome since 'my Liègeois speaks Flemish which is close enough for the needs of the travellers'. Still with an eye to business he wrote, 'This town of Augsburg is famous for the number of engravers to be found in it and the cheapness of their work so we may sometime have works to be done and books to be published.'

He collected some post from Scotland, including a draft preface to *The Ruins of Spalatro* by William Robertson. 'I cannot enough express my surprise and admiration of Willie's preface . . . If any thing can make me think more highly of his abilities than I did for his History it is his masterly penning of my preface. It is beautifully said and in a few words contains the full sense of what would have taken many pages from any other historian of his age but himself . . . I beg you will send Willie a present of 20 dozen of Maxwell's best claret on my account.' Work had only just been started on the etchings for the book and not a word of text had been written, but Robert was confident enough to commission a preface. He was always a great admirer of his learned cousin and when in Rome, and trying to retain the shape of a building or the wording of an inscription, he wished he possessed Robertson's prodigious memory.

* Make a sketch of.

His final letter from his Grand Tour was to Helen on 17 December 1757 from Rotterdam. 'Antwerp I saw with pleasure, the pictures were very fine with respect to effect and colouring, but in drawing defective. It is otherwise a very noble city and the gothic tower is magnificent. But all the places without acquaintances are good for nothing and I tired of it immensely especially as there was no species of public amusement, neither comedy nor concert.'

Robert could not live without a vivid social life. He had great confidence that Frederick the Great would conquer all his enemies and, although there were fireworks to celebrate the Austrian victory over the Prince of Bevern and the ensuing surrender of Breslau, Robert's admiration for Frederick the Great grew. 'That is without doubt the greatest man that ever God had the honour of making.' Almost as an afterthought he decided to stop off in Amsterdam 'to finish his drawings'.

Then on 17 January 1758 Robert wrote to his mother that he had safely returned from Helvetsluis to Harwich and that he intended to take up temporary lodgings in London with the Misses Hays. He said that he had experienced 'a most agreeable passage', although a page later he reported: 'I spewed the whole night on the packet'. He was understandably happy that he managed to get everything past the customs without charge, and 'saved £10 or £12'. His goods from Venice had arrived but the heavyweight Roman goods were coming under convoy from Gibraltar some time later. Hoping to see his family in London soon, he signed himself, 'I am ever my dearest mother's British boy'.

The London firm of the brothers Adam could now start business.

CHAPTER SIX

A Great Diversity of Ceilings

৵

Britain in 1758 was a country on the brink of great prosperity. There was little direct involvement with the war in Europe while in Canada and India the British armies were gaining the upper hand. William Pitt had taken personal command of the forces and his breadth of vision was starting to pay dividends. All of this created a confidence which could be seen in the physical expansion of the capital city itself.

There was now a second bridge across the Thames at Westminster where William Hawksmoor was adding the towers to Westminster Abbey and the western limit of the city pushed itself beyond Hyde Park and Park Lane. The area adjacent to Park Lane itself was already celebrated for its May fair and for the market run by Edward Shepherd, now called Shepherd Market. A popular verse said:

> Pease, cabbages and turnips once grew where
> Now stands New Bond Street and a newer Square[1]

The 'newer square' was Grosvenor Square and other great noblemen, the Lords Cavendish and Burlington, were following Sir Thomas Grosvenor's example by commissioning town houses, often surrounded by formal squares. At Covent Garden towards the east the fourth Earl of Bedford supervised the setting out of a huge piazza designed by Inigo Jones, and surrounded by town houses available for rent. He asked Jones to provide a church, but since the church, unlike the piazza, would produce no rental income for the earl, Jones was instructed to keep the design simple, 'not much better than a barn'. Jones replied that he would build the earl the handsomest barn in Europe and the result is St Paul's church, Covent Garden.

This elegance contrasted sharply with the squalor of, for example, 'Alsatia', a district between the Temple and the Fleet river inhabited by some of the poorest of London's people. There were many similar areas, such as Seven Dials, where thieves and escaped criminals found refuge and only the most foolhardy would venture into these 'rookeries' or urban jungles after dark. Elsewhere petty theft was rife and the news sheets of the time abounded with advertisements promising rewards for the return of watches, snuffboxes and even handkerchiefs. In general the streets were a place of danger at night and most people travelled as little as they could after dark and then only in groups with the gentlemen carrying swords. Wise men knew how to use their swords, and fencing masters, who were not only concerned with the niceties of the duelling code, prospered.

Entertainments of all sorts were available. Handel had dominated the recent musical life of London and the theatre flourished at Covent Garden under John Rich where, in 1728, *The Beggar's Opera* by John Gay had 'made Rich gay and Gay rich', while David Garrick at Drury Lane was the most famous actor in Britain. There was also music and pantomime at Sadler's Wells and opera at the Opera House in the Haymarket.

By the banks of the river were the two great pleasure gardens of Vauxhall and Ranelagh. At Vauxhall – entrance one shilling – one disembarked from a boat to enter a wonderland of twelve acres. There were bandstands in the treetops playing Handel, pavilions serving cold suppers, triumphal arches and ruined grottoes. Three thousand coloured lanterns gave a magical light while there were plentiful shady bowers where the ladies of the night made male revellers welcome. 'It was a Disneyland for grown-up gallants.'[2] Across the river and on the site of what are now the gardens of the Royal Hospital, Chelsea, stood the more sedate Ranelagh where one entered the Great Rotunda to take tea in one of the boxes and to listen to the resident orchestra.

As society had moved west to Mayfair, so the character of some areas had changed and at night the arcades surrounding Covent Garden had become a haunt for prostitutes. Sir John Fielding, a magistrate at Bow Street, said, 'One would imagine that all the prostitutes in the kingdom had picked upon that blessed neighbourhood for a rendez-vous, for here are lewd women enough to fill a colony.'[3] *Bagnios*, or bath houses, provided sexual satisfaction of every sort. At the Shakespeare's Head tavern, one of the waiters produced a regularly updated guide book, *Harrison's List of Covent Garden Ladies, or the Man of Pleasure's Kalendar*. If the taste for diversion was still not sated then there was a choice between viewing public executions, carried out by various methods, or simply visiting the Bedlam, where for a penny one could mingle with, and taunt, the lunatics. The London in which Robert Adam had arrived was a city of extremes.

On 1 February 1758 he wrote to Helen that James and he were in furnished lodgings in St James's Place in the heart of the fashionable new West End. The street ran from St James's Street westwards to the edge of Hyde Park and the brothers set up an establishment 'at a damned high rent' with Robert's two draughtsmen, a manservant and a maid, but with no mention of Donald, who may have been despatched to Scotland. Here they had enough room to put Robert's drawings on show, hopefully for the inspection of prospective clients. But the brothers lacked linen – which, clearly, had not been included in the rental. There was an urgent request for four pairs of fine sheets (for Robert and James), and three pairs of coarse ones (for the draughtsmen), along with appropriate pillow slips and tablecloths, 'anything passes down with batchelors [sic]'. Much to James's amusement Robert 'chatters away in Italian' while James practised his French with Dewez.

The two brothers, however, were infected with a quiet desperation as they now had to find commissions; and to find them urgently before their stock of capital ran out in the cripplingly expensive city. Robert was using every contact or introduction he had made to call on the nobility from morning to evening and these early days were filled with a constant round of visits. The brothers had, as yet, no coach and together they had to trudge their way through the freezing streets of London's West End to make these calls, mostly to no avail. It was certainly a necessary task and there was a hopeful window of opportunity for the brothers since Colen Campbell, Lord Burlington, William Kent and James Gibbs were now all dead and architecture in London was dominated solely by Chambers.

Chambers had been the architect of choice for Frederick, Prince of Wales, for whom he had built the giant Chinese pagoda in Kew Gardens. Royal patronage was, of course, the most profitable, but was unlikely while George II, Frederick's father, was on the throne. It was rumoured that the heavily German-accented George had been shown a painting, the *March to Finchley* by Hogarth, and announced to an unsurprised audience, 'I hate bainting and boetry too!' However, Frederick had died unexpectedly in 1751 – he was only 46 years old – and his son George had, in his turn, become the Prince of Wales. The Scots nobleman John Stuart, Earl of Bute, groom of the stole* in the 20-year-old prince's household, was his close adviser and had appointed Chambers as architect to the young prince. Robert had met Chambers in Rome and, as we have seen, regarded him as the principal obstacle to his success in London. Now Chambers made the first move towards the brothers. 'Chambers was to wait on Bob, but missing him, left his name.' The brothers, in turn, visited Chambers in his lodgings in Russell Street, between Covent Garden and Bow Street, no longer a fashionable area. James wrote, 'We called on him, found him drawing in a poor mean lodging up a long dark stair. He showed some of these designs he is going to publish which are wretched. He mentioned the prince more than once, and showed us a design of his, simple enough . . . We did not reckon it very polite, the repetition of so great a name, but Bob was excessively polite.' The brothers, as newcomers to London, were snobbishly surprised to find Chambers so far away from Mayfair, but did not realise that Chambers no longer needed to meet the expense of

* This is a corruption of the mediaeval position of 'groom of the stool' when a nobleman would care for the royal commode. By the eighteenth century he was simply a favoured adviser.

Mayfair since fashionable London now came to him. The brothers also failed to notice that Chamber's lodging was above Tom's Coffee House, the preferred rendezvous of London's literary and artistic sets, numbering among its habitués Oliver Goldsmith, Samuel Johnson and Clive of India. Lord Clive would later become a client of Chambers. The brothers had a lot to learn about networking in eighteenth-century London.

The brothers did benefit from the presence of a considerable Scots community already established in London. Furthermore, Allan Ramsay had succeeded in getting Robert accepted as a member of the Society of Artists, later known as the Society of Arts. This meant that Robert could exhibit at the society's rooms in the Strand. John Home, the clergyman turned playwright, was in London hoping to persuade Garrick to mount his play *Douglas* and William Robertson was looking for a publisher for his *History of Scotland*. Adam Ferguson was lodging in Harrow while working as a tutor in nearby Barnet. This group of exiled Scots was given cohesion by the always sociable Alexander 'Jupiter' Carlyle.

'As Ferguson had one day in the week when he could be in town, we established a club at a coffee-house in Savile Row or Sackville Street where we could meet him for dinner, which we did every Wednesday at three o'clock. There were J. Home, and Robertson, and Wedderburn and Jack Dalrymple, and Bob Adam, Ferguson and myself . . . As Ferguson rode back to Harrow, we always parted between five and six o'clock; and it will hardly be believed that our reckoning never exceeded 5s a-piece. We had a very good dinner, and plenty of punch etc., though no claret for that sum.'[4] Alexander Wedderburn was later Lord Chancellor as Earl of Rosslyn and Sir John Dalrymple was a Scottish judge. Home's *Douglas* was now the most popular play in London and his success was acknowledged when Lord Bute appointed him to be his private secretary. Garrick immediately set about befriending this once rejected but now influential playwright.

Robert had two other friends of influence in Gilbert Elliot of Minto and his friend from Roman days, Robert Wood, the artist of Palmyra fame. Wood had promised to advance Robert's cause with the Duke of Bridgewater and was now an Undersecretary of State at the Admiralty, a position of some influence and possible financial gain for little or no effort. Wood claimed however that no public building could be contemplated during the current war, and as far as the Duke of Bridgewater was concerned, he had just engaged the engineer James Brindley to start work on the Manchester–Worsley canal, described by one economic historian as 'the nearest thing to a licence to print money'. This particular window of opportunity had slammed shut.

As a Lord of the Admiralty, Gilbert Elliot was a different matter. He was also a personal friend and admirer of Robert's work which he saw in St James's Place. He was certain that town houses would be in great demand when the young Prince of Wales came to the throne and, more immediately, set about the negotiations which would allow Robert to be introduced to the immensely influential Earl of Bute.

Bute was pivotal to gaining patronage in eighteenth-century London. He had been born John Stuart in Edinburgh in 1713 and was educated conventionally at Eton and Leyden in Holland. In 1736 he married Mary Wortley Montagu, the only daughter of Edward and the redoubtable Lady Mary Wortley Montagu, a marriage which eventually brought the vast wealth of the Wortley estates into the Bute family. 'He spent ten years in obscurity, devoting himself to botany and to his family, a man with a cultivated mind and a well turned leg. But by making a fourth at cards when rain stopped a cricket match in which the Prince of Wales was engaged, he edged into court favour.'[5] In 1750 the prince appointed Bute to his position as a groom of the bed-chamber and Bute was now an integral member of the Leicester House set surrounding the prince, later becoming the confidant of his widow Princess Augusta and tutor to her son, the future George III. There were many scandalous and ill-founded rumours that Bute was Augusta's lover. After initially supporting Pitt in opposing George II's Hanoverian policy against France the two men quarrelled and Bute found himself in opposition to Pitt but with the increasingly poor heath of George II he became the man with the greatest influence over the future George III. 'The nobility and gentry of England had paid court to him with such abject servility when the accession of his pupil came near, and immediately after it took place that it was no wonder he should behave to them with haughtiness and disdain, and with a spirit of domination.'[6] His patronage could unlock the most important doors in England.

On his own behalf, Robert was working as hard as he could to become known to the nobility and, on one occasion, James returned to their flat without his key and could not raise any answer. He guessed, correctly, that he might find Robert in Half Moon Street, near Piccadilly, where Lord Lindores had a house and Lady Lindores had now established a salon for the Scottish aristocracy in London. When James arrived he found Robert deep in conversation with the Earl of Moray. Thanks to his attendances at Lady Lindores's salon, Robert received the promise of a small commission from General Bland, the governor of Edinburgh Castle who wanted an extension to his country house, 'particularly of a large room'. As James wrote to Edinburgh, 'small things begin to cast up and large, I hope, will follow soon.' All Robert's new acquaintances were invited to see his drawings, although he decided to wait until his larger trophies arrived from Venice before meeting Lord Bute.

Echoing that hope of large things to follow, Robert found a house in Lower Grosvenor Street near to the Mount Coffee House which was available for £2,000. He negotiated a loan of £1,400 at four per cent from John and moved in, immediately summoning Janet, Elizabeth and William from Edinburgh. In November 1756 Robert had estimated that he would earn no more than £300 at first in London which would just cover the cost of house, servants, hired hackneys and chaises, while 'living and clothing in the most frugal way', although Dewez and Brunias would cost about £150 more. Robert's idea of 'frugal' would mean that debt was inevitable unless there were rapid commissions.

The location of his house was crucial and Lower Grosvenor Street was ideal. Fashionable London was bounded by St

Martin's Lane in the east, Pall Mall in the south, Oxford Street to the north and Hyde Park to the west. The great men, noble or simply very rich, occupied the houses in the squares and on the principal streets, and 'lesser gentry, higher professionals and people of independent means inserted themselves into side streets as best they could, thickening in numbers as the distance from St James's increased.'[7]

Needless to say, Robert could not entirely abandon his social habits and he regularly attended Drury Lane with Alexander Carlyle. Garrick, still trying to gain the favour of Home, Bute's protégé, included Robert on an expedition to his house at Hampton. This was an invitation,

> which he did but seldom. He had told us to bring golf clubs and balls that we might play on Molsley Hurst. We accordingly set out in good time, six of us in a landau. As we passed through Kensington, the Coldstream regiment were changing guard, and, on seeing our clubs, they gave us three cheers in honour of a diversion peculiar to Scotland . . . Garrick met us by the way, so impatient he seemed to be for our company. They were John Home, and Robertson, and Wedderburn, and Robert and James Adam and Colonel David Wedderburn . . . Immediately after we arrived, we crossed to the golfing ground which was very good. None of the company could play but John Home and myself . . . We returned and dined sumptuously, Mrs Garrick, the only lady, now grown fat, though still very lively, being a woman of uncommon good sense, and now mistress of English, was in all respects most agreeable company.[8]

Garrick had married Eva Marie Violetti, a Viennese dancer in 1749. The day continued with toasts to Shakespeare at a temple Garrick had erected in his honour and with Carlyle showing off his trick golf shots. Home tried to drive his ball through a tunnel and landed it in the Thames from where it was retrieved by a giggling Garrick. A perfect Augustan picnic.

This social whirl could not continue indefinitely and so, as James was expected to return to Fort George for profitable employment, he left London early in May in the company of Carlyle, Home and Robertson. Since 'the Adams are a wonderful loving family'[9], Robert, Margaret, Elizabeth and William accompanied the party as far as Uxbridge where they all held a 'very cheerful evening'. Uxbridge was the overnight coaching stop on the Oxford road and there were plenty of inns to choose from. Next morning the north-bound party set off for Oxford and Woodstock where James defended Vanburgh's Blenheim Palace, saying that he had seen few palaces which had more 'movement' than Blenheim. This he did with such authority that Carlyle presumed, wrongly, that James had already seen 'all the splendid palaces of Italy'.

Robert's much hoped-for interview with Lord Bute was now to take place. Lady Mary Wortley Montagu had written to her daughter, the Countess of Bute, from Venice, 'I saw some months ago, a countryman of yours (Mr Adam) who desires to be introduced to you. He seemed to me, in short visit, to be a man of genius, and I have heard his architecture much applauded. He is now in England.'[10] Robert had sent Bute a copy of Piranesi's *Campus Martius* with the dedication to himself, along with a sketch for a snuffbox, but all to no purpose. When Robert arrived with Carlyle, Bute did not formally receive them himself. When they were finally shown into Bute's presence he was already 'booted and spurred' which was taken as an excuse for not asking them to sit; it was clear that their time with him would be as short as possible. 'Our reception was so dry and cold that when he asked when we were to go north, one of us said tomorrow . . . We very soon took our leave and no sooner were we out of hearing, than Robert Adam, who was with us, fell a-cursing and swearing. "What! Had he not been presented to all the princes in Italy and France. And most graciously received, to come and be treated with such distance and pride by the youngest earl but one in all Scotland!" '[11] On 17 June he vented his spleen to James. 'Lord B is the same dirty wretch I have thought him for these many months past. He has never once received me and yesterday sent back your Piranesi with a card and his compliments. I returned his thanks for the book of architecture and so ends that affair, nor has he ever had the manners to say the least thing about the drawing for the snuffbox or anything else. I wish it may ever please God to give me an opportunity of letting him know (without hurting myself) what an ill mannered slave he is.'

The slight still rankled when on 11 August Robert wrote to Alexander McMillan, Deputy Keeper of the Signet in Edinburgh. Carlyle described McMillan as 'loud and jovial, and made the wine flow like Bacchus himself'.[12] Robert clearly found him a fellow spirit.

It is evident that our tempers were pretty much tuned to the same string and to so convenient a pitch that we either sang Homesick Pastoral or Buffoni as the fancy struck us . . . Lord Bute lays himself out to be father, patron and friend and that in so private and hidden a manner that, egad, I have never seen or heard of him since I was with you. Then his returning me that book of Piranesi's was another polite and masterly stroke. He kept it for 3 months till he got intelligence of some more copies coming by another ship from Italy which he instantly bought one of from David Wilson and returned me mine. Gibby Elliot and I had a long conversation about that affair before he went last to Scotland. Gibby defends him and blames J.H. [John Home] for ever having mentioned my name to him. This delay, caution and prudence does exceeding well for Admirals and Admirals' Lords. But damn me, if any free Scot can acknowledge it to be right. At the same time I know not puffing should be done with judgement, otherways it hurts. But in the present case where real merit comes to support the praise, Ay, Sandy, where there is very little danger, I know some people through ignorance of the works and genteel company would call this self-conceit. But I think it is not amiss for a man to have a glint of that infinite merit he is possessed of . . . I shall certainly be revenged on Bute for this conduct. I have a great mind to go out to Kew and when he and Madame la Princesse are striving together, I'll have them put in a boat naked and brought down the river like Adam and Eve, and I'll fell him dead with Piranesi's 4 folio volumes from Westminster Bridge as they are going to pass under the Yoke and Robert Adam. If you disapprove, write me a better scheme. I consult with none living but you.[13]

Clearly, Madame la Princesse was Princess Augusta, and Robert could not resist continuing the rumour of Bute being her lover.

Here Robert had received three blows, one after another. The Duke of Bridgewater, who had seemed his friend in Rome, had no interest in commissioning anything from him; Wood, who had given him enthusiastic encouragement, brushed him off with vague excuses about the state of the economy, and now Bute, who had been the object of a careful campaign, treated Robert like an inconvenient lapdog. His contacts made in Italy were proving ineffectual.

On 17 June 1758 Robert had written to James with a scheme to finish his revisions of Desgodetz with Clérisseau which would have to wait until Clérisseau returned to Rome. Robert proposed to give Clérisseau one third of the profits, but not to allow the book to carry Clérisseau's name. 'After the work is ready for the press to tell him that a French name would spoil the sale in England and as he is not known there it would do him no honour and in order to make amends for this offer him £50 more than his ½ or ? to desist from it.' He told James that he was canvassing nobility hard but he did admit to one failure – Lord Bute. However, Robert was making better progress with the Duke of Argyll whom he already knew and who kept more or less open house in London. Robert would have been pleased that the height of the Duke's gambling was sixpenny whist. In April, Robert and Dewez had visited the Duke's house at Whitton Park, to the west of Richmond, and he told James that 'Brunias is making a large view of Inverary'. These pictures would be gifts to the Duke, all intended, if not to grease the ducal palm, then at least to convince him of Robert's amiability. Robert's campaign to get commissions would continue.

A small thing had 'cast up', as James had foretold, when General Bland's invitation, issued during socialising at Lady Lindores, to sketch an extension to his house at Isleworth turned into a commission including a greenhouse. But a bigger thing swam into view when Lady Lindores introduced Robert to Edwin Lascelles. Lascelles had inherited an estate at Gawthorpe in 1754. After his Grand Tour he had decided to demolish the existing house and then to build a new house and village at nearby Harewood, south of Harrogate in Yorkshire. To Robert's delight, Chambers, who had already submitted designs for the house, had been rejected, and a local architect, John Carr, had been selected. However, Robert wrote to James, 'Lascelles' house is now well advanced, I have made some alterations on it, but, as the plan did not admit of a great many, that has prevented the fronts from being much changed likewise. The portico I make projecting and bold dressings round the windows. The pavilion fronts are quite different and the colonnades with columns also, and look well. Statues etc. adorn the whole, and an enriched frieze – being done to a large scale, it is magnificent. PS. I have thrown in large semicircular back courts with columns betwixt the house and the wings.'

Although the original plans and elevations were by Carr, the alterations specified by Robert to James do seem to have been carried out and Harewood is probably more than half an Adam building. The interior decoration, which was started in 1765, was largely designed by Robert and drawings of projected schemes never achieved – a dressing room ceiling, for example – are preserved in Sir John Soane's Museum in London. A later Earl of Harewood undertook some modernisation a hundred years later with severely deleterious results and much of the original decoration disappeared under a torrent of Victorianism.[14]

Robert was still keeping abreast of affairs in Venice where Clérisseau was supervising the engraving of the plates for the book on Spalatro and sending Robert proof copies or 'pulls'. Robert now had engaged Michael Angelo Rooker and Paul Sandby to make engravings in London. One of their tasks was to create 'rustics' in the general views; the frontispiece shows a Dalmatian lady selling chickens and pigeons, oblivious to the group of western gentlemen making sketches of the ruins while in Plate XX of the Peristylum all the vividity of the Orient takes place. Rooker was only working for Robert in a break from his job as a scene-painter at the Theatre Royal in the Haymarket. Robert however would tolerate nothing less than complete devotion. Rooker, 'was such an idle worthless fellow that he would do nothing . . . for now the plays begin he will never work an hour in a fortnight'. In August he wrote to James, 'As to Spalatro, I think it goes poorly on. If Clérisseau was not present to keep Bartolozzi at work that the plates would not be done these three years and he believes that it will be the best part of two years before they are done at any rate. Clérisseau himself says he cannot yet tell me to a week when they will be done but that he is contriving two or three ways to bring them on faster by getting a clever boy to engrave the outline so letting Bartolozzi fill up the shadows.' Final features were being added in London by three engravers who had been at work on the plates since before James's departure north. 'Paton has finished very neat, Walker has likewise finished the Porta Aurea and Green goes on with the outside walls. Rooker I hope will do the front of the temple of Jupiter which you was present at the formation of [sic]. If well engraved ought not to be ashamed of Palmyra or Baalbec . . . Rooker has done a most charming Corinthian entablature for Chambers's *Civil Architect*.' Chambers's book was the *Treatise on Civil Architecture*, published in 1759 and setting out Chambers's views on correct styles. 'In a measure reflecting his unostentatious and reserved personality, his architecture would be decoratively discreet. [The *Treatise* was] a work of empirical and discriminating eclecticism, ranging selectively over the whole of the classical tradition.'[15] Robert was grudgingly admiring of Chambers's book and still feared him as his chief rival.

His resentment at the arrogance of the nobility had increased by his rebuke at the hands of Bute and now Dundas as well as the Duke of Argyll came in for his spleen.

I wrote to you that Laurie Dundas had got a plan for a Court of Offices from me, which whilst I was making some corrections upon, he went off to Scotland [and] left the plans in my hands without once saying a syllable about them. Nobody thinks of paying and when they do, give nothing worth taking, so may the Divil damn them altogether, I'll turn soap boiler and tallow chandler, [while] they grow rich and eat turtle. The Duke of Argyll, when I carried home his view of Inverary, gave a £20 note to give to my Italian. But I, who are more needy than he, gave him £5.5 of it and with the rest paid £6 for the frame and £3 for the cloth, colours etc, and twenty shillings for a frame to his small view of it so that you see I clear myself of all charges which would have been very ridiculous for me to be at and retain near £5 to myself. Brunias is as happy as a prince . . . I would not have Johnnie to make Delacour's views too cheap it will make the Duke more sensible of that favour I did him.

The 'Italian' was, of course, Agostino Brunias and John had obviously been acting as a go-between for the Duke and William de la Cour who was shortly to be appointed as the first master in Edinburgh's School of Design.

In spite of his resentment at aristocratic arrogance Robert was keen that his relationship with the duke remained properly grateful. 'Let Baron Maule make the Duke aware how much I appreciated his getting 'my stuccos, drawings etc, brought ashore without search or duty. But we must keep the pictures a dead secret that they came by the same ship because I kept it snug that there was pictures else I never would have obtained leave and was affrighted that they would have been opened and discovered. But a little well timed bribery prevented such consequences. Nobody knows of this affair but Willie, Betty and myself.'

Robert's Italian purchases had now arrived and he set about the interior decoration of Lower Grosvenor Street. 'I still go on with Morland cleaning my pictures. He does them vastly well. My Amigonis, my two landscapes of Teniers, my St Francis by Guido Reni and the figures riding the Coliseo all hang in the parlour framed and cleaned and have a charming effect. In my dining room I propose hanging my Domenichino, Carlo Marotte and St Katharine by Guido and some other choice pieces.' Visitors would pass through the house, 'their eyesight dazzled with vain pomp' to a *casino* or 'little house' especially erected at the far end of the garden where the collections of sculpture he had acquired in Italy were on display. 'The Casino, artificial as it was, succeeded in what it set out to do – to put the Adam brothers and the Adam style on the map. It explained visually and physically . . . the critical standards they now imposed on the new architecture.'[16] In time, James would add to these treasures and the brothers would turn their house into a personally curated gallery where visitors could see that they were in the presence of men of taste. Finally Robert would produce his own sketches and drawings. Robert's drawing office with its draughtsmen was in New Bond Street, probably on the corner of Maddox Street, only a few hundred yards from Lower Grosvenor Street. This was a very carefully planned establishment, since there was nothing in Lower Grosvenor Street which indicated that it was anything but the fashionable home of gentlemen aesthetes.

Robert was still chasing income through sinecures – a traditional source in the eighteenth century – and was passing intelligence on to James. He had started to enquire about public positions which the Duke of Argyll could facilitate. Since the Duke had appointed Roger Morris to the Board of Works he might be persuaded to do the same for Robert. There was a certain desperation in Robert's reviewing the state of health of various sinecure holders and then, should they die in office, suggesting himself as a replacement to the duke. 'The Architect of the King's Palaces in Scotland [an available and profitable post] is now in the possession of the Laird of Dundas who Jenny tells me is quite failed. I talked only to Betty Stuart of it who says that Mrs Calderwood has more to say with Baron Maule than all the world and would tease him to death till he worked it out for me . . . I know the D would like to have an opportunity of obliging me . . . Surely I can never be suspected . . .' Robert presumed that the duke was the kind of eighteenth-century aristocrat who acted entirely on whim. He probably did not know that the duke was by no means a typical uninformed aristocrat of the time. His library not only contained a 1552 edition of Vitruvius, but he also acquired the *Builder's Pocket Companion* in 1771, showing that the duke kept himself informed about the practicalities of the trade. Robert even suggested that he would advance Lord Arniston – the Laird of Dundas – two or three years' salary to retire early. The post was not very demanding and, as Robert told James, 'a place of £300 yearly, without doing anything for it, is not to be neglected'. He even contemplated posts in the Board of Ordnance and hoped that Skinner at Fort George might advance his cause. Unsurprisingly, nothing came of this application.

Meanwhile, there were some other small commissions. 'Adam Ferguson and I came to town this morning from Archie Stewart's country house. He is going to throw a wooden bridge over two different rivulets in his garden and I am to make him out drawings for them. On such pitiful objects is my attention bent.' Robert wanted to sell his shares in two whale fisheries. He was also starting to doubt the commitment of Edwin Lascelles to employing him at Harewood House. 'As yet not a scrap from Lascelles so that I begin to suspect him. Had he been pleased surely he would have said so sooner. I hope he'll pay me for the plan at any rate and I may venture to say it will make as good a figure in print as Chamber's does, which he did for some gentleman and put into his Civil Architecture.'

It was now settled that James would be the first of the remaining brothers to visit Italy. From Robert's point of view this would allow James to visit some of the sites he had had too little time to visit and to make drawings of them. There was a hope that Greece, or even

Egypt might be included, and a precise intention that James would supervise the completion of the Spalatro book which Robert felt was dangerously late. Robert suggested that John let George Richardson, a draughtsman, go with James to Italy to facilitate his recording of sites. Later he would send James a shopping list of carvings, grotesques, and ornaments he was to buy for the partnership. Continuing what Robert felt was lacking in James's education, Jenny went to Edinburgh with a book of ornaments, 'particularly those that have the griffins and foliages as it will fix the antique manner in your head before you see them. I have likewise made Brunias copy over the large drawing by Pietro di Cortona which is one of the best things for setting one's hand to these things that I know.' Robert did not know that James had his own ideas on how he would spend his time in Europe, ideas which would have horrified him.

Robert was worried over a clause in the partnership agreement concerning the outcome of money from Dumfries House, which was not yet entirely complete. Robert could not draw on that account until the whole was finished and so William, who was now the financial controller of the London practice, could not close his accounts. General Bland and his wife returned from Bristol and Bath to see the extension to their house at Isleworth: 'The stucco work pleases them much and I am convinced will please generally, though *entre nous* it is not executed in the antique taste as it is impossible to get English workmen who will leave their angly, stiff, sharp manners. However, as they know no better in England they cannot be so vexed as I am myself. Nay, perhaps they like it better than they would the other manner.' Robert knew enough not to disagree with a pleased client, since one pleased client could lead to another.

Presumably while seeking out vacancies in the Board of Ordnance, Robert's conversation had wandered from the main subject. 'In a conversation I had with Mr Fredericks of the Ordnance about statues I mentioned a statue of Marcus Agrippa I was about buying without mentioning the place where it was or anything of price. He immediately told me he had seen a glorious statue of that kind in Venice and that he had offered £600 for it and that he could not get it but that it was worth any money. I told him that General Napier and Colonel Watson thought if it was safe in England it was worth £1,500 or £2,000 and that it was worthy of a crowned head.' Robert immediately instructed Clérisseau to give 300 zecchinis for it, including in the offer a picture he had previously offered for another 20 or 30, 'all of which would not come to £200'. Robert was scenting a huge profit and set about maximising it. 'I will make a vast puff by advertising the arrival of it, by fixing a day of the week in which it was to be seen by all the nobility and gentry in my court yard.'

Entrepreneurship went hand-in-hand with architecture. It was all too necessary since the practice could not support the London establishment solely with greenhouses and wooden bridges, and there were sleepless nights in Lower Grosvenor Street. With James now about to go abroad, John's Edinburgh practice would be the sole source of income while Robert was only contributing tiny amounts and aristocratic promises of work to come. By December Robert proposed to have the King of Prussia added to the subscribers for Spalatro. 'I have also thought of the Pope and all the College of Cardinals.'

Then came eleventh-hour salvation at the hands of Robert's sister Helen. 'Nelly says she just hinted my introduction to Sir Nathaniel Curzon by Lord Charles Hay. I went to his house and in two hours after Sir Nathaniel came to mine to see my drawings and was struck all of a heap with wonder and amaze; everything he converted to his own house and every new drawing he saw made him grieve at his previous engagement with Brettingham. He carried me home in his chariot about 3 o'clock and kept me to 4 seeing all of Brettingham's designs and asked my opinion. I proposed alterations and desired he might call them his own fancys [sic].' It would be a major coup if Robert could conclude an agreement with Sir Nathaniel Curzon. He was 33 years old and had succeeded to the baronetcy in the previous year. He had inherited Kedleston Hall, near Derby, a house which he intended to pull down and replace with a design based on Holkham Hall in Norfolk. Holkham had been, in its turn, designed by William Kent who based the house on Palladio's unbuilt Villa Mocenigo, while the actual building had been carried out by Matthew Brettingham. Curzon, who had already commissioned Brettingham to build Kedleston presuming that his designs, albeit at least third-hand, were the height of fashion, was hugely impressed with what Robert had shown him.

'I went back on Saturday evening at six o'clock and sat two hours with him and his lady who is a daughter of Lord Portmore, Lady Caroline Collyear, sister to the celebrated Lady Julian Collyear. Lady Caroline Curzon is one of sweetest women I ever saw, excessively beautiful, free of pride and affectation, so that you need not doubt that I spent my time agreeably. I revised all his plans and got the entire management of his grounds put into my hands with full powers as to temples bridges, seats and cascades. So that as it is only seven miles around you may guess at the play of genius and scope for invention – a noble piece of water. A man resolved to spare no expense with £10,000 a year, good tempered and having taste himself for the arts and little for game.' 'Lord Chas [Lord Charles Hay] tells me also he has a brother with very nearly the same money who very probably will lay out some of it in the same manner. (Now for a secret) You must know Sir Nathaniel brought me out a design of the great Athenian for his rooms which he begged me for God's sake not to mention to anyone.' The great Athenian was James Stuart, a leading proponent of Greek architecture, and a possible emergent rival. Robert was scathing in his views of Stuart's designs. 'They are so excessively and so ridiculously bad that Mr Curzon immediately saw the folly of them and said so to some people which so offended the proud Grecian that he has not seen Sir Nathaniel these 2 years and he says he keeps the drawings sacred in self defence. He made a gallery only 5 feet high so that one would think that the modern Greeks diminished in size as well as in spirit but forgot that Britons were taller.' He continued to pour scorn on Stuart and quoted Lords Nuneham and De la Warr who met in a room the 'Archipelagian had decorated for Lord

Nuneham. Lord De la Warr said, 'For shame my Lord, pull it down and burn it.'

Robert was recommended to wait on Lord Portmore, and 'putting on a face of brass', did so. He was admitted and Lord Portmore said he would do 'everything he could. To serve me, would seek every opportunity of doing justice to my character both as a friend and countryman.' More to the point, on 12 December he met again with Sir Nathaniel and 'carried many drawings and amongst others the "Nabobs Palace" to show Lady Caroline. Sir Nathaniel was so much struck with it he swore that if he had £300,000 he would begin it directly. I am to begin soon to his temples and to ornament an organ for him and to go to Derbyshire as soon in the spring as I can.' The 'Nabob's Palace' was one of Robert's fanciful sketches – the drawing is nine feet long – for a fantasy palace suitable for anyone returning from India in possession of massive ill-gotten gains. According to Sir John Summerson, it was 'A perfectly colossal palace of Babylonian extravagance.'[17] There was never any intention of putting these sketches into practice.

Pursuing one more of his contacts from the Grand Tour, Robert arranged a meeting with Captain Rodney, guardian to the Earl of Northampton. Like Curzon, the Earl of Northampton had only just succeeded to the title. Robert had met him in Padua as the Honourable Charles Compton and he had high hopes of this contact. 'I think from Lord Northampton's own promise and from Captain Rodney's interest and from Lord Portmore's engaging the Duke of Marlborough to speak to him, I am sure of having both the house and grounds with an estate of £17,000 per annum to work upon.' Captain Rodney invited Robert to Castle Ashby for an inspection of the grounds.

At Kedleston Sir Nathaniel had already contracted James Paine, a fashionable architect, to undertake Brettingham's designs of a central block with four wings. Paine had built the north entrance according to Brettingham's strictly Palladian design but was quite happy to hand over the remainder of the building to be designed by Robert. An exception to this was the huge entrance hall which, at the behest of Sir Nathaniel, was to be a copy of the Pantheon in Rome, the most revered of classical buildings. As Robert's father had discovered at Mavisbank, few buildings escape without unwonted contributions from the patron.

Robert also had to contend with the fact that Paine had already started work on the house and the north side of the building was already in place. It had a pedimented portico with Corinthian supports reached by two sets of steps to the main entrance, while curved ranges stretched out to end in pure Palladian pavilions. This accorded strictly with all the classical principles but had no originality. However 'the south front of Kedleston is as near being wholly Adam as the predetermined plan of James Paine would allow.'[18] Here Robert produced a fine example of what the brothers always referred to as 'movement' in his design. The approach to the front door was by curved steps leading to the main front which is, in fact, modelled on the Arch of Constantine in Rome, with statues in niches on either side of the door. This opened into the circular saloon with a domed roof based, as Sir Nathaniel had insisted, on the Pantheon, which, in turn, led to the great hall where a collection of classical statuary was displayed under a second, shallower dome. Thus the exterior statues would lead to their interior counterparts. The convex dome over the great hall would contrast with concave colonnades stretching out to the pavilions, a chapel on one side and a music gallery on the other. There would be contrasting curves from external stairways, colonnades and a dome, while the external statuary led from a circular saloon into the internal display in a rectangular hall. This contrast between shapes merging into a harmonic entity is exactly what was meant by 'movement' and was what had excited Robert in the Roman baths and palaces. 'Movement is meant to express the rise and fall, the advance and recess, with other diversity of form in the different parts of a building so as to add greatly to the picturesque of the composition. For the rising and falling, advancing and receding, with the convexity and concavity and other forms of the great parts have the same effect in architecture that hill and dale, foreground and distance swelling and sinking have in landscape. That is they serve to produce an agreeable and divertified contour that groups and contrasts like a picture and creates a variety of light and shade, which gives great spirit, beauty and effect to the composition.'[19]

'Movement' was also carried on in the contrast between the decorative styles of the exterior and interior. In his Introduction to *The Works in Architecture by James and Robert Adam*, Professor Reed tells us, 'He would have the client reject the heavy interior ornament of his predecessors which was derived from the exterior detail of the ancient Romans and, instead, have him accept the delicate interior decoration of the same Romans.'[20]

The passage through the rooms themselves was now spectacular. The first interior room was the circular saloon – 42 feet in diameter and 55 feet in height – while the rectangular great hall had 16 columns and 4 half columns all built of local red-brown alabaster with Corinthian capitals in white marble, the light provided from above by three oculi in the ceiling. In contrast to the vivid colour of the columns, the floor was of grey and white marble. The relationship between the hall and the saloon was the same as that between the atrium and vestibulum of Diocletian's palace.

Although the curved colonnades to the southern pavilions were never built – Sir Nathaniel having run out of money – the effect of what remains is awe-inspiring. The standard of finish in the interior was far superior to anything else of the time, with gilded door frames, painted and corniced friezes and ceilings. In the circular saloon were four twelve-foot wide niches with half domes decorated with diamond-shaped coffering, each surrounding cast-iron Roman funerary vases on podia with griffons and bas-reliefs on their sides. While these provide a more than satisfactory focal point for these niches, they are in fact hot air outlets from a form of central heating devised by Robert Adam. Elegance and practicality were to become hallmarks for the Adam brothers. 'Every detail was brought into the scheme – furniture, grates, fire-irons and fenders, all testify to the thoroughness and comprehensive character of his work as an architect.'[21] H.H. Reed aptly described Robert Adam's talents and innovation in his Introduction to *The Works in Architecture*, a view echoed by Geoffrey Beard in *The Work of Robert Adam*. 'What Robert Adam did, in his inclination to design everything that went into a house, was to extend the province of the architect. Besides the ceremonial interiors, he did the domestic apartments. By turning to Roman interior detail, as well to Etruscan, Greek and French, without forgetting the decorative work of Raphael as found in the Vatican loggias, he produced an ornament that could readily find a place in any house no matter how small. There lay the key to his extraordinary success and influence.'[22]

Much of the carving was carried out by Michael Spang, a Danish sculptor destined to become a regular member of Robert's team. Work on Kedleston continued well into the next decade when William Hamilton painted vistas of Roman ruins to hang in the saloon. Hamilton was the son of one of Adam's assistants and Robert had sent him to Rome to study under Zucchi before he returned to London and entered the Royal Academy. No detail was neglected to the extent of gilding the sash-bars on the exterior of the windows, thus earning the disapprobation of Dr Johnson, who called it 'Labour disproportionate to its utility'[23].

In the park at Kedleston Robert created a fishing house, an orangery and an elegant gate from the outer roadway. There is a possibility that Robert even contemplated a ruined temple for a hermit, but the plan never came near to fruition. One elegant extravagance occurred elsewhere when Robert, totally unnecessarily, widened the small stream in Sir Nathaniel's grounds so that it could be spanned by a magnificent triple-arched bridge. The solution to the problem of a narrow and unsightly stream was to render it more pleasing to the eye by widening it rather than diverting it. This is a wonderful example of the eighteenth-century mind at work where elegance could combine with practicality.

Kedleston was visited by Dr Johnson and James Boswell on

19 September 1777 when the work had been completed. Boswell 'was struck with the magnificence of the building; and the extensive park, with the finest verdure, covered with deer, and cattle, and sheep delighted me. The number of old oaks, of an immense size, filled me with a sort of respectful admiration; for one of them sixty pounds was offered. The excellent smooth gravel roads; the large piece of water formed by his Lordship from some small brooks, with a handsome barge upon it; the venerable Gothick church, now the family chapel, just by the house: in short the grand group of objects distended my mind in a most agreeable manner.'[24] Johnson, who had lived much of his life in squalor, reacted aggressively to the splendour and thought that the house would 'do excellently for a town-hall, the large room with the pillars (said he) would do for the judges to sit in at the assizes; the circular room for a jury-chamber, and the room above for the prisoners'. When Boswell remarked that the proprietor of all this must be happy, Johnson replied, 'Nay, Sir, all this excludes but one evil – poverty.'[25] Samuel Johnson was too aware of the vast gulf between the desperately poor and the hugely wealthy to admire the craftsmanship of Adam and his workmen without qualification.

Like no other building, Kedleston marked Robert out as a brilliantly innovative young architect. Here was no workmanlike application of the accepted rules, making full use of the existing pattern books, but a wholly new style where classical components were used inside an individual design. Personal concepts were allowed free rein, moderated only by individual taste. Reason was the slave of the passions. Kedleston was the Enlightenment built in stone. The eminent architect Sir John Soane has said, 'In this superb structure he has united in no considerable degree the taste and magnificence of a Roman villa with all the comforts and conveniences of an English nobleman's residence, and though some hyper-fastidious critics may endeavour to wrest from that great artist his well-earned fame, and smile at his efforts to reconcile the idea of blending an ancient triumphal arch with the exterior of a modern building, for myself I can only regret

Above left. William Adam. Born on 30 October 1689, he rose from humble beginnings to be a successful architect, building contractor and property speculator. He died, a rich man, on 24 June 1748. (*William Adam* by William Aikman. In a private collection)

Above right. Mary Adam was an outstanding example of a loving mother. Born in 1699 she bore thirteen children, three of whom died in infancy. (*Mary Adam* by Allan Ramsay. Yale Center for British Art, Paul Mellon Collection)

Left. John Adam. The eldest brother looks deep in thought. With the grandiose ambitions of his brothers to deal with he had need to be. (*John Adam* by Francis Coates. In a private collection)

Robert Adam, turning a page of an edition of *The Works in Architecture*. Painted in 1775, he was at the height of his powers. (*Robert Adam* by George Willison © National Portrait Gallery, London)

Right. Detail of a chimney piece, from *Diverse manieri d'adnoare I Cammini* by Piranesi Gianbatista, Rome 1749. These may have been his sources for the Etruscan style. (Trustees of the National Library of Scotland)

Below. The Lanthorn of Demosthenes from *The Antiquities of Athens Measured and Delineated* by James Stuart. Atmospheric rather than Architectural. (Trustees of the National Library of Scotland)

Osterley Park Eating Room. Horace Walpole found that the lyre backed chairs gave 'a pleasant harmony'. (The Courtauld Institute of Art, London)

Osterley Park Etruscan Dressing Room. Robert introduced the colours and patterns of Etruria. (National Trust)

Syon House Long Gallery. Books do furnish a room. (Collection of the Duke of Northumberland. Photograph by John Blakey)

Croome Court Tapestry Room. Walls, carpet and furniture are of a unity. (National Trust)

Syon House Eating Room. The calmness of classicism. (Collection of the Duke of Northumberland. Photograph by John Blakey)

Syon House Drawing Room. Both Robert and the Duke of Northumberland felt that the ceiling was a mistake. (Collection of the Duke of Northumberland. Photograph by John Blakey)

Syon House Ante Room. The splendour of colour which led to...
(Collection of the Duke of Northumberland. Photograph by John Blakey)

Syon House, Entrance Hall. Robert used black and white to contrast with…
(Collection of the Duke of Northumberland. Photograph by John Blakey)

Kedlston House, Saloon. The simplicity of the design is echoed in the muted colours.
(The Courtauld Institute of Art, London)

Detail of a Palace. Possibly the 'Nabob's Palace' shown to Sir Nathaniel Curzon?
(Sir John Soane's Museum)

Kedleston House, South Front. A Roman triumphal arch dominates the entrance to an English
country house. (The Courtauld Institute of Art, London)

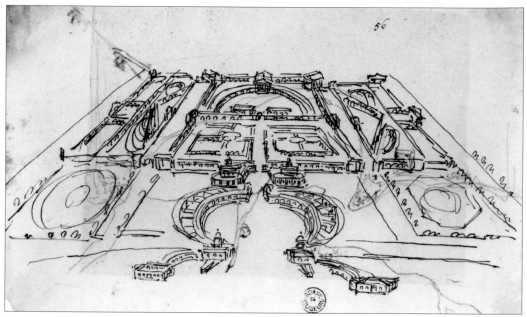

Sketch for rebuilding Lisbon. This takes no account of the topography of Lisbon and was no more than a hopeful dream. (Sir John Soane's Museum)

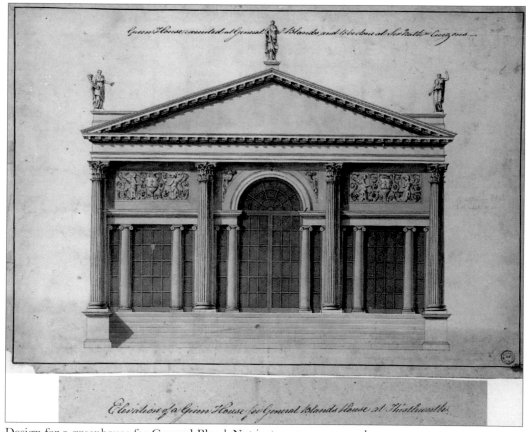

Design for a greenhouse for General Bland. Not just an average greenhouse. (Sir John Soane's Museum)

Above. View from Within the Rotunda of the Pantheon, by Robert Adam. From almost the same viewpoint Robert makes the Pantheon oval and the oculus is only suggested. He was still learning. (*Clerk of Eldin Album,* RCAHMS © Sir Robert Maxwell Clerk, 11th Baronet of Penicuik)

Left. Medallion of Robert Adam by Piranesi. Robert was very proud to be associated with the great Piranesi. (*Campus Martius* by Piranesi, 1762)

View from Within the Rotunda of the Pantheon,
by Clérisseau. This drawing is accurate and
dramatic. (*Clerk of Eldin Album,* RCAHMS
© Sir Robert Maxwell Clerk, 11th Baronet
of Penicuik)

Caricature of Clérisseau by Pier Leone Ghezzi. A somewhat unkind caricature of Robert's teacher at work in the sunshine. (© The Trustees of the British Museum)

Inverary Castle. A drawing by James Adam c1754. An unhappy compromise. (Sir John Clerk Collection)

Above. Dumfries House. Calm classicism.

Right. Grand Tourists pause with their exhausted tutor. Robert's patron looks cynically bored. (*Portrait of Charles, Lord Hope, and the Hon James Hope, with their bear leader.* Major P. T. Telfer Smollett Collection)

Left. James Adam by Pompeo Batoni. Painted by the most fashionable painter in Italy, James wished to be seen as a visionary emerging from a classical background (Baroness Knut-bone Collection)

Below. Fort George. A model of military engineering.

Left. Frontispiece from *The Ruins of the Palace of Spalatro* by Robert and James Adam. A skilful blend of the themes of the book. (Trustees of the National Library of Scotland)

Below. 'View of the Inside of the Temple of Jupiter', from *The Ruins of the Palace at Spalatro*. The figure sketching is thought to be Clérisseau. (Trustees of the National Library of Scotland)

Right. Carpet design for Mrs Montagu.
(Sir John Soane's Museum)

Below. Ceiling Design for Mrs Montagu.
Robert Adam was not acceptable to the
Bluestockings. (Sir John Soane's Museum)

The Adelphi by Thomas Malton from *Picturesque Tour, 1796.* Spalatro-on-Thames? (Trustees of the National Library of Scotland)

Above. The Church at Mistley. (Courtesy of *Country Life*)

Left. Adam's sketch for the Bath House at Mistley. One is now a ruin; the other was only a dream. (Courtesy of *Country Life*)

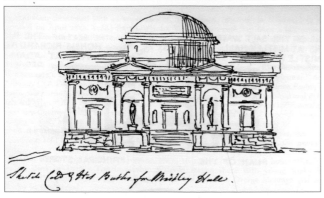

Register House, Edinburgh.

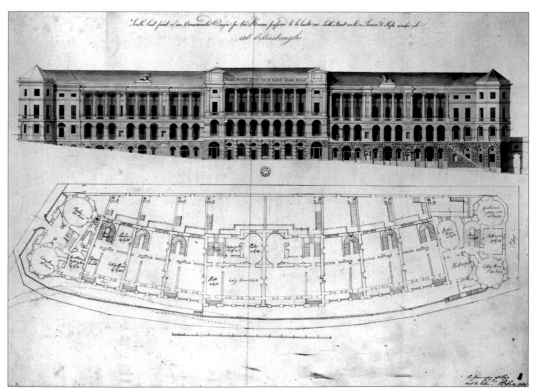

Leith Street Elevation, Edinburgh.
(Sir John Soane's Museum)

Robert Adam's idea for the South Bridge in Edinburgh, from *Architectural Heritage No XV* (Sir John Soane's Museum)

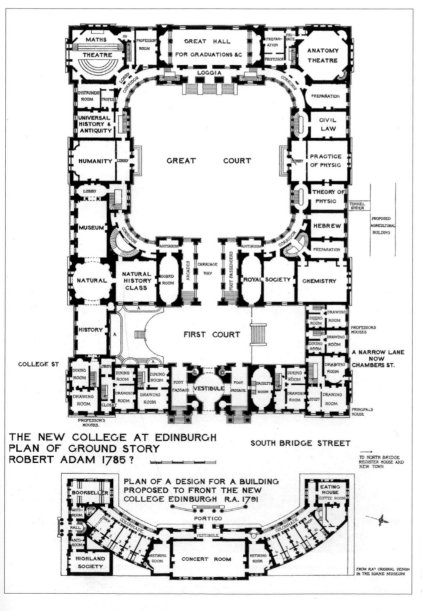

THE NEW COLLEGE AT EDINBURGH
PLAN OF GROUND STORY
ROBERT ADAM 1785?

Edinburgh University Ground Story. (Courtesy of *Country Life*)

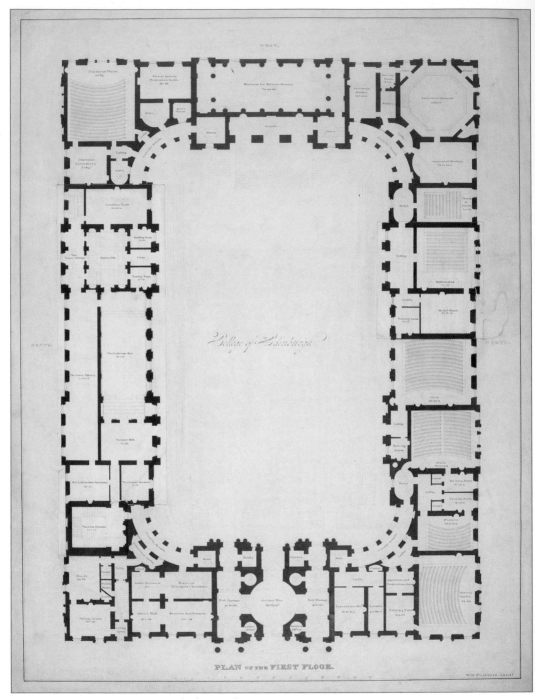

PLAN OF THE FIRST FLOOR.

University as Built. A memory of what might
have been. (Edinburgh University Library
Centre for Research Collections)

Above. Charlotte Square, Edinburgh. North side, Adam's 'Palace Front'

Left. Charlotte Square, Edinburgh. West side, Reid's interruption

Above. Culzean Castle.
Exterior Gothic

Right. Culzean Castle, Oval
Staircase. Interior Classical.
(The Courtauld Institute of
Art, London)

that more and happy attempts are not made to display the powers of pure architecture.'[26]

Ten years later the Rev. Stebbing Shaw visited Kedleston, whose fame had now spread. 'Lord Scarsdale's noble palace at Kedleston which for magnificence and elegance eclipses every other seat in this county . . . The Egyptian hall is thought to be one of the finest rooms in England.'[27] Sir Nathaniel Curzon was now Baron Scarsdale.

The designing and building methods Robert used with a client had varied very little from Tudor times. In *King Henry the Fourth, Part 2, Act I, Scene III*, Shakespeare's Lord Bardolph says:

> When we mean to build,
> We first survey the plot, then draw the model;
> And when we see the figure of the house,
> Then must we rate the cost of the erection;
> Which if we find outweighs ability,
> What do we do then but draw anew the model
> In fewer offices, or . . . leaves [his] part-created cost
> A naked subject to the weeping clouds . . .

At the start of discussions Robert would show a client sketches, often in a very rough form. If they were acceptable as a concept, there might be a site visit with the client when Robert would talk, still in the most general terms, of what might be needed. In fact Robert Adam made very few site visits and usually gained agreement with the client from detailed sketches, drawn in duplicate, with dimensions and indications of colour. One set of the drawings would be left with the client while the duplicate went to the drawing office where it would be used by the draughtsmen as the basis for detailed plans. These would then be used by the contractors to construct the building itself. These detailed drawings were the property of the client, who paid for them whether the enterprise went ahead or not. If the building was completely original (and few were, since the habit was for modernisation of existing structures), a model might be carved in wood. Wren made one of St Paul's showing a design that was never used and James Gibbs's model of St Martin-in-the-Fields went so far as to have a removable roof. There are, however, very few references to models by Robert in surviving bills.

When all plans were agreed, work on site would start with the levelling of the ground while the masons and carpenters built workshops. The masons found their stone as locally as they could to minimise transport costs and it would arrive cut roughly to size before receiving its precise shape in their workshops. The cheapest mode of transport for heavy loads was by water and much use was made of rivers and coastal shipping. Ironically the canals which Bridgewater was building were the ideal solution. When the outer walls had reached five feet from ground level the carpenters started to construct scaffolding from timber planks which they kept as part of their normal stock: 6 to 9-inch diameter poles of 20 or 30 feet in length were lashed with ropes, sometimes using diagonal posts, across which tread boards would be laid. Great care had to be taken over the lashings in wet weather to check for stretching or contracting. The structure would be kept stable by being affixed to 'putlogs'. These were holes in walls to be filled in on completion, although they are still visible in many mediaeval buildings. The carpenters would then start cutting the timber needed for the interiors on saw pits in their workshops. They would also construct and erect any cranes and lifting machinery. Other craftsmen would erect workshops as they needed them. Painters would grind their colours and, although there were ready-mixed paints, most of the colours specified by Robert had to be created on site. The stucco had to be mixed, the woodwork carved and the glass cut to size all under the watchful eye of the master-of-work who would be drawn from a trusted company of workers, who, in their turn, would recruit local workmen to carry out the actual construction.

Robert would make site visits from time to time to ensure that the original concepts were still being observed and that the inevitable compromises were as few and as slight as possible. He could also contribute detailed sketches for door furniture, stucco wall decoration, wood carving, carpets and even silver and glass-ware. In all of these cases detailed drawings were made. 'Clients wanting an Adam carpet had to pay for at least two and sometimes three drawings, a finished watercolour of the whole design and an accurate colour sample of one quarter of the pattern painted in oil or distemper to be given to the manufacturer.'[28] One of the reasons why Adam buildings were expensive was the profusion of ornament, all of which had to designed and drawn at no small cost. Also, if Robert took personal charge of the surveying, an additional charge of between four and five per cent was levied.

At the height of its activities the firm of William Adam & Company employed over 2,000 people in all capacities, and on 27 June 1772, David Hume wrote to his friend Adam Smith that he feared the brothers 'must dismiss 3,000 workmen, who, comprehending the materials must have expended above £100,000 a year'.[29] However, given that Robert had complete trust in his employees, many worked for him over and over again. These men also operated as freelances, dividing their time among several masters. Cabinet makers, such as Thomas Chippendale, were well able to create their own designs and, although Robert was a regular customer, his preference for a particular manufacturer came from a coincidence of styles rather than as a result of the craftsmen slavishly following Robert's designs. However, as far as other craftsmen were concerned, 'regardless of form or degree of finish – often only a quarter of the pattern is sketched in – the ideas of the architect were followed quite closely in the finished drawings. Very little room was left for creativity on the part of the draughtsmen'.[30]

Sir John Summerson said of Adam's drawings, 'The freedom of these designs and the feeling that the artist is designing "out of his head", the occasional introduction of Romanesque and Gothic themes, is very remarkable and something entirely new for English architecture. Adam was probably the first English architect to break with the spirit of servitude to antiquity in this arrogant way. He knows he is, or is determined to be, a man of original genius.'[31]

An idea of the complexity of the work can be had from an invoice for Kedleston:

Bricklayers £2,685.12.0
Masons (Joseph Hall and Francis Battersby) £6,596.1.0
Slaters (Pratt and Co) £344.18.0
Glaziers (Joseph Taylor and William Cobbett) £477.10.11½
Copper Smith, etc. and skylight (William Kinsman)
   £307.0.0
Plumbers £1,354.4.6
Painter (Thomas Smith) £113.17.0
Carpenters/Joiners £5,104.8.0
Plasterers (Abraham Denson [Plain] Joseph Rose & co
   [Decorative]) £1,520.12.0
Ironmongers and Smiths' work £478.12. 0
Carvers, (Joshua Hall and George Moneypenny) £2501.3.0
Chimney pieces to 4 rooms (Joseph Pickford and Michael
   Spang) £990.0.0
Total Inc sundries £22,508.9.4½.[32]

Obviously masons and carpenters were the most expensive in that their costs for raw materials and transport were the highest.

These designs were not exclusively interior and Adam has been unfairly accused of being merely an interior decorator. 'He [Adam] realised that an interior could not be pleasing so long as the furniture and fittings bore no relation to the architectural treatment. He perceived that there must be consonance through-out and that if the work was to achieve true excellence, one scheme of effect must govern the treatment as a whole, and that the carpets ceilings, walls, and fittings, together with the smallest pieces of furniture and sundry features, must all be designed in accordance with the general scheme.'[33]

These early commissions did not signal the opening of the floodgates which Robert had hoped for but there was a sign of some success in Robert's networking when he was commissioned by the 40-year-old Mrs Francis Boscawen to undertake some refurbishments of her house at Hatchlands, near Guilford, in Surrey. Mrs Boscawen was a regular attender at Lady Lindores's salons and was the wife of Admiral Edward Boscawen. The naval connection, possibly facilitated by Gilbert Elliot at the Admiralty, would prove fruitful. Admiral Boscawen was the 48-year-old son of Viscount Falmouth and nephew to the Duke of Marlborough. He had had a distinguished and adventurous naval career and was currently in command of the British fleet in the Mediterranean where his principal task was the containment of the French fleet in Toulon. In the best tradition of military wives Mrs Boscawen decided to redecorate while her husband was in service abroad.

Their house was comparatively recent and showed the influence of William Kent, whose Palladian designs Robert might have been expected to follow. However Doreen Yarwood commented that 'the design is, however, original, totally different from the Palladian and rococo interiors and distinguishably Robert Adam.'[34] In fact, Adam was only being asked to remodel a house probably designed by Thomas Ripley. What established the design as 'distinguishably Robert Adam' was its originality, Robert making full use of the Roman motifs he had seen rather than relying on the pattern books of others. Some designs did come from Raphael in his Vatican Stanze decorations and the drawing room ceiling – a frieze of dolphins alternating with anthemions and flowers – owed a great deal to the Villa Pamphili in Rome. The dolphins appeared elsewhere, along with sea horses, mermaids and mermen as well the drums, flags, cannons and anchors suitable to the house of an admiral. The library ceiling was designed with panels showing Neptune, Fame, Justice and a figure of Victory with laurels and palms. Robert also used wood carving – some of it mahogany – in place of stucco for window frames, dado rails and door cases. One of the similarities between Robert and his father was their fondness for marble fireplaces and here he created one with the mantel shelf supported by caryatids. The total effect of his decoration is one of high quality work reflecting the taste and status of the patron.

This is a taste the patron may not have known he possessed but Lady Boscawen viewed the work as 'simplicity improved by art and care'.

The naval connection was undoubtedly crucial in Robert's next commission, although once again Robert was being asked to follow in another man's footsteps. In the 1720s Thomas Ripley had designed the Admiralty building in Whitehall which was boringly unoriginal. With its Ionic portico it was disproportionately tall and narrow for the site but, being set back from the street, could be discreetly hidden with a screen and entrance. The screen also gave security to a government building with an entrance onto a busy thoroughfare. Undoubtedly Gilbert Elliot would have been instrumental in proposing Robert for the alterations while he had the wholehearted recommendation of Admiral Boscawen. The gossip of the admiral's wife as to Robert's sociability would have reassured their lordships that they were dealing with a gentleman.

This screen would have to stand comparison with two of London's most celebrated buildings. Directly across Whitehall from the Admiralty building stood the Banqueting Hall of Inigo Jones, built about 1620 and the perfect example of Palladio as adapted to English tastes. To the left of the Admiralty was the recently finished Horse Guards building, designed by William Kent and embodying all the Vitruvian principles Kent had used at Holkham Hall. Robert was therefore to display his skills in the face of Vitruvius and Palladio as seen by two of the greatest English architects. Having no interest in easy victories, he relished the challenge.

He placed pavilions with pediments at either end, directly in front of Ripley's wings, and then built a low screen along the breadth of the site with Roman Doric columns in front of a plain wall. The gateway itself has a small triumphal arch with sea horses supporting a balustrade. Elsewhere two boys hold dolphins' tails. These decorations make use of the same themes as at Hatchlands, but were carried out by the sculptor Michael Spang, who had worked for Robert at Kedleston. The screen succeeded in unifying the buildings at the northern end of Whitehall but managed, at the same time, to keep the individuality of each. One had come from the *Quattro Libri* of Palladio, one from his classical precursor Vitruvius, while the third carried aspects of each but was clearly the product of a fresh mind rather than a slavish adherent. It was an Adam building and the Lords Commissioners of the Admiralty were delighted. Robert no longer had only his sketches on display at Lower Grosvenor Street, there were now actual buildings to view, one of them in the heart of the metropolis.*

Also in 1758 came another request for the decoration of an existing house. This was Shardeloes, near Amersham, and the property of William Drake, the local member of parliament. The previous architect had been Stiff Leadbetter, a West Country man devoted to the strictures of Palladio and he had produced a dully correct mansion. Adam immediately gave it a huge increase in style by adding a two-storey pedimented portico with four slender Corinthian pillars rising directly from the ground and corresponding pilasters straddling the windows and doors. The hall, however, was in the Roman Doric order with the three principal rooms leading from it. Here he introduced almost all of his ideas, even though they were still experimental. There was a 'great diversity of ceilings, friezes and decorated pilasters' but for all the decorations 'the house reveals Robert Adam as the designer of an English home.'[35] His decorations were visible throughout the house and in the dining room there were stucco reliefs filling all the wall panels. For this room he always preferred to have wall decoration in stucco rather than in tapestry, damask, or leather which were the popular wall coverings, and this followed the growing fashion for hard surfaces in 'eating-rooms'. Much of the decoration was in carved and gilded wood, although there was plasterwork on the ceiling decoration. This plasterwork was carried out by Joseph Rose of Rose and Company, one of Robert's most frequently used craftsmen. Rose, like so many of Adam's

---

* The screen was mutilated in 1827 to provide additional entrances but repair work in the 1940s restored some of its former beauty.

team, had a claim to be an artist in his own right, since, as a respected artisan, he was not only a member of the Worshipful Company of Plasterers, but also, nine years later, in 1768, he would visit Italy with Gavin Hamilton and Joseph Nollekens. Not only did Robert use the finest materials available, he also used the most expert craftsmen. They themselves benefited from working for Robert and Rose carried out many Adamesque decorations.

As the decade came to a close Robert should have been able to look back on considerable success. In the year since his return from Europe he had established his household in Mayfair, admittedly on borrowed money, and had made his name known in the salons of London. He had undertaken commissions for Admiral and Mrs Boscawen to their satisfaction, been obliging to Archie Stewart with a garden bridge, built extensions for General Bland, and modified Shardeloes. In Whitehall the screen for the Lords of the Admiralty was under construction, accompanied by great praise for his plans, and Kedleston was going ahead satisfactorily. Although that too was not wholly original, the house would stand as an Adam design. To have patrons such as Nathaniel Curzon and Edwin Lascelles, later the Earl of Harewood, in one's first year of practice provided hope that more than James's 'small things' would 'cast up'.

The major setbacks had been the change of direction by the Duke of Bridgewater to invest in canal building and Robert's abrupt rejection by the Earl of Bute. Robert was becoming inured to the high-handedness of people like the Duke of Argyll and the delays in payment by his fellow aristocrats. Waiting for audiences in antechambers was merely the overture to waiting for commitments and the even longer wait for payment. There had been minor casualties by the wayside in this hectic year. Robert had been commissioned to design a new library for the Royal College of Physicians of Edinburgh which he had provided, presumably without ruffling John's feathers, although the building itself was never constructed.

Another disappointment was the invitation by Paul Sandby to provide a Temple of Venus for Vauxhall Gardens. Jonathan

Tyers, the proprietor of Vauxhall, had set aside £5,000 for the project. Given the popularity of the gardens and the nature of the night-time trysts which took place there, a temple dedicated to Venus would seem to be more than appropriate. Robert was well aware that such a building would bring him to the attention of fashionable London. 'He hopes to do a Temple of Venus for Mr Synes, the director and proprietor of Foxhall [Vauxhall], who will spend £5,000 on it. But you may easily judge that it is one of the most critical undertakings for a young beginner and requires more to be perfect than anything I know. For here the universe are [sic] the judges, whereas in a private garden it is only the narrow public and clamour.' Since there is no trace of even preliminary sketches for this project it clearly came to a halt in its early stages.

In every case Robert's designs had been seen to be original and anyone who troubled themselves to find his sources would discover that they came from the original precepts of classical Rome. Robert had no need to feel any guilt over the expense incurred during his extended stay in Italy as 'Bob the Roman'. The rigidity of previous thought was being replaced with the flexibility to choose whatever was the most pleasing aesthetically. Architecture – an art form of solidity and definable dimensions – was becoming enlightened.

Anyone would have been justified in feeling some satisfaction at these achievements, but Robert's ambition was still a long way from being satisfied. His dream – the dream of a man who felt confident at 27 years of age to design a capital city for Portugal – was to create a large public building – a cathedral, a university or a palace – entirely from start to finish. But in the meantime he needed to consolidate his position as an architect, to move from 'up-and-coming' to fashionable and reliable, to oversee the publication of his book of engravings of Spalatro which would enhance this reputation, and also to supervise brother James's proposed visit to Italy with a view to making it profitable to the firm's future. At least now there was no doubt that, however vulnerable, the firm of the Adam brothers had a future.

CHAPTER SEVEN

Foundation Stone Laid

❧

A promising start had been made with the London practice, and Robert was full of expectation that the impetus could be maintained, but first of all his existing plans needed to be brought to fruition. The Spalatro book was not progressing as fast as could be wished, although Robert was sure that James's presence in Venice would give it the necessary boost. James had returned to Edinburgh, but was preparing to leave for Italy. Arranging his visit to Italy was therefore of prime importance, and the advice which flowed to Edinburgh in a steady stream was now mixed with precise instructions for the journey. This was not to be a Grand Tour, such as Robert had enjoyed, but a more precisely focused business trip.

Meanwhile, Robert's drawing office had suffered a serious setback when Robert sacked Dewez in December 1758. This was probably because he was showing demonstrably greater skill than Robert. Dewez returned to his home country to become the leading classical architect of the Netherlands. He died in 1812. Robert, who now needed George Richardson, a relief draughtsman, to come from Edinburgh, told James of his dilemma. 'I am to write to Johnnie about the draughtsman George, for at this juncture, when friends' business and hurry threaten to take hold of me, has the Liègois thought fit to take to his heels and has gone to Brussels without warning or without even telling Brunias of his intention.' The 'Liègois', or Dewez, had accused Robert of secretly putting him under what was virtual indentured servitude and he refused to return to the practice without an attestation that this was not so. Reluctantly, Robert told James, he would have to agree. Some of the artists employed by Robert were made to sign a seven-year agreement to work exclusively for the brothers with a clause incurring payment of the unenforceable sum of £200,000 for breach of contract. 'But George Richardson in the meantime would be a great relief.' One can sympathise with Dewez in that working for Robert, a driven man and a total workaholic, was difficult. He would expect the same devotion from his employees as he himself gave to the firm and would quite forget that they might not share his single-minded obsession. Robert had unburdened himself to James since he was aware that he had weakened the Edinburgh firm with his loan for the purchase of Lower Grosvenor Street and was now taking a principal draughtsman from John's drawing office. Although John was the eldest brother and Robert felt he should be deferred to, Robert preferred to organise the partnership by reference to James whom he probably thought was the more malleable. However, John would have been well aware of the advice and sketches that had been arriving for James, and that James had been working hard at Fort George to amass funds for his projected trip to Europe, although he could have had no idea of what James was planning for his trip.

It is no surprise therefore that on 8 March 1759, the ever cautious John set off for London to clarify the position of the London practice. Was it to be the mainspring of the brothers' partnership or merely a prestigious adjunct to Edinburgh? Robert had no doubt whatsoever that London was now the driving force, ignoring the fact that without the injection of money from John's operation, it had only a limited future. On the journey John was accompanied by the solicitor John McGowan. His progress was leisurely, and inevitably the expedition became an architectural tour of England, with John, surprisingly, admiring the Gothic aspects of much that he saw.

The Earl of Northumberland's Alnwick Castle had stucco work on walls and ceilings by James Paine 'in a very good Gothick style' and at Belford, a few miles north of the castle, John admired a neo-Gothic tower by the same architect. The vast palace of Castle Howard was 'out of proportion. The inner columns have two pedestals which have a very disagreeable effect'. In York the new Assembly Rooms by Lord Burlington were dismissed, but the Minster was 'a magnificent pile' worth all of a three-hour visit. The new classical buildings of Cambridge – the Library and Senate House – were insignificant beside the soaring fan vaults of the Perpendicular ceiling in King's College Chapel. 'Delicate circular compartments springing like rays from their various centres. The chapel is a totally Gothic building with no trace of neo-Classicism . . . It excels everything here and perhaps everything of its kind that we know of.' Twenty days after setting off from Edinburgh John was in Lower Grosvenor Street.

Given Robert's total dismissal of what today are considered the Renaissance jewels of Italy, the tastes of the two brothers only coincided occasionally, John's being clearly more catholic. Robert had made sketches of Gothic buildings on his first visit to England as well as on the Rhine on his return from the Grand Tour but his taste had narrowed to the strictly classical. However, the conversations held in the fortnight the brothers spent together in London were more likely to concern money and prospects than differences in architectural taste. Today we would say that the brothers were 'formulating a business plan', something which Robert always tried to avoid. He simply wanted more work at all times.

John, still accompanied by McGowan, and possibly Robert, then rode to Norfolk to visit Holkham Hall, the epitome of eighteenth-century Palladianism designed by William Kent in 1734 for Thomas Coke, Earl of Leicester. The main block also owes much to Colen Campbell and to Lord Burlington. John admitted that it had 'a pleasant effect from the colouring of the bricks' but felt that the whole effect was over-fussy with details which 'mince a great thing into too many small pieces'. Damned with faint praise.

The tour of England continued, now concentrating on great gardens, especially that at Stowe, after which John returned to

Edinburgh to travel on, as seems likely, to Fort George with Colonel Skinner. What passed between Robert and his brother in the spring of 1759 remains a mystery, but since there was no change in Robert's plans or way of life, we can presume that either John approved or was persuaded by his younger and more ambitious brother. Robert spent the remainder of 1759 consolidating his work at Kedleston, supervising the Admiralty Screen and designing a conservatory for the Earl of Coventry at Croome Court near Worcester. Although this was a relatively insignificant commission it fitted perfectly with the idea of an introduction which might lead to greater things. At that moment the 'greater thing' was about to originate from the Earl of Northumberland. Whether John had met the Earl when he visited Alnwick Castle is not known, but it was during 1759 that Robert started work on plans for the restoration of the earl's country house near London. This was Syon House and, more than any other commission, it would seal his reputation.

Early in 1760 James arrived in London, accompanied by George Richardson, so John had clearly approved both the draughtsman's absence and James's tour of Italy. First, James would have to travel through a Europe which was still very much at war although much of this war was being fought elsewhere. In India Clive had been victorious over French forces at Plassey, French power in Canada had been fatally wounded by Wolfe's capture of Quebec and in Europe Lord George Sackville had been instrumental in the victory at Minden. 1759 is remembered in Great Britain as the *Annus Mirabilis*, but a travelling Scotsman might be less than welcome in France. Fortunately, General Graeme, the 'hearty old cock' who had been crucial to Robert's visit to Spalatro, was in London and was only too happy to indulge in the pretence that James was an ex-officer in the Jacobite cause and therefore the friend of France. He could travel as an assistant to the general who was himself, technically, a servant of Venice and, therefore an enemy of Austria and a friend of France. Deception in the eighteenth century could be elaborate.

On 7 May 1760, while at Harwich, James told his mother, 'I still have the greatest reason to believe I am fortunate in my general, he seems easy obliging and good humoured and speaks all the languages we shall now need very fluently.' As a hint of what was to come he also told her that he was 'wearing Bob's red embroidered vest with my own coat and Brussels lace.'

Robert no doubt expected that James would scamper across France in order to reach Venice, Clérisseau and the Spalatro plates as soon as he could, but he was to be disappointed. First there was a ball at The Hague with the Prince of Nassau Weilburg and then, a few days later, another with the Prince of Hesse Philipstall at Breda. James had previously met the prince with Robert so the disguise of being a Jacobite could obviously be used or discarded at will. If warfare interrupted the affairs of society, then it would be ignored. This was not likely to be so easily done in Paris which, 'surprises me, the streets are narrow and bad except along the river . . . the dirtiness of the French is really inconceivable, even to a Scotsman'. But questions were asked of his landlord by a lieutenant of police as to James's true identity and, although the landlord assured the police that he was an attendant of the general and never went out without him he stayed only long enough to buy two suits, one of silk and one of velvet, before leaving for the south.

The sea voyage which Robert had taken would now be dangerous and the trio of James, Richardson and the general made the crossing of the Alps, which James found, even in June, to have 'snow in greater quantities than ever I saw at this season'. The descent into Savoy was made through a pass which was 'a colossal representation of Killiecrankie' in man-hauled barrows which James thought was 'in the manner of Scotch beggars'. After a few days rest with the British Envoy in Turin and with the flimsy disguise abandoned, the trio arrived in Venice on 25 June where Clérisseau was waiting for them.

Clérisseau, who had been fiercely loyal to Robert and had admired his skills as a draughtsman, was ready to accord James the same loyalty. But James was completely out of his depth in this 'aquatic city', which now had very few English residents. Parisian silk suits were impressive enough for a man who had spent most of his adult life at Fort George but they made little impression on the Venetians who were world experts at the slippery art of profitable flattery. James was unaccustomed to being bowed to by everyone and always being addressed as 'Your Excellency'. His first reaction was to take flight and he instructed Clérisseau that they should leave at once for Rome. Clérisseau pointed out that the heat in Rome and Florence during July was such that even the local population left for the hills and, anyway, he wanted James to spur Bartolozzi, Santini and Zucchi, the engravers of the plates, into greater action. The work of engraving a reverse image of Clérisseau's finished drawing onto the copper plates, cutting them in precisely varying depths with steel tools, was painstaking in the extreme. In a Venetian summer the engravers could be excused for slowing down, although, according to Doreen Yarwood, even in winter the engravers also 'slipped back once more into the usual Venetian way of spending the winter – doing nothing.'[1] There was also the problem that Clérisseau had finished the drawings, which had been seen by many English visitors, thus making it difficult for Robert now to claim them as his own. Robert was furious at what he saw as a personal betrayal. 'Why should he, out of a piece of idle vanity, prostitute these antiquities . . . I cannot help being enraged at the inconsistency of his actions.' The final compromise was that the individual plates would be signed, not by the men who had drawn them, but by the engravers.

Robert was also having trouble with the execution of the Admiralty Screen whose building was controlled by the Board of Works. 'The Board of Works have taken such a time to turn a drain that carries water from the river into St James's Park as they might have pulled down and rebuilt the whole Admiralty . . . none of them sets a stone or puts a bit of timber without my positive instructions.' Robert far preferred to work with his chosen and trusted workers who could proceed unsupervised, as at Kedleston where he and Sir Nathaniel had been discussing publishing Robert's drawings for the house.

Robert was also pleased with his work for General Bland. 'The Green House turns out in the execution handsomer than it is possible to conceive and surprised myself as infinitely prettier and more antique like in the reality than in the drawing.' At this time he also visited Kenwood House in north London and talked, although only in generalities, with Lord Mansfield. It was more important to establish oneself as a convivial companion of near equal status than to suggest that a library-cum-drawing room might be added with advantage to the house. Robert's 'softly, softly' approach was effective and a commission for just such an extension would come later.

Meanwhile, in Venice, James made the usual rounds, meeting Resident Murray and Consul Smith as well as travelling to Padua in August 1760 to sit at the feet of Lady Mary Wortley Montagu, who 'said I would surely return to England much more accomplished than most of my countrymen'.[2] But James was, in fact, achieving very little. His proposed visit to Greece was now to encompass the entire Levant as research for a giant publication, *The Antiquities of Magna Greciae*, but he also wanted to open up trade routes for his brother William – who knew nothing of the scheme – dealing in Greek and Cretan wines, Ionian honey and Paros marble. Clérisseau and Zucchi were to accompany him as his grasp of languages was still weak. However the venture was mercifully postponed while Clérisseau attempted to improve James's skills in drawing, especially in anatomy and perspective.

Attempting to follow in some respects in Robert's footsteps, he did hire a felucca on 3 September and sail to Pola [now Pula], the southernmost town on the Istrian peninsula. It possessed some antiquities, although nothing on the scale of Diocletian's palace. He was provided with letters for the Podestà, or governor, but the Podestà refused to receive him. James flew into a Scots fury and he returned to Venice without anything to show for his trip.

James wrote congratulating Robert on his commission to build the Admiralty Screen. 'It is agreeable to have something executed in the eye of the public.' And on his own account he asked Robert to supply him with 'some intelligence of what is requisite for Parliament House and its attendants.' Robert, realising that this was no more than a fraternal pipe dream, replied that he was too busy. The scheme to rebuild Parliament House, first proposed by Lord Shaftesbury who had engaged William Kent, was not undertaken until after the fire of 1835. James also proposed publishing plans of the Baths of Agrippa, which might not be profitable in themselves but would 'extend our names as travellers to the uttermost ends of the earth'. Robert also ignored this non-profitable scheme. In August Robert had had a first 'dummy' made of the *Ruins* and he was extremely unhappy with the result. According to Robert, Clérisseau was being over imaginative, 'he wants to do something on the inside of the Imperial Apartments, but I am afraid that is pushing the joke too far'. There were also 47 plates as yet unaccounted for and sharp instructions were sent to Venice.

James started to keep a journal of his travels in Italy, but, like so many of his enterprises it is only partially complete.[3] His account is a litany of socialising combined with his comments on architecture. He arrived in Rome on 24 February and lodged at the Villa di Londra – 'an extravagant inn' – and three days later he was established in Robert's old apartment at the Villa Guarnieri but in considerably more style. He listed his '*Personaggi della Commedia*' as headed by '*Cavaliere Inglese altre volte architetto scozzese*'. Clérisseau was registered as *segretario al Cavaliere*, followed by five draughtsmen, a cook, a valet, a footman and a coachman. James was proud that people felt he had a greater retinue than the Duke of Marlborough and Abbé Grant had never known artists with such splendour as the brothers Adam. Gossip of his wealth in the Vatican made him the equal of a cardinal. This far exceeded the lifestyle Robert had adopted to differentiate himself from the artistic colony, but shortly after his arrival James was horrified to find himself at a dinner party composed almost entirely of painters and architects. He made very sure this never happened again and cultivated the aristocracy with a vigour surpassing even that of Robert's.

It had been clear since James's arrival that Clérisseau was

disappointed in the young man's attitude which was much more that of the rich dilettante than of Robert's aspiring aesthete, and the Frenchman made it clear that he resented being treated by James as an employee with a lower status than that of a tutor. Clérisseau's attitude of devoted application to Robert's ambitions bored James, who found the Frenchman, 'extremely entertaining on all subjects concerning our own art but extremely insipid on all others.' There was eventually bound to be friction between the two men and Clérisseau fired the first shot, writing that James was neglecting his studies and losing himself in the Roman beau monde. James petulantly complained that Clérisseau was behaving as his equal and accused him to Robert of making copies of drawings which he would eventually pass off as his own. Neither man spoke to his opposite number in this but passed their disquiets back to Robert in London, who wisely ignored the feud. The two men would never be friends or have the relationship that had existed with Robert, but they would continue to work together and James greatly reduced his socialising.

On 9 May 1761 James took time to formulate his views on architectural theory to Henry Home, Lord Kames. Kames was a leading character among the polymathic members of the Scottish Enlightenment who trod the pavements of Edinburgh. He was born in 1696 as Henry Home, a close neighbour of, but no relation to, David Hume's father, who also spelled his name 'Home'. Like Hume's father, Henry practised as an advocate in Edinburgh and was raised to the bench in 1752 as Lord Kames. David Hume called him 'the best friend I ever had' although disagreements between the two men were frequent as they debated every subject with passionate vigour in the various philosophical societies in the city. Kames's 'daily round started at five when he prepared for court, after which, in late morning he walked with friends . . . before dinner and study. He would then go out to the taverns where he would sit late and drink hard.'[4] A genuine polymath, he once said, 'Anatomy is the only science I've never studied'. On this occasion, he had asked James to report on 'the ancient state of architecture'. James was only too happy to assume the position of an aesthetic arbiter. 'It is now about two months since I came here, during which time I have been employed in visiting most of the antiquities of this place, which you may be sure I saw with the greatest relish. I soon discovered that there was a certain *je ne sais quoi* in those magnificent remains that I had never met with in any modern performance. Though I had studied with great attention the works of Palladio and the celebrated modern masters at Verona, Venice and Florence . . . it is indeed amazing how much is to be learnt from the venerable monuments of antiquity. One is perpetually gathering new and great ideas from them.'[5] James was comparing the ancient with the modern and 'had an excellent opportunity of finding out the causes of that difference which everyone must be sensible of and which, found, will be like fixing a standard for beauty and rules for the composition in this art.'[6]

In May 1761 Robert thought that the end to the work on the Spalatro book was finally in sight when he sent the final ten plates to Rome for re-touching. Clearly he trusted James's artistic acumen to undertake this last stage of the preparation and he knew that with Clérisseau to oversee the craftsmen he could rely on the result.

James, however, did not intend to remain long in Rome but to continue his tour to Sicily, Calabria, Egypt, Turkey and Greece. His draughtsman, George Richardson, who was loaned by John, wrote to an Edinburgh friend of his expectations, 'of our going to those places of ancient glory and to examine works of so many ages and celebrated performance of ancient Hellas and every day I think more of our noble journey'.[7]

But James was not so focused as his assistant and what equilibrium he had was seriously disturbed when, at the end of July, John wrote to him with the unwelcome news that, since their mother had returned from London, her health had declined beyond the possibility of a cure at Moffat. A further letter from Robert confirmed the worst: Mrs Adam had suffered a heart attack and was dying. James's response was to write, not to John or Robert, but to Willie, bemoaning the distress the news was causing him. He left at once for Frascati, vowing to keep on the move, 'for I have no pleasure in company'. A few days later a letter arrived sealed with black wax which James 'opened but was afraid to read the consequences'. On 7 August 1761 he wrote to Jenny, 'Though I expected by every post from this fortnight the melancholy account of an event we all have such reason to bewail. Yet when I received Peggy's of 21st July yesterday I felt the deepest regret at seeing my past anxiety determined in such a manner . . . Though I felt strong desire of learning every circumstance yet I am much pleased Peggy has given me so few.' This letter James also sealed with black wax as a proper sign of mourning and he did not return to red wax until nearly a year later.

It is all too easy to criticise James for his reaction, lacking any sign of regret, to his mother's death after 13 years of widowhood. The Adam family had always maintained the closest of bonds, no matter how widely they were spread geographically, and now the first of these bonds had been broken. John and William would bear the loss with Scottish stoicism. John was surrounded by his own family in Edinburgh, and William was consoling his sisters in London, while Robert threw himself into a frenzy of work, but James was enjoying what was a well-nigh profligate holiday in Italy surrounded by servants and new acquaintances. He simply did not have the emotional equipment to grieve for his loss, and today we would excuse his behaviour by saying that he had 'gone into denial' and was covering his inexpressible grief with activity.

Mary Adam had been a faithful mother to a brood of children who might be seen as having left her behind as the family split itself between London and Edinburgh. Her husband, William, had been fiercely ambitious and had neglected his family in exchange for making a fortune. In widowhood she had ignored her poor health to continue with her motherly duties. A year before her death, while still seeking a cure at Moffat, she had written to Margaret, John's wife, with advice for the unmarried daughters. 'I forgot to tell you three young folks before I left the town not to go with any young gentlemen unless you have some married lady to escort you, young folks character is very soon hurt. Let them resort to prevent it. It is not enough your having two or three young ladies with you.' Like many mothers with successful families, she became isolated, but continued to care about their various activities until her own death. The effect on the brothers was grave and James, typically, reacted with a determination not to allow his grief to prevent his continuing his Grand Tour.

Therefore, at the end of August, James set out for Naples, in spite of a warning from the ever-cautious Clérisseau that malaria rendered such a voyage suicidal. On the way, at Capua, 'for half an hour after going to bed I was so attacked in flank, front and rear by six battalions of bugs and four squadrons of fleas, exclusive of several companies of *zampones* or *muschetoes*, that I was soon put to flight and obliged to take up my nights quarters upon three straw chairs in the middle of the room. I rose early, drank chocolate, dressed and waited upon Colonel Docherty of an Irish regiment'. Clérisseau and Zucchi wisely did not join the two Scots until September.

The turn of the year did not bring any of the hoped-for improvements with the *Ruins*, when on 4 February 1762, another 'dummy' was shown to Robert. He was appalled. There were errors in the table of contents, and a translation of the text into French had been added although there was to be no French edition. Both James and Clérisseau had wanted such an edition and James had made enquiries of printers in Paris during his journey south, but Robert was firmly opposed to the scheme. Added to these annoyances, the plates still had inaccuracies – for example, the Temple of Aesculapius had the wrong number of steps. The text also described the temple as being made of brick faced with marble, whereas Robert knew that it was made from stone. His visit to Spalatro may have been brief and beset by political problems, but his notes were thorough. Finally the dummy edition had only 56 plates while the prospectus had promised 60. With acid humour he asked James if he could create any more or stretch the existing drawings. His temper was wearing thin.

James had returned to Rome where he would now bring off a commercial coup almost validating his protracted absence from the firm, and going some way to calm his fretful brother, although the initiative for the enterprise came from Robert who kept the scheme under his own remote control. James had, as well as filling Robert's shopping list of antiquities and ornaments, been collecting pictures and statuary for some time, although an Apollo 'in need of some repairs' and a Germanicus 'perfectly entire unless in one hand which is restored' leads one to feel that his pieces were not all first rate. However, word had reached Robert in London of a collection which was of the highest quality. Cardinal Alessandro Albani, with whom Robert had been on good relations during his visit to Rome, and from whom Robert had bought much already, still owned a colossal collection of drawings originally in the possession of his uncle Pope Clement XI, who, in turn had bought the albums of Cassiano del Pozzo, a close friend of Poussin. It was the finest collection in Rome and Robert could see a huge opportunity if he could acquire it on behalf of the new king, George III.

Through the good offices of John Home he was now reconciled to Lord Bute and, along with Chambers, had been jointly appointed Royal Architect, thus having a chance to broach the topic of acquiring the collection to Bute and to the king. With their agreement James was told to negotiate the purchase and immediately approached the Contessa Cheroffini, the aged cardinal's mistress. She was keen for the cardinal to augment his fortune since she was about to marry off her eldest daughter and needed money for a dowry. The parentage of this daughter is unknown, but the circumstance of her impending marriage gave Cheroffini considerable influence with her lover which she was prepared to use, provided, needless to say, that a *douceur* was paid to herself. Winkelmann, the cardinal's librarian, opposed the sale since he was possibly in negotiation himself with the King of Spain. James, however, held the trump card in having the contessa's good will and soon he was able to tell Robert that he could buy the collection for 14,000 *scudi* as well as a payment of

500 *scudi* for Cheroffini. Since an English pound was worth approximately four *scudi*, this was an enormous sum and James justified the contessa's sweetener as, 'A present to the lady of 500 who really has been most indefatigable in the affair'. Along with Clérisseau and Zucchi, James visited the Palazzo Albani, inspected the 200 folios of drawings and made an offer of 10,000 *scudi*. Unsurprisingly it was rejected and James, who had now been told to make what bargain he could, had to pay the original amount. On the same day as the acceptance, 8 May 1762, a carefully watched cart delivered the collection to the Casa Guarnieri and two months later they were shipped to England. On 10 July James wrote, 'God send them well into England. I shall direct them simply to His Majesty'. They now form the core of the royal collection of drawings in Buckingham Palace.

Robert's success in acquiring the drawings could have been expected to improve his position with he king and his appointment as co-Royal Architect should have brought him much-desired royal commissions, but it was Chambers who profited from the position. He was given the task of modernising Buckingham House (now Buckingham Palace) as well as building lodges at Windsor Castle. Chambers was aiming to be comptroller of the royal works while Robert was looking for fashionable commissions, although both men hoped for a large royal project from George III. None was forthcoming.

Earlier in 1762, Robert had, like his brother, been in communication with Lord Kames who clearly still wanted to improve his understanding of architecture and had written to Robert asking if any rules applied to the use of the various orders of columns. Robert responded on 31 March: 'The practice of architecture rushes so fast upon me that I have but too few moments to dedicate to theory or speculation'. The Doric order should appear 'simple and solid' with no fluting nor carved mouldings of bases or capitals. 'Fluting leads to ornamentation. This degree of enrichment I would seldom use without doors [out of doors], but is very proper in Halls, Temples, etc. I have ventured to alter some parts of this order . . . but it is a dangerous experiment for more retailers of the art who have neither eyes nor judgement.' The capital of the Corinthian order demanded delicacy and richness and Robert poured scorn on the legend surrounding its origins. This was the Fable of Callimachus as told by Vitruvius. In it, Callimachus, a metalworker, saw, on the grave of a Corinthian girl, a basket surrounded by acanthus* leaves and with a tile covering the top of the basket. He then used the image as a capitol head. To Robert's eighteenth-century mind there was 'an absurdity in supporting any weight by a combined cluster of foliage'. In a prime example of ignoring one's own advice Robert used the Corinthian order on many occasions. 'The Ionic Order ought only to be used in gay and light buildings.' He dismissed the composite orders. They are 'by no means so fine as the Corinthian and the Doric Order can, without great variation, supply every purpose of the Tuscan . . . If any of these observations are worth your lordship's remarking, I should be obliged to you not to mention them as coming from me.'

He then moved to more general observations.

> Painting and sculpture depend more upon good architecture than one would imagine. They are the necessary accompaniments of the great style of architecture and a building that makes no provision for them I would at once pronounce to be wretched . . . My brother James writes with that enthusiasm and love of architecture that no one could feel who has not formed very extensive ideas of it . . . The architect who begins with minutiae will never rise above the race of the reptile architects who have infested and crawled about this country for these many years . . . I expect to be very little in London all this summer having business all over England, which I am with difficulty able to get managed with honour to myself and satisfaction to my employers.[8]

* Acanthus is the name of a genus of flowering plants, common in the Mediterranean area.

It is the brisk and business-like letter of one who is a practitioner with little time for theory.

The argument over the correct use of the orders may seem aridly academic to us today but the disputes raged on into the nineteenth century. When Sir John Soane delivered the second of his Royal Academy lectures on the subject in 1810, he caused such a riot by criticising a living fellow academician that the lecture was abandoned and the lectures themselves were postponed for two years.

Pursuing James's schemes, on 8 May 1762 Willie, in London, signed the charter papers on a Danish ship the *Fliegende Engel* to deliver a cargo to Città Vecchia, a port slightly to the north of Rome, and to place itself under James's orders. This would carry him to the Levant and bring back the first cargoes of his proposed trading mission. Unfortunately, the ship was seized by the Spanish navy and taken as a prize to Algeciras. There was an outbreak of plague in Turkey and the plan, like so many of James's, was quietly dropped. Instead he spent his time in Rome buying antiquities on request from Robert and in a now reduced round of socialising.

He did maintain his friendship with Johann Winkelmann and showed him the latest dummy of the *Ruins*. Winkelmann wrote, from Castel Gandolfo, to his friend J.J. Volkmann on 18 June 1762: 'There is soon to be published a magnificent work in English . . . it has been thought of with great intelligence and taste.' [9]

On 27 November 1762 James once again set down his thoughts on architecture in a personal memorandum of which a fragment remains in a notebook: He wrote as if he were experienced in building: 'I myself have followed an idea of the ancients and have placed on the top of a high pediment a figure in a triumphal chariot drawn by four horses.' This feature appears in James's rather fanciful design for the Houses of Parliament. There was always hope that the existing parliament building would be replaced and that James's design might be adopted. Also James probably drew it to demonstrate his skills to his more talented brother and his new friends in Rome. He gave rules for the levels of storeys in houses whether in town or country and ended limply by preferring that which 'is most pleasing to the eye'. The essay contrasts with Robert's letter to Lord Kames as no more than the theoretical outpouring of a dilettante.

Robert wrote to his brother telling him that the war would shortly end and a building boom would start in England. It was a plea for James to come home. James replied, 'I swear I give up my idea of travelling with regret' although he must have been privately relieved. Thus, in April 1763 James and George Richardson turned north. Clérisseau remained in Rome while Zucchi and Cunego went their separate ways. On their zig-zag route home James and Richardson met up with Willie in Bordeaux who was en route for Granada where he hoped to buy vineyards. By October 1763 James was back in London.

Clérisseau was left in Rome to act as agent for the brothers and it is unlikely that they ever met again. His influence on James had been minimal but his governance of Robert had been crucial. When the two men met, Clérisseau was already an established draughtsman while Robert had little or no experience of the classical roots. His time at Fort George had given him a grasp of the practicalities of architecture and his self-education had sharpened his taste to the point where he knew that he would never be a slavish follower of the current fashions. Expressing these ideas in practice meant gaining facility with a pen or brush and it was Clérisseau who taught Robert the crafts of perspective and drawing, while exposing him to the jewels of ancient architecture. Robert could learn the 'free manner of drawing' and while Clérisseau was being paid by Robert he could not work for anyone else. Clérisseau knew that he did not possess the flair of the younger man but he produced the raw materials which Robert fashioned into the enlightened neo-classical style. Neither could have done it without the other.

After James's departure Clérisseau continued to work in Rome, creating what is surely one of the great oddities of decoration. A century before the Romantic Revival he decorated a room in the convent of Santa Trinità dei Monti as a ruin with *trompe-l'oeil* holes in the walls giving on to an abandoned garden and with the roof appearing to be open to the sky. It is still extant. He married in 1763, shortly after James's departure, and started to undertake a series of designs for Catherine the Great. Clérisseau was certainly in touch with the brothers in 1765, when a payment of £300 was made to him, possibly for the purchase of some art work, but this does seem to be their last contact.[10] He returned to France in 1767 and published Volume I of *Antiquities de la France*. Although he visited England in 1771 he does not seem to have renewed his somewhat uneasy relationship with the Adam brothers and he returned to Paris in 1775. Such was his international reputation by now that he was consulted by Thomas Jefferson over the design of the Capitol building in the state of Virginia. He sent Jefferson a design and a model, both of which were highly influential. In 1804 Clérrisseau was granted a pension of 600 francs by the Emperor Napoleon and, on the restoration of the Bourbon line in 1815, was made a Chevalier de la Legion d'Honneur. The old man died on 19 January 1820, aged 99, and at auction his house and furniture fetched 34,250 francs. 'He had completely outlived his time, though he had been honoured by both Napoleon and the Bourbon Restoration within the previous decade – his death and the sale of his possessions seemed to have created little stir.'[11]

In Britain, the increase in prosperity and optimism forecast by Robert was in full flood on James's return to London in October 1763. Under the Peace of Paris, signed in March, Britain gained Canada, all of Louisiana east of the Mississippi, Tobago, Dominica, St Vincent and the Grenadines in the Caribbean, Minorca in the Mediterranean and the sub-continent of India. France retained fishing rights in the St Lawrence, as well as the islands of Martinique, Guadeloupe, Mariegalante, Desirade and St Lucia in the Caribbean. It was the most advantageous treaty in terms of territory gained that had ever been made and was the foundation of the British Empire.

James, however, had brought back nothing except an indifferent collection of art and an unfinished portfolio of drawings for a new parliament building which he had proudly displayed at a 'levée for gentlemen' in Rome. The drawings were abandoned on his return and all that remained of his three years in Europe was the polished veneer of one who had made the Grand Tour. The portraits of the two brothers make an interesting comparison. James is portrayed in 1763 by Batoni, the most expensive painter in Rome, holding a roll of plans while classical figures hover behind him. In another portrait, his pen is poised above a drawing. In contrast, in the portrait by George Willison, Robert sits comfortably holding a copy of *The Works* in a presentation binding and looks inquiringly at the viewer. James chose to be the inspired genius of pure aesthetics, while Robert is the man of practice. James's future lay in providing the firm with an air of social sophistication in which clients could be sure they were dealing with gentlemen.

On his return to London, James found the atmosphere in Lower Grosvenor Street entirely different from the one he had left behind in 1760. Work was well under way on the Admiralty Screen, Kedleston and Shardeloes were under construction, and the Adam home buzzed with messengers coming and going from the various sites. Robert had reached a rapprochement with Lord Bute and there had been a change of king. Much was expected of George III, but he turned out to be a disappointment, building no palaces for himself and commissioning no public buildings. However, on 7 December 1761, a year after the king's accession, Bute had persuaded George to appoint Robert and Chambers as 'Joint Architects of his Majesty's Works' at a salary of £300 a year. Bute's appointment put Robert on an equal footing with his rival and in that same month of December he was admitted a fellow of the Society of Antiquaries. Robert Adam had arrived as an innovator exactly as new wealth allowed the aristocracy to seek such new ideas. As Sir John Summerson has commented: 'English architecture, in short, was in the dumps, landed there by Palladian dogma and by the stream of text-books and pattern books which had, in thirty five years, inculcated that dogma with grinding thoroughness . . . [Adam was] a gentleman by birth and estate, who could therefore adopt a certain lordliness towards the whole business of building and yet be completely the professional. He held all the cards.'[12] When Piranesi's book *Campus Martius* was published in 1762, with an engraving of Robert's head on a medallion, his status as a fashionable architect was assured.

A 'cloud no bigger than a man's hand', but which would grow to considerable proportions, was now forming without Robert's knowledge. As typified by Robert's first meeting with him, Bute's social graces were few, added to which he had the knack of making enemies. He was happier amongst his own countrymen and, when he became Prime Minister in May 1762, he set about the usual round of patronage. Robert's appointment, along with that of Chambers – another Scot, although he, politically, always claimed to be Swedish – was taken as Bute's chauvinistic largesse towards his fellow countrymen. This attitude spread to an astonishing extent and loathing of the Scots became widespread. On 8 December 1762 James Boswell was at Covent Garden when two Highland officers came in. 'The mob in the upper gallery roared out 'No Scots! No Scots! Out with them! They hissed and pelted them with apples.'[13] Boswell was patriotically furious, but suspicion of the Scots would remain, even after Bute's fall from power, and the Adam brothers would be subject to it in the next decade.

Work had begun in James's absence on the decoration of Syon House on the Thames, just west of Chiswick. Elisabeth Seymour was the heir to the great estates of the Percy family. Sir Hugh Smithson, on his marriage to her, changed his name to Percy and acquired first the Earldom, and then, in 1766, the Dukedom of Northumberland. These huge estates comprised not only Alnwick Castle in Northumberland and Northumberland House in London, but also Syon House. This had been a Bridgettine convent founded by Henry V in the fifteenth century. It had subsequently been castellated and in Tudor times was used as a convenient place of exile for recalcitrant queens and princesses.

The house was given to the Percy family by James I and was now in the hands of the new earl. Vastly wealthy, he set about turning it into his country dwelling near London, sparing no expense. Horace Walpole said of him that 'the earl was spending by the etiquette of the old peerage . . . in short they will soon have no estate'. And so greatly did the earl embrace these ideas of what was expected of the aristocracy that the countess maintained her own pipers while her husband had Swiss porters and became the last nobleman in England to keep a personal jester, which he did until 1789. He wanted Robert to turn his mediaeval pile into an eighteenth-century mansion without equal, but unfortunately, also without altering the 'ruinous and inconvenient shell'. 'In the year 1762 the Duke [sic] of Northumberland came to the resolution of fitting up the apartments of Syon House in a magnificent manner . . . the expense unlimited, and the Duke himself a person of extensive knowledge and correct taste in architecture, I endeavoured to render it a noble and elegant habitation.'[14]

However much the exterior is a hybrid in styles, the interior of Syon House is one of Robert Adam's most magnificent achievements and it is one of the marks of true genius that while compromises have had to be made, all that is evident is originality. Only with the finance and freedom provided by the duke could Robert translate his well-formed theories into the reality, and by examining the structures of Syon, we can arrive at a clearer understanding of Robert's principles.

The entrance to the grounds was through a triumphal arch flanked by a screen supported by Corinthian pillars and surmounted by the Percy lion 'statant' with his outstretched tail streaming out behind him. Robert's first problem in the house itself was that the ground was uneven and thus the entrance hall was below the level of the other principal rooms. If a visitor is faced with the immediate barrier of a flight of stairs, the approach is daunting rather than welcoming. Robert stated the problem succinctly: 'Some inequality in the levels of the old floors, some limitations from the situation of the old walls, and some want of additional heights to the enlarged apartments were the chief difficulties with which I had to struggle, These difficulties, I flatter myself, are in a great measure surmounted, so as not only to procure much convenience in the arrangement of the apartments, but likewise an elegant form and graceful proportion in the principal rooms.'[15] Once again Robert stresses the need for 'movement' in his planning and there is a continuity of function through the succession of rooms in Syon.

In the centre of Syon was the original monastic court, a circular space which Robert intended to turn into a giant rotunda. Unfortunately this feature joined the ranks of concepts too expensive even for the wealthiest. However, on one occasion in 1768, when the empty space was given a temporary covering, it easily accommodated three hundred guests who dined with the King of Denmark.

Entering the main house through the Tudor fortified doorways in the west wall, the visitor arrives in the centre of an entrance hall. Robert would have preferred almost anything else, since the idea of 'movement' was now almost impossible to achieve. Instead the eye is given a contrast. On the left is a coffered apse, originally intended to house a statue of Laocoön, but instead made a home for a copy of the Apollo Belvedere by John Cheere which was bought for £21 in 1764. The décor of the hall is largely black and white but Robert was at pains to point out that the visitor would be met by servants in livery, who would provide the colour. In the walls behind the statue are doors leading to apartments for servants not in livery. Full-size figures from antiquity by John Rose decorate the walls and the floor is laid in a black and white chequer pattern. On the right is the access to the rest of the house and it is here that the rise in ground level occurs. The necessary stairs are partially hidden behind a screened archway with Roman Doric columns whose bases are at the height of the room beyond. To make the change even more dramatic, between the columns is another piece of statuary. While the Apollo and the wall statues are white and upright, this piece, a copy of the Dying Gaul by Valadier, bought by the duchess for £300 in 1773, is black and horizontal. The contrast draws the viewer towards it and the short staircases behind it where Robert has managed to achieve his beloved 'movement' in the most awkward of spaces. In the *Works in Architecture* he said, 'The inequality of the levels has been managed in such a manner as to increase the scenery and add to the movement so that an apparent effect has been converted into a real beauty.'[16]

Climbing the steps, the visitor passes from the black and white severity of the entrance hall into probably the most lavishly decorated room Robert ever designed. It was here that his hosts waited to welcome their visitor. After the awkward rectangular entrance hall, the anteroom is similarly rectangular but Robert created the impression of a square room by placing 12 Ionic columns against the walls. The south wall was pierced by windows and here Robert set the columns apart from the wall by eight feet, thus marking out a square floor space. In this vast room Robert controlled the awkward space simply by effortlessly altering it. Although this was a technical solution, Robert used it to allow the introduction of brilliantly coloured splendour. The columns are of *verde antico* and had been bought by James after being dredged from the bed of the Tiber in Rome. However Geoffrey Beard strikes a cautionary note: 'It is, however, known that some of the columns are made of scagiola so that a Tiber origin for them all must be discounted.'[17] On 22 April 1765 James was able to tell the duke that his columns had 'sailed from Città Vecchia on the 7th of last month with a fair wind and in a few hours were out of sight'. The volutes and necking of the Ionic columns are taken directly from the Erectheuem on the Acropolis in Athens, but Robert used necking designs from Roman baths and then transposed the Greek design to the frieze of the entablature. 'This specific case is typical of the freewheeling malleability which was, perhaps, the quintessential feature of the Adam style.'[18] There is a space of over six feet between the Ionic capitals and the ceiling which is filled with life-size classical figures, entirely gilded. The gilding continues on a blue background in a panelled frieze under the white and gold ceiling. Also in blue and gold are panels of military trophies on the walls between the pillars while the floor, in *scagliola*, is a circular pattern within an octagon.

It would be easy to believe that Adam's imagination had run riot here with no thought for the practicalities of life, but the space of eight feet where he had brought columns forward from the south wall formed an ambulatory which led to a privy hidden beside the door case leading to the dining room.

Robert had to contrast the classical splendour of the anteroom with the room which followed it and, as an eighteenth-century gentleman, he was particularly fond of dining rooms as a focal part of the elegant living practised in Britain. However he qualifies his enthusiasm for English manners:

> To understand thoroughly the art of living it is necessary, perhaps, to have passed some time amongst the French, and to have studied the customs of that social and conversible people. In one particular, however, our manners prevent us from imitating them. Their eating rooms seldom or never constitute a piece of their great apartments, but lie out of the suite, and in fitting them up little attention is paid to beauty or decoration. The reason for this is obvious; the French meet there only at meals, when they trust to the display of the table for show and magnificence, not to the decoration of the apartment; and as soon as the entertainment is over they immediately retire to the rooms of company. It is not so with us. Accustomed by habit, or induced by the nature of our climate, we indulge more largely in the enjoyment of the bottle. Every person of rank here is either a member of the legislation or entitled by his condition to take part in the political arrangements of his country and to enter with ardour into those discussions to which they give rise; these circumstances lead men to live more with one another, and more detached from the society of the ladies. The eating rooms are considered as the apartments of conversation, in which we are to pass a great part of our time. This renders it

desirable to have them fitted up with elegance and splendour, but in a style different from other apartments. Instead of being hung with damask, tapestry, etc., they are always finished with stucco, and adorned with statues and paintings, that they may not retain the smell of victuals.[19]

This quotation illustrates the depth of thought which Robert Adam put into planning rooms and their layout. Also, if we take his views as a generalisation of all his clients, it tells us whom he regarded them to be: men of influence, whose voices would be heard in government, and who would linger long, and, as we shall hear, often raucously, over their port or brandy. The room would be occupied more by men than by the ladies of the house, who would simply eat their food, make polite, but unimportant, conversation, and then retire to let the true business of the room commence. The domestic dining room was merely an extension of the masculine atmosphere of the gentleman's club in which ladies' chatter would never be heard, while at home, it could be tolerated for a short time. Lady Mary Wortley Montagu would have been appalled, but not surprised to read such a statement.

The room itself is decorated largely in white and gold in contrast to the vivid colour scheme of the anteroom. At each end are a favourite feature of Robert's designs: semicircular apses with screens supported by Corinthian columns. Thus the visitor has seen the Doric order in the entrance hall with a coffered apse at one end and a columned screen at the other, then the Ionic order in the anteroom. Now there are coffered niches with elaborately gilded Corinthian screens at each end of the room. The walls are comparatively plain with six niches holding casts of classical statuary which James had acquired in Rome following Robert's precise instructions. Luc-Francois Breton had been commissioned to copy sculpture in the Museum Florentinum the size and attitude of which would fit exactly into the dining room niches. These figures stand on either side of the white marble fireplace which has a bas-relief of the Three Graces, also carved by Breton in Rome. It is flanked by Corinthian pilasters with a gilded pediment above it. The dining room was deliberately plain, 'to parade the conveniences and social pleasures of life' and was the first of the sequence of rooms to be finished – in 1763 – but so perfectly does it fit into a progression that it is clear that Robert had the designs for all the state rooms in a very advanced state before the start of work.

Through a white and gold Corinthian screen a door leads directly into the red drawing room, so named since the walls are covered in red Spitalfields silk. The white and gold of the dining room has been replaced by warm colours and vivid decoration. Robert attempted to emulate the ceiling by Raphael in the Villa Madama and he covered it with octagons linked by diamonds, each octagon – there are over 200 of them – carrying an individually painted medallion. The effect is startling, but the ceiling dominates the room with its over-fussy style. Chambers claimed that it resembled nothing so much as a host of dinner plates that had been skied in some mad revel. In the *Works* Robert defended the concept of compartmented ceilings: 'Inigo Jones introduced them into England, with as much height, but less fancy and embellishment.'[20]

The roundels in the compartments were painted by Cipriani – 'in the best manner' – for two guineas each, and neither Robert nor the duke was entirely happy with the result, although the duke and duchess had insisted on choosing the colour scheme. Giambattista Cipriani had met Robert briefly in Florence in 1755 when he was about to depart for England as a draughtsman working for Chambers, but after the 1760s he became one of Robert's 'regiment of artificers'. Robert thought he was 'the best natured lad in the world who draws in the most delightful manner imaginable in the styles of all the great masters.' Since the room was 'a splendid drawing room for the ladies *en route* for the Long Gallery' it was not meant for lingering and the skied dinner plates could be excused. The pilasters and entablatures of the doors and fireplaces are decorated using ormolu, the first time Robert had used this material in favour of the more traditional gilded stucco. Since much of this work was carried out by Matthew Boulton it may be that he, not Robert, was the innovator, although Robert would have supervised every detail closely. The carpet was woven by Thomas Moore but to a design by Robert; the latitude he allowed to trusted craftsmen extended only to their interpretation of his designs.

The duke showed that he had a keen aesthete's eye for detail and he insisted that some mouldings be returned and remade since he would allow nothing to be installed in Syon that was not entirely to Robert's satisfaction – and, by implication, his own.

The last of the public rooms, the Long Gallery, is also the largest, running the entire 130 feet length of the east side of the house. According to Robert it was too low and too narrow to provide any scope for an elegant reconstruction. However, 'it is finished in a style to afford great variety and amusement; and is, for this reason, an admirable room for the reception of company before dinner or for the ladies to retire to after it: For the with-drawing room lying between this and the eating room prevents the noise of the men from being troublesome; and for this reason we would always recommend the intervention of a room in great apartments to prevent such inconvenience.'[21] This is another insight into the social behaviour of Robert's clients.

The eastern wall of the gallery is pierced with ten floor-to-ceiling windows, looking onto the river Thames, as well as a central window recessed in a bow. The facing wall has three doors and two fireplaces, around which Robert put apsed niches to hold antiquities. Michael Pergolesi carved 62 pilasters for this wall at three guineas each which flanked the doors and bookcases which, in turn, were filled with uniformly bound books, the colour of the bindings providing the keynotes of the colour scheme. Above the bookcases is a frieze with landscapes and, in lunettes, portraits of the Percy family. Finally, at either end of the gallery are small secret rooms, one circular and one square where, among collections of porcelain and glass, one could read in comfortable seclusion. These were closets, or miniature bou-doirs for the privacy of the ladies. The design of the carpet, which complements, but does not directly echo the pattern of the ceiling, was, according to Damie Stillman, 'probably inspired by a mosaic such as one of the second century found in Ostia'.[22] Robert's problem with the gallery was that it was much wider than it was high and with its great length any conventional architect would be left with the option of making the space a prettily decorated tunnel. His introduction of pilasters framing the doors and bookcases divided the gallery into sections around which chairs – also designed by him – could be grouped, thus distracting the eye from the vast length. Sir John Summerson said of it: 'The gallery at Syon may, I think, possibly be the place where the Adam Style was actually initiated. The room presented to the designer a rather special challenge and elicited a correspondingly original response . . . A style which is a carefully balanced pattern of verticals and horizontals, with a lacy, racy accompaniment of arabesque ornament painted or in relief, a style gay, delicate and rich, but never without a strict underlying discipline.'[23]

As to the rooms in the remainder of the house they remain 'undescribed', since, 'in these little form is necessary, and none is here attempted, except that may serve in some measure to diversify the scene.'[24] This was not snobbery – a duke's dressing room is no ordinary retiring room – but these were private apartments where public show was unnecessary and therefore utility reigned over splendour. In *The Works* there is a description of some of these apartments which gives us a clear picture of the service required by a duke and duchess. 'In Syon the private apartments are now the only part of the place undescribed; on one hand is the Duchess's bed-chamber, an anti-room for the attendance of her maids, her toilet or dressing room, her powdering room, water closet, and outer anti-room, with a back stair leading to intersols for her maids' bed-rooms and wardrobes etc. On the other hand there is a dressing room for the Duke, a powdering room, writing room, water-closet and stairs to intersols for his Grace's Valet-de-chambre, and wardrobe. In these little form is necessary.'[25]

By the time the decoration of Syon was completed the order

book of the brothers Adam was full and, even by the completion of the dining room in 1763, Robert's reputation was secure. He could now choose his clients. He had achieved this reputation in just over four years, a seemingly meteoric rise after his initial disappointments.

This was, however, an era of furious artistic progress and innovation. Joshua Reynolds had established himself in London in 1753 and, by 1755 he had painted a phenomenal 120 portraits, setting up a studio in Leicester Square with an income which would reach £6,000 a year by 1760. David Garrick arrived in London as a penniless wine merchant in 1737 and in ten years became the patent holder at Drury Lane where he set about changing theatre from the haunt of whores and pickpockets into a respectable place of recreation. The style of production moved to more realistic presentation, while both he and Sarah Siddons were received at court. His friend and fellow midlander, Samuel Johnson, started work on his Dictionary which would bring a sense of order to the language, while, in 1726, Alexander Pope's *Dunciad* and Jonathan Swift's *Gulliver's Travels* held the follies of society up to ridicule. Philosophy and politics were entering the modern world with David Hume's *Treatise of Human Nature* in 1739 and Adam Smith's *Theory of Moral Sentiments* in 1759. Change and innovation were in the air and the most innovative architect in Britain was Robert Adam.

CHAPTER EIGHT

A Regiment of Artificers

❧

In the 1760s Robert Adam's establishment at Lower Grosvenor Street had become an established success and Robert was the architect of choice for most aristocratic property developers. He juggled several projects simultaneously and in this decade he worked on 11 major houses at Syon, Kedleston, Kenwood, Osterley, Harewood, Bowood, Mersham-le-Hatch, Nostell Priory, Newby, Croome and Landsdowne. According to Damie Stillman, 'the success of his early career in London, as well as his subsequent efforts was also due to his organisational ability'[1]. Another art historian said of him that 'an inordinate craving for success also partakes in the making of the Adam style. It drove him to amass the largest classical vocabulary, to be a superior draughtsman, to be continually and infinitely novel, and thus to eclipse his colleagues and overwhelm his patrons'.[2] Patrons were not the only people to feel overwhelmed by Robert. On 22 October 1762 James wrote to Peggy, 'I think from what I can perceive, he makes plans [of entire houses] faster than I can make cornishes [cornices]'.

Clients were beating a path to Lower Grosvenor Street and demanding results, causing Robert to complain that he was never allowed time to think in the abstract about the concept as a whole. Instead he had to produce instant results, and deal with the clients' often unhelpful suggestions. With John now being sidelined in Edinburgh, Robert, as head of the firm, had to undertake the unpleasant task of extracting payment from clients. A firm with such enormous outgoings – most houses were built on a shaky scheme of trust and credit – was dangerously vulnerable to the vagaries of aristocratic fortunes.

Robert not only astonished James at his plan-making facility but produced detailed drawings and sketches of the tiniest details. 'The extraordinary range of Adam's invention, including everything from beds to inkwells, is a constant and valid source of amazement.'[3] At the same time he was, with the help of James, pursuing his contacts among the nobility and gentry. He knew very well that a publication like *The Ruins of Spalatro* would not only enhance his reputation, but also enable him to reach a far wider clientele. 'The thrustingly ambitious young Adam had viewed his book on the palace of Diocletian as something akin to a very grand publicity brochure for a rising architectural practice, or as the crowning achievement of an elaborate public relations exercise aimed at the glorification of Adam the man, rather than the site he purported to honour.'[4] Robert had rejected the pressures of James and Clérisseau to publish a bilingual version in English and French as well as James's suggestion that the publication of the engravings alone without the text might prove a better seller than the full edition. Such a version might have exposed the fact of Robert's minimal contribution to the plates as opposed to the team of engravers led by Francesco Bartolozzi. Nothing less than the complete work would be enough; Robert insisted that the book carried Robertson's much praised foreword with the full descriptions of each plate and by 1762 it was, at last, ready for publication.

An unpleasant surprise came with the appearance of *The Antiquities of Athens Measured and Delineated by James Stuart, F.R.S. and F.S.A., and Nicholas Revett, Painters and Architects*. The publication of this work had been delayed due to a difference between the two men over the layout, which eventually led to Stuart buying out Revett's interest; what was finally published can be taken to be all Stuart's work. To Robert's horror, 'Athenian' Stuart began by making clear that any similar publications concerning themselves with Rome were simply describing the work of what was an inferior and derivative civilisation. Without naming Robert, Stuart's introduction did as much as possible to denigrate his proposed book. 'The ruined edifices of Rome have for many years engaged the attention of those who apply themselves to the study of architecture; and have generally been considered as the models and standard of regular and ornamental building. Many representations of them drawn and engraved by skilful artists have been published.' There was more. The Greeks 'distinguished themselves by a pre-eminence and universality of genius, unknown to other ages and nations. Painting, sculpture and architecture, it should be observed, remained all that time [the reign of Pericles 490–429 BC] in a very rude state among the Italians.'[5] Having thus demolished Roman architecture Stuart then decries Vitruvius and Desgodetz as being incompetent in their descriptions of the Doric and Ionic orders. Curiously, after such a definite statement, all but one of the buildings in Volume 1 are from either the Hellenistic (c 350–150 BC) or Roman (c. 50 BC–250 AD) periods and do not fall inside Stuart's own definition of pure Greek architecture. But Stuart 'seemed to feel that everything in Greece was Greek.'[6]

In the main body of the book the frontispiece is a panoramic view of Athens by Stuart followed by detailed descriptions of the sites giving their history as well as recounting Stuart's personal recollections of his visit. The introductory plates are elaborate reconstructions of the present condition of the sites with notes on their history. For example, Plate 1 in Chapter 4 is of a building said to be 'The Lanthorn of Demosthenes' and since, at the time of Stuart's visit, it was a Capuchin Hospital we are given a charming engraving of the garden with a monk contemplating a skull and looking much like St Jerome, although without his lion. This informal and historically informative tone continues throughout the book. In all there are five chapters with 55 plates accompanied by highly detailed drawings of architectural details where everything was carefully measured in feet and inches

The publication of *The Antiquities* confirmed Stuart's place as a leading architect – he was now, without doubt 'Athenian' Stuart. Volumes 2 and 3 were published posthumously by Stuart's widow and the architect William Reveley in 1790 and 1795. Other volumes were brought out in 1809 and 1830, while so popular was the book that in 1837 a pocket-sized version of the text alone was published as a guidebook for tourists to the Greek sites.

While Robert's irritation was understandable since Stuart's first volume was well received and there was the threat of two more volumes appearing shortly, the publication of Stuart's book should not have been a total surprise since it had been known in London that the work had been in preparation since 1754. Robert's reaction to his family was predictable. 'I can't say I like this sort of forestalling much. I wish I had been first.' Had his interests been entirely academic there was no reason why he should not publish *The Ruins* immediately, since he was describing an entirely different site of a different period, but Robert was seeking fame and celebrity, and therefore he needed exclusivity in the market place. With the tenacity and determination of a true star he delayed for two years.

Building continued on various projects in 1763, but the brothers never forgot their maxim that 'little things may lead to large' and Robert followed up the smallest commission, even for a proposed riding school in Edinburgh. On 21 May he sent plans to John Fordyce, the agent to John Mure of Caldwell. 'I have avoided all extra ornament, and used no more than what was necessary to make the façade decent and genteel. Mr Mure approves of it only says it is too little ornamented.' The plans showed the building ready for plastering but Robert was worried about the amount of available light and proposed alternative places for windows, but, not having seen the proposed site of the building could offer nothing more positive. 'Mr Mure and I have had many conversations on the extension of your scheme, and forming a complete academy for fencing, dancing and having houses for the different masters all formed on a regular plan; making this riding house the centre building.' He asks for a more complete ground plan and goes into detail.

> The rooms I call for the gentlemen at the end of each lobby
> are proper for dressing and undressing in. The closets in

these rooms will hold boots, whips, etc. and, as there is a communication twixt them and the stables, in bad weather the horses may go that way from the Riding house to the stables, and the chimneys may be used for boiling drinks for the horses; and I would have these rooms with Dutch clinkers. The rooms above would answer for the clerks to keep your accounts, or for a person to sleep who has the care of the Riding House till such a time as a proper house is built for the Riding Master. But these things I only fling out as they occur. I wish my plans may please you and you will make me happy by letting me hear from you when they have been inspected.[7]

This letter indicates that the partnership would respond to any possibility of work and would give it their full attention, even including facilities for heating the water for the horses to drink. As at Kedleston – with its elegantly disguised central heating system – there is practicality combined with style. The riding school was built, with Angelo Tremamondo, an internationally renowned fencing champion, in charge. Paid for by the city, it was a great success, and since it faced the university, 'the Riding House is great benefit to the students, who in the shortest time possible have the advantage of taking these wholesome exercises.'[8] It was destroyed in 1829 to make way for Playfair's Surgeons' Hall.

Now John was dividing his time between the Edinburgh practice and enjoying more or less bucolic retirement as a landowner at Blair Adam in Kinross. He was also making wise investments in the purchase of land in Edinburgh. He, of all the brothers, was his father's son. From the London practice either James or Robert – normally James, who only left London for short periods – would be present to run the drawing office. Robert would be more or less free to seek new projects and James would keep a watchful eye on what projects were passed on to Robert. The Edinburgh Riding School would have been one of them, although once in Robert's hands, the project was entirely his, except for William's control of the financial aspects. They made a highly effective brotherhood.

Their book which finally emerged in 1764 was well worth the wait. It was printed on sumptuously thick paper, bought especially in Rome, in large folio, or crown size – as had been Stuart's. In today's measurements this is 15 inches (380mm) by 21 inches (535mm). Great care was taken over the bindings for the presentation copies, designed by Robert himself, with the king's copy bound in red morocco with gold embossing. Less lavish embossing appeared on volumes for lesser luminaries but still with great attention to detail. Knights of the Garter had copies bound in blue leather, while the copies for Knights of the Thistle were in the dark green of their order. Unlike Stuart, Robert gave a list of 519 subscribers. After the Royal Family came 'a selection of the aristocracy that reads like a page from Debrett. After the names of the great libraries, subscribers of interest listed include the Hon. Horace Walpole, the Archbishop of York, Joshua Reynolds, David Garrick, Allan Ramsay, Michael Rysbrack and the Rt Hon. Robert Lord Clive. The twenty eight foreign subscribers include the Duke of Parma, the library of St Mark in Venice and the Venetian Ambassador.'[9]

Lord Bute had ordered ten copies, while the Duke of Argyll took two sets and Major General Skinner one set.* A surprising omission from the list of subscribers is Edward Gibbon, although he certainly consulted the book when he gave his own description of the palace: 'For this account of Diocletian's palace we are principally indebted to an ingenious artist of our own time and country whom a very liberal curiosity carried into the heart of Dalmatia. But there is room to suspect that the elegance of his deigns and engraving has somewhat flattered the objects which it was their purpose to represent.'[10]

Flattery was expected of the author of such a book and Robert was only too glad to oblige. After the title page, which read:

---

* In the eighteenth century books were sold unbound as 'sets'. The new owner could then have the set bound to his own taste.

RUINS OF THE PALACE
OF THE EMPEROR DIOCLETIAN
AT SPALATRO IN DALMATIA
BY R. ADAM F.R.S. F.S.A.
ARCHITECT TO THE KING
AND TO THE QUEEN
PRINTED FOR THE AUTHOR
MDCCLXIIII

came the dedication:

TO

THE KING

I beg to lay before your Majesty the RUINS OF SPALATRO. Once the favourite Residence of a great Emperor, who, by his Munificence and Example, revived the Study of Architecture, and excited the Masters of that Art to emulate in their Works the Elegance and Purity of a better Age.

All the Arts flourish under Princes who are endowed with genius as well as possessed of Power. Architecture in a particular Manner depends upon the Patronage of the Great, as they alone are able to execute what the Artist plans. Your Majesty's early Application to the study of this Art, the extensive Knowledge you have acquired of its Principles, encourages every Lover of his Profession to hope that he will find in George the Third, not only a powerful Patron, but a skilful Judge.

At this happy Period, when Great Britain enjoys in Peace the Reputation and Power she has acquired in Arms, Your Majesty's singular Attention to the Arts of Elegance, promises an Age of Perfection that will complete the Glories of your Reign, and fix an era no less remarkable than that of Pericles, Augustus or the Medicis.

I am, may it please Your Majesty.

Your Majesty's most dutiful Servant and faithful Subject, Robert Adam.

Robert's message was clear. Seemingly on behalf of all architects, but in reality on his own behalf, he pled that George III should commission some large-scale public buildings. In this he was to be disappointed. Then came the Preface, written by William Robertson, but entirely with the agreement of Robert. At its time what it put forth was true, not only of architecture, but also of all Augustan taste.

> The buildings of the ancients are in Architecture, what the works of nature are with respect to the other arts; they serve as models which we should imitate, and as standards by which we ought to judge: for this reason, they who aim at eminence, either in the knowledge or in the practice of Architecture, find it necessary to view with their own eyes the works of the ancients which remain, that they may catch from them those ideas of grandeur and beauty, which nothing, perhaps, but such an observation can suggest . . . At a time when the admiration of the Grecian and Roman architecture has risen to such a height in Britain, as to banish in a great measure all frivolous and fantastic tastes, and to make it necessary for every architect to study and to imitate the ancient manner, I flatter myself that this work, executed at considerable expense, the effect of great labour and perseverance, and which contains the only full and accurate designs that have hitherto been published of any private edifice of the ancients, will be received with indulgence and may, perhaps, be esteemed an acquisition of some importance.[11]

With the publication of Stuart's book, Robert was obliged to allow Greek architecture to stand beside Roman, but he would have excused his beloved 'grotesques' in decoration as not being 'frivolous' or 'fantastic' since they had their own classical roots, and, of course, the assertion that this book 'contains the only full and accurate designs' is complete nonsense. Not only Stuart but Wood in his *Ruins of Palmyra* and *Ruins of Baalbek* had done just that.

The 'Descriptions' which followed were a guided tour of the site as the reader proceeded from Porticus to Vestibulum – where the sacred fire on the altar of Vesta, goddess of hearth, home and family, burned continually – and finally to the Crypto Porticus, the 'gradation from less to greater, of which some connoisseurs are so fond, and which they distinguish by the name of a Climax in Architecture'. This was a justification for the theory of movement, which Robert asserted was essential to prevent dullness. Modern architects 'are apt to fatigue us with a dull succession of similar apartments.' There were detailed descriptions and judgements – always favourable – on some of the finer points. A cornice 'seems to have been kept simple . . . and the whole is far from having a bad effect'. As Iain Gordon Brown points out, 'Adam would "improve" upon the Romans by representing some architectural features – such as a pilaster capital of unusual form which he found in the Peristyle – not as they actually were, but as he thought they *ought* to be.'[12] But Robert kept an eagle eye on such errors as he felt Clérisseau had committed. The inside of the Vestibulum was built of 'brick, and covered with a hard cement for receiving an incrustation of marble.'[13] There were also, as there had been in Stuart, plans with exact and detailed dimensions.

The *Capriccio* plates, or general views, started with a frontispiece engraved by Bartolozzi showing the ruins with two eighteenth-century gentlemen sketching hard, while a rustic lady carries out her trade of selling chickens and pigeons. Later in Plate XXXIII the sketcher is thought to be a caricature of Clérisseau while, for local colour, a cripple is gesticulating wildly while being wheeled around on a low cart. This plate was labelled the Temple of Jupiter although the building is now known to be the Mausoleum of Diocletian.

Robert's text was less detailed and not as anecdotal as Stuart's. It was popular enough for an edition of the text alone to appear in Italian in 1764; the *Rovine del Palagio dell'Imperatore Diocleziano nella Città di Spalatro in Dalmazia* was signed by Francesco Egidi and is described as the work of a '*diligente Inglese*'. According to

Iain Gordon Brown the Venetian text (which bears Adam's name) should 'most probably not be regarded as a pirated edition but as one having the author's imprimatur'.[14]

The delay in publication meant that the impact was not what Robert had hoped for back in 1762, when he was still only an emergent talent. Now, in 1764, the publication was no surprise and merely confirmed his position as a leading architect who had moved, as James had hoped, from small commissions to major undertakings. The *Ruins* demonstrated Robert's expertise in building, but he was also now much in demand as an interior designer.

It was not uncommon for a client to employ several craftsmen in the construction and decoration of his house and, although there would be a supervising architect who might recommend others, it was still possible for a patron to use several designers on one project. This could, of course, involve considerable internal reconstructions and the subcontracting of specialised artisans such as painters, carvers, gilders, and so forth. It was even possible for different architects to be commissioned to design various buildings in different parts of the estate. In 1759 Robert had been designing a rather grand greenhouse for the Earl of Coventry at Croome Court in Worcestershire. It resembled a Greek temple with its six Doric pillars supporting a pediment decorated with festoons of botanical cornucopia. This beautiful conservatory led to a commission to decorate the interior of the earl's house.

The house itself had been designed by Lancelot Brown, a man who, on inspecting a prospective client's estates was reputed always to comment, 'My Lord, your estate has the capability of great beauty'. Capability Brown was born about 1716, the fifth son of a Northumbrian farmer, and started his career as a jobbing gardener. By 1741 he was head gardener for Lord Cobham at Stowe and worked there with William Kent and James Gibbs, first as a gardener, but eventually as an architect, designing a number of buildings including the various temples and bridges at Stowe, where he also laid out the gardens. During the 1750s Brown had more than 40 commissions and his annual turnover averaged £8,000, rising to £10,000 in 1759. He frequently worked for no fixed fee, allowing his clients to pay what they felt his achievements merited. In modern terms, they seem to have merited nearly £1 million during the 1760s, although he often had difficulty in extracting the sums he was owed. For example, Sir John Griffin of Audley End and Ambrose Dickens of Branches were reluctant to pay, although as close neighbours the two men may have conspired to delay payment for as long as possible.

Capability Brown hoped that the artificiality of his designs would not be noticed. In his obituary it was said of him: 'he was the happiest man [when] he will be least remembered, so closely did he copy nature that his works will be mistaken'.[15] He took great care to produce contrasts in his landscaping, with deer parks seeming to adjoin cultivated land and rough pasture approaching the house in which it stood. All of this was the landscaping equivalent of Robert's desire for 'movement'. No fences could be seen and Brown was an expert in the use of the ha-ha to provide invisible barriers. At Swynnerton in Staffordshire he created a vista of a large lake which was, in fact, composed of smaller lakes at different unconnected levels. He was also a technical expert in agriculture, bringing seemingly infertile pasture to life with gardens, shrubberies, kitchen gardens, or even arable land. Lord Coventry said, 'Croome was entirely his creation, and I believe, originally as hopeless as any spot in the nation.'

Robert was happy to erect a greenhouse here, picturesquely surrounded by cedars planted by Brown*, while Brown demolished a church and raised a hill to display its reconstruction by Robert. This is probably one of the very few churches Robert designed. He certainly rendered accounts for a painted window and a Gothic chair, as well as for decorating the interior of Brown's house for his lordship. The ceilings and fireplaces are

* Sadly, today the trees have partially destroyed the conservatory.

among Robert's finest with niches holding statuary in the gallery much as in the dining room at Syon, and with full-sized caryatids supporting the chimney pieces. But the Earl of Coventry had seen something while on his Grand Tour which gave him an idea and Robert had to accede to it. The idea was that the walls of a room were to be hung with tapestries, called *alentours*, complete with woven representations of picture frames, and revealing wall paintings of rustic scenes by François Boucher. The tapestries also surrounded door cases and fireplaces as well as having woven representations of cornicing. A set of these surrounding tapestries by Boucher had been made at the Gobelins workshop by Maurice Jacques from designs by Germain Soufflot, and the earl had seen another set by Jacques [probably James] Neilson, a Scot. Soufflot also seems to have supplied designs for the furniture as well as sending specially woven fabric for chair covers. Whether Adam approved or not is not recorded but like a good artist he accepted his client's instructions and the Gobelin tapestries were hung around his fireplaces. The entire set was bought for £50,000 by the Metropolitan Museum of Art in New York where the room has now been reconstructed.

Neither Robert Adam nor Capability Brown dominated the other during their work at Croome and they often worked elsewhere on different aspects of a single house. At Bowood Adam designed the portico, some interiors and the 'Diocletian' wing, and he built a mausoleum for Lord Shelburne on the top of a hill overlooking a lake created by Brown. 'Adam could hardly have hoped for a more advantageous setting.'[16] On the other hand, at Corsham Court in 1772, Adam merely contributed four console tables, while Brown created not only the grounds, but the entire house, with plasterwork by Stocking, a Bristolian plasterer never used by Robert. Indeed, there is no evidence that Adam and Brown ever met. Their backgrounds were entirely different as were their commercial approaches, Robert being by far the more commercial, while Brown was seemingly humble. A life-long sufferer from asthma, Brown died of a stroke on 6 February 1783, aged 67, when returning from a visit to Lord Coventry in

London. His obituary claimed that 'his great and fine genius stood unrivalled' and his biographer Dorothy Stroud summed him up as 'one of the most remarkable characters of the eighteenth century, a man of few enemies and many friends; whose list of employers reads like Debrett, whom Walpole described as having, "wit, learning and great integrity", who after thirty years of work in this country could afford to refuse the Duke of Leinster's offer of £1,000 on landing if only he would go to Ireland, excusing himself on the grounds that he 'had not yet finished England.'[17] He was buried at Fenstanton, his estate in Huntingdonshire, and at his death in 1783 his estate was valued at £10,000.

Another close contemporary of Robert's did not find fortune so easily. He was Thomas Chippendale, born in 1718 in Otley, Yorkshire, and like Robert, born into the career he would follow. His father and most of his male relatives were joiners or general woodworkers, so his earliest memories were of wood and glue and, as soon as he was old enough, he was apprenticed to Richard Wood, the leading cabinetmaker of York. By 1752, in his mid thirties, Chippendale was living in Somerset Court, near London's Strand, and had married and fathered the first of nine children. He was working as a cabinetmaker providing furniture for the rich, usually according to other men's designs. However, having his own creative ideas only used occasionally was unsatisfactory to Thomas and he started to collect his own working drawings until, in 1754, he changed his way of life completely. He joined a Scots merchant, James Rannie, and set up his own workshop as an independent designer in St Martin's Lane. For a year Chippendale had been collecting subscribers for *The Gentleman's and Cabinet-Maker's Directory*, a large folio book (£1 14s bound, or 2 guineas after publication) showing, 'Elegant and Useful Designs of Household Furniture in the Gothic, Chinese and Modern Taste' lavishly illustrated with 161 plates. It was dedicated to Adam's patron at Syon, the Duke of Northumberland, whose, 'intimate acquaintance with all the arts and sciences that tend to perfect and adorn life' would surely attract him to the book. This was a triple-pointed approach and was aimed at his fellow tradesmen and architects as well as the 'gentlemen' who were choosing furniture for their new houses. On publication Chippendale had 308 subscribers, of whom 259 were fellow tradesmen, but for the first time what was essentially a furniture catalogue had been bought by 49 members of the upper classes. It ran to three editions and by 1762 both Catherine the Great and Louis XV had copies. By August 1754 the firm of Chippendale and Rannie was in full operation.

Fortunately, Robert was in London en route for Europe at the time and visited Chippendale's newly opened showrooms in their first few days. He ordered 'superfine silks and damasks' for the decoration of Dumfries House and saw the 'thousand temptations' which he told his family he had resisted purchasing 'for our habitation.' It is, however, likely that he only placed the orders for the furniture for Dumfries House since it was not delivered until 1759 after Robert had inspected it on his return from Italy. The furniture was sent by sea, insured and accompanied by a representative from the workshop, but Chippendale still paid £9 for repairs to a mirror and a girandole. Unfortunately, with the ability to make repairs locally and, given the availability of *The Directory* with its easy access to Chippendale's styles, clients often sought out local, cheaper craftsmen to execute the pieces. Alexander Peter, an Edinburgh craftsman, copied a sideboard and a set of bed cornices directly from the pattern book. 'The Duke of Atholl, having received a pair of candle stands from Chippendale, promptly had another four copied by a local man, John Thompson.'[18]

In spite of this disadvantage what seems to have been an auspicious opening was maturing into a financial success when disaster struck. Only seven months after the opening of Chippendale's workshop the premises burned down. Overcoming this difficulty, Chippendale managed to flourish again employing 40 or 50 artisans 'including cabinet-makers, upholsterers, carvers, gilders, chair-makers, polishers and packers. The names of his specialist carvers or *marqueteurs*, who must surely have been

amongst the most accomplished in London, are not known.'[19]
'Perhaps the most compelling proof of Chippendale's reputation
is the fact that Robert Adam, who was notoriously fussy about
equipping the rooms he had designed, entrusted him with
furnishing many of his finest interiors.'[20]

Nostell Priory had received a new wing and interior decoration
from Adam in 1766 and Chippendale had provided the furniture.
Adam had, as at Kedleston, taken over from James Paine and
the internal work was all under his aegis. However there are
pier glasses which, while indistinguishable from Robert's style,
are, in fact, by Chippendale. This is only one instance when
confusion between the two men has arisen, to the point where
some historians have even suggested that Robert simply provided Chippendale with sketches, a practice for which there is
no concrete evidence. Robert did render an account to Sir
Lawrence Dundas 'to design sopha chairs for the salon' at
Sir Lawrence's house at Arlington Street, for £5, although the
execution of these designs was by Chippendale. This is the only
occasion on which Adam provided designs for the other's workshop. Lady Knatchbull dealt directly with Robert over furniture
for her house at Mersham-le-Hatch when she 'had half an hour's
conversation with Mr Adam concerning the furniture of our
drawing room'.[21] Not only is there no correspondence between
the two men, but their clients dealt with each individually. On
occasions there were complaints about furnishings – usually
about excessive costs or late deliveries – in houses designed by
Robert, but these complaints always went directly to Chippendale. However, in the case of Kenwood in 1769 Chippendale
delivered ten mirrored plates of glass for £340 0s 0d directly to
Robert.

Both men operated in the closed world of eighteenth-century
aesthetics and both men changed the established view of what
was acceptable. In some areas their views diverged – Chippendale was more influenced by France than Rome – while in others
they converged, with Robert designing some lyre-backed chairs
similar to ones Chippendale had made. Horace Walpole wrote to

the Countess of Ossory in June 1773 with the weak joke that he found the designs of the chair backs were 'taken from antique lyres and make a charming harmony'. It is inevitable that some overlap would occur given the output of the two men, with over 600 pieces coming from Chippendale's workshops alone. He would furnish a house in its entirety, including servants' rooms and he would design the kitchen and cellars where needed. His most expensive items were his mirrors, using only mirror glass imported from France and therefore liable to customs duty. His reputation as 'the Shakespeare of English furniture makers' was based on his innovative design and the high quality of his workmanship. In this Thomas Chippendale was, like Capability Brown, the equal of Robert Adam. Robert understood this well enough to work with the two men as equal partners and not simply as employees or suppliers. He regarded Chippendale as 'the most accomplished exponent of neoclassical furniture in London and trusted him to equip his most elegant interiors with decorum. This interpretation implies a handsome compliment from the leading architect to the most confident furniture maker of the age.'[22]

Chippendale's establishment in St Martin's Lane put him geographically on the boundary between tradesman's London and fashionable London. As a tradesman Chippendale was one 'of the middling sort' whom Dr Johnson defined as 'within reach of those conveniences which the lower orders must necessarily want', in other words in 'the middle station in life.' Tradesman's London comprised the environs of Covent Garden and included the theatres, brothels, bagnios, and intellectual coffee houses. Chambers could count among his neighbours Fielding and Goldsmith, Zoffany and Hogarth, while Sheridan used the Piazza Hotel as his coffee house and Garrick lived in Southampton Street. Robert Adam did not include himself as part of intellectual London. One other huge difference between him and Chippendale was that Chippendale asked for advance payments and importuned his clients for payment, thus marking himself as a tradesman, while Robert, backed up by the social skills of brother James and removed from the direct financial dealings by the acumen of William, had all the appearance of a gentleman, even if he was not ever secure in his self-appointed position in society. At his death, the tradesman Thomas Chippendale's estate was valued at a meagre £28 2s 9d.

Neither Chippendale nor Brown could be defined as close collaborators of Robert Adam; they were independent artists whose work occasionally coincided with Robert's and they were never part of the Lower Grosvenor Street practice. Here the drawing office was headed by Agostino Brunias who had accompanied Robert from Rome and remained with him in London. Brunias was, however, independent enough to exhibit under his own name at the Free Society of Arts in 1763, as Robert's practice was reaching its peak of activity. Around 1773, and after exhibiting at the Society of Arts and the Royal Academy, Brunias made the fatal mistake of gaining a reputation to equal that of Robert and the two men inevitably quarrelled. Brunias left Britain for St Vincent in the West Indies where he pursued a successful career as a painter of architecture and botany. James had also brought two draughtsmen with him from his tour of Italy, Agostino Scara and Guiseppe Sacco, and they were, in turn, joined by Giuseppe Manocchi and Guiseppe Bonomi, both of whom had probably been summoned thanks to recommendations from Clérisseau. Although we have heard that George Richardson worked for the practice for some time the common language was clearly Italian and the atmosphere was too hectic to allow for the presence of British apprentices, whose pupillage would have been expensive for the partnership and could have slowed the productivity. Robert was a fast worker and expected his staff to equal his pace and not to expect too much in terms of reward. Although some of the office draughtsmen were expensive, energetic Italians keen for a foothold in Britain fitted the bill perfectly.

Robert was naturally cautious about expenditure which was not directly to his own advantage and had often been on the verge of treating Clérisseau with miserly caution. John, who had financed Robert and James, was now excluded from the London practice and had settled very comfortably into the society of Enlightenment Edinburgh, where he maintained the strong friendship between the Adam family and David Hume. To the strictly practical John, Hume's philosophy was so much 'intellectual rope-dancing'. On one occasion Hume called unannounced to find John absent and he was entertained by the Adam daughters who greatly enjoyed the conversation of the great man. Unfortunately Hume was as great in figure as he was in reputation and the chair on which he was seated gradually gave way until, finally, the philosopher landed on the floor to the accompaniment of girlish giggles. Hume's response was, 'Young ladies, you must tell Mr Adam to keep stronger chairs for heavy philosophers,'[23] and collecting his hat and tucking his pet Pomeranian under his arm Hume took his leave, his shoulders heaving with laughter. However laughter was soon to be in short supply in Merchiston.

As in the rest of the United Kingdom, Scotland in the mid eighteenth century was a country of growing prosperity. In Glasgow the import of tobacco had led to the meteoric rise of the 'tobacco barons' who brought vivid colour to the streets with their scarlet capes and gold-topped canes. Three private banks, the Ship, the Arms and the Thistle had opened primarily to answer to their needs. Nationally, the Bank of Scotland, founded in 1695, had, according to Bruce Lenman, been 'tainted by Jacobite associations' and was now rivalled by the Royal Bank of Scotland, founded in 1727. The demand for extended credit by expanding industries such as the Carron ironworks led to a huge increase in the money supply and, between 1744 and 1772, the number of banknotes in circulation increased by an astonishing 1,500 per cent. These boom times also saw the establishment of numerous private banks operating on extended credit from the two principal houses. One of these was the bank operated by Adam and Thomas Fairholme, who were Dalkeith Academy school friends of John Adam's and among the most successful of the independents. John Adam had entrusted his financial investments to the seemingly respectable Fairholme Bank. Adam

Fairholme had been the treasurer of Edinburgh City Council and Thomas had been a director of the Bank of Scotland. Together the brothers had moved the bank to London and by 1763 it was worth £70,000 – at least on paper. However, a year earlier, Fairholme had been warned, first by the Royal Bank of Scotland on 8 February, and then by the Bank of Scotland on 10 February, that no further credit would be available and by 1764 the brothers were bankrupt. Adam Fairholme fled for France, but while his ship was still tied up in an English harbour it was boarded by two Bow Street Runners. Fairholme, presuming that they had come to arrest him, dived overboard but, being unable to swim, he was drowned and John Adam faced ruin. However since John had a preferential claim on the bank, he managed to regain £18,000 in 1767, but the effects were severe.

This disaster caused concern to the 'fat philosopher' David Hume and he wrote to his friend Hugh Blair from Paris on 26 April 1764: 'What you tell me of John Adam gives me great consolation. I had heard the alarming news of his connexions with Fairholme, and things were put in the worst light. I was just ready to write to Ferguson to get from him a just state of the case; but if he has 15 or 18,000 pounds remaining, his industry will recover him, and he may go on, in his usual way of Beneficence and generosity. The family is one of the few to whose civilities I am much beholden, and I retain a lively sense of them.'[24]

It seemed that John went immediately from being a solid mainstay of the firm to being a fragile outpost. As architect to the Board of Ordnance he had been responsible for building a powder magazine in Edinburgh Castle – later the basis for the Military Hospital – and in 1752 he had been awarded the commission to design the City Chambers, although, as we shall see, his bid for the construction contract failed. Now he was threatened with bankruptcy and managed to stay afloat only by selling the Merchiston house and moving his family to Blair Adam. He opened negotiations with a London publisher to sell his father William's drawings as *Vitruvius Scoticus*, although he managed to avoid the necessity. They were finally published by a desperate William in 1812. John retained enough credibility to be consulted over the layout of Edinburgh's New Town and over the construction of the North Bridge spanning the now drained Nor' Loch. Since the bridge collapsed shortly after its opening his contribution to its construction, happily, remains obscure. Less obscure is his part in the building of the Jamaica Street Bridge over the Clyde in Glasgow. The design of this bridge was by William Mylne, brother to the Robert Mylne, who had been ignored by Robert Adam in Rome in 1756 and had been the builder of London's now also demolished and rebuilt Blackfriars Bridge, and John was involved only as contractor. The Glasgow bridge has also been demolished. John's most cherished enterprises were the development of Blair Adam and his extensive property speculation in Edinburgh.

As a result of John's plight, 1764 saw the formal foundation of William Adam & Company with a credit balance of £6,620, almost £40,000 in today's terms. The Philadelphian motive for this enterprise, the protection of John, became less necessary when he was paid the £18,000 owing to him on account of his preference shares in the wreckage of Fairholme's Bank. The account for William Adam & Company was held at Drummond's Bank at Charing Cross. This was an area heavily populated by Scots entrepreneurs and 'it was to provide for their needs that Andrew Drummond, a Perthshire goldsmith of good family and of strong Jacobite sympathies set up shop in 1712 in the Scottish heart of London.'[25] Within four years the firm's account stood at £12,359 5s 11d and by 1771 it was a more than comfortable £40,123 11s 11d (£2,407,380 today). Lower Grosvenor Street was now undoubtedly the principal focus of operations for the Adam brothers.*

From time to time Lower Grosvenor Street was visited by independent artists summoned by Robert for specific tasks of decoration and the most frequent of these was Antonio Pietro Zucchi. Zucchi was born in Venice in 1726 and had been

---

* Drummond's Bank was absorbed into the Royal Bank of Scotland in 1924.

engaged by Robert in 1757 to join the team of engravers working on *The Ruins* although he did not accompany them to Spalatro. He met James in Venice and did travel with him on his ill-fated trip to Pola, living with the *cavalieri* and his entourage in Rome in 1761. By 1763 James thought Zucchi 'a worthy honest lad, a most singular character in this degenerate country.' Most probably as the result of an open invitation, Zucchi came to London with his elder brother Guiseppe in 1766 and quickly established himself as one of Robert's principal decorative painters. One of his first tasks was to paint four panels in the dining room at Kedleston which he filled with representations of the four seasons, embodied by Bacchus, Aeolus, Venus and Apollo. The execution of the paintings would have been left to Zucchi while the overall concept would have been Robert's in consultation with Sir Nathaniel Curzon. On the ceiling are four circles showing the continents of Europe, Africa, Asia and America while the central panel shows Love encircling Fortune. Zucchi's four seasons are very well fitted into the mythical theme dictated by Robert.

At Harewood House, in spite of later restoration, Robert's flair for coordination is visible with martial trophies in plaster bas-relief by Joseph Rose in the entrance hall and large-scale paintings of classical sites by Zucchi in the music room. The ceiling is painted by Angelica Kauffman, of whom more later, and who may have met her husband-to-be Zucchi while working at Kedleston, while the carpet design is by Robert himself. When the partnership undertook the designing of a house, Robert brought all the available skills at his disposal to bear.

This principle applied everywhere, no matter how small the commission might seem. An outstanding example of this is to be found in Kenwood House. The house was magnificently situated on a hill to the north of London and in *The Works* Robert described the site: 'Over the vale through which the water flows, there is a noble view let into the house and terrace, of the city of London, Greenwich Hospital, the river Thames, the ships passing up and down, with an extensive prospect, but clear and distinct on both sides of the river. To the north-east, and west of the house and terrace, the mountainous villages of Highgate and Hampstead form delightful objects.'[26] The house was originally given by the Duke of Argyll to his nephew Lord Bute who sold it to William Murray, Lord Mansfield, Chief Justice of the King's Bench, of whom Dr Johnson, had to admit, slightly grudgingly, that 'much may be made of a Scotchman, if he be caught young'. Mansfield asserted that slavery could not be held to be legal in Great Britain and his judgements revised the laws of evidence as well as establishing the laws of copyright. 'Lord Mansfield exhibited some of the best features of the really great lawyer who can rise above the minima of the law and bring it into the scope of a great agent of civilisation. Law, as a rational science, founded on the basis of moral rectitude, but modified by habit and authority.'[27] This could well be a definition of the ideal in human behaviour as defined by David Hume in his *Treatise*. Lord Mansfield, this personification of the Enlightenment, asked Adam to design a Great Room which would act as a library but was also capable of receiving company.

In the introduction to the drawings in *The Works* Robert said, 'Whatever defects, either in beauty or in composition, shall be discovered in the following designs, they must be imputed to me alone; for the noble proprietor, with his usual liberality of sentiment, gave full scope to my ideas.'[28] This, of course, means that any credit is all his.

Adam solved the problem of dual purpose with great ease, putting his favourite half-domed recesses at each end with bookcases in the apses and then furnishing the central space as a drawing room. Arthur Bolton, in his *Architecture of James and Robert Adam* writes: 'This truly magnificent salon ranks high among the great chambers to be found in England, and takes a leading place in the list of the architect's achievements.'[29] The central portion of the room is a double cube and the half-domed recesses are divided from it by a beam supported by Robert's favourite Corinthian columns. Robert was keen to point out that here he used light tints of pink and green to 'take off the glare of white, so common in every ceiling till of late. This has always appeared to me so cold and unfinished, that I ventured to introduce this variety of grounds. At once to relieve the ornaments, [and] remove the crudeness of the white.' (This is a lesson we are still learning.) Joseph and Anne Rykwert in *The Brothers Adam – The Men and the Style*, point out that however much their credo was one of personal choice from a combination of ancient styles, 'they were men of the environment of Hume and Smith and Ferguson, whatever they might have done to submit antique examples to the demands of individual genius, they could not dismiss geometry as a rational discipline for the designer.'[30] Robert himself could be rigid over the definition of the orders. 'We only acknowledge three Orders, the Doric, the Ionian, and the Corinthian, for as to the Tuscan it is, in fact, no more than a bad and imperfect Doric, and the Composite, or Roman Order, in our opinion is a very disagreeable and awkward mixture of the Corinthian and Ionic, without either grace or beauty.'[31]

On the exterior of the building Robert used stucco manufactured according to Liardet's system, whose patent the brothers had acquired – unfortunately, as we shall see – and it failed, resulting in repairs which, according to Lord Mansfield, would have been cheaper in the most expensive Parian marble. Robert provided a new entrance portico supported by four Ionic columns with a pediment concealing a new attic storey. In *The Works* he is at pains to point out that he put on the new roof before the old one was removed 'thus the house was left habitable and unexposed to the injuries of the weather during the progress of this useful alteration'.[32]

The internal plasterwork was again by Joseph Rose while Zucchi painted Hercules in a central oval, with four lunettes showing Justice embracing Peace – a reference to Lord Mansfield's enlightened view of the law – as well as Commerce, Agriculture and Navigation, his lordship having also reformed maritime law. There were ten other paintings of classical subjects in the compartments of the apses as well as in panels on either side of the fireplace. In all Zucchi painted one centrepiece, four lunettes, eight panels and six large paintings for all of which he was paid £152 5s 0d. As John Swarbrick points out, this was not a meagre amount since Hogarth, at the height of his fame in 1735, had only received £184 8s for his *The Rake's Progress*, a series of eight large canvases, although, for the bulk of his income, Hogarth relied on reproductions of his prints. What is of greater interest is the manner in which Zucchi submitted his account. It is written in French – even the dimensions are given as 'pieds' and 'pouces' rather than his native Italian 'piedi' and 'pollici' – and we can immediately presume two things. Firstly, Lord Mansfield, who had doubtless made a Grand Tour, spoke French but no Italian and Zucchi, in spite of having lived in London for three years was still reluctant to express, in whatever English he had learned, the delicate matter of an invoice. Secondly, since the account is rendered to 'Son Excellence, my Lord Mansfield' and only subscribed as 'examined by Robert Adam' it is clear that Zucchi had not been subcontracted by Adam, but was employed directly by Mansfield. Adam trusted Zucchi's technique and would have delineated the spaces to be filled but the decisions as to subject matter would have been made between Zucchi and his lordship – no doubt with Adam in close attendance. Since Robert spoke Italian his services as an interpreter could have necessitated his attendance at such meetings and allowed his artistic opinions to be heard. At any rate, these were quasi-social encounters, allowing Adam to maintain his position as a gentle-man go-between while Zucchi was clearly an artisan – albeit an artistic artisan.

Zucchi, unlike Robert, did maintain at least one pupil, William Hamilton, whose father had been in the direct employment of Robert as clerk of works at Kenwood. It seems that Robert paid for William to study for nine years in Italy and, on his return, Hamilton used his classical training to paint the landscapes which hang in the circular saloon at Kedleston where they are flanked by mythological scenes painted by Biagio Rebecca in grisaille. Rebecca, as a master of painterly techniques, specialised in such work, producing *trompe-l'oeil* bas-reliefs. He painted panels for Elizabeth Montagu who thought they were 'exquisitely done and much surpass what they are meant to imitate. I afterwards called on Rebecca and saw designs for the pictures over the doors: they are beyond my expectation in composition and effect'.[33] He used his skill for countless practical jokes, on one occasion painting a *trompe-d'oeil* silver coin on the floor and gleefully watching aristocratic courtiers trying to pick it up. At Audley End, where he was working for Robert, he painted a black tea kettle which he left on Lady Howard de Walden's white satin armchair. Like most of the artistic community, he worked cheerfully for a number of masters, including Chambers at Somerset House, with no sense of breaching loyalty with any of them.

The most fascinating of all Robert's contemporaries was the Swiss-born painter Angelica Kauffman, who is well worth a biography of her own. She was the only daughter of Johann Kauffman, himself a painter from Bregenz in Austria, and she was born on 30 October 1741 in Chur, Graubünden, Switzerland. By the age of 13 she was in Milan where she painted the duke, the archbishop and other members of the nobility. Her self-portrait of the time shows her between the figures of music, since she was considering a career as a professional singer, and painting, but in 1759 she decided on painting as her life's work. She became one of the most successful painters in Rome, producing not only history paintings but portraits of David Garrick and the Earl of Exeter among other Grand Tourists. Her relationships with Grand Tourists led to Lady Wentworth taking her under her wing and accompanying Angelica to London in June 1766. Within a week the vivacious 25-year-old immigrant became a close friend of Joshua Reynolds and he, recognising her talent and not a little swayed by her charm, unlocked the doors of society for her. Angelica was immediately thrust into the life of Georgian London, moving into a house in Golden Square to which came a steady stream of aristocratic subjects for portraits. Access to 16 Golden Square was often blocked by the carriages of 'Miss Angel's patrons'. A hundred years previously, Artemesia Gentileschi, existing in an even more male-orientated society, had to suppress her femininity to have any chance of success as a painter, while Kauffman undoubtedly used her flirtatious nature to advance her position. In London she became rich enough to attract the attentions of Count Frederick de Horn, a wealthy Swedish nobleman whom she rashly married in 1767. He was soon revealed as a penniless fraud and, after threatening Angelica and her father with violence, was arrested, signed a deed of separation and left Britain for ever. Her talent and charm combined to allow her to rise above this disaster – as she had risen above the rumour that she was the mistress of Reynolds – and her career continued to prosper.

Art historians have differed widely on whether she ever worked directly for Robert but what is quite certain is that Angelica's ambition was to be accepted as a painter and not as a decorator. In her article in the *Oxford Dictionary of National Biography*, Wendy Wassing Roworth is quite definite: 'Kauffman may have provided some sketches for Adam, but she was not responsible for the many decorative works attributed to her.' Fanny Burney records that Angelica carried out decorations for Elizabeth Montagu at her house in Portman Square which was under the overall design of Stuart, while she is credited with painting the ceiling of the music room at Harewood House, this time for Adam. In this case she had painted pictures on behalf of Joshua Reynolds who had been commissioned to supply them. She is also accepted as the painter of the walls of the dining room and all the ceilings in Stratford House, Stratford Place, off Oxford Street, as well as many other houses. Given Robert's often intolerant attitude to other talents, it is likely that he avoided a conflict of tastes, always preferring to use decorators who would work according to his close instruction. Wendy Wassing Roworth, in her *Angelica Kauffman, a Continental Artist in Georgian England*, has said, 'The myth has endured, reinforced by the fact of her marriage to Antonio Zucchi who did have a long and close association with Robert Adam.'[34] She painted four ceiling panels for the council chamber of the Royal Academy, of which she had been one of the founding members in 1768. Since this was in Somerset House, designed by Chambers, she, like her colleagues, clearly worked for whoever would employ them. These ceiling panels are now in the entrance hall of the Royal Academy's current premises in Burlington House, Piccadilly. Nowhere does her name appear in Robert Adam's accounts with Drummond's Bank.

On 14 July 1781 she married Antonio Zucchi and five days later the couple left Britain for Rome with her earnings of £14,000 – approximately £840,000 in modern terms. The couple became respected members of the international artistic community, and from Zucchi's death in 1793 until her own in 1807 aged 66 she remained a focus for all those interested in painting who passed through Rome, including Goethe, Canova and Sir William Hamilton. Angelica Kauffman had a probably well-founded reputation as a flirt, but the tales of her as Goethe and Canova's mistress are most probably no more than deliciously scandalous invention.

Robert had acted as a successful go-between for the aristocratic house builders and the various artists they employed and he was a landowner in his own right. But it was a tiny parcel of Scottish land and could not equal the acres of Yorkshire or Worcestershire owned by his wealthy patrons. He had been welcome at their tables in Rome, but in London, he was on a lower rung.

An account of Mrs Elizabeth Montagu's character and relations with Robert give a clue as to his place in society. James Adam claimed that she was a distant relative, having been once a Robinson or Robertson, but there is no evidence for this claim. She had married Edward Montagu, the grandson of the Earl of Sandwich and the couple owned houses at Sandleford Priory, near Newbury, and at Hill Street in Mayfair. Hannah More said of Mrs Montagu and her house, 'She is not only the finest lady I ever saw, she lives in the highest style of magnificence; her apartments and tableware are in the most splendid taste', and Dr Johnson thought: 'The lady exhibits more mind in conversation than any person I ever met with.'[35] In the 1750s Elizabeth had commissioned Gilbert West to redecorate her huge dressing room in London in the Chinese style. Ten years later she had tired of this décor and asked

'Mr Adam and his workmen' to visit her. 'He came at the head of a regiment of artificers, an hour after the time he had promised, the bricklayer talked about alterations to be made in a wall, the stone-mason was as eloquent about the coping of the said wall . . .'[36] In short the lady became bored with Adam, dismissed him and sent for Stuart. He was just as unsatisfactory and Robert was forgiven, although she wrote to a friend, 'Mr Adam is a traitor to betray me into the vanity of a marble chimneypiece'.[37] On 11 October 1766 Robert wrote to her:

> I hope this month we shall nearly finish your room in Hill Street. The gilders are at work and I am doing all I can to push them on . . . The paintings are almost finished, and the moment the gilders are done I shall put them up. I cut away that disagreeable projection over the chimney alto-gether, so that now the cornice runs round the whole room without interruption and the ceiling becomes square the effect of which you will like . . . I should also wish it done, that you may see the effect of the whole at once, as I am not without hopes that it will have a striking one and should not be a little happy that it met with your approbation.[38]

As always here is the artisan's anxiety for approbation, without any of the arrogance of a self-styled great artist. By 8 January 1767 he had completed his work for her and she was happy. 'My dressing room is wonderfully pretty. Mr Adam has done his best, he has exerted much genius on the doors in emulation of his rival Stewart [sic]. I assure you the dressing room is now just the female of the great room, for sweet attractive grace, for winning softness, for delicacy, for *le je ne sais quoi* it is incomparable.'[39] By the early 1770s this room, decorated with flowers and cupids, and later to be known as the Cupidon Room, was large enough for receptions to be held in it.

Mrs Montagu's Cupidon Room was a focus for a certain exclusive branch of London society, for it was here that the 'Bluestockings' met. Along with the Anglo-Irish Elizabeth Vesey

– wealthy after her marriage to Agmondesham Vesey, member of parliament and accountant general for Ireland – Elizabeth Montagu founded a series of evening assemblies for literary and artistic conversation. According to the poet Hannah More these gatherings provided 'Learning without pedantry, good taste without affectation and conversation without calumny'.[40] There were no cards or gaming and talk of politics was discouraged. An early attender at them was the naturalist Benjamin Stillingfleet, one of whose many eccentricities was to wear blue stockings. When he ceased attending, 'his absence was felt as so great a loss that it used to be said, "We can do nothing without the blue-stockings"'.[41] Admiral Boscawen's wife was another regular guest and the admiral applied the name 'Bluestockings' to the entire company which, from time to time, included Samuel Johnson, with his attendant biographer Boswell, Sir Joshua Reynolds, Edmund Burke, David Garrick and, inevitably, Horace Walpole. However neither of the brothers Adam are ever mentioned in her guest lists; for all their efforts they were people of 'the middling sort' and were perceived as lacking the status which would allow them social equality. Since architects were employed and rendered accounts to be paid, then, as employees, no matter what their skill and artistry might be, they could never be invited to join this level of society. 'The alliance of money and gentility was calculated to maintain the morale and sense of superiority of propertied people. Politeness was the mark of an immensely vigorous but also a remorselessly snobbish society.'[42] The club certainly existed until 1815 when Rowlandson lampooned its meetings in his cartoon 'The Breaking up of the Bluestocking Club', showing a bare-breasted fist fight with flying furniture and overturned chamber pots. Of the plentiful underwear on view there are no blue stockings.

In her letters Mrs Montagu often linked 'Mr Adam and Mr Brown' as though they were partners in a retail firm and she clearly shopped for architects much as she would for bonnets, regarding her architects as no more important than her milliners.

Lady Shelbourne went shopping in 1768 and made an entry in

her diary. 'Saturday we went first to Zucchi's where we saw some ornaments for our ceilings . . . from there to Mayhew and Inch where is some beautiful cabinet work . . . from thence to Cipriani's where we saw some beautiful drawings and crayon pictures . . . from thence to Zuccarelli's where we also saw some pictures doing for us and from thence home it being half an hour past four.'[43] The penetration of the decoration market by Italian craftsmen is clear as is the glee with which their offerings were taken up by the fashionable arbiters of taste. To the aristocratic mind, craftsmen provide *objets d'art* while architects provided houses and decorations.

Thus architects were not regarded as part of the intelligentsia and Reynolds said of their art, 'It remains only to speak a few words of architecture, which does not come under the denomination of an imitative art. It applies itself like music, (and, I believe, we may add poetry) directly to the imagination, without the intervention of any kind of imitation.'[44] On another occasion the Adam style was described as 'little more than a new combination of those images which have been previously gathered and deposited in the memory'.[45] Horace Walpole found Adam's work 'gingerbread and sippets of embroidery'. Robert was a robust defender of architecture as an art form in its own right and in *The Works* he gave a spirited defence. 'Architecture has not, like some other arts, an immediate standard in nature, to which the artist can always refer, and which would enable the skilful instantly to decide with respect to the degree of excellence obtained in any work. In Architecture it must be formed and improved by a correct taste, and diligent study of the beauties exhibited by the great masters in their productions; and it is only by profound meditation upon these that one becomes capable of distinguishing between what is graceful and what is inelegant: between that which possesses and that which is destitute of harmony.'[46]

Robert Adam did little to ingratiate himself with the existing establishment of artists, preferring that his reputation spoke for itself, but possibly thanks to Robert's casual arrogance, Reynolds did not invite the brothers to become academicians, although, under his presidency, two architects did become members of the Royal Academy, one being the egregious Chambers.

Chambers's mind then became focused on founding an organisation which would act as an academy for artists; an idea which he formalised in a paper proposing such a 'well regulated School or Academy of Design' which would also hold an Annual Exhibition. This proposal, endorsed by 22 others including Zuccarelli, Bartolozzi, and Kauffman he presented to George III on 8 December 1768. Events moved at amazing speed, with the king attaching his signature on 19 December and the first meeting of what had become the Royal Academy of Arts taking place on 14 December 1768. Chambers was to be the treasurer of the Royal Academy while Joshua Reynolds, after some hesitation, accepted the Presidency; he 'declined to accept the honour until he had consulted his friends Dr Johnson and Edmund Burke and that it was not until a fortnight later that he gave his consent.'[47] There were 36 founding members, including Angelica Kauffman and Thomas Gainsborough, but not including either of the Adam brothers.

Although Robert had been given the largely meaningless title of Royal Architect and was now the most fashionable architect in Britain, the insecurity of the incomer still burned inside him. Chambers held the royal favour, while others worked regularly without the cachet Robert so desperately sought. Robert longed to have the opportunity to build an entire house from its very beginnings, but with the possible exception of Dumfries House such an opportunity had evaded him. It came with a commission to build at Mersham-le-Hatch in Kent. The house was built for Sir William Knatchbull, who sadly died in 1763 when the construction was only in its first year. The building is unique in that only Robert and William Rose were involved in the plain elegant and classical design of the two-storey house with flanking wings. Built entirely of brick – three million are said to have been used in its construction – it stands alone as Adam in its entirety, free from interference by the client and without the need to adapt or alter what already existed.

But Robert wanted more. He wanted to build a great public building and this would almost certainly mean having a share of the scant royal patronage, although even there limitations were being imposed and Prime Minister Grenville had drastically cut back Chambers' plans for the refurbishment of Buckingham Palace. This was an early sign of the conflict between king and parliament, but without influence in either place Robert stood little chance. Chambers had the king's ear, and therefore Robert must take another route.

He would enter parliament. 'Men went there to "make a figure", and no more dreamt of a seat in the House in order to benefit humanity than a child dreams of a birthday cake that others may eat it; *which is perfectly normal and no way reprehensible.*'*[48] There was to be a general election in 1768 and Robert would stand as a prospective member for Kinross.

The House of Commons of the 1760s, with its 558 members, bore little resemblance to our present assembly. After the Act of Union of 1707 Scotland returned 60 members, 45 in the counties and 15 from the burghs, voted for by 2,600 electors in the counties and 1,500 in the burghs. Most of these seats had members who 'held the interest', that is to say, they were the nominees of great landlords with their own interests at the forefront of their membership. 'It was even easier there for the dispenser of official patronage to control the representation by the more dignified and cleanly methods of influence and favour . . . In the counties the electors were so few that it was generally possible for a member to be on visiting terms with most of his constituents.'[49] The idea of members being 'party' men had not yet gained currency and their alliances were defined by personal interest. This had caused the separation of the king's supporters from the government led by William Pitt the Elder, who confused the issue even further in 1766 when he took the title of the Earl of Chatham and decamped for the House of Lords, leaving the Commons under the control of Lord North. 'There was a period

* Author's italics. RG.

of uneasy calm at Westminster, the Stamp Acts had been passed in 1765, taxing the American colonists, who were only beginning to be a political force of any great power, the Seven Years War was over and the revolutions of the 1770s were still to come. The General Election of 1768 took place at a curious time in politics: there was a lull between two periods of intense conflict.'[50]

There was, however, intense conflict in Kinross in the years leading up to the election. Kinross only elected a member in every second election, alternating with Clackmannanshire, and the seat was currently held by John Bruce Hope. From 1764 John Adam began to create an opposition favouring either himself or his brother Robert. There were 26 voters in the electorate and in 1766 Hope had put his support behind William Bayne, his nephew. In 1766 one candidate standing against John was William Bayne, supported by Hope, another was General Irwin – presently on garrison duties at Gibraltar – but represented in Britain by his agent Lord George Sackville. Robert now declared his interest and, as an opening compromise, agreed to stand aside in return for the rotten borough of East Grinstead – a constituency largely composed of the Ashdown Forest. This borough was owned by the Duke of Dorset, and it returned no member. The duke merely said that the seat was quite adequately represented by a black stone in the wall surrounding his estate. Since General Irwin had already bought two votes and Lord George, in an early version of an opinion poll, claimed that 'the temper of the country is to wish the affair might be accommodated and that you [General Irwin] may be the representative'[51], no compromise was acceptable. The general returned from Gibraltar and set about forming an alliance with William Bayne, but this antagonised Bayne who combined with John to support Robert, and on 5 April 1768 Robert Adam became the Member of Parliament for Kinross by sixteen votes to three. The other seven voters abstained in one way or another. Robert held the seat for six years, until 1774, when it was Clackmannanshire's turn to be represented. He never showed any interest in standing again and in 1788 all the votes in Kinross were bought by George Graham, a returning nabob.

In the constituency Robert was more notable for his absence than his presence, but in 1771 he did refurbish the County Hall in Kinross, adding a three-storey bowed extension to the south front, complete with a plaque commemorating that this had been built at the expense of 'Robert Adam, Knight of the Shire', or in modern terms, member of parliament. It is a significant building in the town and the plaque leaves no one in doubt as to who presented it to the town. Architecturally, it is of interest since it stands on the corner of two streets and in the elbow of a bend in the main street. Thus the bowed front becomes a circular diversion for the eye, acting as a hinge for the bend. Much later, in London, John Nash used the same device at the much grander junction of Upper Regent Street with Portland Place with his church of All Souls, Langham Place acting as the pivot. Even his most humble buildings were given all of Robert Adam's expertise, and his innovations were incorporated into the general vocabulary of architecture and town planning by later generations.

In the House of Commons, Robert was an infrequent speaker, but a regular attender, usually supporting Bute or the Duke of Argyll and revelling in the gossip which he relayed with glee to his friends. Alexander Carlyle wrote: 'I then lodged in New Bond Street with my aunt, and resorted often at supper to Robert Adam's, whose sisters were very agreeable, and where we had the latest news from the House of Commons, of which he was a member, and which he told us in the most agreeable manner, and with very lively comments.'[52] As told by Alexander Carlyle, Robert – at least for the time being – used the House of Commons as his club. He was clearly a clubbable man who could leave the considerable worries of the day behind him to relax with friends. Much later in 1778 when troubles had gathered around him Boswell said of him: 'An ingenious gentleman was mentioned concerning whom both Robertson and Ramsay agreed that he had a constant firmness of mind: for, after a laborious day, and amidst a multiplicity of cares and anxieties, he would sit down with his sisters and be quite cheerful and good-humoured. Such a disposition it was observed was a happy gift of nature.'[53] He was happy among his fellow Scots, in spite of the phobic atmosphere of eighteenth-century London, and their regular meeting place was in the British Coffee House, in Cockspur Street. Perhaps they felt that the name of the coffee house gave them some camouflage. Robert had redesigned the building in 1770. He gave free rein to his imagination with a site only 20 feet wide providing a large public space on the ground floor with two private rooms for 'company' on the first floor. On the exterior the ground-floor windows are flanked by six columns in the 'Spalatro' order, while the first floor has Ionic columns with Corinthian on the second floor. These floors have tripartite windows and, on the first floor, the windows are flanked by giant urns. The effect of the façade is welcoming and fanciful, fronting a building in which one would expect to meet men of character and imagination, similar to the architect.

Robert's election to parliament did mean that he had to resign as joint architect to the Office of Works and he passed the position on to James. The coveted position of Comptroller of the Office of Works had been held since 1758 by Henry Flitcroft, a rigid traditionalist, who died in 1769 at the age of 72 to be succeeded by Chambers. With the royal patronage in the hands of Chambers there was now no realistic hope of a large public project coming to Lower Grosvenor Street.

CHAPTER NINE

Four Scotchmen by the Name of Adams

आई

Two other major projects were occupying the draughtsmen of Lower Grosvenor Street in the late 1760s and one of them was conveniently under construction only a few hundred yards away. Lord Bute had acquired some land on the south side of Berkeley Square and intended to build a palatial town house on the site. It was screened from Piccadilly by Devonshire House and would stand at right angles to the square. Lord Shelburne had owned the site and had agreed plans with Robert but, by 1762, he had sold the land along with the work in progress to Bute. Bute's unpopularity was growing and he fell out spectacularly with Pitt over the Treaty of Paris, although the treaty was regarded by everyone else as a huge success. He was eventually forced from office when he supported a bill to introduce a tax on cider. When Bute left the government in April 1763 his direct influence as a source of patronage went with him, although he retained the king's ear and was now known simply as the 'Favourite'. He continued his correspondence with George III from his house at Luton Hoo in Hampshire which Robert had been building for him since 1767. In *The Works* Robert said of Lord Bute, 'We are happy in having this opportunity of expressing to the world that gratitude which we never ceased to feel, for the protection, favour and friendship with which we have always been honoured by his Lordship.'[1] Robert had clearly recovered from the slight he felt at first meeting Bute.

A certain Mrs Delany visited Luton Hoo on 14 September 1774 and wrote to the Viscountess of Andover. 'I lead you to where I have lately been to Luton Park. To a very fine house, a very fine park a fine situation, (the house not finished). It is very capacious and elegant, and after walking through a grand apartment with a delightful saloon, and a magnificent and most agreeable library nobly furnished, your ladyship must please go up 42 steps to a very long gallery, which conveys you to at last 4 complete apartments of large and lofty rooms, all elegantly furnished without ostentation, but well suited. As to pictures, vases, marbles, and a long et cetera of curiosities it would be endless to recount them!'[2]

Dr Johnson, who visited in the company of James Boswell, approved of the house and preferred it to Kedleston. 'It is a very stately place, indeed; in the house magnificence is not sacrificed to convenience, nor convenience to magnificence. The library is very splendid; the dignity of the rooms is very great.'[3] When Boswell pointed out that among the sites they might visit there was a botanical garden, Johnson responded, 'Surely, sir, all gardens are botanical?'

Having no longer any need for a town house, and discovering that he would have his bitter enemy the Duke of Devonshire as a neighbour, on 16 September 1765 Bute sold the now finished house back to Lord Shelburne. It had been designed very much with Lord Bute in mind and since 'the earl spent much of the day in his libraries'[4], Robert produced no fewer than four detailed drawings for the library which consisted of two domed and shelved octagons linked by a gallery with columns enclosing a screen of more shelves. As well as agreeing to complete the building to Adam's design at his own expense, Bute had to surrender this sumptuous library to Shelburne. According to the *London Chronicle* of October 1765, the price was £22,000, but Shelburne paid only interest of £900 a year for eight years and then settled the payment of the capital. Bute spent the rest of his life in semi-retirement either in Italy or on his estate in Hampshire. However he still had the king's ear and wielded enough influence for the general distrust of Scotsmen to continue – as the Adam brothers would discover.

Lord Shelburne had started his career as Sir William Petty, an aide-de-camp to George III and close friend of Pitt. He was responsible for negotiating the Treaty of Versailles which, in 1783, gave America its independence, and was created Marquess of Landsowne. The house on Berkeley Square therefore became Landsdowne House.

By January 1766 the Shelburnes were cheerfully treating Robert as a jobbing craftsman as Lady Shelburne's watch was passed to him by his lordship to have the chain mended. He even supplied six slates for Lady Shelburne 'to model on' for six shillings, and she 'consulted Adam on the furniture for my painted antechamber'. Robert was already well known to the family since he had built a mausoleum for Shelburne's mother on their estate at Bowood in Wiltshire. Robert had also carried out extensive renovation and decoration inside the house; one of his most beautiful ceilings is that of the Great Drawing Room, now incorporated in Lloyd's building in Leadenhall Street, in the city of London.* In Berkeley Square the town house was built in the grand style with typical Adam features. There were two drawing rooms linked by a rotunda – to add 'movement' – one of which is now in the museum in Philadelphia. The dining room is today in New York's Metropolitan Museum, where the frieze has been erected upside down. Shelburne was strongly recommended to let Adam have his own way: 'it is his own plan, disturbed by nobody in any respect, and, according to the ground, nothing I think could be better.'[5] The only discordant note was when the earl visited Italy in 1771 and took the advice of Gavin Hamilton to acquire sculptures for the great gallery and undertake designs by the Roman architect Pannini. This gallery was never built. What was immediately important was that Robert had now been responsible for a great town house in the most fashionable quarter of London. This was a significant step forward in his career.

However, Robert's burning ambition was still to build a 'Grand Project'. This had been rehearsed, albeit in a small way, in 1766

* A detailed account of the technicalities involved in the transfer of the ceiling can be found in *Architect and Surveyor*, vol. 61, no. 2, April 1986, p. 16.

when the brothers were asked by Sir James Lowther, later the Earl of Lonsdale, to design and build a model village for his tenants and workers near Penrith in the Lake District. During the 1768 election Lowther tried to unite the counties of Cumberland and Westmoreland, for which he would be the sole member, and he used the influence of Bute to achieve it. The model village scheme produced an architectural oddity and as a benevolent gesture towards the workforce it was a failure. It was visited in 1802 by Richard Warner, who stopped to smile at the 'fantastical incongruity of its plan; which exhibits the grandest features of city architecture, the Circus, the Crescent and the Square, upon the mean scale of a peasant's cottage. These groups of houses were built for the labourers of Lord Lonsdale but from their desolate deserted appearance it should seem that no sufficient encouragement had been held out to their inhabitants to continue in them.'[6] The model village had been only partly built, was now clearly deserted and lasted only as an example of the brothers' willingness to undertake any commission. In fact, the commission may simply have been given by Lowther as a sweetener to a known friend of Bute's which would explain the brothers' lack of interest in, and the workers' lack of enthusiasm for, the village. Lowther's scheme of amalgamating the constituencies also failed.

Nearer to London, Robert had been involved throughout the 1760s in a building in the Middlesex countryside at Osterley, now a stop on the Underground railway line to Heathrow airport. The construction of the house lasted well into the next decade and showed quite clearly Robert's facility for experimentation and novelty. It had originally been built in Elizabethan times as Osterley Park, and had been the property of Francis Child. He had sold the house to one Nicholas Barbon, a building speculator, on a mortgage which Barbon failed to repay. When Child repossessed the house he discovered that Barbon had pulled down much of the Elizabethan structure and rendered the house uninhabitable. The Child family had become spectacularly rich dealing in the City of London in that most attractive of commodities, gold bullion. Rebuilding the framework of the house appears to have started while Robert was in Italy under an unknown architect, but Francis Child, a younger son of the original Francis, approached Robert early in 1761 for a reconstruction.

This would not be the complete creation that Robert aspired to since some work had already been done, possibly by Chambers, but in 1761 Adam submitted plans for a very conventional eighteenth-century house with a central courtyard surrounded by projecting wings. Before this could be built, however, Francis Child died and the estate passed to his brother Robert who agreed to fresh plans from the brothers Adam. At the western front there were curved steps meeting in a perron with an Etruscan style grotto under its platform. The forecourt was extended greatly and acquired a deep hexastyle portico with an elegant pediment over it. The Elizabethan frontage had completely gone and the portico gave on to an open courtyard with the appearance of a roofless drawing room. The hall is, much like that at Syon, rectangular, with domed and niched apses at either end, but each now contains fireplaces. The walls are decorated in grey and white, with a black and white floor reflecting the decoration of the ceiling. Although both might seem coldly formal to the arriving visitor it must be remembered that these rooms were where visitors would be greeted by servants in livery. Adam was particular about fitting function to design, even designing the keyhole plates. A door to the right led across a narrow service corridor to the eating room and library.

'We have adopted a beautiful variety of light mouldings, gracefully formed delicately enriched and arranged with propriety and skill. We have introduced a great diversity of ceilings, freezes [sic] and decorated pilasters, and have added grace and beauty to the whole, by a mixture of grotesque stucco, and painted ornaments, together with flowing *rainçeau*, with its fanciful figures and winding foliage.'[7] Eileen Harris comments that 'Adam's eye for the picturesque encouraged him to regard rooms as scenery'[8].

The eating room, thus, has a warmer ambience, with wall panels in duck-egg blue decorated with white stucco and medallions painted by Zucchi. The walls themselves are pink contrasting with the white marble fireplace under a painting of *An Offering to Ceres*, also by Zucchi. The ceiling, too, is in blue and pink, and has an oval centrepiece, itself inside an oval of bound reeds garlanded with *rainçeaux* of vine leaves. As promised by Robert it was a very suitable setting for the consumption of food and wine.

Beside the eating room is the library where Robert took ideas he had already used in the gallery at Syon to surround the bookshelves with Ionic pilasters, the shelves holding books bound to Adam's designs. In both the library and eating room are carved chairs with backs shaped in the manner of lyres. They were made by John Linnell, a carver and gilder who had worked previously for the brothers at Kedleston and Shardeloes. Other lyre-back chairs by Chippendale are at Nostell Priory and the style quickly became widely fashionable. 'The light and elegant ornaments, the varied compartments in the ceilings of Mr Adam, imitated from the ancient works in the baths and villas of the Romans, were soon applied in designs for chairs, tables carpets and in every other species of furniture . . . such was the electric power of this revolution in art.'9

There now was a gap of some seven years while work continued in other parts of the house. On 21 June 1773, during this gap, Osterley was visited by the ubiquitous Horace Walpole who gave his impressions to his friend the Countess of Ossory:

Oh! The palace of palaces! – and yet a palace *sans crown sans coronet*, but such expense! Such taste! Such profusion! And yet half an acre produces all the rents that furnish such magnificence. The old house I have often seen, which was built by Sir Thomas Gresham, but it is so improved and enriched that all the Pierces and Seymours of Syon, must die of envy. There is a double portico that fills the space between the towers of the front, and is as noble as the

Propyleum of Athens. There is a hall, a library, breakfast room, eating room, all *chefs d'oeuvres* of Adam, a gallery one hundred and thirty feet long and a drawing room worthy of Eve before the fall. Mrs Child's dressing room is full of pictures, gold filigree china and japan . . . and then in the drawing room I mentioned, there are door cases, and a crimson and gold frieze, that I believe were borrowed from the Palace of the Sun; and then the park – is the ugliest spot of ground in the universe – and so I returned comforted.[10]

Robert turned his invention to a sequence of three rooms: a Gobelins tapestry room, a velvet state bedroom and a painted Etruscan dressing room. Eileen Harris in her *Guide to Osterley* points out that the rooms were in French, English and Italian styles with the colours red, green and blue symbolising fire, earth and air, and the mirrors representing water. The state bedroom had an outrageous and overpowering bed with richly decorated pier glasses. As was his custom, Robert was also designing intimate objects for Mrs Child, including a work bag and a fire screen with the Child family crest of an eagle which his patroness embroidered herself. So we can presume that client/architect relations were still good and that Robert's designs were in accord with his patrons' tastes.

The bedroom was flanked on one side by a room hung with tapestries from the Gobelin workshop designed by Boucher and Neilson, who had also been responsible for the tapestries at Croome Court. While the concept of this room might be thought to be looking backwards, the dressing room flanking the bedroom on the other side was the most advanced yet attempted by Robert. Its designs were Etruscan and caused an immediate stir. In 1778 Walpole was forced to revise his previous opinion and was horrified. He approved of the bedroom and the Gobelin tapestries, but, 'the last chamber after these two proud rooms chills you . . . it would be a pretty waiting room in a garden . . . It is called Estruscan and is painted all over like Wedgwood's ware. It is like going out of a palace into a potter's field.' Walpole, who had probably never been in a potter's field in his life, was always repelled by novelty – unless it was introduced by himself – and Etruscan decoration was an undoubted novelty. Chambers added his voice, criticising the 'trifling gaudy ceilings, which, composed as they are of little round squares, hexagons and ovals, excite no other idea than that of a dessert upon the plates on which are dished out bad copies of different antiques.'[11] He had said much the same of the ceiling in the red drawing room at Syon. It is also worth noting that at Syon it had been Walpole who recommended placing Etruscan funerary urns along the wall of the long gallery, but now this was the style he described as 'gingerbread with sippets of embroidery!'

In *The Works* the brothers claim that this decoration differed from anything 'hitherto practised in Europe'. This was a rash claim since it must have been seen in Italy at around 500 BC. They did claim to have consulted a library full of learned works but tactfully ignored two key publications. The first of these was the catalogue of Sir William Hamilton's collection of antique vases, *Recueil d'Antiquities Etrusques, Grecques et Romanes*. Hamilton claimed his vases were Greek, although they were clearly Etruscan, and were illustrated in four volumes of drawings in 1767. The second was *Diverse Maniere d'adornare i Camini*, published in Rome in 1749 by their old friend Piranesi. The full title of Piranesi's book is *Diverse Manners of decorating Chimneys and all other parts of Houses taken from Egyptian, Tuscan and Grecian Architecture*, and it was published in Italian, French and English in a single volume. The idea that they had used this book as a sole source of patterns is false since, as its name implies, it is composed of largely heavily worked illustrations of fireplace decorations. However, the designs of the overmantels strongly show the Etruscan influence. Piranesi gives a closely argued justification for using designs from any source provided they achieve a 'union of taste and ornamentation.'[12] The style had been adopted by Josiah Wedgwood in his new factory at fashionably named Etruria Works and he threw six black vases each inscribed with '*Artes Etruriae Renascuntur*'. All of this was enough of a seed planted in Robert's fertile mind to allow the style to grow over an entire room. Sheets of paper with a pale blue-grey background were painted by Peter Borgnis in black and terracotta then pasted onto canvas before being mounted on the walls. Playing boys and dancing figures appear in the traditional Etruscan colours on a black background. Robert had planned a similar decoration in 1773 for a room in Lord Derby's house at 23 Grosvenor Square, which has now been demolished, but changed his plans and used the style at Osterley. In *The Works* the brothers claimed this use of the style as a completely original idea, particular to themselves. 'The style of the ornament and the colouring of the Countess of Derby's dressing room are both evidently imitated from the vases and urns of the Etruscans, yet we have not been able to discover, either in our researches into antiquity, or in the works of modern artists, any idea of applying this taste to the decoration of apartments.'[13] Both Robert and James had seen such designs on apartments at Herculaneum.

With grand houses now in construction all over England, a large town house being built in Berkeley Square and a reputation as the most fashionable architects in Britain, the brothers could be excused for relaxing. The firm still had time for small commissions and in February 1770 they were in correspondence with the Earl of Findlater over the building of a suitable coach.[14] They had produced plans, sections and elevations for the earl in 1767 but nothing had been built. Sir William Chambers was a rival, but the brothers had enough commissions to be able to exist in healthy competition.

Now a new threat to their position arrived in the person of the 24-year-old James Wyatt. Wyatt was the son of a prosperous farmer and builder in Staffordshire and had come under the patronage of Sir William Bagot, his rich neighbour. Bagot sent the boy to Italy with his own brother, who was secretary to the ambassador in Venice, where he might receive an education in the arts. Wyatt's younger brother, John, was established as a surgeon in London and on James's return both brothers went into partnership with P.E. Turst who owned a site in Oxford

Street. Their idea was to build a 'Winter Ranelagh' as a weather-proof pleasure garden with the same range of entertainments and the shareholders invested the huge sum of £60,000. Wyatt exhibited his drawings for the scheme at the Royal Academy and, as a result, in 1770, was elected an associate member. He would become a full member in 1785. The principal feature of what became the Pantheon was a vast dome, as the name would imply, based on the Pantheon in Rome, which Robert had already interpreted at Kedleston Hall. To ease any construction difficulties Wyatt hired most of the workmen who had worked for Robert at Kedleston. The Pantheon opened in 1772 to universal acclaim, with even Horace Walpole calling it 'the most beautiful edifice in England'. Commissions flowed to Wyatt. The building was criticised only for its extravagance as it was lit with thousands of candles which only enhanced its reputation as a place to be seen. Like its fellows at Ranelagh and Vauxhall it was a lively marriage market:

> There I beheld full many a youthful maid,
> Like colts for sale to public view display'd

wrote the satirist William Combe. 'At the Pantheon it seemed that vulgarity was dimmed and only the politeness illuminated.'[15] It was burnt down in 1792. Sir John Soane said of it, 'The Pantheon in Oxford Street affords another melancholy example of the effects of fire. Even a slight inspection of this drawing will cause every lover of architecture to lament the loss of this masterly composition.'[16]

The emergence of Wyatt merely acted as a spur to the ambitions of Robert. The threat of war with the American colonies had caused the aristocracy to express caution over large investments and the building boom of the 1760s was coming to an end. It seemed plain that if the firm of the brothers Adam was to expand, a new direction had to be found. It was also clear that there were unlikely to be any commissions for great public buildings; George III was largely uninterested in building for posterity and, if he were, the most likely recipient of such favours would be Chambers. The great palace at Spalatro still burned in the brothers' memory and a development of luxury apartments on the banks of the Thames constructed on a similar scale was in the forefront of their minds. Nothing like it had ever been built in Britain and the risk would be enormous.

In Lower Grosvenor Street, Robert dreamed, James followed and William worked out how to afford such a project. Then he wrote to John on 20 February 1768, 'Bob and Jamie have secured Durham Yard for the brotherhood at £1,200 per annum for 99 years which you will say is a bold stroke . . . Lord Mansfield told Bob yesterday when he dined with him that he would give him 100 percent for his bargain . . . before Bob comes down the survey will be made and the plans put into some form for your examination, approbation and amendments. It is at present our Hobby Horse.'[17] On 25 March 1768, a 99-year lease was granted by the trustees of the Duke of St Albans for £1,200 annually. The duke was bankrupt and in 1770 he was imprisoned for debt in Brussels so the trustees were glad of the money. There was a delay in signing the lease and it did not become effective until 23 June 1769. John was another signatory to the lease and had come to London to assist in the project. So great would be the expense that it could easily break the finances of the entire family and therefore the complete agreement of all four was necessary. We can be confident that, at least in Lower Grosvenor Street, the argument was most vigorously expounded by Robert. Publicly, the development would commemorate the brothers' combined skills and would carry their name. It would be, in Greek 'ἀδελφοί', 'The Brothers', and in English, 'The Adelphi'.

Robert had fervently wished for a royal palace, a university, a ministry or hospital which would carry the name of the Adam brothers for posterity, but this development would go a long way to satisfy this ambition. In *The Works* Robert had said:

Public buildings are the most splendid monuments of a great and opulent people. The purpose for which they are intended admit of a magnificence in the design and require solidity in the construction. Such buildings must, of course, contain great and spacious apartments for the meeting of numerous assemblies, and consequently they are susceptible of more grandeur, as well in their external decoration, as in their internal distribution. The frequent, but necessary, repetition of windows in private houses, cuts the façade into minute parts, which render it difficult, if not impossible, to preserve that greatness and simplicity of composition, which by imposing on the imagination strikes the mind. The master who has not an opportunity to distinguish himself by displaying his abilities in works of real greatness, will naturally betake himself to other resources, and, following the most approved examples of Greece and Rome, endeavour to call forth the admiration of mankind by the beauty and variety of his forms, by the richness and delicacy of his ornamental decorations. All these may be adopted with great propriety in small rooms and private apartments.[18]

The riverside site leased by the brothers was large, running from north and south, between the Strand and the river, and east to west from the Savoy to the estate of the Duke of Buckingham. That estate comprised George Court, Villiers Street, Duke Street, Buckingham Street, and to complete his name, Of Alley. The Adelphi site had held Durham House, the one-time home of Sir Walter Raleigh, converted in 1609 to the New Exchange, and replaced in 1737 with 11 houses. One of these had been improved by Robert for his friend James Coutts. Coutts was the son of the ex-lord provost of Edinburgh and a partner in the bank of Campbell and Coutts whose premises were at Durham Court on the Strand. The rest of the area was in a ruinous and wretched state but with the expansion of London, both eastward from the West End and westward from the City and Covent Garden, this was a prime site.

This fact had not escaped Robert's fellow architect John Gwynn who lived in nearby Leicester Fields. His house was actually in the garden of James Paine. Gwynn had drawn up a plan driving streets north and south to the river and, in the centre of the development, building a square to supplement Covent Garden. The plan appeared in 1776 in his publication *London and Westminster Improved*, but it was too late. 'At the very time, however, that this was written, four Scotchmen, patronised by the unpopular Lord Bute, were contemplating the transformation of the site on a plan of the most daring originality.'[19] The City of London did not like seeing what they considered their own property being snatched from under their feet by upstart 'Scotchmen'. But the 'Scotchmen' had been drawing up plans for this project for some time before signing the lease; some are dated early in 1769 and on 13 September of the same year a joint bank account of £7,502 1s 10d in the names of Robert and James Adam was started with Drummond's Bank. The brothers were eager to start work. This initially involved clearing the site and levelling the ground. The project would consist of ten multistorey apartment buildings facing onto the river at Royal Terrace, flanked by Robert Street and Adam Street, both of these streets having further apartments. Behind the main apartments was John Street, bordering the rear court of Coutts' private house. This was important since Coutts had negotiated an agreement ensuring that the view of the river from his rear windows would be unimpeded. Beside Coutts' house lay James Street, and then William Street divided his house from his bank which itself fronted onto the Strand. The two buildings were thoughtfully linked by a bridge. The Duke of Buckingham would have been proud of the naming of the streets. The entire site would provide 69 houses bringing in a rental income of well over £7,000 annually.

Before the Adelphi affair reached its height the Adam family had time to take a break at fashionable Lyme Regis in Dorset where they met Fanny Burney who gave her forthright opinion of them in her diary. Of Peggy she thought,

> she is about twenty-six or seven, ugly in person and too
> reserved in manners to permit me to judge of her, but I will

imagine she has some remarkable qualities . . . Mr Adams, very sensible, very polite and very agreeable, the most so . . . of the whole party. Mr [James?] Adams, his younger brother, a well behaved good sort of young man. During the time of rest, I was much happier than in dancing, for I was more pleased with the conversations I then had with Mr Dundas, [newly elected MP for "Linlithgowshire"] Mr Adams and others . . . Mr Dundas and Mr Adams are quite high conversers. I was never more pleased. When supper was over, all who had voices worth hearing were made to sing – none shone more than Mr Adams; though in truth he has little or no voice . . . yet he sung with such taste and feeling that very few *fine* voices could give equal pleasure: I cannot but much regret the probability there is of my never seeing him again. I may see many fools ere I see such a sensible man again.[20]

This was the calm before the storm, although Robert certainly seemed to be exercising his enviable facility to put anxieties away and relax in company.

Back on Thames-side, building works were rapidly going ahead. The severe slope of the ground from the Strand down to the river was to be accommodated by supporting the entire structure on warehouses and cellars, running underground for 236 feet, but which would have level access to the river at a wharf under Royal Terrace. The commercial leasing of these warehouses to the Board of Ordnance was estimated as providing an annual revenue of £2,281 10s 0d which would defray much of the huge building cost. There never had been such a project in London with its combination of planning, commercial viability and elegance. It was a total embodiment of the eighteenth-century ethos or artistry combined with grandeur.

The river, unfortunately, curved awkwardly into the bank from Inigo Jones's water gate at the foot of Buckingham Street and at high tide it backed up, forming a small bay with a foul-smelling mudflat, something which had been a cause of complaint for years. But there had been no commercial advantage in doing anything about it and therefore nothing had been done. The brothers saw there was a simple remedy – to alter the course of the Thames – and promptly applied to parliament to gain permission for the diversion. With an MP as a partner it did not prove too difficult and so in 1771 an Act of Parliament was passed.

The Act starts by pointing out that the bend in the river caused 'mud and silt' on the north and 'a very extensive sand bank' on the south to the 'manifest injury of the public'. This was obviously true and the answer was that 'navigation might be greatly improved and the said nuisances and inconveniences considerably diminished by an embankment on the north part of the said river within the bay or hollow of the said bend, which by advancing the unequal and irregular fronts of the said wharfs into an uniform line would give a proper direction to the stream, and, by narrowing the unnecessary width of the bed of the river in this part would considerably deepen the channel thereof.' This sounded totally altruistic and made no mention of the commercial gains from the wharves and docks which could now be constructed.

The work would be carried out by the brothers, along with 'James Paine, architect, Dorothy Monk, Widow, Clementina Pawson, Widow, and William Kitchener, Coal Merchant, having interest, [who] will execute such embankment in the front of their respective properties at their own expense.' Paine, as we have already noted, was known to the brothers and was the architect of the adjacent site, so his inclusion was inevitable. Nothing was to be built on the embankment higher than within 20 feet of high water but with the creation of this Act there was now a terrace officially called the Adelphi. However, the mayor, commonalty and citizens of the City of London were recognised to be able to claim a right to the soil of the River Thames and on that account the named ought to make satisfaction to them. If not, the Act stipulated that the City could go to trial for satisfaction as could the Dean and Chapter of St Peter in Westminster.

Such a project, undertaken by four Scotsmen – still a group

tainted with the unpopularity of Bute – could not be allowed to happen unopposed under the very noses of the City of London and battle was promptly joined. The City of London vowed to stop the scheme before it went any further and at a Court of Common Council held on 3 May 1771 it was decided to petition the king directly. 'The sheriffs, attended by the City Remembrancer went to St James's and presented the said petition to His Majesty.'[21] At the same time in the *Gentleman's Magazine* for May 1771, the following was printed:

A petition to the King's most excellent Majesty. An act for enabling certain persons to enclose and embank part of the river Thames adjoining to Durham Yard, Salisbury Street, Cecil Street, and Beaufort Buildings in the county of Middlesex . . . The provisions of this bill appearing to be destructive of the ancient and valuable rights and property of the City of London, rights granted by charters of your Royal Majesty's predecessors and enjoyed without interruption through a succession of many ages . . . It is now become our duty to represent to your Majesty that the soils and ground of the river Thames, in that part of it which the present bill transfers to private persons for their particular emolument is the ancient property and inheritance of the City of London . . . and. consequently is now vested in your Majesty in right of your crown . . . Such an injury, we believe is without precedent in the annals of this kingdom . . . We are sure that the sanction of your royal name can never be given to a proposition not only absolutely false, but known to be false by the very persons who allege it. We therefore humbly implore your Majesty to refuse your assent to this bill.[22]

Despite a protest in the House of Lords, on 8 May 1771, George III signed the bill. The furore continued, although a letter in the *Morning Advertiser* pointed out that private persons could own property up to the high-water mark as the City itself had leased houses and wharves in Blackfriars in similar circum-stances. A second appeal was made to the King on 10 July, including a request 'to give peace to this distracted nation by removing your present and despotic ministers.'[23] The king administered a severe rebuke to the petitioners, but the affair was too good an opportunity to miss for the anti-Scottish faction:

> Four Scotchmen by the name of Adams,
> Who keep their coaches and their madams,
> Quoth John, in sulky mood to Thomas,
> 'Have stole the very river from us.'

An anonymous satirist under the name of 'Londiniensis Lib-erty' was more direct:

> Ye friends of George, and friends of James,
> Envy us not our river Thames,
> The Pr . . . ss, fond of raw-boned faces,
> May give you all our posts and places;
> Take all – to gratify your pride,
> But dip your oatmeal in the Clyde.[24]

The Pr . . . ss was the Dowager Princess of Wales, long thought to be the mistress of Bute. Thus the brothers were included in the general Scotophobia prevalent at the time. When the actor Charles Macklin appeared at Covent Garden as Macbeth, and in Scottish clothes, he was booed from the stage. Doubly unfair since Macklin was an Irishman. Wilkes in the *North Briton* wrote, 'The public were told that Mansfield, the Lord Chief Justice, came from Scotland and so did Loudon who commanded the British forces in Portugal, Sir Gilbert Elliott and James Oswald of the Treasury Board, in addition to Ramsay, the Court painter [Alan Ramsay Junior was appointed portrait painter to George III in 1767], and Robert Adam the Court Architect [in fact Robert had resigned his position when he took his seat as an MP].' It was declared that Scotland was 'the home of want and that England, a land flowing with milk and honey, was being thrown open to the Scotsmen and betrayed'.[25] Added to this the brothers were now unfairly linked with the jobbery of Bute and could expect no favours from anyone having a connection with the City of London. Their aspirations to be taken as 'gentlemen' were becoming perilously fragile in that all too snobbish society.

Although their account at Drummond's was more than comfortable in 1771, financially they were now dangerously overstretched, with battalions of workmen employed on the site and, as yet, no properties let. There were, however, wild rumours about the industrial activities on the river front. 'In a spirit of nationality that seems ludicrous, they had brought all their masons and bricklayers from Scotland and the work was stimulated by the monotonous drone of the Bagpipe. The labourers, however, soon found that this cheerful music made them insensibly give more work than was quite profitable, and with a spirit, in its own way as national as that of their employers, they presently struck work.'[26] Another rumour had it that when the Scots labourers discovered what could be earned in London, they thanked Robert for the transport to England and promptly left his employment for richer pastures.

A more bitter blow fell when the brothers heard from the Board of Ordnance that they would have no need to lease the basements and the main bulwark of their finance collapsed. They would now be reliant solely on leasing the apartments. The apartments facing south across the terrace comprised a lower basement with kitchen, the kitchen rising over two floors as was the common practice, to absorb the heat; a cellar and butler's accommodation; then an upper basement with more servants' rooms. On the ground floor there was an eating room facing the terrace, with a parlour at the rear, while on the first floor were two drawing rooms. The second floor had two bedrooms and a dressing room, with three more bedrooms and two dressing rooms on the third floor.

Among the first to lease an apartment there was David

Garrick. 'Garrick was taken with the situation, and through Lord Mansfield's interest, obtained the promise of one of the houses on advantageous terms, even before it was completed.'[27] In modern terms, Garrick bought 'off plan' and Robert could not have wished for a better tenant. Outside the realms of aristocracy and politics he was the most famous man in London, now inside the bastion of respectability, and could pick his friends as he chose. One of his friends, and a successful playwright at Garrick's theatre at Drury Lane, was John Home, through whom Garrick had previously met Robert. Robert had already done some work for Garrick at his villa at Hampton and relations between the two men were jovial. At one point Garrick wrote to Robert that he was 'always ready to obey the commands of those unprincipled gentlemen and vile architects the Adams. Mrs Garrick sends her detestation.'[28] Fanny Burney recorded: 'The centre was allotted to Mr Garrick but none of them were quite suited to him, as his health was then declining, and the bleak situation was ill contrasted with his own warm and sheltered situation in Southampton Street, but he was tempted at last to make the experiment and acceded to the proposal. Thus Garrick returned to the same spot where he had begun life as a struggling wine merchant in Durham Yard.'[29]

On 14 March 1772, however, 'Mrs Garrick is almost killed with the fatigue of moving to the Adelphi. Mr Bauclerk is to be our neighbour.'[30] Garrick had engaged Chippendale and Sons to provide furnishings, to repair and shift the furniture from Southampton Street and to move material up from Hampton. There were 30 horse-loads of 'Sundry Goods' and Garrick's beds followed. He was now in residence at Number 5 Adelphi Terrace where he had 24 rooms at his disposal. On the ground floor Garrick reversed Robert's plan and placed the eating room, with Chippendale furniture, at the rear. He made the front parlour his library where he could watch the river traffic with his newly installed telescope. His first-floor drawing room had a ceiling painted by Zucchi, furniture by Chippendale, green silk damask curtains and three large green Venetian blinds. Between

January 1771 and April 1772 Garrick ran up bills of £931 9s 3½d. with Thomas Chippendale and Sons alone. 'All my ready money is exhausted. I have some on mortgage too.'[31] Among his first guests was the indefatigable Miss Burney, 'We were so happy as to be let in to Mr Garrick's, and saw his new house in the Adelphi Buildings. The house is large and most elegantly fitted up.'[32]

Given the collapse of the brothers' arrangement with the Board of Ordnance they were in even deeper financial straits than David Garrick. A contemporary newspaper reported: 'The Adelphi buildings were mortgaged for a loan of £70,000 and it is said that the Messrs Adam had laid out as much more upon them; so that in the course of five years, these gentlemen expended £140,000* to raise palaces upon an offensive heap of mud, and circulated an immense sum to make a palpable nuisance a principal ornament to the metropolis.'[33]

In fact, the Adelphi was becoming a success, with prospective tenants vying with each other to acquire properties. Their private bank account was still healthy, but this did not reflect the other loans on various banks in Scotland and in the City. However the Adelphi was now a desirable address. A bookseller, Thomas Becket, desperately wanted a prime site on the corner of Adam Street and asked Garrick to intercede for him. The actor duly obliged. 'My Dear Adelphi, I forgot to speak to you last Saturday about our friend Becket. We shall all break our hearts if he is not bookseller to the Adelphi, and has not the corner house that is to be built . . . Make your peace with heaven by an act of righteousness and bestow that corner blessing – that is the prayer and petition of your affectionate and devoted, David Garrick.'[34] Becket moved to 73 Strand on the north-west corner of Adam Street in January 1774.

Robert and James moved into Number 4 with their sisters, and relocated the drawing office to Number 13, while William moved into Number 6 Adam Street, presumably with the business

---

* Approximately £8,400,000 in today's terms.

offices. In contrast to the general ill-will towards the brothers, a couplet welcoming them circulated:

> 'Twas as the brothers at that pile arrived,
> Where elegance and taste revived.[35]

This was written by George Keate, an aesthete whom Robert had met on the Grand Tour. He lived with his collection of books, coins and medals in Charlotte Street where, in 1777, Robert decorated a house for him, complete with an octagonal room for the display of his collection. This had a ceiling 'in the Etruscan style' – painted at about the same time as the apartment at Osterley – although it collapsed and resulted in a law suit in which Keate sued the brothers. He lost and they somehow gained £16 14s. 4d in damages.

In 1778 Robert and James moved again to 3 Robert Street, where they were joined by William in 1782. Number 3 Adelphi Terrace was taken by Topham Beuclerk, a great-grandson of Charles II and Nell Gwynn. He was the epitome of dilettantism and a prodigious book collector. Married unhappily, but profitably, to Diana St John, Viscountess Bolingbroke, the daughter of the Duke of Marlborough, Beauclerk was a close friend of Dr Johnson. Eventually his book collection of over 30,000 volumes moved with him from the Adelphi to Great Russell Street, where Walpole said 'it has put the British Museum's nose quite out of joint.'

At Number 6, flanking Garrick, was the celebrated Dr Graham. He arrived at the Adelphi in 1779 and, after refurbishing the house to his requirements, declared it open as a Temple of Health. His handbills announced that: 'This evening exactly at eight o'clock the celestial brilliancy of the medico-electrical apparatus in all the apartments of the temple will be exhibited by Dr Graham himself. Admission by night 5s in the day 2s 6d.' A couple spending the night in Dr Graham's electric bed would be guaranteed conception. The price for this was £200 and Walpole called it 'the most impudent show of imposition I ever saw!' Graham was the son of an Edinburgh saddler, and was assisted in his demonstrations by the voluptuous Emma Lyon who left Graham's establishment to marry Lord Hamilton and go down in history as the mistress of Lord Nelson. Graham moved out in 1781 and died, insane, in Edinburgh in 1794.

Probably the most lasting monument to the original concept of the Adelphi is the building housing the Royal Society of Arts. Robert had been elected a member in 1758 and James in 1764, so when the Academy advertised for new premises in March 1770, the Adam brothers were obvious candidates to provide them. A site at the end of John Street was reserved and plans and elevations were delivered. Back in 1757 Chambers had proposed a grandiose structure in the Strand, but the Society had prudently let the proposal lie. On 28 March 1772 the foundation stone was laid. The final agreement on rent was £270 for 92½ years and on the same day £1,000 was paid to the brothers in the Adelphi Tavern.

Had the Society known the true state of the brothers finances they might have delayed and made an even more advantageous deal. Occupation of the Adelphi was successful but it was slow and without the Ordnance contract the rents were falling far behind the expense of the building. By January 1772 the cost of work required to finish the project was £29,812 6s 2d. There were debts of £124,000, a gap of nearly £60,000, although there was the promise of a loan from John. Then, on 8 June 1772, the bank of Neale, James, Fordyce and Down collapsed. Fordyce himself owed £243,000 and he absconded with what he could rescue. This was the domino that started the fall leading to the collapse of most of the Scottish banking system. 'There was consternation among the Scottish merchants and bankers in London, most of them with strong Edinburgh connections.'[36] By July there were unpaid bills held on agreement with sundry Scottish banks amounting to £117,545 8s 10d. The brothers had funds in at least two Scottish banks: £1,500 with Charles Ferguson & Sons and £9,000 with Fordyce Grant & Co. (a subsidiary of the now failed Neale, James, Fordyce and Down).

They recovered 5s in the pound from Charles Ferguson & Co. and 6s 6d from Fordyce Grant, a net loss of £7,200.[37] A sympathetic view of the brothers' plight is given by David Hume in his letter to Adam Smith of 27 June 1772, written five days after the collapse of the Ayr Bank. 'Of all previous to the late unhappy failures of the banks, the sufferers I am most concerned for are the Adams, particularly John. But their undertakings were so vast that nothing could support them. They must dismiss 3,000 workmen who, comprehending the materials, must have expended above £100,000 a year . . . People's compassion, I see was exhausted for John in his last calamity and everybody asks why he has incurred any more hazards . . . To me the scheme of the Adelphi always appeared so imprudent, that my wonder is how they could have gone on so long.'[38]

In June 1772 Hume would not have been surprised that the situation could not go any further, and *The Scots Magazine* reported: 'The poor men had begun work in the morning before the melancholy news of their masters' misfortunes was communicated to them; when informed of it they came down the walls in silence and stood for some time in the street in a body; and at last went off one by one, with every mark of regret for the fate of their masters, whose business had supported them and their families for several years.' The bagpipes – if they had ever existed outside an Englishman's imagination – fell silent and all work came to a standstill. The brothers were now in a very dangerous position. The bulk of their available capital was locked in agreements for building the Adelphi, and to go cap in hand to the City asking for extensions to loans would lead to certain rejection. They were the 'Scotchmen who stole the very river from us'. They were friends of Bute and Mansfield, and City financiers could cheerfully sit back and watch the brothers drown. In any case, bank closures brought on by unwise extension of credit in Scotland had spread to the City and the brothers now faced almost certain bankruptcy.

However, creditors did realise that completing the Adelphi would increase the net worth of the company and work restarted on 26 June. The brothers were themselves personally wealthy since their earnings as architects were independent of the company and, in any case, the company owned a successful timber business with large stocks of mature timber in store at Thames Bank worth £17,000 and brickworks in London and Essex valued at £7,700. In addition William Adam held a majority share in Adam Campbell & Sons, builders' suppliers, worth £6,000, as well as a stone and paving business and John had a profitable interest in the Aberdeen granite quarries. Even at this early stage the Adelphi rents were worth £2,005 annually. Obviously the current debts had to be paid off, preferably without damaging this infrastructure, and construction costs would have to be met from the brothers' private accounts – a dangerous practice.

There were two possible alternative ways out of the morass, neither of them pleasant and, even together, probably not enough for a complete rescue. The first solution was for the brothers to sell off part of their art collection and, since Number 4 Royal Terrace was considerably smaller than Lower Grosvenor Street, this probably seemed a convenient solution. The collection was vast and was sold at auction by Christie's over five days, starting on 25 February 1775, at their gallery in the Strand. The first three days saw the sale of the pictures – 220 in all – including two Rembrandts, a Tiepolo, four Poussins, four Veroneses, as well as 61 by Clérisseau, Pecheux, Zucchi and other artists. Not only the drawings themselves, but prints of the drawings were sold off. On the fourth and fifth days 104 casts and sculptures came under the hammer; these items alone fetched £3,115.[39] Needless to say, Fanny Burney attended the sale. 'The undertaking was, I believe too great for them, and they have suffered much in their fortunes. I cannot but wonder, that so noble and elegant a plan should fail of encouragement . . . As I have neither knowledge nor judgement in these matters, I venture no further opinion than that to me the sight was a great regale. We saw many of our friends of the Scotch party but were not known to any, probably not seen as we sat very backward.'[40] Sadly, the sale was, in fact, a failure and the brothers were forced to buy back 'the greater part of 218 lots'[41].

Other means had to be found to clear the growing mountain of debt. On 1 December Robert wrote to Baron Mure of Caldwell asking him 'to visit Blair with Adam and Alex Ferguson in order to set our affairs at ease'[42]. He wrote again on 28 December and thanked Mure for the valuation of Blair. 'We flatter ourselves to be able to make out the loan we desire which will make all our affairs perfectly easy.' So John, who had returned to Scotland, dutifully mortgaged Blair Adam and contributed his share while the brothers looked at what they possessed in London. The second possible solution was to sell off their London properties by lottery, which could raise more money that a straightforward auction. There already was a popular National Lottery but permission to hold a private lottery would require an Act of Parliament. This was not, however, impossible to obtain since one of the brother's most useful possessions was parliamentary influence and Robert duly used it to obtain the requisite Act of Parliament. This was actually 'an enabling Act', allowing 'John, Robert, James and William Adam to dispose of several houses and buildings in the Parishes of St Martin in the Fields and St Mary le Bow, in the county of Middlesex, and other of their effects, by way of chance, in such manner as may be most for the benefit of themselves and creditors.' In other words, the Act gave them the permission to hold the necessary lottery, which the brothers then publicised in a pamphlet, *Particulars concerning the Prizes in the Adelphi Lottery*. In a rather apologetic tone they state, 'the Messrs Adam engaged in this undertaking, more from an enthusiasm for their own art than from a view of profit; at the same time being eager to point out a way to public utility, though even at an extraordinary expense; they will be perfectly satisfied if they should only draw, from this lottery, the money laid out by them on a work which they readily confess, they have found to be too great for their private fortunes.'[43] To make this statement represented a great alteration of stance, especially for Robert and James. No longer could they behave as dilettantes on the edge of gentility. The mention of money now reduced the brothers to membership of the 'middling sort of people'. They were acceptable company, cultured enough, though perhaps a little too learned, certainly well dressed and even clean – itself quite a novelty for the eighteenth century – and even allowed entrance at the front of the house, which they had probably designed, but finally, no more than superior tradesmen with an acknowledged artistic flair. Gentry did not reveal their financial shortcomings in the public prints nor did they run lotteries. Gentry became bankrupt and went to live on credit in Aix-la-Chapelle.

This lottery consisted of 4,370 tickets at £50 each, with total prize money of £218,500, backed by their various properties. The first prize was £50,000 and lesser prizes descended in stages from £10 to £800. The last ticket drawn would win £25,000. The draw began on 3 March 1774 in Jonathan's Coffee House and continued for six days. Portions of tickets were sold at various lottery offices and many tickets were themselves sold over and over again as the draw became more and more popular. The cash for the prizes was not instantly available but represented shares in various properties, the sales of which the brothers guaranteed would be completed. Robert's friend, Baron Mure of Caldwell took ticket number 342 and Robert wrote that, 'The lottery goes swimmingly,' and they were already paying off their mortgages. 'This is a real felicity to honest minds.'[44] By a happy coincidence the last ticket drawn – worth £25,000 – was held by the brothers themselves.

They were saved from disaster, although their private fortunes were hugely depleted. It had been a very narrow squeak. They were still admired for their skill and artistry in architecture, but the monster of poverty had brushed his tattered robe against them. They were still be admitted at the front entrance and Robert was doing more and more work for the aristocracy, but their astonishing architectural success went nowhere in elevating their status.

The Adelphi had been an idea of grandeur and something entirely new in London's town planning. Inevitably Walpole thought it disgraceful. 'What are the Adelphi Buildings? Warehouses laced down the seams, like a soldier's trull in a regimental old coat.' The twentieth-century town planner and architectural historian Steen Eiler Rasmussen took a different view. 'In the case of the Adelphi the *commercial* idea is no less grand and full of imagination than is the *artistic* one. The scheme is a fantasia upon antique motifs. The financier was an artist and the artist a financier.'[45] Another contemporary commentator thought, 'These are serious and monumental structures. They could make us wish that Robert Adam had designed Imperial Delhi! Willing hands did more damage to London than a German landmine.'[46] The site, where George Bernard Shaw, H.G. Wells and J.M. Barrie among others, had followed in the trail of David Garrick, is now a sad relic of a hubristic dream.

The brothers had no time to dream. Although they had been able to pull back from financial ruin, they could not afford to stand still, and set about reinforcing their architectural reputation. They acted immediately and, possibly, without enough forethought. On 16 January 1773 the *Public Advertiser* announced that, 'in a short while will be published *The Works in Architecture of Robert and James Adam of the Adelphi.*' The book was published in numbers at a guinea each to avoid the 'ignorant rabble' and to avoid wholesale copying by 'every dirty artist in London'. It would eventually be a three-volume work, with Volume Two appearing in 1779 while Volume Three was published posthumously in 1822. The format for the book was a familiar one, with a general foreword followed by individual introductions to each section and explanations of the plates themselves. There were extracts from James's essay on architecture and from Robert's letter to Lord Kames. The opening paragraph of the foreword gives us an idea of what was to come.

Some apology may perhaps be requisite for giving to the world a book of architecture, after so many works of this kind have been published in Italy, France and England during the last two centuries. The novelty and variety of the following designs will, we flatter ourselves, not only excuse, but justify our conduct, in communicating them to the world. We have not trod the path of others, nor derive aid from their labours. In the works which we have had the honour to execute, we have not only met with the approbation of our employers, but been with the imitation of other artists, to such a degree, as in some measure to have brought about, in this country, a kind of revolution in the whole system of this useful and elegant art. These circumstances induced us to hope, that to collect and engrave our works would afford both entertainment and instruction.[47]

Robert goes on to claim that 'to the observation of the skilful' there would be seen a remarkable improvement and 'to the decoration of the inside, an almost total change.' He leaves the reader in no doubt as to who has instigated this change. Massive entablature and the ponderous compartmented ceilings have been replaced with 'light mouldings, gracefully formed, delicately enriched and arranged with propriety and skill'. The footnotes to this section press home Adam's scorn for what has gone before. He claims that St Peter's in Rome and the church *des Quatre Nations* at Paris are the only forerunners of Kedleston. The early Italian artists mistook the original intentions of the Romans and so 'all Europe has been misled and has been serviley [sic] groaning under this load for these three centuries past'. Inigo Jones introduced compartmented ceilings, 'with as much weight, but less fancy and embellishment. Vanburgh, Campbell and Gibbs followed too implicitly the authority of this great name.' The brothers – the book is presented as a joint effort, although Robert's opinions, as already expressed to Lord Kames, dominate – acknowledge that Kent was more skilful, but 'his works, however, are evidently those of a beginner.' They allow that Mr Stuart has 'contributed greatly to introducing the true style of antique decoration'. The essay continues with a glossary and even that manages to attack the architecture which has gone before. 'We hope this minute explanation of these terms will be excused. It is intended to supply in some measure a general deficiency we have found upon this subject, in all the encyclopaedias and technical dictionaries.' As to previous or other contemporary architects, they are largely ignored and there is no mention of Chambers or Wyatt.

In the foreword to the Kenwood plates they set out their aims of entertainment, instruction and observation. 'As in this work we aim not only by affording entertainment to the connoisseur, but wish also to convey some instruction to the artist; we shall, from time to time, make observations as naturally arise from the work before us. Should we differ in any of these observations from the opinions of either ancient or modern authors, we do not mean to engage in any controversy, being only desirous of submitting our ideas to the consideration of the public.' Clearly the brothers would brook no argument from their contemporaries. 'Many of the disputes among modern architects are extremely frivolous . . . We, by no means, presume to find fault with the compositions or to decry the labours of other authors; many of whom have great merit and deserve great praise. Our ambition is to share with others, not to appropriate to ourselves the applause of the public; and if we have any claim to approbation, we found it on this alone; that we flatter ourselves, we have been able to seize, with some degree of success, the beautiful spirit of antiquity, and to transfuse it, with novelty and variety through all our numerous works.' They explain that some of the plates are coloured so 'that the public in general might have an opportunity of cultivating the beautiful art of decoration, hitherto so little understood in most of the countries of Europe'.

In the first two editions of *The Works* the brothers managed to antagonise the few supporters they had in the artistic world but not until the publication of the second volume in 1779 was there a printed riposte. This was a pamphlet purporting to be a preview of the Royal Academy Exhibition in its new premises at Somerset House and written by Roger Shanhagen, Gent., which was a pseudonym for Robert Smirke, the architect and academician.[48] The pamphlet is a satire in which the writer despairs at what might be exhibited. The works would be so predictable that he vowed to publish a catalogue with opinions of all future exhibitions thus obviating any need to visit the exhibitions. Jeered and insulted by the current exhibitors he went home and was visited by a spirit carrying *Arcana Cabalistica* who showed him the works of the Adam brothers. Since the brothers were not members of the Royal Academy the reader can be sure that he has entered the realm of fantasy. The designs are for 'a Temple of Northern Patriotism' – a reference to the brothers' Scottishness – a design for a Temple of Virtue, and a section of a lady's dressing room. 'We have long considered the remains of ancient magnificence as the sources from whence every architect must derive his ideas of excellence . . . but the works of these artists convince that the opinion is erroneous . . . The world believed it impossible to attain magnificence in building, without order, symmetry and proportion, but the Adams erected the Adelphi and convinced the world of its mistake.' Smirke accuses the brothers of making architecture 'contemptible by decking her in the flutter of a courtesan'.

He continues,

Genius is a happy madness that decides and determines without thought, reflection or foresight. Such is the genius of the Adams, irregular, elevated and magnificent. Like Michael Angelo they look down with contempt on all the inferior excellencies, and, like him, astonish by a grandeur of style that can never be imitated . . . As they are placed high, and my eyes are dim, I cannot see them; but, doubtless, men of perfect sight will find them more instructive than many volumes . . . But nothing so much displays the wonderful extent of their abilities as the Preface to their Works with its Notes. Some have indeed insinuated that this Preface was not their performance; but of those I would ask, who but the ostensible authors could be so sensible of the merits of the artists? . . . No writers they remark were ever so arrogant as the Adams, if the Adams are the authors of that preface . . . they are elevated far above the usual elevation of men. Philosophy has advanced them to heaven. They are wrapped in clouds through which shame cannot penetrate, nor yet the hisses of derision and envy.

He then continues with more complimentary surveys of Cipriani, Kauffman and Reynolds. He says of Chambers, who had submitted drawings of Somerset House as well as some temples: 'Sir William Chambers is an Architect of inferior merit when compared with the Adams. His genius is not original . . . Sir William treads the beaten path of the old Italian masters. In regular architecture he seldom deviates from the cannons which he has so well illustrated.' Wyatt is praised in retrospect for the Pantheon: 'England never before possessed a building where the genius of architecture was so conspicuous.' He criticises Chambers for designing interiors as though they were exteriors; although Stuart cured Adam of this, 'Adam fell into the contrary extreme and while he aimed at elegance within, covered the outside of his buildings with frippery . . . most of the white walls which Mr Adam has speckled this city are no better than models for the Twelfth-Night decoration of a pastry cook.'[49]

Smirke was not the sole author of the pamphlet and his collaborator on the work was William Porden, an assistant in Wyatt's drawing office, and an architect in his own right, responsible for Eaton Hall in Cheshire. Ignoring the inevitable anti-Scottish jibes, however, a lot of the satire is well aimed since the text of *The Works*, while intending to be a manifesto for the personal style of the brothers, does not allow for the existence of any other form of architecture. Wounded pride at the financial failure of the Adelphi is not sufficient excuse for the tone – the Adams brothers felt themselves to be the finest architects in Europe and were unashamed to assert their primacy. After Robert's death other commentators would rush to the attack.

Robert's ambition had been only slightly moderated by the financial collapse of the Adelphi and he was not a little relieved when a similar scheme for a giant open-ended square in Portland Place consisting of grand villas gradually withered. Reluctant to lose their grip on such a prestigious site, however, two of the great houses on the street are by James Adam. For some of the construction of the street James had gone into partnership with John Elwes, a member of parliament and building speculator. Elwes was best known as a miser and he would leave his house in Welbeck Street at four in the morning, dressed as a beggar, to inspect building progress. James must have been relieved when 'in 1789 he appointed Mr Gibbon the builder, in place of Mr Adam'.[50] According to Bolton, 'The American war had a fatal effect on the development of Portland Place, for its final completion was delayed until the next century, then falling into the hands of Nash, when the Crown Estate to the North was developed in the days of the Regency.'[51]

Other town houses were occupying the practice at this time as the nobility beautified their London residences. Chandos House in Chandos Street, 20 St James's Square and Derby House in Grosvenor Street were all remodelled between 1771 and 1773. All of them presented the problem of having an existing breadth and depth, giving Robert less than the scope offered by a country house. Nevertheless he contrived to find scope for invention in every case with no two layouts being similar and each room having an individual flair. 'Robert had reached, in these town houses, a virtuoso's skill in fiddling the changes on a simple plan within narrow confines.'[52] Derby House (now demolished) even received one of the last flourishes of Adam's Etruscan style. Still extant and in use is 20 Portman Square. Now an exclusive private members' club, it had been owned by the 60-year-old, twice-widowed Elizabeth, Dowager Countess of Home, known in her time as the Queen of Hell. In 1776 she engaged Wyatt to decorate her town house but his lack of raid progress caused her to move with an alacrity typical of her fiery personality as she peremptorily sacked him and employed Robert Adam. Her house was across the street from where Stuart was building Mrs Montagu's new house. In fact, Mrs Montagu also displayed the iron whims of society ladies when she became disenchanted with Stuart's dilatory behaviour and replaced him with Joseph Bonomi.

The interior of 20 Portman Square certainly shows us Robert at his most inventive. Given a five-bay house he created a square hall with his favourite apsidal recess containing a stove. Then he constructed a curved staircase under an elegant lantern that seems to defy both gravity and geometry. He also gave the house an Etruscan room and showed his deep debt to Piranesi with the chimney piece and overmantel in the music room. This faced an organ of suitable domestic size, but the jewel of the house is the music room ceiling with stucco roundels 'as complex and fine drawn as a spider's web upon a frosty morning . . . among the most elaborate works of Robert Adam in this class.'[53] 'It was the constraints imposed by the house already built and partly decorated by Wyatt, and the unique challenge of giving a star performance on his rival's stage that galvanised Adam's creative genius and brought it to a higher peak than it would have reached had he designed the house from scratch.'[54] These four houses are among Robert Adam's greatest achievements.

Outside London, Robert had been contacted by Sir William Johnstone-Pulteney who wished to develop the suburb of Bath-wick by connecting it to the city of Bath by a bridge and expanding the region into a new town. Robert designed the bridge based on the Ponte Vecchio in Florence but the new town scheme died a peaceful death. A keen planner – this was, after all, the man who at the age of 28 had offered to rebuild Lisbon – Robert had drawn up plans for the new town which were never used.

However his skill as a town planner was again called for when he was asked by Richard Rigby to work for him at Mistley Hall in Essex. Rigby was the inheritor of a fortune made in the South Sea Bubble, had completed the Grand Tour, and been elected as a member of parliament. Due to his friendship with Charles James Fox, Secretary to the Treasury, he was appointed Pay-master-General of the Forces, a post he held for 12 years. The American war produced 'an unexpected source of wealth' lead-ing to his being prosecuted for corruption – almost uniquely in the eighteenth century – and forced to repay £10,000. 'Thus persecuted on all sides Rigby naturally turned with disgust from statesmen and politicians and sought his own domain to partake of those comforts in retirement which his benevolence had spread around it.'[55] He had inherited Mistley Hall near Manningtree on the River Stour in Essex. 'Mistley Hall stands pleasantly on an eminence, with a good prospect, especially to the north. It was newly built by Richard Rigby and much improved by his son the Right Hon Richard Rigby Esq., with fine plantations of trees, etc.'[56] This was a view endorsed by David Garrick in 1777 when he was a guest of the hospitable Rigbys. 'While I am writing this in my dressing room, I see no less than 50 vessels under sail, and one, half an hour ago, saluted us with thirteen guns.'

Today the river is heavily silted and the idea of Mistley being either a thriving port or a fashionable watering place seems absurd. But it was not absurd to Rigby since on 25 June 1745, Horace Walpole had reported: 'I have been near three weeks in Essex at Mr Rigby's. It is the charmingest place by nature and the most trumpery by art that ever I saw. The house stands on a high hill on an arm of the sea, which winds itself before two sides of the house. On the right and left, at the very foot of this hill lie two towns; the one of market quality, and the other a wharf where ships come up. This last was to have a church but by a lucky want of religion in the inhabitants, who would not contribute to building a steeple, it remains an absolute antique temple with a portico, on the very strand.'[57] It would clearly take very little for an architect of Robert's imagination, and a convivial host of Rigby's quality to bring about a stunning transformation.

Rigby had already 'built several granaries, warehouses, a large Malting office, and made good quays and Coal-yards and there is now a large trade carried on there. The new church stands at the thorn. It is a neat edifice.'[58] Walpole had personally made some improvements in 1749 but a formal approach was not made to Robert until 1777. He had already been designing an elegant set of salt water baths for Rigby, proposing that Mistley should become a spa. Rigby, who was ill, was convinced of the efficacy of sea bathing, and making a profit from his private cure was an attractive thought. There were hot and cold, private and public baths with a portico supported by Corinthian columns leading to a rotunda, itself giving on to a peristyle overlooking the river. The baths were fed from a fountain reservoir supplied from the sea. For the hall Adam designed a pilaster and pediment frontage. A new wing with a drawing room and eating room looked over the Stour, although this, being a later addition, may not have been by Adam. There was a drawing for an entrance screen with arches and twin lodges, of which only the lodges were built, again at a later date and after Robert had left the project. Drawings still exist for an elaborate ceiling and carpet design.

Sadly, not only did Rigby not build Robert's new frontage, but the bath house was likewise ignored; today there is only a small pond with a replica swan swimming desolately in front of a group of four cottages to mark its site. In 1870 the Great Eastern Railway Company built its line to Harwich on an embankment which completely obscured the view over the Stour from the hall and Mistley Hall was finally demolished. What was built at Mistley was, uniquely, an entire Adam church. Robert built around the existing 'neat edifice' by adding transepts with towers and lanterns. He added pillared porticos on the north and south walls, producing a unique design. The church had the oddest fate in that only the two towers remain, saved from destruction by their usefulness as navigation landmarks. It needs a great deal of imagination to recreate the dreams of Sir Robert Rigby and his improving architect beside the River Stour.

CHAPTER TEN

Certain Public Works in the City of Edinburgh

The decade of the seventies displayed a marked change in the practice of the brothers. Work continued on their projects in the south of England and on the great town houses in London but in 1769 the Duke of Northumberland, owner of Syon, wanted renovations to his property at Alnwick castle. The castle had been visited by John in 1759 but was new to Robert so he duly travelled north and contributed some interior decoration, the style of which was heavily Gothic, with a fan-vaulted ceiling based on King's College, Cambridge. The duchess was strongly attracted to the past and Thomas Percy dedicated his *Reliques of Ancient English Poetry* to her. 'It is prompted by natural curiosity to survey the progress of life and manners . . . but this curiosity, Madam, must be stronger in those who like your ladyship, can remark in every period the influence of some great progenitor, and who still feel in their effects the transactions and events of different centuries.'[1] The duke 'out of complaisance to his duchess ornamented it in the Gothic taste which he himself did not like, but he did it with so much taste that he made it one of the most superb buildings of that kind in Europe'. In the park, Robert designed the Brizlee Tower, a purely Gothic folly, supposedly on the spot where Malcolm Canmore, the son of Macbeth, was killed in 1093.

Louis Dutens, for many years the guest of the duke, recounted the ducal expenditure. 'For 20 years he spent annually £7,000 in building his castle at Alnwick . . . his *maison de plaisance*, Syon, costs him £2,000 in taxes and upkeep, Northumberland House, [the duke's London house, now destroyed] £1,000, Alnwick, £3,000, his parliamentary interest, £5,000 annually – he has spent more than £200,000 on building.'[2] The Duke of Northumberland was a useful patron for an architect.

About the same time Robert was called to work further north, well inside the Scottish border at Mellerstain, near Melrose. This house belonged to George Ballie, brother of the Earl of Haddington who had inherited it in 1759 having returned from his Grand Tour – where he had met Benjamin Stillingfleet of the blue stockings. The existing house had been built by William Adam, Robert's father, and was very much a 'castle', complete with battlements and machiolations. It was evident that the further north one travelled the stronger the preference for castles became and Robert was now called upon to design and decorate many of them. They were, of course, not built with any idea of defence nor had they military aspirations, but towers, arrow slit windows and battlements were *de rigeur*.

Architectural historians have spilt much academic ink in attempts to define Adam's 'castle style' but Adam was quite capable of adapting his style as fashion changed and clients demanded differing results. Robert was, after all, the owner of a castle himself when he inherited Dowhill Castle from his father. He had sketched Gothic architecture on his travels and although his Grand Tour was closely focused on classicism, in Rome he could not have been unaware of the massive bulk of Castel Sant' Angelo: once Hadrian's tomb, but in Robert's day the wholly mediaeval papal castle from whose ramparts Benvenuto Cellini shot at invading soldiery. Robert was not required to construct castles according to the principles of military engineering, although he was experienced in that, but to design structures which pleased both himself and his clients

In 1766 Robert had written to Mrs Montagu about the plans of Sir James Lowther, the wildly ambitious landowner who had asked him for a model village at Penrith: 'Sir James seems to impose on me the arduous task of placing a castle upon this principality. It is a work worthy of the chief artist of Olympian Jove, and not for a narrow genius of this world; I am not at all surprised that you found the castle of Inverary so defective. The surrounding mountains would humble a nobler piece of human art, the pyramids of Egypt if situated near a Ben Lomond, or Skiddo [sic] would look mean and despicable, even the most admired efforts of the Greeks and Romans would appear altogether insignificant if placed near these unparalleled works of nature.'[3] Robert drew up plans for Sir James's castle but they were too ambitious and joined the long list of projects that came to nothing.

Robert did agree that the Gothic style adopted by his father was suitable for the rugged landscape in which Mellerstain is set. His earliest drawings, dated before 1770, are simply for ceilings. In fact, his major contributions to the house as it stands today are in the interior decorations. Robert used a freer imagination here, with discreet dancing girls, centrepieces showing the ritual slaughter of oxen – equally discreet – and the hint of Etruscan influences in some of his frieze designs. He added a novelty for the time, a basement bathroom and dressing room complete with dolphins and stoves for heating water.

In *The Architecture of James and Robert Adam*, Arthur Bolton points out that the drawings for these decorations are not in the style of the Adelphi office and may have been done locally.[4] Robert and James had an office in Edinburgh with three permanent staff until 1772 and Robert, who visited the city annually for a month or two every summer, was well aware that in his home city the firm could find plenty of employment.

During his visits he lodged with 'Mrs Drysdale' at 14 Nicolson Street on Edinburgh's rapidly expanding southside. Mrs Drysdale was Robert's sister Mary, now the widow of the Rev. Dr John Drysdale, minister of the Tron Kirk. Number 14 was the first house to the south of the Riding School.

By 1791 he was using Mrs Drysdale as his agent during his absences and there is a note in his pocketbook on 15 July of £15 10s od paid to Mrs Drysdale for Mr Paterson, his local clerk of works at Craigwell Quarry. The pocketbook also records that he had bought Mrs Drysdale a dozen dessert spoons on 21 June and four salt cellars on 2 January 1792 for a total of £11 8s od. A detailed breakdown of his domestic expenses with Mrs Drysdale during this period showed:

House rent from Whitsunday 1791–1792 £29 0s 0d,
Taxes on the house £5 10s 0d,
Servants wages and tea £4 2s 6d,
One years coals to 1791 £6 3s 11d,
Do. from March 1791 to Jan 1792, £7 6s 2d,
Candles £5 0 0d,
Water £1 4s 0d
Living during the time of my residence in Edinburgh £69 9s 1d.

Robert's figures do not add up but perhaps he included and did not note the hire of horses and chaises.[5] His detailing of expenses was enthusiastic, probably due to constant reminders by William, but somewhat fanciful. As Rasmussen said, 'The financier was an artist'.

In 1752, while Robert was serving under Colonel Skinner at Fort George, George Drummond, the ex-lord provost of Edinburgh, and Sir Gilbert Elliott, Member of Parliament, had published *Proposals for carrying on certain Public Works in the City of Edinburgh*. This was one of the most far-sighted pieces of civic planning ever proposed. 'What is astonishing about the *Proposals* of 1752 is that they outlined a scheme which, in the course of the following eighty years was actually carried out . . . Seldom has the promised land glimpsed by one generation been so swiftly and accurately reproduced and carried out.'[6] The situation was that the old city into which the brothers had been born was literally bursting with over population and had no room for expansion from its spine of rock. The *Proposals* offered alternatives. The document conceived of a New Town to the north of the city on the other side of a drained Nor' Loch and linked to it by bridges. It also envisaged a Merchants' Exchange and a place for storing the national records. Demolition of old houses in the High Street – possibly including the birthplace of David Hume and the manse of John Knox – provided so much earth that a mound of waste now stretched across the loch to the north side. It answered the need for at least one of the proposed bridges and was unimaginatively named 'the Mound'. Parallel to it, work started on the North Bridge in 1765 and in 1766, bids for planning the layout of the New Town were requested. By 21 May six anonymous plans had been received and on 2 August 1766 Plan no. 4 by James Craig was adjudged the best by Lord Provost Drummond with John Adam acting as an adviser.

No formal invitation to tender had been made to Robert and this opportunity arose at a time when he was working on 11 major houses at Syon, Kedleston, Kenwood, Osterley, Harewood, Bowood, Mersham-le-Hatch, Nostell Priory, Newby, Croome and Landsdowne, among others. It was the one time in his career when the putative designer of Lisbon had enough work to avoid entering into competitive projects. In any case, Craig's original plan is now lost and what was adopted in July 1767 was the result of serious consultations by the council, Lord Kames, John Adam and various members of the great and the good. Robert would not have borne this interference.

As part of the modernisation of the city, Drummond had determined that a Royal Exchange for the Edinburgh merchants be built. A private venture had built an exchange in 1680 in Parliament Close but the Edinburgh merchants preferred their old ways of dealing in the open street and the exchange was never used. It vanished in a fire in 1700 and Drummond wanted to tidy up the streets by having the merchants indoors. John Adam, in partnership with Robert, submitted drawings on 21 August 1753 with an estimate of £25,484. The plan was accepted but John was not given the contract to build the new exchange which went to five 'gentlemen belonging to Mary's Chapel'. The 'gentlemen' were 'a mason and three wrights directed by John Ferguson, an architect.'[7] The execution of the building was under the Deacon of the Crafts. Mary's Chapel was Edinburgh's leading Masonic lodge, and shared its premises with the Trade Incorporation which appointed the Deacon of the Masons, a town council member. Thirty-six years later Robert, himself a member of Dalwhinnie Number 2 Lodge, would suffer from another demonstration of local Masonic power.

Craig's plan, for what would be called the New Town, was a

very simple scheme with eight blocks of housing transversed by a broad boulevard with garden squares at either end. The boulevard, inevitably – if sycophantically – to be called George Street, would have parallel streets beyond the blocks which overlooked the drained loch to the south and, to the north, the valley of the Firth of Forth. These streets would be St Giles' Street – St Giles being the city's patron saint – and Forth Street, while the garden squares were to be named after St Andrew and St George. Lanes parallel to George Street would give access to the coach houses and were to be named Rose Street and Thistle Street. It was all very neat and the plan was duly submitted to George III. The final layout saw St Giles' Street become Princes Street, Forth Street become Queen Street and, for complex local reasons, St George's Square was renamed Charlotte Square. There is a nice story that Nancy Orde, daughter of Baron Mure of Orde, took chalk from her purse and, on the side of the new house of David Hume, whom she had been visiting in a yet unnamed street on the south-west corner of St Andrew Square, wrote 'St David's Street'. This may only be a legend (did Edinburgh ladies carry lumps of chalk when making social calls?) but the street name remains. Craig's plan had included churches at the end of both the terminal squares, but, in the case of St Andrew Square the site was already occupied by the house of Sir Lawrence Dundas, built by Chambers. This has been described as 'a triumph of power and money over town planning'.

Robert had been forestalled but, in 1785, he did build an adjacent house for Andrew Crosbie, the vice-dean of the Faculty of Advocates. Meanwhile Baron Mure had bought a site at Number 8 Queen Street, the most northerly street on Craig's plan of the New Town, facing a view of the Firth of Forth over formal private gardens; Robert designed the house for his old friend in 1770–1771. It had a doorway flanked by four quasi-Corinthian pillars, but surprisingly not surmounted by a fan-light. More surprisingly, Robert designed a separate annexe in the garden to the south for the kitchens and servants' quarters. The laundry room was in a basement but there was no drying green, so, at a later date, a tunnel was driven under Queen Street which emerged onto a drying green in the private gardens opposite. Otherwise it is an elegantly classical, undecorated three-storey house sitting easily among the other houses in the street. Many of these houses are of a later date and, while none are by Robert, they fall into the class named by Horace Walpole as 'Adamitic', though they would have lacked the ceiling plaster-work Robert drew out for his friend.

Robert had written to Mure on 5 November 1770, saying he had been in Scotland: 'Stayed only two days as I had an appointment at Edinburgh about the Register Office business'. He had met with a broken shin which kept him housebound for six weeks but he promised to send plans soon. He saw John Home and had 'schemed 2 wings for him to give him the conveniences necessary for a married man'.[8] John Home was the nephew of David Hume who was expanding the family home at Ninewells, Berwickshire.

Robert's plan for Register House, a building to house the National Records, is dated 1771 and on 30 July 1772 Lord Frederick Campbell, the Lord Registrar, reported to the trustees that he had employed Messrs Robert and James Adam to draw up a plan. The contract stipulated that either Robert or James would visit the work annually or bi-annually. The fee payable to them would be 2 ½ per cent of the cost of the building as well as expenses of 50 guineas to be paid for each journey they made to Edinburgh. The plans would be lodged with James Salisbury who was appointed clerk of works at a fee of £100 annually. Salisbury and his family were to be housed, rent free, in a house in adjacent St Andrew Square.[9] The building, 'so much wanted and so exceedingly necessary for the preservation of the public records of that country,' was begun, and on 27 June 1774 the foundation stone was laid.

This building was undertaken when the brotherhood was at its most vulnerable. They had weathered the financial crisis of the Adelphi – but only just – and the pressure on them for constant vigilance in London was enormous. The precise amount earned by the brothers for the building of Register House is difficult to calculate, although there is a record of Robert being paid

£1245 16s 6d, while Salisbury was paid a total of £1,800. This was enough for Salisbury to become a property speculator himself, and he bought plots in the nearby Leith Street building scheme. Robert also contributed drawings for the development of this steeply sloping site for which he was paid, reluctantly, since his plans were never used. There were posthumous payments to Robert of £75 10s 0d and there would have been other miscellaneous payments during the building, but given that the mason's work was priced at £6,810 8s 4½d, it was not a hugely profitable enterprise. The fee of 50 guineas – £3,150 in today's money – may seem exorbitant for a return trip to London, but the journey could take 14 days in all, with the cost of lodging at inns, horse changes and loss of productivity while travelling to be included. So serious were these additional costs that Wyatt had a coach constructed with folding drawing boards so that he could continue working while on the road. Architects, perhaps more than other artisans, had to travel to where the work was available.

Ground had been bought for the site of Register House at the eastern end of Princes Street facing the North Bridge. Where the bridge met the street there was a small piazza where the Theatre Royal had been built in 1768, for which Boswell wrote a dramatic prologue. It is interesting that in building a New Town the earliest buildings were the Public Record Office and a theatre. Churches came later. By the end of 1778 work on Register House ceased, and Adam, realising that this was only a pause, advised that a temporary roof of planks be built. His advice was ignored and pigeons occupied the half-completed building. In 1779 Hugo Arnot wrote, 'Edinburgh may indeed boast of having the most magnificent pigeon-house in Europe.'[10] However in 1789 the transfer of records from the old Parliament House began.

The finished building, now known as Register House, has one of Robert's most easily viewed frontages. Set back from the thoroughfare with a double flight of steps leading to the doorway, there is a rusticated lower storey. Above the doorway four Corinthian columns support a low pediment, while pavilions at each end of the building are surmounted by a turret with a small dome on a square base. The southern faces of these turrets carry a clock to the west, and a wind vane to the east. There is a low dome all but invisible from street level, in the Roman style, but splendidly visible from the North Bridge. This view of Robert's building is now ruined by an equestrian statue of the Duke of Wellington placed directly in front.

In the interior the visitor moves from a spacious entrance hall to a rotunda, or main reading space, covered by this dome and flooded with light from it. This succession of spaces leading to the largest surviving Adam ceiling, provides the movement in the building. Since the rotunda is larger and more spectacularly lit than the entrance, the impression of size is greatly enhanced as the visitor moves from daylight into a comparatively dark entrance hall and then progresses towards greater light. In the Guggenheim Museum in New York Frank Lloyd Wright used the same technique to lead us through a small entrance to a vast rotunda. This technique derives from the Pantheon in Rome, still exerting its influence in the last century.

Robert's method of heating the rotunda in the Register House by hot air grilles in the floor is simply an adaptation of the Roman hypocaust system. Sadly Robert died before the building was completed in 1800 and the rear portion, including the Research Room, was built by Robert Reid. Reid was not only the king's architect in Scotland from 1808 to 1856, he was the son of Alexander Reid, a bitter enemy of Robert's. Although he was a much inferior architect, he was able to complete works which were far superior to his own, but the building shows all the signs of compromise and committee limitation. Sir John Soane believed that, 'the British Coffee House at Charing Cross shows more novelty and fancy and does as much honour to the memory of Robert Adam as the great structure he raised to contain the public records of Scotland.'[11]

To be fair, Robert worked within the boundaries of taste displayed by the Trustees, men devoted to the classicism of Edinburgh's New Town, a style not entirely to the liking of Sir John Soane: 'The Old Town of Edinburgh by the variety and breaks in the outlines of its buildings is more beautiful and possibly not less convenient than the new town, with all is regularity and polish.'[12]

There exists a sketch – no more than that – for a piazza facing Register House including the already existing Theatre Royal. This plan was never expanded in detail and it remains an architect's doodle. However, combined with Robert's detailed plan for an extension eastwards towards the Calton Hill and for a colonnaded street leading towards Leith, north-eastwards from Register House, there would have been an elegant eastern New Town. The extension towards Calton Hill would have passed over the proposed Calton Viaduct, a Roman-style bridge with shops and storehouses below it, and continued to the city's Bridewell*, built in the Gothic style in 1791 to Adam's design. With an eye to the coming fashion for Romanticism, Robert even conjectured that the hill itself might have some classical ruins built on it. Ironically these were supplied in the next century by still half-finished monuments celebrating Britain's victory over Napoleon. 'Had each of these schemes been executed they would have provided the eastern boundaries of Georgian Edinburgh with a succession of classical terraces which in their impact, would have been equal to those built in Regent's Park by John Nash.'[13] Sadly none of these schemes came to fruition.

It was an enormous stimulus for Robert to see the multiplicity of building taking place in his native city and back at 4 Adelphi Terrace Robert's pen flew over designs for streets and terraces which might come to a later fruition. The building of Edinburgh's New Town continued until well into the next century and it was a boom time for architects and builders. When the Rev. Stebbing Shaw visited the city in 1788 he reported:

> Such is the present rage for building that streets are daily rising to the surprise of everybody, and I was informed by a principal architect that near 12,000 workmen are now employed for this purpose . . . There is also another parallel

* The term derives from the Tudor St Bride's Hospital for the destitute in London, later converted into a prison.

to the north one [bridge], formed entirely out of earth taken out of the foundation of the new town begun in 1783, and now brought almost level . . . The Register House is a very noble structure of the Corinthian order, about two hundred feet long and one hundred and twenty wide. In the centre is a large dome, fifty feet diameter, and eighty high; but as it is intended for public use and divided into small offices, the visitor will be much disappointed with the inside, after a display of so much magnificence. This was begun in 1774 and not yet finished. The expense will amount to £40,000 . . . The university, or college of King James, is in a ruinous condition, and rather a disgrace than an ornament to a place of such high reputation for the study of physic . . . The deportment of the higher class is stiff and reserved, and in all their communications, self interest seems to be their predominant passion and rule of action . . . the women are, in general handsome until they approach twenty, when much of their beauty vanishes and they become large and masculine.[14]

The brothers who, as native Edinburghers, already had experience of coping with a haughty 'higher class' and their masculine wives, were to come into direct conflict with this establishment.

However, the mid 1770s saw another unwanted problem arrive on the brothers' doorstep. The quality of the stucco they used for decoration had always been problematical, especially on exteriors, and we have heard how the decorations on Kenwood House had to be replaced. In 1765 improved 'stucco-duro' was invented, and patented, by David Wark of Haddington and then a Swiss clergyman, Liardet, produced and patented another improvement. The brothers, wisely, bought the patents in 1776 and called the product 'Adam's new invented patent stucco'. They ensured their rights to use the new material by Robert obtaining an Act of Parliament making them the sole manufacturers and merchandisers. But even this new stucco was faulty and they were sued many times, notably by Lord Stanhope in 1778, with disastrous financial consequences. When another entrepreneur, Johnson, produced what he claimed to be an improved version, the brothers felt that his method had infringed their patent and they sued and won. The case was heard before Lord Mansfield and to nobody's surprise the verdict was given in favour of Adam & Co. Liardet then claimed that the fault in the stucco arose from its manufacture and the brothers had to pay him considerable damages.

As was painfully clear in the Adelphi affair, the brothers' business skills were limited. Robert's talents lay in architecture and design and James concentrated on attracting clients, while William was ineffectual in controlling his imaginative siblings. They set up the Battersea and Sand End Company making saltpetre and barrels, something totally outside their field of expertise; the company collapsed with debts of £30,000 when their partner in this enterprise, one J.P. De Bruges, absconded with what money there was left. John wrote to William, 'Everybody at this distance cried out that he must be a cheat, and did not understand what he pretended to. So the event proves and a sad event it is.'[15] John had now distanced himself from these wild enterprises and took to confiding his fears to William as the business tottered. The London business manager Henry Robertson emigrated to America in 1780 and his replacement Archibald Campbell quarrelled and left the firm in 1782. In 1776 the balance had been £8,854 1s 2d in the red, by 1780 the deficit had increased to £27,008 5s 3d while total debts stood at £95,000 with £4,750 interest payable annually. By 1784 the deficit had risen by a further £10,750 although in 1790 some slight economies brought it down to £34,971 7s 10d. John despaired of the improvidence of Robert and James and after 1781 had little contact with the London office. He wrote to James, 'Let us now (I hope to God it is not yet too late) take the contrary system and at least obtain honour and honesty as our reward, if we should not be able to accomplish riches. You shall always find in me and mine [a readiness] to enter cheerfully into every view of that kind . . . without which sham and confusion must ensue.'[16] However, since Robert and James paid their fees into their private accounts they felt no responsibility for the dire circumstances of the partnership and continued to pursue art and glory rather than profit. The brothers' father, William Adam, must have been spinning in his grave in the Greyfriars churchyard.

Back in England in 1775 the brothers undertook a new speciality with vigour when they were asked to recreate the Market Hall and theatre in Bury St Edmunds. Robert had, in 1761, built Little Market Hall in High Wycombe, adapting the existing Shambles [slaughterhouse] and Butter Market into an elegant fusion of mediaeval and classical styles. In Bury St Edmunds the existing building had an open market at ground level which he adapted by rusticating the walls and opening up the interior by removing some of the supporting piers. Stairs at one end of the hall led to a theatre on the first floor, allowing Robert the licence to introduce panels in the exterior walls showing the masks of tragedy and comedy. Most of the features were lost in a fire in 1908 but the building has now been lovingly restored.

More extensive were the improvements Robert made to Covent Garden Theatre at the request of his old friend David Garrick. Garrick had, for some time, been imposing stricter discipline on his audiences. In the 1750s attendance at the theatre was a social event in which the performance of the play was almost an irrelevance. Long before the performance began, seats – all of which were unreserved – would be occupied by servants on their masters' behalf. The servants were supplied with food and drink and engaged in conversation and occasional song until the owners of the seats arrived. The best seats were on the stage itself which was protected by armed guards to prevent any spontaneous interruptions by members of the audience. After making private financial arrangements with the staff, audience members were quite accustomed to climbing onto the stage and walking backstage during the performance, usually in search of actresses in *déshabillé*. When the searches were successful, which they usually were, assignations would be made and flirtations started. The aristocratic audience would often hold conversations across the stage, oblivious to the action of the play.

In the auditorium, eating, drinking, conversation and shifting of places continued. There were boxes with direct access to the playing area, and passage through them was frequent. The general impression was that a play was being performed in the centre of a rowdy party and it took actors of considerable presence to silence the audience and hold its attention. Garrick had determined to change all this, not without resistance. In spite of remonstrations and having to endure a loss of takings, Garrick banished patrons from the stage and prevented them from going backstage during the performance. To make some of these reforms permanent, he asked Robert to redesign the theatre.

The Covent Garden Theatre became 'the prettiest and most elegant theatre that London could ever boast.'[17] In 1775 Robert redecorated the auditorium to hold an audience of 3,000, with three tiers surrounding the pit which had ten rows of benches. There were three tiers of boxes at the back of the pit and nine rows of stepped benches were divided into nine boxes. The flat plaster ceiling was painted into a *trompe-l'oeil* dome. The boxes on the stage still remained, but direct access from them to the stage itself had disappeared. An orchestra pit ran across the full 30 feet of the stage, so that access on either side was limited and the stage invasions of the past were now all but impossible. There was no longer any need for armed guards to the left and right of the stage. The *Public Advertiser* on 30 September 1775 reported: 'I was a good deal surprised to find that by some means or other the ingenious artists had contrived to give an appearance of greater magnitude to the house . . . the sound of the music and the actors voices were both improved . . . All the people around me agreed with me in this fact, and owned they found it a very uncommon effort of art . . . it perfectly answered my ideas of elegance and splendour.'[18] Over the proscenium arch was a large oblong panel depicting, 'The Apotheosis of Shakespeare supported by the Tragic and Comic Muses.'

The interior had a grand and spacious air. The theatre seems to have been wider than it is now, and more in the shape of a square, and the seats were disposed in galleries, rather than boxes. Every one could see and hear to the best advantage. The exterior front was given a new entrance in Brydges Street [now Catherine Street] and was resurfaced with Liardet's Stone Paste. A balcony with an iron balustrade ran across the three window bays on the first floor with offices behind. The decorations were in the Italian style, then in fashion, overlaid with the garlands and flowers which spread over the Adelphi houses, and even over the chimney pieces we see in old mansions of this era.[19]

'The façade was fitted with pilasters, pediment, balcony and colonnade, and crowned at the top with the singular device of a military trophy – a helmet and a coat of mail. At one corner was a lion, at the other a unicorn. Great improvements were made in the approaches to the boxes, and part of the Rose Tavern in Bridge Street was taken to give more room. "It was noble", he said [Garrick].'[20] Uniquely in Robert's exterior designs there was a continuous balcony at first-floor level with an iron balustrade under which lamps illuminated the main entrance.

The theatre had changed from a place of raucous entertainment provided by people little better than vagabonds and whores to an art form in its own right. David Garrick had made it respectable and Robert Adam had made it convenient.

Adam was now, at the age of 48, travelling even longer distances than he had as a young architect. When not using his own coach, he would travel in a hired chaise with a coachman, covering about 50 miles in a day, while occasionally stopping to make local contact or even to draw sketches of buildings which intrigued him: a notebook has one such sketch of Northampton church. He also carried 40 guineas in cash for day-to-day expenses, but since dinner, bed and breakfast cost him between 10 and 14 shillings this seemed a lavish sum to carry around. He quoted the expenses he allowed for a clerk, or foreman, as horse hire, 2s 6d, horse maintenance, 2s, breakfast, dinner and supper, 3s, drink, 2s 6d, total 10s; then he adds, 'but you might get one for 8s 6d.'[21] For himself he allowed nearly 6 guineas daily or 126 shillings!

One of his longer voyages in 1770 took him to Culzean Castle, a site which would occupy him for 20 years. In this case Robert had to deal with a building worthy of its name, owned by Thomas Kennedy, Earl of Casslis, who died unmarried in 1775, having spent £30,000 transforming the estate and modernising the castle. His brother David Kennedy, another bachelor, continued the work until his death in December 1792. The family, and the castle, traced its history to Gilbert de Kennedy, who in 1466 was one of the regents of Scotland in the reign of James III, and its position proclaimed the family's power. Situated on a rocky headland on the coast of Ayrshire, it is easy to see how the Kennedys had been the principal agents for the Excise in an area thick with smuggling and illicit distilling.

There was no possibility of adapting the original structure to eighteenth-century fashion and Robert left the mediaeval brew houses and bakeries alone. The interior of the rectangular block at the centre of the castle was modernised and Adam then built a circular tower with adjoining wings between it and the sea. The centre of the existing tower had a light well running the full height, which Robert used to accommodate an oval staircase reaching all three floors. This staircase has galleries with Doric columns on the ground floor, Corinthian columns on the first floor and Ionic columns on the top floor. This may seem a trivial point of decorative detail but it is a complete reversal of the convention – although Adam had flirted with this innovation at Osterley – and Adam's enlightened view of conventions allowed him to throw out of the window the pattern books so slavishly followed by his contemporaries. On the first floor the circular tower is entered through a vestibule and provides breathtaking views of the sea through its seven floor-to-ceiling windows. On the floor above he splits the circle to provide two semicircular bedrooms with, incredibly, three-and-a-half windows each. This allowed the exterior asymmetry to be undisturbed and the castle to have more of a mediaeval aspect than before Robert's modernisation. It represents the satisfying idea of a mediaeval castle with all the conveniences of the eighteenth century. Stebbing Shaw visited Culzean in 1787.

> We now approached the noble castle in view, which toward the sea had all the appearance of antiquity, built upon a perpendicular cliff of one hundred feet at least from the surface of the water, but a nearer inspection presented us, on the opposite side with a very elegant front of castle like features wrought in fine stone, which you approach over a large bridge, so constructed and discoloured, as to have every appearance of ancient Gothic. All the outward buildings are grand architecture of the same style. What rooms are finished in the castle are very elegant, and the whole on a scale best adapted for use and enjoyment. But I was informed His Lordship, not content with the present extensive pile, intends adding a similar front to the sea, which will be a most arduous undertaking from the vast depth of the foundation necessary to be formed. At present it does great credit to Adam, the architect, and his Lordship's peculiar taste, and will, when complete, stand unrivalled in its way.[22]

Robert's plans for the ceilings and carpets, some made locally, were all carried out, and the castle, still being completed two decades after Robert's death, now stands as one of his finest achievements. So fine, in fact, that, in 1945, a suite of rooms in the castle was put at the permanent disposal of General Eisenhower, as thanks for his part in the allied victory in Europe. Any person who confines the idea of the 'Adam Style' to strictly classical sources would be immediately contradicted by Culzean. Inveraray is Gothic, and there the existing structure was preserved with little in the way of amendments, but at Culzean Robert drew on all his experience to demonstrate the confidence of a great architect in full maturity.

The partnership continued its work in London on properties in the capital where their personal investments were not always fruitful. The brothers had decorated a house in Portland Place for the Earl of Findlater in 1775, but five years later found themselves short of ready funds; on 17 May 1780 they sent his lordship a begging letter for £2,000 which the earl supplied. In April 1783, presumably when the loan was due for repayment, they wrote, confessing that they had failed to sell a house in Portland Place, due to a recession in the property market, even after a drop in the asking price, and they could not repay the £700 due on that date. Finally, on 2 September 1785, the partnership paid £500 and assured his lordship that they had sent the chimneys he had ordered to Cullen House in Banffshire.[23]

In Edinburgh Robert and James had to admit that they had so far been excluded from the building of the East End of the New Town and that the dream of an elegant piazza in front of the Register House was no more than that. In 1776 James Craig was making surveys for the construction of an observatory on Calton Hill to the east of Princes Street when he encountered Robert: '. . . upon seeing the intended observatory founded on the top of an high and abrupt hill, which terminates in a precipice, he [Robert] conceived the idea of giving the whole the appearance of a fortification, to which it was excellently adapted. Accordingly the line was chalked out for inclosing the limits of the observatory with a wall constructed with buttresses and embrasures, and having Gothick towers at the angles. The beauty of the design was so much admired, that the main object was forgot . . . Here is a building which the folly of its contrivers led them to begin, without considering that by their poverty they were unable to finish it.'[24] Only the Observatory House includes the tower of Robert's 'Gothick' folly; the observatory was completed by William Playfair in the nineteenth century, and the hill is surmounted with a motley collection of buildings. Dominating all is the National Monument, a proposed replica of the Athenian Parthenon, also by Playfair, and abandoned in 1829 for lack of funds.

Robert's plans for the southern approaches to the North

Bridge were ignored, but the extension of the South Bridge towards the university was still, it seemed, open for debate, although it was to be a tangled tale of intrigue. To oversee the construction of this street eleven trustees, answerable to the town council, were appointed, including the provost, Sir James Hunter Blair, himself a freemason and member of Mary's Chapel, Henry Dundas, one of the most influential members of parliament, who acted as chairman, and Dundas's half-brother Robert. With them were the Duke of Buccleugh, the Rt Hon. Islay Campbell, the Lord Advocate, Sir William Forbes of Pitsligo and the notorious judge, Lord Braxfield. Believing that someone with technical knowledge might be an asset, they appointed James Brown, an architect, as a further trustee. Brown was also a property developer and had started the speculative development of George Square to the south of the New Town. The square was initially developed from Ross Park by John Adam, who sold it profitably to Brown in 1761. Brown named it after his brother, George, thus disrupting Craig's idea of naming the square to the west of George Street after the English patron saint, and balancing St Andrew Square to the east. It is now Charlotte Square, named for Charlotte of Mecklenburg-Strelitz, George III's queen.

In May 1785 the South Bridge Act was passed, allowing for a general tax on all citizens with any profits from the leasing of properties to be spent on the refurbishment of the Old College of the university. Robert Kay was appointed as surveyor and inspector, although his role seems to have been that of a coordinator of the various plans that were considered.

While Hunter Blair was in London steering his South Bridge Act through parliament he met with Robert and discussed what might be done. Adam was helpful in guiding Hunter Blair through the pitfalls of both the House of Commons as well as the Lords and the two men discussed the possible designs for the street. Adam promised to send plans to Edinburgh and on 25 June he wrote: 'I am really ashamed and vexed at having so long delayed sending your lordship the plans of the street and bridge over the Cowgate and still more so at not having explained the cause of the delay in answer to your obliging letter which I had the honour of receiving a month ago . . . You will have them either by private hand or by the fly within a fortnight.'[25] Adam had experienced difficulty since his draughtsmen had become seriously ill. This did not prevent the brothers submitting their invoice before sending the plans. On 12 July they sent an invoice for £98 15s od. for plans and 'various attendances at meetings of the Trustees in London at the houses of Lords and Commons. To the clerks £5 gns for drawing up the invoice.'[26] Then on 14 July he sent the plans, 'taking into account the discussions' he had had with Hunter Blair in London. 'I have endeavoured as much as possible to make them agreeable to the information I had from your lordship in London.'[27]

Hunter Blair had obviously been worried that a colonnade would render the shop fronts dark and obscure, but Robert assured the provost that he has compared the columns with those in the Admiralty building and 'the light of the shops would not suffer in the smallest degree from the footways being under cover'. The colonnade would keep the rain off window-shoppers and there would be grates between the columns. Adam also proposed an inn to the south which would be called the Arms of the City of Edinburgh and a staircase from South Bridge Street which would lead down to the Cowgate 'on the level of the old entry to my father's old house'. He enclosed plans for houses and shops in Leith Street. 'I hope your lordship will prevent the drawing from being copied or going into bad hands, it is easy to find fault and criticise, though not so easy to invent.'[28]

The plans Robert produced were for a pillared colonnade in front of a terrace of shops surmounted by dwelling houses. The rising ground from the Cowgate was to be filled with warehouses, while the lower road itself was to be covered by an elaborate bridge with twin towers over a lower balustrade carrying lions on either side. On the western side of the street the dwelling houses were to have three pediments supported by Ionic pillars with an iron balustrade running the length of the building. It echoed the elegance of Italian cities with their shaded loggias, neatly solving the problem of the steeply rising and falling ground while also providing the trustees with a large number of dwellings and shops for rent. Two days later, on 14 July, Robert wrote to the trustees: 'I have endeavoured to overcome all the difficulties particularly those owing to the risings and fallings of the ground which are puzzling in regular buildings and where a continuation of straight lines gives great beauty.'[29] William reported to John Clerk of Eldin that 'the plan Bob produced today was much admired'. Robert's plan went far beyond what the trustees were envisaging. He designed a new façade block to screen the old university buildings with an elegant circus opposite them containing re-sidences for the professors. He also proposed extending the route of the street southward as far as the inn, to mark the entry point to Edinburgh with a new set of assembly rooms opposite and adjacent to the university. It was to be both elegant and triumphalist, but ignored some crucial facts of local politics.

Since James Brown had only recently built the nearby George Square Assembly Rooms in Buccleuch Place – a venture which much interested Braxfield and Dundas, both residents of Brown's newly fashionable George Square, and investors in the scheme – Robert's grand idea was destined to get short shrift from the trustees. They wanted indemnities on possible losses and could not agree on anything concerning the precise route or extension of the street. They promptly adjourned for a 'sennight'. The Duke of Buccleuch prophesied that the project would be botched, but on 1 August 1785 the foundation stone was laid. Robert was attempting to negotiate from London, which was itself an irritant to the native Scots, and was doing so without any firm grasp of the internal politics and financial interests of the trustees. He was fighting with his eyes shut.

However he continued his efforts, writing directly to Hunter Blair:

It is seldom that such an opportunity occurs for an architect to show his talents. It is therefore very natural for me to wish for the sake of my own reputation that if my designs are to be adopted they should be properly carried into execution. But from what I have heard this is not likely to be the case. It may become as ugly and as deformed a piece of work as ever disgraced a great city . . . For these reasons I feel myself exceedingly anxious to have this business put on some proper footing especially as my name is at present connected with it . . . When I was at Edinburgh and proposed to superintend the whole of this work the emolument I was to receive seemed to be a bar to this proposition, but I do assure your Lordship it was not as much the pecuniary disadvantage I looked to as the desire and ambition I felt to see this noble work properly done. If therefore it were agreeable to your Lordship and the Trustees to put this business under my direction I am ready to engage to survey it and see it properly carried into execution for a modest salary and the expense of my journeys.[30]

On 6 February the provost replied. 'The Trustees cannot accept any plan which diminishes the value of the ground lots at a public sale. The Trustees have already engaged their private fortunes to the extent of more than £20,000.' In spite of having held an invoice from the brothers for over six months Hunter Blair asked for another. 'The Trustees do not wish you to be at any more trouble until it is known whether the plan of a new college can be carried into execution.' This was not only a caution to stop importuning the trustees, but also a lightly veiled threat that the brothers Adam might not be considered for the building of the new university. Robert ignored the threat.

In February 1786 the trustees made a contract with Alexander Laing, a local architect and mason, but the following month Robert wrote, 'Your lordship and the Trustees have been far too precipitate in pushing on the works'. Robert had been given various plans of the ground and some were found to be erroneous, with mistakes in the ground level surveys. 'But it is not too late and the new plan will not affect the value of the lots.' He was still fighting to protect his colonnade although the trustees thought of taking 'some house in the New Town as a model and repeating that through the whole length of the new street [which] would certainly produce a very tiresome and bad effect. I have given my sentiments freely, I am sorry to find they differ so much from your Lordship's and the Trustees, but I cannot help feeling as others do, extremely disappointed on thinking that so uncommon and so fine an opportunity which does not occur once in a century should be lost both to your Lordship and to myself and to the public'.

The Trustees made 'Remarks on the plan now carrying into execution by the Trustees for the South Bridge in Edinburgh' which contrasted with what Robert proposed. 'The great beauty of the street will be destroyed by not running in a proper direction.' The houses would slope 'producing a most disagreeable effect. The colonnade would darken the shops. The small arches proposed by Mr Adam for the footway, passengers would make an improper use of and become receptacles of nastiness.' By April 1786 Hunter Blair and the Trustees were in London to negotiate a second Act of Parliament and met with the brothers to no great avail in 13 Albemarle Street, to which he and his family had moved from their apartments in the Adelphi. It was Robert's last permanent address, a few hundred yards from his original headquarters at Lower Grosvenor Street.

On 21 April Robert, accompanied by William, met with the trustees in Edinburgh to put their case in person: 'The whole side of the street being one connected design, every separate house makes only a part of the whole, which forms the symmetry that pleases the eye, without having the dull effect of a repetition of one thing without meaning and without design.' Here Robert was suggesting that the street should be designed as an architectural entity with the individual houses merely forming parts of the whole. This was a design he would bring to fruition in the so-called 'palace fronts' in Edinburgh's Charlotte Square. As to the bridge, Robert found the existing design tawdry: 'the Trustees may depend on it that it will meet with universal condemnation when executed'. Again he stressed the commercial

gain to be had from his revisions: 'All these circumstances
contribute to make the Trustees risk upon Mr Adam's new plan
less than upon that which they now propose to carry into
execution.' In sober fact his new scheme increased the rentable
value of the site by £6,608

In a long letter of May 1786 Robert points out that his plan
would save the trustees £4,058 while their plan would lose them
£3,384. But the Adam plan was, inevitably, rejected and in 1787
the brothers submitted a final invoice for £1,228 11s 0d. This
resulted in an appeal on 28 August 1787 when the trustees agreed
a payment of £500 on account and left judgement on settling the
remainder entirely to Henry Dundas. Finally in November
Dundas agreed, through a Decree Arbitral, to pay a further
£400, a not inconsiderable sum for a design that was never built.
This was a plan which, had it been built, 'must have made the
bridges the most famous Neo-Classical street in Europe.'[31] 'But
the real reward would have been to be awarded the contract for
rebuilding the College.'[32]

John Adam, who was by now almost completely estranged from
his brothers, managed to sell the trustees a house in the north-west
angle of Adam Square for £1,800. He had reason to believe that he
had been used harshly by his brothers. They had been of little help
during his financial troubles following the failure of the Fairholme
bank in 1762, and he had been forced to mortgage Blair Adam
peremptorily to provide security for their Adelphi scheme. John
was now living in Fountainbridge in Edinburgh and had invested
wisely in property in the rapidly growing city. His sale of Hope
Park to Brown for development as George Square established him
as a major player in the commercial development of Edinburgh.
He was respected enough to be consulted over the adoption of
Craig's plan and the building of the North Bridge.

Unfortunately the trustees of the South Bridge would not trust
their money to Robert's plan although it would have created a
spectacular and innovative entry point into Edinburgh for travellers from the south. He was greatly disappointed by this rejection
in his native city.

Alistair Rowan believes the Adam schemes for the South Bridge foundered for two reasons: '(1) the brothers entered into the debate about the best form which the bridge and street would take after the work had already been begun by a group of Trustees for the Town Council on the basis of a utilitarian design overseen by a local man, and (2) they were too distant . . . Local interests and opportunities were threatened by the intervention of such great men from the capital. Ultimately Edinburgh business managers saw off the brothers' challenge.'[33] Added to these reasons was the underlying resentment against any person returning to his roots, having established himself and been successful elsewhere. The nabobs, returning from India having shaken fortunes 'out of the pagoda tree', were only just tolerated as figures of enviable fun, but to return from London as a polished Englishman was unforgivable. It is a mark of Adam's reputation that he was given any civic work at all. Sadly, the South Bridge is now a dismal collection of sordid buildings housing discount shops: a dream of elegance replaced by unimaginative commercialism at its most tawdry.

Equally tawdry at the end of the eighteenth century was the state of the university. Captain Topham had noted in 1776 that 'the College is a very ancient and irregular building, consisting of three courts on different planes, which are small, and contain rooms for the professors to read their lectures. I do not find any of the professors inhabit the college, except the principal. As the University of Edinburgh is celebrated throughout Europe . . . the number of young persons that crowd here from different countries is prodigious.'[34] An anonymous commentator in *Fugitive Pieces* added to the condemnation: 'The University is in the same ruinous condition that it was in 1763, and the most celebrated university in Europe is the worst accommodated.'[35] On 23 December 1767 a *Memorial* spelt out the necessities: 'The whole fabric has a mean, irregular, and contemptible appearance. Some of the houses which were found upon the area when it was purchased were converted, as they stood, into a part of the University's buildings and many of the schools of teaching rooms are at this day crowded into what was the Marquis of Hamilton's house. A stranger, when conducted to view the University of Edinburgh might, on seeing such courts and buildings, naturally enough imagine them to be alms houses for the reception of the poor.' However the pamphlet also suggested the appointment of a group of 43 trustees, making it the most unwieldy committee imaginable.

The author of the *Memorial* was William Robertson, who was principal of the university from 1762 until 1793, 'perhaps the high point in its history'.[36] He was a minister of the Church of Scotland at Greyfriars Kirk where his tomb stands beside that of Robert's father, William Adam, and Robert Adam was William Robertson's cousin. An eminent historian, Robertson abolished the necessity for religious tests to be applied to professorships and befriended the progenitors of the Scottish Enlightenment. 'He was concerned to build bridges, so to say, between Jerusalem and Athens'.[37] His *Memorial*, however, fell on deaf ears.

The problem of the decaying university premises would not go away and in 1779, the historian Hugo Arnot, in a fit of Republicanism, suggested that the university relocate itself to the Palace of Holyroodhouse, which, apart from the Young Pretender's brief visit, had stood empty since 1707. No one took this proposal seriously.

More serious was an open *Letter to the Rt Hon Henry Dundas* written by James Gregory, Professor of the Theory of Medicine: 'The university itself is the boast of our city and our country, the buildings belonging to it are a disgrace to both. It is common . . . to dissuade strangers from going to visit the buildings.' The letter goes on to describe the precise needs: 'No better situation for a new college can be required than the site of the old. By means of the new South Bridge, it will have such easy and immediate connection with the rest of the city, that it may be regarded as near the centre of it.' The development of the new South Bridge had clearly brought the plight of the university into public debate. Among the other plans for this bridge ' . . . we were much gratified lately with the sight of a plan and elevation of the east wing of a new college designed by Mr Robert Adam, and would no doubt, be much gratified were we favoured with a complete plan of a new college from the same masterly hand.'[38] The letter went on to make a similar plea for the erection of a Bridewell to house short-term detainees, debtors and lunatics. This would have allowed the removal of the old Tolbooth jail in the High Street and facilitated the clearance of the Lucken-booths, a motley assembly of shops built against the north side of the High Kirk of St Giles, while the alternative prison in the Canongate would continue in all its squalor. The letter was written by someone far-sightedly concerned for the future development of the city.

Events now moved with almost dizzying speed. On 19 October 1789 Principal Robertson told the university senate that the town council had ruled that the foundation stone for the new university which would be designed by Robert Adam, architect, would be laid on 16 November. The next day Robertson and his colleagues met with Provost Thomas Elder and the town council, and also present was Robert Adam, architect. *The Scots Magazine* reported that, 'on 25 October the Trustees with Henry Dundas and Robert Adam of London resolved that the new buildings for the university within the City of Edinburgh should be begun to be erected with all convenient speed, conformably to a plan prepared by the same Robert Adam which has met with general approbation'.[39] Significantly Robert was also named as surveyor. This was important since it meant that Robert would choose the various tradesmen to whom contracts would be awarded, thus inevitably, antagonising the losers. He would also have authority beyond that of Alexander Reid, Deacon of the Masons, who claimed his own right to have first refusal of any civic contract and to charge whatever seemed reasonable to him without further supervision. Robert had powerful support from Principal Robert-son, Lord Provost Elder – and James Stirling, Elder's replacement in 1791. It cannot have hindered his cause that Andrew Dalziel, Professor of Greek, was Robert's nephew by marriage, but Robert's most powerful ally was undoubtedly Henry Dundas.

Henry Dundas was born in 1742 and became a member of the College of Advocates when only 21, rising meteorically to be Solicitor General three years later. In 1774 he was elected member of parliament for Midlothian, and a year after was appointed Lord Advocate, as which he was noted for his tolerance towards Roman Catholics. Positions of power and patronage poured in and on 31 July 1782 he became Treasurer of the Navy, then Privy Councillor and Keeper of the Signet. As such he held the patronage of all government places in Scotland. On 3 September 1784 he took charge of the Board of Control for India, as well as controlling the restoration of estates forfeited during the 1745 rebellion. In 1790 he became the member of parliament for Edinburgh and in 1791 he was appointed Home Secretary. Not for nothing was he nicknamed 'Harry the Ninth.' His family home at Arniston had been built by Robert's father, William, and Dundas had been sympathetic to Robert during the fiasco of provincial favouritism in the building of the South Bridge.

Yet Dundas had reservations about Adam's total control of building at the university and he refused to confirm him as surveyor. The result was fast and furious. On 31 October Robert wrote a long letter to Principal Robertson:

> I have considered Mr Dundas's letter to you of yesterday in which he seems to think that it would be improper to insert the clause in the subscription paper appointing me to survey the execution of my own plan. I have been very much pleased with the candid and handsome manner in which Mr Dundas has hitherto acted in the business and I am confident that he will approve of my speaking and my feelings on the subject of the clause in question. It was in order that everything might be upon a fair and even footing that I insisted on the clause being inserted and I was of the opinion that the same committee that authorised the subscription papers fixing the adoption of my plan could also appoint me to have the direction of the building. I wished that this might be done immediately as the very best way of preventing all

jealousies. At the same time it was always my intention to employ any tradesmen or artificers recommended by the Town Council with the approbation of the Trustees. I have hitherto proceeded in this business upon the faith that I was to have the direction of the work nor could I consent to the execution of my plan in any other mode, as I know it would not otherwise be done either to my own satisfaction or that of the public. And as I have bestowed so much passion and thought upon it, and exerted myself to the utmost to make it as perfect as possible, and though the money is no indifferent object to me, yet I am anxious I have been infinitely more educated by the motive of leaving behind me a monument of my talents, such as they are, than by any hope of gain whatever. As Mr Dundas has already so deservedly gained the greatest praise from all descriptions of men for the firm and spirited part he has acted in this business, I flatter myself that he will not hesitate upon further consideration to adhere to his former opinion. If not, I must freely say that I shall though with the greatest reluctance be under the necessity of declining all further concern in this business. I, after spending so much time and pains, have the mortification of returning immediately to London with the disagreeable reflection that my plan has not had the effect to accelerate this grand and important work which I had so much at heart and while the public was so impatient to see executed. I beg you will communicate this with Mr Dundas without loss of time, as his answer must determine me whether to go or not, and I hope well of all other proceedings on this building.[40]

Adam's threatened resignation was enough and he was confirmed as surveyor on 14 November 1789, two days before the foundation stone was laid.

CHAPTER ELEVEN

Monuments of His Taste and Genius

❧

The laying of the foundation stone of Edinburgh University was the commencement of the enterprise Robert had always sought. It would be a great public building.

In every other enterprise in which Robert Adam had been involved he had been able to operate with a comparatively free hand, subject only to the whims of his patron, but now the building was under the control of a board of trustees. This had been true with the Register House but here the conflicting interests were far more complex. The university interest was represented by Principal Robertson, Robert's relative and ally, but the vested interests of the Edinburgh architects and trades-men would have to be considered and appeased. The city's freemasons did not take kindly to being thrust aside by a man they regarded as an incomer, and, worse than that, an Edinburgh-born incomer who had made his reputation in London. At the laying of the foundation stone of all his other buildings Robert would have been central to the activity, but this was Edinburgh and the city refused to be impressed by its new architect.

The foundation stone of the university was duly laid on 16 November 1789 with all the ceremonial pomp that Edinburgh freemasonry could muster. A crowd of 30,000 watched a proces-sion of over 300 dignitaries in their most splendid regalia, accompanied by the Town Guard and a detachment of the 35th Regiment of Foot, make their way from Parliament Close to the front of the university. Lord Napier, Grand Master Mason of Scotland, performed the ceremony of laying the stone, which had been prepared by Alexander Reid, as Deacon of the Masons.

Coins and crystal bottles, along with manuscripts describing the history of the university were buried and the stone was sealed with a metal plate bearing a Latin inscription recording the event and asking for the blessing of God. It acknowledged Lord Napier's involvement in the 'aera of Masonry 5789', a system of dating beginning with the presumed foundation of Solomon's temple. All of this arcane ritual was witnessed by Thomas Elder as provost of Edinburgh, William Robertson as principal of the university, and finally, by Robert Adam as the architect. Dundas was given an honorary LLD, as was Lord Napier, who was also given the Freedom of the City. No one should have been under any delusions that Adam was any more than a hired artisan.

According to Adam's elevations, the frontage was to have six huge columns supporting a balcony over a frieze decorated with ox skulls in roundels, the façade pierced by triple arches and flanked by two-storey buildings, the basement level rusticated, with pedimented windows above. Due to the awkward ground, rising steeply from east to west, Adam's plan led the visitor upwards into a series of vistas. The triple gateway led into a first court with living accommodation for professors and the principal around it. This was the first part to be built; after the principal's lodging was completed there was a lengthy delay in further building, giving rise to the rather weak joke: 'There is only the principal gate. It is a gate only for the Principal.' It was not to be the only delay. The entrance continued through a rising carriageway under a bridge, when the approach opened out into the Great Court. At the western end of this, and on account of the rising ground, a flight of steps led to an arcaded loggia beyond which was the Great Hall for graduations and other college ceremonies. This plan again illustrated Robert's great love of 'movement'. Around this court were the various lecture theatres. The pattern was continued on the second storey with the addition of a library and, daringly, the university chapel was placed on the bridge above the carriageway from the first court. It provided everything the university needed and with a crescent of houses facing the front was a masterpiece of elegance. Sadly most of it was never built and the existing building is a weak compromise.

In the autumn of 1789 Robert met John on the street in Edinburgh and, since John noted that they had a 'civil exchange', we can deduce that the relationship between the two brothers had cooled as Robert's business had expanded dangerously and John often found his position in Edinburgh compromised by his more famous brother. Understandably, he was careful to have as little to do with Robert and James as possible. John reported the gist of the meeting to his sister Susan: 'I understand now he intends spending a great portion of his time in this place and Mrs Drysdale is to take a larger house . . . as the sisters, draftsmen, etc. are also to come down . . . as if his employment in London was totally gone so he must hang on here like a man in dependence.' This was partly unfair since the new-found prosperity of Scotland provided attractive new prospects, although the practice was still involved in urban building in London.

Robert faced his first problem with the awarding of the contract for masonry work, a decision he felt was entirely within his power as surveyor, and he asked Alexander Reid to bid for the work. Reid duly made the application and Robert, feeling his price was too high, refused to accept it and awarded the contract to one James Crichton, who had made a lower bid. This was all within normal business practice, but Reid was appalled. The trustees felt, after some prodding, that, given Reid's position as Deacon of the Masons and a senior member of St Mary's Lodge, he should be given a second chance to tender and on 24 November Robert got Reid to agree to carry out the work, but at Crichton's prices. Face was saved and economic wisdom was observed. As if to refute John's prophecy, Robert immediately returned to London to continue administering the building work from a distance. His clerk of works, John Paterson, would, in addition to all his other duties have to provide almost daily reports on progress while waiting for Robert's response. Communication between the two cities had improved and there were now fifteen coaches every week from Edinburgh to London, a journey of four days, or if you could afford it, a mail coach which reached London in 60 hours – two-and-a-half days.

The storm brewed up in Robert's absence and the day after his departure Paterson wrote to Robert: '26 Nov 1789 Mr Reid called at Mr Adam's office and acquainted Mr Paterson that upon second thoughts he could not proceed further with the works of the College at the prices agreed with Mr Adam.'[1] Reid cancelled his orders to the quarry and all deliveries of stone stopped. On 1 December 1789 Paterson replied to Reid: 'I have had a conversation with some of the Trustees in which they were surprised you are not at work. I beg you will write me by bearer your reasons for not going on with the work that I may lay it before the Trustees.' Reid repeated his reasons on cost and Paterson replied the same day that he would now lay Reid's letter before the Trustees and send a copy to Robert. The Trustees asked for secret competitive bids but Paterson pointed out that it was difficult to get secret bids as in Edinburgh everyone knew everyone else. However, understandably, on 8 February he told Robert, 'I wrote you that the Provost wishes you down soon, I wish it were in your power to come, your presence would do a great deal just now'. Reid had relinquished the contract in favour of Crichton, but had merely retired, Achilles-like, to plot his next attack.

The motives for Reid's extraordinary loathing of Robert are complex. They were fellow freemasons and so sworn to brotherly love, but Robert had usurped many of the functions over which Reid felt he should have control. Robert behaved high-handedly as a Londoner and did not mingle with the contractors and workmen in Edinburgh. He was a Scot with a well known brother who was embedded in Edinburgh society, but he had chosen to emigrate to London and now returned insisting on pursuing projects according to his own inclinations. All of this was disturbing enough to Scots who had never worked outside their natal country, but above all, Robert was costing Reid money as he watched contracts he felt were his by right being given to this arrogant incomer to award. The antipathy was deep.

In Robert's next letter, on 25 February, the extent of Robert's Scottish enterprises can be seen. He had sent Paterson his estimates for a house for the Earl of Weymss at Gosford, East Lothian and Paterson 'had a very full conversation with the current Provost Mr Stirling, Mr Cockburn, the Sheriff and Mr Smith, Dean of Guild about the Bridewell and the most proper place for its situation on the Calton Hill'. They discussed the road leading to the Bridewell and 'I said they had it in their power to make one of the finest approaches into Princes Street in the world'. This accorded totally with Adam's ambition to have a spectacular eastern approach to Princes Street.

The Bridewell project was coming near to a decision. In 1782 *The Scots Magazine* printed 'A Proposal to build a Bridewell'[2] in which it pointed out that public whippings had 'scarcely ever been inflicted on any offender who was not mortally intoxicated', but now they could be carried out in the Bridewell on sober offenders on top of the surrounding wall so that, 'those individuals that take pleasure in such exhibitions, will resort at the time appointed to the outside of the wall, where they will have an opportunity of gratifying the strangest of all passions in greater peace and security than they can possibly enjoy at present.' It also reported that, 'The depravity of the present manners of the youth of both sexes among the lower class of people in and about this metropolis is truly alarming to society'.

In March 1790 Reid accused Paterson of having doctored Crichton's figures for the trustees so that he and Crichton could share the difference. Paterson had, wisely, discussed the matter with Dalziel, a trustee, before finalising the situation with Crichton and the matter was dropped. Paterson reported to Robert that 'A malicious and ill founded report was spread abroad', that masons had been employed by graft and advances of cash had been made to Crichton for 'more than his work amounted to'. At a trustees' meeting Paterson had shown his accounts and the provost said 'he was certain he [Paterson] had shown none'. Paterson agreed that there was no partiality in the accounts, but, oddly, accepted that, if there had been 'it had been to the advantage of the Trustees and the public.' Alexander Reid had studied the accounts for ten days 'to find out faults' without success. The result was that Crichton's prices had saved the Trustees £3,488 1s 3½d.

In spite of all this acrimony by Reid and his faction, work on the site had begun in the same month with Paterson concentrating on the frontage and the north-west corner of the main building. This allowed teaching to continue in the remainder of the existing structure while Robert dealt, at long distance, with the specialised needs of various professors. Alexander Monro was Professor of Anatomy and as Monro *secundus*, was the midpoint in a distinguished trio of father and son professors. It was rumoured that Monro *tertius* actually lectured verbatim from his grandfather's Latin notes, made in 1719 when he had studied under Boerhaave in Leyden. Monro requested that underground facilities – including a lime pit – be constructed to receive the remains of his dissection classes. Robert provided the burial pits and on 31 March Monro himself laid a foundation stone for the Anatomy Theatre.

The trustees also received a letter from Joseph Black, Professor of Chemistry. In the letter he praises Robert's plans, but with a sting in the tail: 'In this plan in which utility and beauty are in general so happily combined there is an ample provision of lecturing halls for all the professors.' He then notes that houses are provided as accommodation for some professors, but 'there is no professor whose office stands in more need of this privilege than the Professor of Chemistry'.[3] He lists the amount of work involved in the preparation of experiments and the recording of results, pointing out that the amount of time he spent in front of students was an inaccurate measure of his needs. Robert saw the importance of Black's argument and provided a house in a revised plan.

On 11 May Paterson received the welcome news of Robert's return north. 'I am happy you have been able to form a plan of the intended alteration in the parliament house, to bring with you – the most part of the advocates are impatient to see you with their plan.' Robert had prepared plans and elevations for a new

'College of Justice and of a Library for the Dean and Faculty of Advocates and also a Library for the Writers to the Signet', a two-storey building with a rusticated ground floor and a pillared and pedimented first floor under a small dome. The frontage faced west and the rear of the building fitted neatly into the corner of Parliament Square without destroying the existing seventeenth-century Parliament Hall. It was never built.

In October 1790 Paterson was told by the quarrymen at Craigleith that the giant flanking columns for the frontage were ready. In the style of the Pantheon in Rome and of the columns at Syon House, they were not carved into drums for ease of assembly, but were entire, each 3 feet in diameter and 22 feet high. They were also prodigiously heavy and Paterson was deeply concerned as to which route to the university the columns might take. They could be taken over Ravelston Hill to join the Water of Leith at Bell's Mill in what is now the Dean Village; from where they could be taken easily by barge to Canonmills. They would then be transferred to carts for the steep haul through Broughton to the east end of Princes Street. Now Paterson was faced with the problem of whether the North and South Bridges would carry the weight. The North Bridge had collapsed in August 1769, burying five people in the ruins, and Paterson delayed testing the bridges for five months. If the bridge would not bear the weight, then Paterson would have to cut the columns into drums; although this was was normal practice, it had not been done by the Emperor Hadrian's architect in Rome. Robert was determined to follow in the imperial foot-steps.

In the same month Provost Stirling told Paterson that he wanted Adam to produce designs for the fronts of the buildings in Charlotte Square, and Robert produced a plan of the square with elevations of the east side. Robert would later provide elevations for the other sides of the square. Stirling now voiced the city's objections to Robert's scheme for a road from the east end of Princes Street to the Bridewell. At that time Princes Street ended abruptly with a sharp decline turning north-east into Leith Street, off which St Ninian's Row turned steeply downhill into the back of the Canongate. Robert's plan would bridge St Ninian's Row and continue due east, through Butler's Land, then past the Calton Burying Ground and the proposed Bridewell to his eastern approach boulevard. Provost Stirling felt that the houses in Butler's Land were too valuable to demolish, that the people owning the Calton Burying Ground would not approve any curtailment of their property, and, lastly, that there must be no houses near the Bridewell. Paterson argued with the provost against the objections and even proposed placing the Bridewell on top of the Calton Hill. Robert had already rejected this plan since the building would then be higher than the reservoir on Castle Hill, thus giving the jail no water supply. Paterson believed that with 'the assistance of a machine the people in the Bridewell might work it in themselves', but he was grasping at straws and Robert's plan of a grand boulevard entering Edinburgh from the east had to be abandoned.

November brought more problems, with Reid was now complaining about the system used for the invoicing of stationery. On 12 December 1790 the trustees received a letter setting out the dispute with Reid. [Reid] 'had frequently been heard to say that he would contrive some way or other to embarrass the work'[4]. To add to this Mr Young, treasurer and trustee, but also owner of a carpentry firm, wanted a contract for carpentry work on the same terms as existed for other firms. Paterson quietened him with a promise to mention him to Robert. To add to Robert's problems, the provost agreed that a crescent in front of the main entrance to the university should be built, but caused Robert to redraw his plan entirely by asking for a concert hall to be placed in the centre of it.

At the other end of the city, Robert's plans for Charlotte Square were turned down, as 'you would draw the town into a great expense both for your designs and execution of them'. Robert was not entirely absent from Edinburgh at this time since John records seeing him in the city in December 1790. To the now hostile John this was proof that Robert had, in fact, exhausted his client base in England and there were to be no further great enterprises in that country. Robert was also finding Scottish clients more than normally frustrating. 'All the gentry in this country are architects. They know, or think they know much more than any professional man be he ever so eminent; it has been my constant study to root out this absurd idea of theirs and I flatter myself I am rather gaining ground on them.'[5] This was Robert whistling in the dark. The London practice had always relied on incoming commissions to pay off the debts incurred previously and there were now fewer new commissions coming in.

The effect of all this was to feed Robert's already not inconsiderable arrogance. At the turn of 1790–91 Robert wrote to the trustees re-emphasising his position: 'As Architect and Surveyor to the University of Edinburgh, I take upon me the whole burden of the Building, therefore entitled to employ whom I choose. All contracted prices must be adhered to and all accounts will be laid before the trustees.' He also told the provost that Reid had 'no other reason for being convenor than to watch over Adam and Paterson whom he mortally hated'.

However, another possibility of employment arose on 8 March 1791 when Paterson wrote to Robert that, 'it was agreed I should go to Glasgow with Mr James Stirling and see a piece of ground. The Trades [Association] in Glasgow is going to build a hall and has £6,000 subscribed for it. They are to mention you to the managers of that also and show them the advantages that would arise by bringing you for both . . . talking of beginning the infirmary there soon, no design is fixed for it as yet'. Furthermore, the Provost had not abandoned his idea of having Robert design Charlotte Square 'provided it could be got for little money. He [the Provost] would get the measures of the Square on Monday first to send you. He wishes to keep this a secret from everybody [before] you come down. Mr Baxter has made a design for the Bridewell that they have got it staked out on Calton Hill but whether it is fixed to be built or not I cannot tell.'

Paterson also gave progress reports on Airthrey House in Stirlingshire which was being built to Adam's plans for Robert Haldane; on Seton Castle; on Lord Lauderdale's house at

Dunbar, and on Robert Hogg's house at Newliston. According to Margaret Sanderson in *Robert Adam and Scotland*, at this time Robert was juggling over 30 commissions in Scotland alone, although he would not undertake any work in Glasgow until the next year. Paterson was acting not only as clerk of works to the building of the university, but also as Robert's overseer of the partnership's many projects in Scotland. In addition, he was now being active as an agent procuring future work for Robert. And all for £100 annually!

On his return from Glasgow, Paterson finally had no option but to put the weight-bearing capacity of the bridges to the test and, crossing his fingers, he ordered the lumbering procession with the columns to set out. On 19 March 1791 he wrote to Robert that he had 'the pleasure of informing you that I have got one of them erected at one o'clock this day without the smallest accident taking place and very much to the satisfaction of everyone here.' Three days later another column was erected, but the good news was moderated by a request from Provost Stirling for plans of tea and retiring rooms to be included at the new concert hall. He also wanted Charlotte Square to have 'Lodgings, not houses to let in flats' and not 'much ornaments but with an elegant simplicity'. Robert was paid £200 for the plans for the square and was to be paid 5 guineas for each house he designed. The actual building of the square was largely carried out after his death but the north side gives us a clear idea of his intentions. The so-called 'palace front' looks as if the entire building is a single house on a truly palatial scale but artfully conceals the fact that it possesses several entrances to the 'lodgings'. The lower storey is rusticated along its length while the central bay is a magnificent feature with four Corinthian columns supporting a plain classical pediment. It is flanked by two bays with twin columns, each surmounted by garlanded balustrades. The result is breathtaking. 'Charlotte Square ranks as one of the major achievements in European civic architecture of the period.'[6] The remaining sides were completed by other hands, including that of Robert Reid, Alexander's son, who had completed

Register House. He erected St George's West Church on the west side of the square described by J. Storer in his *Views of Edinburgh* as 'a pile of discordancy seldom to be met with!'; in the *Inventory of the Ancient and Historical Monuments of the City of Edinburgh* the church is described as an 'arresting discord'. Since the man responsible was the son of Robert's 'mortal enemy', it is unsurprising that he had little sympathy with Robert Adam's style. Adam had specified Craigleith stone for the entire square but not a single house exists entirely according to his plan. Robert died just as the sale of the plots in the square was started and in 1794 the first dwelling house was completed. Subsequent fashions have seen Robert's façades altered to accommodate floor-to-ceiling windows and the need for servants' rooms has resulted in a 'rash of mansards and dormers' rising from a 'vista of rising slate roofs – a Scottish feature'.[7]

In April 1791 Robert finally accepted that John Home at Ninewells would never agree to anything he proposed and, politely, he wrote to him later that month, 'To wish to be employed when not agreeable to the employer would be the height of folly in me, disagreements may unfortunately happen in business begun by parties living in perfect confidence, but it has always been a maxim of mine that when confidence ceases the business ought to end as quick as possible – and still better if it is never begun.'

One project that still looked likely never to begin was the Bridewell, with the town council being completely uncertain as to where to site the building. Their latest worry was that if it was overlooked by Calton Hill, then people 'of the lower sort' might assemble there and communicate with the prisoners below. Robert suggested that a guard house be built on the hill to prevent this, but the council, scenting further expense, rejected this and finally agreed to Robert's chosen site under the hill. His plan for the Bridewell owed much to Jeremy Bentham's plan for his as yet unbuilt 'Panopticon'. The latter was a 'D'-shaped building with the cells – three storeys of them – placed around the curve of the 'D'. One guard could sit on the bar of the letter and observe all the cells with ease; hence 'Panopticon'. Robert's plan for the Bridewell allowed for a governor's residence behind the guard room and a space between the guard room and the cells which could eventually house a chapel. There were two wings, one for lunatics and the other for debtors, while the main block would be used for 'the strolling poor, lazy beggars, idle vagrants and common prostitutes' with exercise yards for women, men and boys, all surrounded with a high wall. Finally the plan was accepted by the council without the two wings and a much reduced exercise yard. Paterson estimated it could be built for £10,327 2s 9d.

Robert still had trouble enforcing his position as surveyor for the university. On 5 June 1791 he rode to Hopetoun House to collect the earl's subscription for the university. It was 100 guineas for 5 years, which the earl threatened to withhold from the trustees when some of them, with their tradesmen accomplices, were obstructing Adam's right to fix prices for their workmanship. Eventually the trustees conceded and the earl relented.

On the site of the university Paterson had now completed most of the east façade and all of the north-west corner. The anatomy theatre was not yet complete, but lectures and demonstrations were taking place and the provost complimented Paterson 'on the rapidity of the buildings, the goodness of the work, and the measures taken to accomplish it'.[8] Adam, who had returned to Edinburgh in May, could now supervise the building work himself with a diversion on 30 November when the foundation stone of the Bridewell was laid, again with full masonic honours.

In 1791, the Trades in Glasgow finally resolved to build their hall in Glassford Street and on 9 September of that year the foundation stone was laid. The city already had a building, Pollok House, built by William Adam in 1792 but 'Glasgow had few buildings with large-scale classical pretensions until the arrival of the younger Adams in 1792. This event evidently coincided with an increased desire on the citizens' part for the elegancies of city life.'[9] The brothers certainly contributed an outstanding example of classicism in the Trades Hall. It was two and a half storeys tall, with, at its centre, an aedicule of paired Ionic columns on a rusticated base, topped by a balustraded parapet with a frieze of circular metopes, under a large carving of the royal arms. In common with his other works in Glasgow, Robert died before its completion. His plans for a new infirmary in Glasgow were not accepted until 1802, ten years after his death, but in spite of the delay, 'the new hospital was much finer than the one it replaced'.[10] The frontage was much the same as at Edinburgh University but with a projecting entrance porch, giant Venetian windows in the wings and an elegant dome. Assembly rooms jointly designed by Robert and James in 1792 were built in 1796.

Astonishingly, in Edinburgh in 1791, Robert sacked John Paterson and replaced him with Hugh Cairncross, who would continue in the post until 31 December 1795. The reasons for this act are unclear and it was certainly not with the consent of Paterson who sued the Adam brothers for damages in the spring of 1792. It was entirely thanks to Paterson that the university was being built, for with Robert in London, all activity would have ground to a standstill, and the same could be said for the Bridewell project. Indeed, it was thanks to Paterson's good offices with Provost Stirling that both the Bridewell and the Charlotte Square contracts were in Robert's pocket. It is not accurate to argue that Paterson was being well paid for what he did, since £100 was not a large amount (roughly £6,000 in contemporary currency) even allowing for the assumed benefits of administering subcontracts, and Paterson, in supervising all the many Adam projects in Scotland, acted well beyond the limits of his job description as clerk of works to the university. So why did Robert cut this paragon loose?

One possible explanation might be that Robert had to be pre-eminent in whatever he did. When he looked as if he might fall into Clérisseau's shadow, there was conflict. His reputation as an engraver was at risk when the true authorship of the Spalatro drawings was made obvious, so he insisted on the device of having the engravers' names in the publication and not the author of the original drawings. When it became obvious that he relied on another for his reputation – or for any part of that reputation – then there was discord. In Edinburgh he may have felt that the name of Paterson was becoming better known than his, even though Paterson was clearly an agent. Robert's backbone might be supple enough in the face of a noble client but it could become militantly rigid if his total authority was threatened.

Also the brothers now had all the work they could reasonably hope for in Scotland and therefore could risk a less enterprising assistant to supervise progress. They had no further need for expansion in the country and on 6 January 1792 Robert left for London in the post-chaise with John Hindsley, his servant, on horseback behind him. His life would now be centred on 13 Albemarle Street and he would never return to Scotland again. Paterson pursued an independent career building Castle Forbes in Aberdeenshire and Castle Lennel in Berwickshire. Architectural historians have commented on the similarity of Paterson's designs to those of Robert Adam but he did become a significant Scottish architect.

Robert Adam had left an indelible mark on Scotland with his elegant country houses and his recently adopted 'castle' style of designing rural retreats. He had accepted a commission from the Duke of Buccleuch to build a Doric bridge on the duke's estate at Dalkeith. A large structure with a span of 70 feet rising on a single arch, it was to be one of Robert's finest bridges and was completed after his death, with the omission of only some of Robert's typical decorations. Robert Adam was elected an honorary member of the Society of Antiquaries of Scotland and a fellow of the Royal Society of Edinburgh. In spite of these honours, his homecoming had been more bitter than sweet and the fault cannot be laid entirely at the door of Scotland.

On 20 October of the previous year, 1791, a meeting took place in the Thatched House Tavern, St James's Street in London. Present were Robert, Chambers, Mylne, Wyatt, and John Soane, among ten others. Together they were the founder members of the Architects' Club, an antecedent of the Royal Institute of

British Architects. The brothers were also regular visitors to the British Coffee House in Cockspur Street, so that for all that Robert felt business prevented him from settling back in Scotland he greatly enjoyed the company of the other exiles. The London practice was much involved with the building of Fitzroy Square which was designed as a unity, with much less evidence of the 'palace fronts' of Charlotte Square. Here the fronts are of Portland stone decorated with Liardet stucco (most of which has fallen off) with a great variety of window groupings and column sizes. 'There was no London development to rival the elegance and compactness as well as the scale of Fitzroy Square.'[11] Most of this was built after Robert's death, but his mark could now be seen on some of the principal streets of the ever-expanding West End of London, and there were hopes that his influence might spread. 'The houses in Portland Place and Mansfield Street held out some prospect of a return to a better style of building, and those on the south and east sides of Fitzroy Square, in their architectural appearance promised still more.'[12]

Since 1784 the Adam practice had been involved in the Herculean task of designing a completion of the quadrangle at King's College, Cambridge. This already comprised, on the northern side, the magnificent fifteenth-century College Chapel, regarded with awe by even the classically bound aesthetes of the eighteenth century, while on the west, stood the severely classical Fellows' Building, erected by James Gibbs 50 years previously. Robert thus inherited a quadrangle with a mediaeval chapel and a classical block facing the Senate House. His solution was typically self-confident. He would build a hall directly opposite the chapel, of similar size and scale, but of contemporary design. It would comprise a giant circular college hall, approached via steps, a portico and vestibule, and flanked by rooms for student accommodation. With a style he was growing more and more fond of, the lower part would be rusticated. Above were Corinthian columns and pilasters, topped by a balustrade. He would build a replica of the Senate House with the library between it and the new structure. Robert's plans were hugely ambitious and were drawn up in great detail but they were never translated into buildings.

Back in Edinburgh, Robert's absence gave rise to continued mutterings among the trustees. But John Clerk wrote to Margaret Adam that Robert was quite securely endorsed as sole supervisor. Lord Hopetoun briefly joined the meeting at which this was agreed and repeated his intention of withholding his subscription 'should anything inimical be continued against Mr Adam.'[13]

In February Margaret reported to her sister Susannah, now Mrs Clerk of Eldin, on another accident to Robert's legs. 'You will have heard of Bob's accident upon his leg which has proved very tedious and troublesome and will not be cured by plantain leaves, which we tried too, but his pain is being ill to heal and his nerves so irritable that he suffers a great deal more pains from anything of that kind than is common. We find the law suit with Paterson is to come on directly. We put our trust in your son John that it will be successful on Bob's side.' Then two days later, she wrote, 'We are impatient to have the finishing of the law suit with Paterson.'[14] The final results of this case are obscure since on 20 November 1795 an inventory of the papers is marked 'Lord Craig to advise'. Presumably in Paterson's favour, since on 28 December 1799 a 'Bond of Caution', was issued against William, as Robert's heir, for £34 12s in Paterson's favour.[15] A small reward.

Robert's unremitting workload began to catch up with him and his doctor recommended he eat a proper diet of rice in various shapes: puddings, piloa*, and rice milk. Mutton, fowl and venison were thought to be very healthy while veal and pork were good for people with diarrhoeas. He was to abstain from malt liquors, legumes, greens and broths. He could have sago or salep†, for a breakfast-time tea. 'The best drink is Tilbury or Bristol water with red wine . . . if it turns sour and gripes him, then substitute brandy or rum for the wine. A warm bath will help to carry off the diarrhoea and gripings and a cold bath will

---

* Piloa is made by suffering rice to stand for four hours in a large quantity of cold water, boiling it for half an hour then straining it in a colander.
† Salep was a drink, or jelly, made from various roots.

prevent a return. Griping – he must have recourse to his rhubarb. After his bowels are cleansed he may eat a tea-cupful of the following composition. 2oz of fresh mutton suet boiled for a quarter of an hour in milk, then add a heaped tablespoonful of starch, boil for another quarter of an hour then add an ounce of loaf sugar and a little cinnamon. Rice-gruel with fifteen or twenty grains of grated nutmeg will make a proper supper on these occasions. Half a pint of lime water twice a day.'

It is very unlikely that Robert paid any regard to this advice, in spite of the best efforts of his sisters. In 1774 Robert had been dosed with cascara, bismuth and liquorice and had been advised to wear a flannel waistcoat next to his skin. Moderate exercise on horseback was also recommended, although moderation was never at the front of Robert's mind. At one time he had been treated with a 'decoction of bark' with two scruples of myrrh swallowed with half a teaspoon of brandy daily. Back in 1787 William had written to John, 'you are not ignorant of the influence that distressful situations have upon Bob's constitution and how much they render him unfit for business'. Two years later, in the autumn of 1789, Margaret referred to 'the complaint in his stomach which has long been a tiresome complaint to him . . .' Robert had 'a griping in his bowels when he waits his dinner too long'.[16] In other words, he was suffering either from stomach ulcers or severe Irritable Bowel Syndrome, or both.

On 1 March 1792 one of the ulcers burst, causing Robert to vomit blood and suffer great pain. Two days later, at the age of 64, Robert Adam was dead. On 3 March, the day of Robert's death, William wrote to Susannah in Edinburgh: 'As I had not time before the post went off yesterday, I desired my sister Mary to communicate to you the very unlooked for illness that Bob had been suddenly seized with in so alarming a manner, of which, however, we at that time, entertained sanguine hopes that this danger was over and it continued for 20 hours, he sleeped very composedly the first part of the night, but all at once the vein opened again at 4 o'clock this morning when he threw up a vast quantity of blood that weakened him to a degree that he appeared then to be quite gone, his pulse being totally gone, he however revived again but in so low and exhausted a state that he only struggled for life in very great pain, till 2 o'clock when he became quiet and went off very easily . . . The suddenness of this cruel event so inviolated me . . . I am sure that you will bear it with that resolution that such trying occasions require. My sisters seem to have been prodigies in that way and they seem not to have suffered in their health by the fatigue.' Due to 'the agitation of spirits' this letter was not posted until 5 March, nor was the letter to Mrs Drysdale: 'My sisters hold up wonderfully. As we are satisfied Bob would have inclined to have left money to you all we have desired Mrs Drysdale to get £200 and divide it equally among your family.'[17]

Robert had been sufficiently in control of his senses the previous day to compose his last will and testament:

> I do hereby leave all my effect whatever they are
> to my sisters Elizabeth Adam and Margaret Adam
> And I appoint my brothers James Adam
> and William Adam both of Albemarle Street my
>   executors.
> London, in the second day of March
> in the year of our Lord one thousand ninety hundred
>   and seventy two.
> Robert Adam.

The will was witnessed by two servants and proved on 8 March. John was excluded, presumably since he had his own establishment in Edinburgh, as had the widowed Mary, now living there with Janet. The remaining sister was Susannah, now quite comfortable as Mrs John Clerk of Eldin.

On 10 March Robert was buried in the south aisle of Westminster Abbey, the coffin borne by the Duke of Buccleuch, the Earl of Coventry, the Earl of Lauderdale, Lord Viscount Stormont, Lord Frederick Campbell and Mr Pulteney, all of whom were, in some respect or other, clients. Adjacent tombs in the

Abbey would be occupied by William Chambers in 1796 and James Wyatt in 1813.

The March issue of the *Gentleman's Magazine* carried an obituary stating that, 'the many elegant buildings, public and private, erected in various parts of the kingdom by Mr Adam, will remain lasting monuments of his taste and genius: and the natural suavity of his manners, joined to the excellence of his moral character, has endeared him to a numerous circle of friends, who will long lament his death.'

After an a brief account of his life, the obituary noted:

It is somewhat remarkable that the Arts should be deprived at the same time of two of their greatest ornaments, Sir Joshua Reynolds* and Mr Adam: and it is difficult to say which of them excelled most in his particular profession . . . Mr Adam produced a total change in the architecture of this country: and his fertile genius in elegant ornament was not confined to the decoration of buildings, but has been diffused into every branch of manufacture. His talents extended beyond the lie of his own profession: he displayed in his numerous drawings in landscape a luxuriance of composition, and an effect of light and shadow, which have scarcely been equalled . . . to the last period of his life, Mr Adam displayed an increasing vigour of genius and refinement of taste: for in the space of one year preceding his death, he designed eight great public works, besides twenty five private buildings, so various in their style, and so beautiful in their composition, that they have been allowed by the best judges, sufficient of themselves, to establish his fame unrivalled as an artist.[18]

The obituary writer's arithmetic was somewhat elastic, but Robert's output had not diminished, with no rejection of commissions on account of size. In his notebook for January 1791 he wrote, 'Mr Jackes agreed for 50 Guineas for the east and south

---

* Reynolds died of liver disease on 23 February 1792.

fronts for the cottage, 2 plans and 2 elevations and a section for £1 1. Mr Bilby Thompson esq., erect near York a gateway for Wetherby Grange.'[19] It might be said that these entries show Robert returning to his beginnings with a bridge and a green-house and that he was always loath to turn down work, but there is a certain desperation in his seeking it wherever it might be found. The splendour of Robert Adam's achievements can easily mask the anxiety of ever-approaching debt – especially in one who aspired to the status and lifestyle of the gentry he served. Margaret felt the injustice of his seeming neglect keenly and after Robert's death she wrote: 'In a period of time when more money has been spent by the public than this country ever knew, in which private luxury has gone to a greater excess than ever was before seen, in which we have had a King and a Prince of Wales professed lovers of architecture, an architect of most sublime genius has been neglected, suffered to remain for 14 years almost unemployed, while in the meantime many buildings have been erected, some of a private nature, some for the public and at public expense, will remain a disgrace to the country to which they belong.'[20] One can excuse the hyperbole of '14 years almost unemployed' when Robert was largely in Edinburgh, in Mistley and planning for Portland Place and Fitzroy Square, but un-doubtedly Robert felt that after the debacle of the Adelphi, his career had declined. Inevitably, the domestic atmosphere of Albemarle Street had been fraught with disappointment.

The work in progress had now to be continued by James and William, and most of the correspondence was now between John Clerk and the London sisters. On 13 March John Clerk wrote to London that he hoped William would come to Edinburgh in six months, although in the meanwhile Mrs Drysdale was proving equal to the task of acting as the brothers' agent in Edinburgh. He was sure that the two brothers, along with Principal Ro-bertson, would be capable of finishing the works projected and already begun. He assured London that, 'nothing can be done without the concurrence of the executors. This will satisfy you about the impropriety and improbability of brother John interfering. Mr [Provost] Blair is positive that not one single iota shall be altered or changed'[21].

John's son William had suggested to his father that he might help in the brotherhood's projects in Edinburgh. In March 1792 Susan Clerk commented: 'That is an odd proposal of William Adams. He certainly does not know the situation of his father, who is so little recovered that he has only been up twice to have his bed made . . . his disease seems to be weakness for he has no complaint and I doubt much if he will ever be able for business of any kind.'[22] No help could be expected from John who was now thoroughly estranged from the London brothers, an estrangement made final by his death, at 71, on 25 June 1792. He was buried alongside his father and mother in Greyfriars Churchyard, Edinburgh, with an epitaph extolling him as 'firm in adversity, not elated in prosperity. The serenity of his temper and the kindness of his nature were the source of happiness to his family and a blessing to all within his influence. His taste and spirit of improvement were the most distinguished'. Largely thanks to the bounding ambition of his younger brother he had had much need of 'serenity of temper'. His son, also named William, after his grandfather, was a 41-year-old lawyer and politician, sitting as member for Ross-shire. He once fought a duel with Charles Fox* and had no interest whatever in architecture, although it finally fell to him to try, however unsuccessfully, to bring order into the chaos of the brotherhood. He died in 1839 and, as befits a politician, his epitaph is several times longer than that of his father.

James succeeded to John's position with the Board of Ordnance and reluctantly continued to supervise the completion of Edinburgh University. This was now beset by financial problems, with a brief respite in November when a royal grant was awarded. In January 1793 France declared war on Britain and wartime inflation pushed up costs to the point where all building stopped. Robert Reid reported on a revised plan for the completion of the building in 1810 and he promptly cut the design, reducing the quadrangle to a single court, in spite of an undertaking to have regard 'to the part

* He wounded Fox, who remarked that William must have been using Government powder with no penetrative power, much like their policies.

already executed, and to the preservation of the architecture of Mr Adam, as far as practicable'. The actual completion was undertaken by Henry Playfair in 1816 with a total disregard for Adam's designs, and apart from the dome, it was completed in 1834. The dome, completely out of proportion with Adam's idea for a smaller domed clock tower, was added by Sir Rowland Anderson, surmounted by a naked golden torch bearer. What was to be Robert Adam's greatest public building is a disappointing hodge-podge of other architect's ideas.

James gratefully returned to England and spent most of his remaining years at his farm in Hertfordshire with a succession of female companions. However, with an unknown woman he had rented a house in London where, on 20 October 1794, he suffered an apoplectic seizure* and died, aged 62. Margaret wrote a long letter to Susan Clerk giving more detail of James's death:

> According to the woman's account it was 12 o'clock on Sunday night that he was seized with a fit. She sent off for my brother Willie who was in the country but was there early in the morning with John Robertson . . . it seemed he had fallen asleep while he was eating his breakfast and the same at dinner and the doctor said that if medical assistance had been called, when that was observed they might have saved his life . . . I do not doubt but you might think it a strange reserve to say nothing, when we were with you, of my brother James's connection with that woman to whom he was so much attached, but being quite uncertain what she might turn out to be and the same time being pretty certain he would dislike it being spoken of to his friends in Scotland, we thought it better to say nothing at all till we were better informed. It is a great comfort to us to find there was no marriage as we are certain now she that she was a woman of no character. Whatever her birth is that we know not.[23]

* In modern parlance, this was probably a stroke.

Apart from this sniff of scandal, abhorrent to an Edinburgh nose, James left the remains of the practice to William. The obituary in the *Gentleman's Magazine* of October 20 1794 mentioned that 'the Adelphi buildings and Portland Place are monuments of his taste and abilities in his profession. Besides his excellent treatise on agriculture, published some years ago, Mr Adam was preparing a history of architecture, which all lovers of the art have reason to lament he did not finish.'[24] There is no trace of a history of architecture, but the third and final volume of the *Works* remained unpublished until 1822, when it appeared with 10 engravings and 15 copper plates, described by Bolton as having been, 'put together by a publisher's hack in a very inferior way, with an absurd preface, and no description of the plates.'[25]

According to the tables drawn up by David King, in the years from 1790 to 1794 the partnership undertook 30 projects, 29 of which were in Scotland. 'There was a tendency for the Adams' practice to move from England to Scotland and to change from extending and decorating noblemen's houses to building more modest residences for people of lower rank. It is tempting to infer from this tendency that their practice declined. It terms of prestige it did, but in terms of architectural quality it did not.'[26]

It is tempting to speculate that, with the brothers dying in such rapid succession, the death of Robert had released a tension which had been gripping the senior members of the family. John had faced the unenviable task of living as a near neighbour to an estranged brother who had, with a minimum of consultation, risked his fortune for a scheme of his own devising. James knew himself to be inferior in talent, but had to smooth the path for an often ungrateful brother and neither sibling can have found life easy. However, there was now no doubt that with the death of James, the architectural practice was over and William was left to hold the business together. It was an impossible task, as it had been kept intact solely by Robert's industry. This ensured that the brothers were constantly racing ahead of creditors and borrowing against future prospects. These were 'penal bonds', a system whereby double the amount advanced would be payable if any default occurred. In 1775, for example, the brothers borrowed £1,000 from Joseph Rose who had worked with them as plasterer and *stuccatore*.

In 1796 the pretence of the firm having a presence in Edinburgh ended and all Robert's drawings came south to William. In the past, every new commission went to repay some of the debts already accrued, but now there were very few new commissions and in October 1801 Margaret reported to Susannah that there was an account in the *Morning Chronicle* that the firm of William Adam had stopped making payments. 'Willie is well in body but dispirited in mind . . . my brother Willlie, will never communicate to me anything of the perilous situation.'[27] The brickworks was failing to meet demands to supply the building works at London Docks for the West India merchants and in 1801 the firm of William Adam & Co. was declared bankrupt.

Susannah Clerk's daughter, also Susannah, remained in Albemarle Street to look after William who, in 1815, tried unavailingly to bid for the recommencement of the building of Edinburgh University. The debts had to be repaid and from 20–22 May 1818 Mr Christie auctioned Robert's collection of pictures, drawings, books and statuary. Elizabeth and Margaret (Bess and Peggy) had died in the same year and did not witness this attempt to clear the debts. Sadly, the attempt failed as the sale realised only £1,091 15s 6d. The situation was still desperate and Susannah and William hung on, in increasing penury, moving in 1820 to a smaller house at 43 Welbeck Street for another two years until, in February 1822 the 84-year-old William, now a broken man, committed suicide. He was buried in one of St Marylebone's parish burial grounds on 9 February and he left everything to his niece, Susannah, 'which, I am afraid will produce little or nothing'.

On 9 and 12 July another attempted sale was held, this time at Albemarle Street, and it included the furniture as well as the copper plates for *Spalatro* and *The Works*. This more or less public humiliation realised £868 5s. There were approximately 9,000 drawings in 54 volumes and Susannah first tried to sell the collection of drawings privately to Joseph Planta, Principal Librarian to the British Museum. When he rejected the offer Susannah returned to Edinburgh where she lived out her days as housekeeper to her brother, another John Clerk, now aged 65 and recently raised to the bench as Lord Eldin. In 1832 an approach was made to Sir John Soane, a known admirer of Robert's work and a purchaser at the earlier auctions. He rejected the offer, saying, 'I saw the collection some years since and thought that the sum then asked for them was too large and I am of the same opinion as to the sum now stated by you to be required by the proprietors.'[28] In the next year the collection was put up for auction in Edinburgh but failed to make the reserve price of £250 and was offered again to Soane for the reduced price of £200. He agreed to this price and on 20 July the drawings left Leith by steamer. They arrived in London four days later and are now one of the jewels in the crown of Sir John Soane's Museum in Lincoln's Inn Fields.

When Sir John Soane delivered his inaugural lectures as the incoming president of the Royal Academy in 1810 Robert's reputation still stood supreme. The Prince of Wales was ready to become Regent in the place of poor mad George III, Wellington was in Spain, but not yet victorious, and Napoleon was master of Europe. The country was groaning under the costs of a war which yet had to provide any dividends, and no one had any ambition for building. When prosperity returned it signalled the start of a rejection of the classical values of the eighteenth century, and turned its back on the love of elegance and fancy which had reached a ridiculous apotheosis in the Orientalism of the Brighton Pavilion. Sir John Soane and John Nash both embraced Greek classicism with its greater love for regularity, without the profusion of decoration beloved of Adam.

In 1808 under the pseudonym of Anthony Fisgrave, Robert Smirke, a pupil of Sir John Soane, had published *Midas, or a serious inquiry concerning Taste and Genius*, in which he argued, satirically, for the control of genius by a 'Supreme Court of Connoisseurs.' He admits that, 'I am naturally inclined to venerate whatever has been sanctioned by our forefathers' and goes on to say that 'the arts have long laboured under a complicated malady. The power of genius may, except under prudent and wise direction, be productive of nothing but error upon error' and 'with no discriminating faculty genius and taste are especially distinct from one another.'[29]

By the middle of the century the Victorians saw greater seriousness in all things and the eighteenth-century's distrust of individual genius had grown. Gone were the excesses of Adam and the Augustans, now seen as the work of intellectual barbarians. The champion of this Counter-Enlightenment was Joseph Gwilt, an architect of no particular talent, whose *Encyclopaedia of Architecture* encapsulated the dull seriousness of the Victorians. Gwilt, the son of an architect and father of two architects, reserved his loathing for Robert Adam: 'Many artists had to contend against the opposite and vicious taste brought by Robert Adam, a fashionable architect whose eye had been corrupted by the corrupt taste of the worst time of Roman art . . . the depraved compositions of Adam were not only tolerated but had their admirers.' In his *Encyclopaedia* he mistook the length of Adam's life, giving his age at death as 94, and commented after a list of some of Robert's buildings: 'None, however, would now do credit to a mere tyro in the art.'[30] Robert Adam's reputation had fallen after his death and Gwilt, writing at its nadir, was merely expressing the popular view.

The possession of original genius had been a matter of grave suspicion in the eighteenth century, a time when the influence of precedent and of academic teaching was paramount. Sir Joshua Reynolds was cautious in his approach, counselling against 'servile copying' and encouraging the artist to 'improve what he is appropriating to his own work'.[31] The poet Joseph Young, author of *Night Thoughts*, and friend of Mrs Boscawen, Mrs Montagu and Samuel Richardson, controversially proposed the existence of personal inspiration in *Conjectures on Original Composition*, part of a letter to Richardson. In Germany, Johann Georg Hannann had said, 'O ye servants of universal rules! How little do you understand art, and how little do you possess of the genius which has created the pattern upon which you want to build art.'[32] Hannann, who admired Hume, but distrusted pure reason, in his *Socratic Memorabilia* of 1759 and *Aesthetica in Nuce* advocated personal dependence on individual passion as the foundation of aesthetic genius. Although his essays were anathema to Chambers and Joshua Reynolds, Hannann was fundamental to the foundation of the German *Sturm und Drang* school of romanticism. His influence has led Isaiah Berlin to nickname Hannann 'the Magus of the North'. The seeds of imaginative expression were planted but would take time to flower.

Sadly, today one will search almost in vain for a complete creation by this 'tyro' in the art. However, thanks greatly to the energies of His Royal Highness Prince Charles, Dumfries House, Robert's first commission, is now preserved as a complete example of his work. Perhaps this is the royal patronage the brothers lacked in their lifetime. In other cases, if the exterior is intact, as at Mersham-le-Hatch, the interior has been remodelled. The frontage may be as Robert designed it, as in blocks of Fitzroy Square, or in some façades of Charlotte Square, but everywhere fashion has changed and 'improvements' have been made. Furniture has been dispersed and entire rooms have crossed the Atlantic. Where rooms and furniture remain untouched they are frozen in public exhibition. The minor waspish cavils of Horace Walpole and the heavyweight demolition of reputation by Joseph Gwilt are slight beside the well-intentioned improvements of succeeding owners.

More important than the bodily transfer of rooms to America was the spread of Adam's influence. We have seen how Clérrisseau influenced Thomas Jefferson, but nowhere is the Adam style more obvious than in the Boston buildings of Charles Bullfinch, while many of the porticoed antebellum houses of the South could have sprung directly from Adam's drawing board. During our own time, a classical broken pediment, more suited to eighteenth-century furniture than twentieth-century building, crowns Philip Johnson's AT&T Building on New York's Madison Avenue. In Russia, where Charles Cameron worked with Clérrisseau for Catherine the Great, Adam's influence is clear, but his legacy lies in much more than stone and stucco.

In many ways Robert Adam controlled his own education

having personally assembled his own tutors in Rome. He had learned much from his father's library and had seen the administration of a large site at Fort George, but his reinvention as a selective neo-classicist was a personal journey. Although he was a member of classical academies, such as San Lucca in Rome, he created his own style and this intellectual freedom from slavish obedience to precedent allowed him to develop his own personal aesthetic. The time Adam had spent on the Grand Tour gave him a wider vocabulary than most of his contemporaries, and he forged a new language with it. He saw how every rule of architecture had originated and he then adapted each one to fit a new grammar of his own devising. As Sir John Summerson said, 'Adam was probably the first English architect consciously to break with the spirit of servitude to antiquity in this arrogant way. He knows he is, or is determined to be, a man of genius.'[33]

Although Adam held to strict rules – 'the proportions of columns depend on their situation' – he used these rules to create buildings and decorations which were individual and original. He took the rules – as strict as the Latin grammar he had learnt as a boy – and observed them in the passionate context of the Porteous mob. This allowed him to let his personal taste dominate his selection of materials, colours and designs, and made the published pattern books of the past almost completely redundant – almost, but not totally, since complete freedom of taste would have required his clients to define their own artistic inspirations. Their attitude was often, 'I know nothing about art, but I'll know what I like when I see it in a book'. Adam took the book away and put personal enlightenment, based on his encyclopaedic knowledge, in its place. The result has been that his name now stands alone as an adjective; the style is not 'Picasso-like', 'Pinteresque', or even 'Gothic', it is simply 'Adam'. This individuality of taste was too demanding for the Victorians and it has taken time for the cycle of fashion to revolve. But now in the twenty-first century, David Hume's 'reason' and the 'passions' are finding an enlightened balance. Robert Adam represents to us the Enlightenment in stucco and stone.

Notes

꙰

The following abbreviations have been used:
NAS: National Archives of Scotland, Edinburgh
NLS: National Library of Scotland, Edinburgh
EULCRC: Edinburgh University Library Centre for Research
  Collections
SRO: Scottish Record Office, Edinburgh

CHAPTER ONE: *Anarchy and Augustans*

1 Chambers, Robert, *Traditions of Edinburgh* (Edinburgh, 1980), p. 48
2 NAS GD18/4981
3 NAS GD18/4736 William Adam to Sir John Clerk
4 Simpson, James, 'The Practical Architect', in *Architectural Heritage 1* (Edinburgh, 1990), p. 75
5 Quoted in Colvin, Howard, *A Biographical Dictionary of British Architects* (London, 1978), p. 56
6 Kay, William, 'The Real William Adam', in *Architectural Heritage 1*, (Edinburgh, 1990), p. 80
7 John Clerk of Eldin, NAS GD 18/4981, 2
8 Gunther, R.T., (ed.) *The Architecture of Sir Roger Pratt* (Oxford, 1928), p. 60
9 Dunbar, J.G., *The Historic Architecture of Scotland* (London, 1978), p. 76
10 Summerson, John, *Architecture in Britain, 1530–1830* (New Haven, 1993), pp. 348–49
11 Colvin, Howard, 'A Scottish Source for English Palladianism', in *Architectural History*, 1974 p. 8
12 Pope, Alexander, *Moral Essays, Epistle IV* (Edinburgh, 1751), lines 193–194
13 Ackerman, James S., *Palladio* (London, 1966), p. 185
14 Fenwick, Hubert, *Architect Royal: the Life and Works of William Bruce* (Kineton, 1970), p. 97
15 Beard, Geoffrey, *The Work of Robert Adam* (London, 1978), p. 1

16 Summerson, *op. cit.*, p. 349

17 Rowan, Alistair, 'William Adam's Library', in *Architectural Heritage* I, (Edinburgh, 1990), p. 12

18 Simpson, *op. cit.*, p. 75

19 Clerk, Sir John of Penicuik, *Memoirs*, ed. John M. Gray (Edinburgh, 1892), p. 114

20 Macaulay, James, *The Classical Country House in Scotland 1660–1800* (London, 1987), p. 63

21 *Ibid.* p. 70

22 Glendinning, M., MacInnes R., and McKechnie, A., *A History of Scottish Architecture*, (Edinburgh, 1996), p. 116

23 Beard, Geoffrey, *Craftsmen and Interior Decoration in England, 1660–1820*, (Edinburgh, 1981), p. 11

24 Fleming, John, *Robert Adam and His Circle* (London, 1962) p. 51

25 Topham, Edward, *Edinburgh Life in the Eighteenth Century* (Glasgow, 1989), p. 7

26 Hume, David, *A True Account of the Behaviour and Conduct of Archibald Stewart*, (London, 1748), p. 10

27 Grant, James, *Old and New Edinburgh Vol. II* (London, 1883), p. 17

28 NAS GD18/4982

29 Phillipson, N.T., and Mitchison, Rosalind, *Scotland in the Age of Improvement* (Edinburgh, 1970), p. 33

30 Clerk, *op. cit.*, p. 22

31 Fleming, *op. cit.*, p. 55

32 'Philasthenes', *A letter from a gentleman in town to his friend in the country relating to the Royal Infirmary of Edinburgh* (Edinburgh, 1739), pp. 1, 2

33 NLS MS 14425, f338

34 Brown, Iain Gordon, *Scottish Architects at Home and Abroad* (Edinburgh, 1978), p. 3

35 NAS GD18/4981

36 Fleming, *op. cit.*, p. 60

37 NAS GD18/4736

38 Ramsay of Ochtertyre, John, *Scotland and Scotsmen in the Eighteenth Century* (Bristol, 1996), p. 231

39 Carlyle, Alexander, *Autobiography*, ed. J. Hill Burton (Edinburgh, 1910), pp. 47–48

40 Hume, *op. cit.*, p. 6

41 Carlyle, *op. cit.*, p. 123

42 NAS GD18/4982

43 Cosh, Mary, 'Building Problems at Inveraray', in *Bulletin of the Scottish Georgian Society*, vol. II, 1973, p. 64

44 *Caledonian Mercury*, 30 June 1748

CHAPTER TWO: *The Search for Foundations*

1 NAS GD18/4982
2 Carlyle, *op. cit.*, pp. 285–86
3 NAS GD18/4981
4 Fleming, *op. cit.*, p. 93
5 NAS GD18/4981
6 *The Scots Magazine*, July 1754
7 Fleming, *op. cit.*, p. 96
8 *Ibid.*, pp. 96–97
9 Carlyle, *op. cit.*, p. 119
10 NAS GD18/4737
11 NAS GD18/4739
12 NAS GD18/4740
13 NAS GD18/4982
14 NAS GD18/4744
15 Virgil, *Aeneid, Book VI*, ed. H.B. Cotterill (London, 1901), p. 663
16 Brown, Iain Gordon, 'Atavism and Ideas of Architectural Progress in Robert Adam's Vitruvian Seal', in *The Georgian Group Journal* (Edinburgh, 1994), p. 70
17 NAS GD18/4745
18 Carlyle, *op. cit.*, p. 319
19 Boswell, James, *Life of Johnson* (Oxford, 1985), p. 742
20 Hibbert, Christopher, *The Grand Tour* (London, 1987), p. 25
21 NAS GD18/4748. Robert Adam's letters from his stay in Europe can be found in NAS GD18/4748–4845. They can be identified by date and, to avoid tedious repetition, will no longer be individually footnoted.
22 Montagu, Lady Mary Wortley, *Selected Letters*, ed. Robert Halsband (London, 1970), p. 117
23 *Ibid.*, p. 117
24 Boswell, *op. cit.*, p. 973

CHAPTER THREE: *The Grand Tourist*

1 Montagu, *op. cit.*, pp. 113–14
2 Summerson, *op. cit.*, p. 408
3 Sitwell, Sacheverell, 'Venice, Florence and Naples', in *Grand Tour*, ed. R.S. Lambert (London, 1935), p. 110
4 Quoted by Hibbert, *op. cit.*, p. 156
5 Montagu, *op. cit.*, p. 182

6 Fleming, John, 'Allan Ramsay and Robert Adam in Italy', in the *Connoisseur*, March 1956, p. 79

7 *Oxford Companion to Art*, ed. Harold Osborne (Oxford, 1970), pp. 151–52

CHAPTER FOUR: *Bob the Roman*

1 Jacks, Philip, *The Antiquarian and the Myth of Antiquity* (Cambridge, 1993), p. 186

2 Fleming, *op. cit.*, p. 80

3 Graham, Roderick, *The Great Infidel: A Life of David Hume* (Edinburgh, 2004), p. 85

4 Tait, A.A., *Robert Adam – Drawings and Imagination* (Cambridge, 1996), p. 19

5 Scott, Jonathan, *Piranesi* (London, 1975), p. 105

6 *Ibid.*, p. 116

7 Stillman, Damie, 'Robert Adam and Piranesi', in *Essays in the History of Architecture Presented to Rudolf Wittkower* (London, 1967)

8 Fleming, John, 'Robert Adam, The Grand Tourist', in the *Cornhill Magazine*, vol. 168, 1955

9 Stillman, *op. cit.*, p. 201

10 Ramsay, Allan, *A Dialogue on Taste* (London, 1757), pp. 32–38

CHAPTER FIVE: *Spalatro*

1 Gotch, C., 'Mylne and Adam', in *Architectural Review*, September 1956, p. 121

2 Gotch, C., 'The Missing Years of Robert Mylne', in *Architectural Review*, September, 1951, p. 180

3 Gotch, 'Mylne and Adam', p. 121

4 Fleming, *Robert Adam and His Circle*, pp. 80–81

5 Small, John, *Biographical Sketch of Adam Ferguson* (Edinburgh, 1864), p. 5

6 NLS ACC 12409

7 Beard, *The Work of Robert Adam*, p. 7

8 Searches have been made in the National Library of Scotland, the British Library, the National Library of Italy and the Biblioteca Vaticana and no trace can be found of this book

9 Gibbon, Edward, *The Decline and Fall of the Roman Empire Vol. 2* (London, 1984), p. 22

10 Quoted by Fleming in *op. cit.*, pp. 241–42

Notes

CHAPTER SIX: *A Great Diversity of Ceilings*

1 Branston, James, *The Art Of Politics* (London, 1729)
2 Graham, *op. cit.*, p. 93
3 Quoted by Felix Barker and Peter Jackson in *London* (London, 1974), p. 204
4 Carlyle, *op. cit.*, pp. 356–57
5 Watson, J. Steven, *The Reign of George II* (Oxford, 1960), pp. 69–70
6 Carlyle, *op. cit.*, p. 376
7 Gatrell, Vic, *City of Laughter* (London, 2007), p. 54
8 *Ibid.*, pp. 359–60
9 *Ibid.*, p. 379
10 Montagu, *op. cit.*, p. 152
11 Carlyle, *op. cit.*, pp. 375–76
12 *Ibid.*, p. 496
13 EUL, CRC, Dc.4.41/101
14 Rykwert, Joseph and Anne, *The Brothers Adam, the Men and the Style* (London, 1985), p. 74
15 Harris, John, 'Sir William Chambers', in *Dictionary of National Biography* (Oxford, 2006)
16 Tait, A.A., *The Adam Brothers in Rome* (London, 2008) p. 16
17 Summerson, John, 'The Adam Style', in the *Listener*, August, 1953, p. 335
18 Summerson, *Architecture in Britain*, p. 400
19 Reed, H.H, ed., *The Works in Architecture of Robert and James Adam* (New York, 1980), p. 9
20 Reed, *op. cit.*, p. v
21 Bolton, A.T., *The Architecture of Robert and James Adam* (London, 1984), vol. I, p. 148
22 Reed, *op. cit.*, Introduction
23 Beard, *op. cit.*, p. 9
24 Boswell, *op. cit.*, p. 844
25 *Ibid.* p. 844
26 Soane, Sir John, *Royal Academy Lectures, 1810–1835*, ed. David Watkin (Cambridge, 2000), p. 216
27 Shaw, Stebbing, *A Tour in 1787 from London to the Western Highlands of Scotland* (London, 1788), p. 88
28 Harris, Eileen, *The Genius of Robert Adam* (New Haven, 2001), p. 3
29 Hume, David, *Letters*, ed. J.Y.T. Greig (Oxford, 1960), vol. II, p. 263
30 Stillman, Damie, *Decorative Work of Robert Adam* (London, 1972), p. 44
31 Summerson, *op. cit.*, p. 394

32 Beard, Geoffrey, *Georgian Craftsmen and Their Work* (London, 1966), p. 186

33 Swarbrick John, *Robert Adam and His Brothers* (London, 1915), p. 63

34 Yarwood, Doreen, *Robert Adam* (London, 1970), p. 99

35 Bolton, *op. cit.*, p. 241

CHAPTER SEVEN: *Foundation Stone Laid*

1 Yarwood, *op. cit.*, p. 102

2 NAS MS GD18/4972

3 *Library of the Fine Arts*, vol. II, no. 9, October 1831, pp. 165–78. Mistakenly titled *Journal of a Tour in Italy by Robert Adam*

4 Graham, *op. cit.*, p. 21

5 NAS MS GD24/1/553, p. 284–86

6 *Ibid.*

7 NLS MS no. 3812

8 NAS MS GD24/1/564/1

9 Winkelmann, J.J., *Briefe an Bianconi*, ed. W. Rehm and W. Diepholder, (Berlin, 1952/58), vol. II p. 237

10 Drummond's bank accounts of Robert Adam, 1765, held by Royal Bank of Scotland Archives, Edinburgh

11 McCormick, Thomas, *Charles-Louis Clérisseau and the Genesis of Neo-Classicism* (New York, 1990), p. 211

12 Summerson, 'The Adam Style', p. 335

13 Boswell, James, *London Journal*, ed. F. Pottle (London, 1973), p. 98

14 Reed, *op. cit.*, pp. 47–48

15 *Ibid.*, p. 48

16 *Ibid.*, p. 48

17 Beard, *op. cit.*, p. 82

18 *Ibid.*, p. 22

19 *Ibid.*, p. 48

20 Reed, *op. cit.*, p. 1.n

21 *Ibid.*, p. 49

22 Stillman, *op. cit.*, p. 33

23 Summerson, *op. cit.*, pp. 335–6

24 *Ibid.*, p. 49

25 Reed, *op. cit.*, p. 3

CHAPTER EIGHT: *A Regiment of Artificers*

1 Stillman, *op. cit.*, p. 41

2 Harris, Eileen, *The Furniture of Robert Adam* (London, 1963), p. 7

Notes

Ibid., p. 25

4 Brown, Iain Gordon, 'Spalatro Redevivus', in *Apollo*, January 1998, p. 32

5 Stuart, James, and Revett, Nicolas, *The Antiquities of Athens, vol. I* (London, 1762), Preface

6 Watkin, David, 'James Stuart', in *Dictionary of National Biography* (Oxford, 2006)

7 Letter from Robert Adam to John Fordyce, *The Caldwell Papers vol. I* (Glasgow, 1854), pp. 180–82

8 Topham, Edward, *Letters from Edinburgh* (London, 1776), p. 221

9 Yarwood, *op. cit.*, p. 111

10 Gibbon, *op. cit.*, p. 53

11 Adam, Robert, *Ruins of Spalatro* (London, 1764), pp. 1–4

12 Brown, Iain Gordon, *Robert Adam and the Emperor's Palace* (Edinburgh, 1992), p. 38

13 Brown, *Ibid.*, *passim*

14 Brown, 'Spalatro Redivivus', p. 33

15 Stroud, D., *Capability Brown*, (London, 1957), p. 202

16 *Ibid.*, p. 91

17 *Ibid.*, p. 202

18 *Ibid.*, p. 8

19 Lomax, James, 'Thomas Chippendale', in *Dictionary of National Biography* (Oxford, 2006)

20 Gilbert, Christopher, *The Life and Works of Thomas Chippendale, Vol. 1* (London, 1978), pp. 17–18

21 Pryke, Sebastian, 'Revolution in Taste', in *Country Life*, vol. 186, no. 16, April 1992, p. 101

22 *Ibid.*, p. 98

23 Adam, William, *The Gift of a Grandfather* (Blair Adam, 1836), pp. 21–22

24 Hume, *op. cit.*, vol. I, p. 436

25 Checkland, S.G., *Scottish Banking, a History* (Glasgow, 1975), p. 70

26 Reed, *op. cit.*, p. 6

27 Bolton, *op. cit.*, p. 306

28 Reed, *op. cit.*, p. 6

29 Bolton, *op. cit.*, p. 310

30 Rykwert, *op. cit.*, pp. 147–48

31 Reed, *op. cit.*, p. 5

32 Reed, *op. cit.*, p. 6

33 Montagu, Elizabeth, *'Queen of the Blues' – Her Letters*, ed. Reginald Blunt (London, 1923), vol. 2, p. 242

34 Roworth, Wendy Wassing, *Angelica Kauffman, A Continental Artist in Georgian England* (New Haven, 2001), p. 114

35 Baird, Rosemary, 'The Queen of the Bluestockings', in *Apollo*, vol. 158, no. 498, 2005, p. 43

36 Montagu, *op. cit.*, p. 255

37 Baird, *op. cit.*, pp. 43–49

38 Bolton, *op. cit.*, vol. II, p. 319

39 Bolton, *op. cit.*, vol. I, p. 153

40 *Ibid.*, p. 11

41 Boswell, *Life of Johnson*, p. 1148

42 Langford, Paul, *A Polite and Commercial People*, (Oxford, 1989), p. 60

43 Bolton, *op. cit.*, vol. II, p. 312

44 Reynolds, Sir Joshua, *Discourses on Art* (London, 1924), p. 141

45 *Ibid.*, p. 13

46 Reed, *op. cit.*, p. 5

47 Hutchison, Sidney, C., *The History of the Royal Academy* (London, 1968), p. 48

48 Namier, Lewis, *The Structure of Politics at the Accession of George III* (London, 1957), p. 2

49 *Ibid.*, p. 6

50 Namier, Lewis & Brooke, John, *The House of Commons 1754–1790* (London, 1964), p. 68

51 *Ibid.*, p. 486.

52 Carlyle, *op. cit.*, p. 544

53 Boswell, *op. cit.*, p. 281

CHAPTER NINE: *Four Scotchmen by the Name of Adams*

1 Reed, *op. cit.*, p. 6

2 Delany, Mary, *Mrs Delaney at Court among the Wits*, ed. R. Brimley (London, 1925), p. 242

3 Boswell, *op. cit.*, p. 1163

4 Russell, Francis, 'The House that Became a Hostage', in *Country Life*, vol. 182, no. 44, 29 October 1998, p. 29

5 Bolton, *op. cit.*, vol. II, p. 5

6 Warner, Richard, *A Tour through the Northern Counties of England*, (London, 1802), vol. 2, p. 88

7 Reed, *op. cit.*, p. 5

8 Harris, *The Genius of Robert Adam*, p. 5

9 Soane, *op. cit.*, pp. 258–59

10 Walpole, Horace, *Letters, Vol. VIII*, ed. Mrs P. Toynbee (London, 1903) p. 291

11 Hardy, John, and Andrew, Caroline, 'The Essence of the "Etruscan Style"', in *Connoisseur*, vol. 208, no. 837, 1981, p. 227

Notes

12 Piranesi, Gianbattista, *Diverse maniere d'adonare i Camini* (Rome, 1749), p. 7

13 Reed, *op. cit.*, p. 13

14 SRO GD248/590/3/1

15 Langford, *op. cit.*, p. 575

16 Soane, *op. cit.*, p. 217

17 Rowan, Alistair, *Vaulting Ambition* (London, 2007), p. 7

18 Reed, *op. cit.*, p. 9

19 Wheatley, Henry, B. *The Adelphi and its Site* (London, 1885), p. 13

20 Burney, Frances, *The Early Diary, Vol. 1*, ed. A.R. Ellis (London, 1907), pp. 90–93

21 Swarbrick, *op. cit.*, p. 225

22 *The Gentleman's Magazine*, May 1771, p. 194

23 Swarbrick, *op. cit.*, p. 226

24 *The Foundling Hospital for Wit*, 1771, *passim*

25 Wilkes, John, *The North Briton*, p. 28

26 Fitzgerald, Percy, *The Life of Garrick, Vol. II* (London, 1868), pp. 267–68

27 *Ibid.*, p. 268

28 Garrick, David, *Letters*, ed. David M. Little and George M. Kahrl (London, 1963), p. 776

29 Burney, *op. cit.*, p. 175n

30 Garrick, *op. cit.*, p. 792

31 *Ibid.*, p. 795

32 Burney, *op. cit.*, p. 168

33 Swarbrick, *op. cit.*, pp. 231–32

34 Garrick, *op. cit.*, p. 744

35 Wainwright, Clive, 'George Keate', in *Apollo*, vol. 143, no. 47, January 1996

36 Checkland, *op. cit.*, p. 129

37 Rowan, Alistair, 'After the Adelphi: Forgotten Years in the Adam Brothers' Practice', in *Journal of the Royal Society of Arts*, September 1974, p. 675n.

38 Hume, *Letters*, pp. 263–64

39 Bolton, *op. cit*, pp. 324–28

40 Burney, *op. cit.*, p. 200

41 *Ibid.*, p. 200

42 NLS MS 19992, f. 198

43 Lees-Milne, James, *The Age of Adam* (London, 1947), pp. 34–35

44 Caldwell Papers, 28 February 1774, pp. 230–31

45 Rasmussen, Steen Eiler, *London, the Unique City* (London, 1984) p. 181

46 Sitwell, Sacheverell, 'Robert Adam and the Adelphi', in *Architecture*, vol. II, 1922, p. 312

47 Reed, *op. cit.*, p. 1

48 Shanhagen, Roger, *The Exhibition, or a Second Anticipation being remarks on the principal works to be exhibited next month at the Royal Academy* (London, 1779) pp. 97–98

49 *Ibid., passim*

50 Topham, Edward *The Life of Mr Elwes, the Celebrated Miser* (Glasgow, 1795) p. 49

51 Bolton, *op. cit.*, p. 111

52 Rykwert, *op. cit.*, p. 156

53 Sitwell, *op. cit.*, p. 312

54 Harris, p. 315

55 Rigby, Richard, *Authentic Memoirs* (London, 1788), p. 11

56 Morant, Philip, *The History of Essex, Vol. I* (London, 1748), p. 480

57 Walpole, *op. cit.*, p. 107

58 Morant, *op. cit.*, p. 460

CHAPTER TEN: *Certain Public Works in the City of Edinburgh*

1 Percy, Thomas, *Reliques of English Poetry* (London, 1767), p. ix.

2 Dutens, L., *Mémoires d'un Voyageur qui se repose*, 3 vols, (London, 1806), vol. II, p. 108–109

3 Bolton, *op. cit.*, p. 319

4 *Ibid.*, p. 257

5 SRO GD18/4968

6 Youngson, A.J., *The Making of Classical Edinburgh* (Edinburgh, 1975), p. 25

7 *An Inventory of the Ancient and Historical Monuments of The City of Edinburgh*, The Royal Commission on the Ancient Monuments of Scotland (Edinburgh, 1951)

8 NLS MS 4945 f58

9 Bolton, *op. cit.*, vol. II pp. 222–34. (Bolton quotes a full account of the proceedings of the Register Trustees)

10 Arnot, Hugo, *The History of Edinburgh* (Edinburgh, 1778), p. 422; also quoted in *Fugitive Pieces* (Edinburgh, 1791) p. 92

11 Soane, *op. cit.*, p. 174

12 *Ibid.*, p. 227

13 Rowan, Alistair, 'Robert Adam's Idea for the North Bridge in Edinburgh', in *Architectural Heritage*, no. 15, 2004, p. 34

14 Shaw, *op. cit.*, pp. 185–206

15 Rowan, 'After the Adelphi:', p. 682

16 *Ibid.*, p. 682

17 Fitzgerald, Percy, *The Life of Garrick*, vol. II, pp. 375–76, London 1868

18 Sheppard, F.H.W, ed., *Survey of London Vol. XXXV* (London, 1970), p. vii

19 *Ibid.*, p. 462
20 Fitzgerald, *op. cit.*, pp. 375–76
21 *Ibid.*, p. 462.
22 Shaw, *op. cit.*, p. 119
23 NAS GD248/590/3/1
24 *Book of the Old Edinburgh Club*, vol. XXII, pp. 245–46
25 NLS MS 20500
26 *Ibid.*
27 *Ibid.*
28 Rowan, Alistair, 'Kinross and Edinburgh', in *The Architecture of Scottish Cities*, ed. Deborah Mays (East Linton, 1997), p. 74
29 SRO GD18/5838/1
30 SRO GD18/5838/5 The remainder of this correspondence can be found under the principal document number (GD18/5838). Individual letters are under their appropriate dates.
31 Rowan, 'After the Adelphi:', pp. 672–73
32 Fraser, Andrew, G., *The Building of Old College* (Edinburgh, 1989), p. 79
33 Rowan, *op. cit.*, p. 77n
34 Topham, *op. cit.*, pp. 205, 208
35 *Fugitive Pieces*, p. 92
36 Horn, D.B., *A Short History of the University of Edinburgh* (Edinburgh, 1967), p. 76
37 Steele, Alan J., *Principal William Robertson* (Edinburgh, 1994) p. 1
38 *A letter to the Rt Hon. Henry Dundas* (Edinburgh, 1785), *passim*
39 *The Scots Magazine*, November 1789
40 NLS MS3431 f. 214

CHAPTER ELEVEN: *Monuments of His Taste and Genius*

1 The Paterson/Adam correspondence is in NLS MS 19992/3 and can be identified by date. To avoid multiple endnotes I will give no further references for this episode.
2 *The Scots Magazine*, 1782
3 EUL CRC gen.875/111/174-5F
4 EUL CRC. La.11.500
5 Rowan, *Vaulting Ambition*, p. 38
6 *An Inventory of the Ancient and Historical Monuments of the City of Edinburgh*, p. 207
7 Gow, Ian, 'Fragmenting Adam's Charlotte Square', in *Fragments, Architecture and the Unfinished*, eds Barry Bergdol and Werner Oechslin (London, 2006), p. 9
8 Horn, *op. cit.*, p. 88

9 Gomme, Andor and Walker, David, *Architecture of Glasgow* (London, 1987), p. 60

10 *Ibid.*, p. 239

11 Rykwert, *op. cit.*, p. 192

12 Soane, *op. cit.*, p. 257

13 NAS GD18/4966/15/2 /91

14 NAS GD18/4961/37/38

15 NAS CS271/410

16 NAS GD18/ 4962

17 NAS GD18/4972

18 *Gentleman's Magazine*, March 1792

19 NAS MS GD18/4968

20 Rowan, *op. cit.*, p. 38

21 NAS GD18/4973A

22 Rowan, *op. cit.*, p. 38

23 *Ibid.*, p. 39

24 *Gentleman's Magazine*, October 1794

25 Bolton, *op. cit.*, vol. I, p. 130

26 King, David, *The Complete Works of Robert and James Adam* (Oxford, 1991), pp. 413–14

27 NAS GD18/4985

28 Brown, Iain Gordon, 'Robert Adam's Drawings', in *Book of the Old Edinburgh Club*, vol. XXII, 1992

29 Smirke, Robert (writing as Anthony Fisgrave), *Midas, or a serious inquiry concerning Taste and Genius* (London, 1808), *passim*

30 Gwilt, Joseph, *Encyclopaedia of Architecture* (London, 1842), p. 224

31 Reynolds, *op. cit.*, p. 107

32 Pevsner, N., *Academies of Art, Past and Present* (London, 1940) p. 190 (quoted by R. Unger in *Hannann und die Aufklärung* (Jena, 1911), p. 298

33 Summerson, *op. cit.*, p. 427

Glossary of Architectural Terms in the Text

꙳

AEDICULE

An area, usually in front of a doorway, with columns supporting an entablature and pediment.

ANTHEMIONS

Ornaments, usually in a frieze with formalised honeysuckle or palm leaves.

APSE

An apse is found when a rectangular space is finished, not with a flat wall, but a semicircular or polygonal recess.

ARCHITRAVE

The base lintel of an entablature, or the moulded frame of a door or window.

ATRIUM

An inner court, often unroofed and used as an entrance hall.

BALUSTRADE

A sequence of short pillars supporting a rail.

BASTION

A large projection from the wall of a fortification.

CARYATID

A female figure used to support an entablature. Spectacularly found at the Erechtheum on the Acropolis in Athens. Both Robert and his father were fond of caryatids supporting chimney pieces.

CORNICE

A decorated range at the top of a wall, often stucco or plaster-work applied to coving.

COVING

A concave moulding at the junction of a wall and a ceiling.

CROCKETTING

A particular feature of Gothic architecture where hooks and spikes, often in leaf-like form, project from spires and gables.

DENTIL

A small square block used repeatedly in cornicing and in Romanesque stone work.

DUTCH GABLES

Correctly refers to gables with curved sides ending in a pediment, but more often used to refer to crow-stepped gables where the gable ascends in a regular series of steps. Often found in Fife cottages.

ENTABLATURE

The topmost part of an aedicule.

ERECTHEUM

A fifth-century Greek temple dedicated to Erichthonius and celebrated for the Porch of the Maidens with six full-size caryatids.

FAN-LIGHT

A semicircular window above a door, allowing light into a hallway. They are normally decorated with glazing bars arranged in the form of a lady's fan.

FRIEZE

The area of a wall below the cornice and coving.

GIRANDOLE

A branched candlestick, ornately fashioned from metal and occasionally mounted on mirrors or wall sconces.

GOUACHE

Opaque watercolour painting.

GRISAILLE

Monochrome painting, usually in shades of grey.

HA-HA

A ditch separating a garden from a field. It is so constructed with a sloping bank that it cannot be seen except at close quarters. The name may arise from surprise at discovering it, or from laughter at watching people fall into it.

HEXASTLYE

A portico with six columns.

ICHNOGRAPHIA, ORTHOGRAPHIA AND SCENOGRAPHIA.

Literally three methods of describing a building, i.e., ground plan, elevation and sketch.

INTERSOL

Small rooms off a staircase, often between floors.

JAPAN

Highly polished lacquer.

LANTERN

A turret, usually circular or polygonal, with windows on all sides.

LOGGIA

An open gallery, usually pillared on one or both sides.

LUNETTE

A semicircular opening.

MACHIOLATION

A parapet which projects outwards on brackets from the top of a defensive wall. Defensive measures can be dropped through the gaps.

METOPE

A square space on a frieze, usually decorated.

NECKING
A circular moulding around a column, usually between the capital and the pediment.

OCULUS
A circular opening allowing light to enter, usually at the summit of a dome.

ORDER
This word refers to the style of column and there are four principal orders: Doric, Tuscan, Ionic and Corinthian. The Doric is sub-divided into Greek Doric and Roman Doric. In both cases the columns have no base and join the entablature with a simple necking. The Greek Doric is fluted, while the Roman Doric is smooth. The Tuscan order is similarly smooth but sits on a simple base. The Ionic order is fluted but joins the entablature under volutes. Some authorities believe these volutes derive from the figures of the goddess Hathor in the Egyptian temples at Dendera on the Nile. The Corinthian order – a favourite of Robert Adam – is fluted and terminates in a garland of acanthus leaves. There are many variations – the Composite order – and rules are frequently broken.

ORMULU
Gilded bronze used in decorations.

PANTILES
'S'-shaped roofing tiles, laid in overlapping layers.

PARTERRE
A level garden space laid out with formal flower beds.

PEDIMENT
A low-pitched gable above a door or portico.

PERISTYLUM
A range of columns around an open court.

PERPENDICULAR
The apotheosis of Gothic architecture in England, with strong emphasis on verticals, delicate tracery and complex vaulting.

PERRON

A platform outside an external door, often reached by twin stairways, sometimes curved.

PIER GLASS

A figure-length mirror.

PILASTER

A fraction of a column projecting from a wall. It may be semicircular or rectangular and will conform to one of the orders.

PORTICO

A roofed space at the entrance to a building.

PROPYLEUM

A type of portico, as on the Acropolis temples.

RAINÇEAU

A continuous garland of flowers and leaves, applied in stucco to ceilings and friezes.

RAVELIN

A 'V'-shaped projection from a fortification, allowing a field of defensive fire on both sides.

ROCOCO

A highly ornamented style of decoration, using complex natural and abstract forms.

RUSTICATION

A masonry style where the individual blocks are separated from each other, often by 'V'-shaped clefts, or are treated to give a rough and unpolished appearance.

SALLY PORT

A gate in a fortification allowing sheltered access to the exterior for a sudden counter-attack.

SCAGLIOLA

A material which, when polished, can be used to imitate marble inset with semi-precious stones.

TROMPE-L'OEIL
A drawing or painting where extremely fine detail is used to falsify perspective.

VENETIAN WINDOWS
Sometimes called 'serliana' after Sebastiano Serlio. Linked triple windows with the central window being arched and larger than the others.

VERDE D'ANTICO
A dark green mottled serpentine which can be polished to resemble antique green marble.

VESTIBULUM
An entrance hall. In Roman architecture it housed the domestic shrine of the goddess Vesta.

VOLUTE
A spiral scroll found above the columns of the Ionic order.

Bibliography

֍

MANUSCRIPT SOURCES
The majority of family correspondence quoted here will be found in the
Clerk of Penicuik papers held on deposit by the National Archive of
Scotland. They range from MS No GD18/4221 to MS GD18/5838.

The Paterson/Adam correspondence is in the National Library of
Scotland MS 1992/3.

Some items of correspondence regarding the building of Edinburgh
University are held in the Edinburgh University Library (Centre for
Research Collections) La.11.500 and La.11.580.

Drummond's Bank accounts of Robert Adam for 1765, are held by
the Royal Bank of Scotland Archives, Edinburgh

JOURNALS AND MAGAZINES
Apollo, January 1998, vol. 143, 1996
Architectural Heritage Edinburgh, 1990, 1993, 2004
Architectural History, 1974 1982
Architectural Review, 1951, 1956, 1958
Bulletin of the Scottish Georgian Society, 1973
Caledonian Mercury, 30 June, 1748
Cornhill Magazine, vol. 168, London, 1955
Country Life, Annual 1958; vol. 186, no. 16, April 1992; vol. 182, no. 44,
    October, 1998
Edinburgh Amusement, 11 July 1771
The Foundling Hospital for Wit, 1771
The Connoisseur, March 1956, vol. 208, 1981
Gentlemen's Magazine, May 1771
The Listener, London, August 1953
The Scots Magazine, November 1789

SECONDARY SOURCES

Ackerman, James S., *Palladio* (London, 1966)

Adam, James, *Practical Essays on Agriculture*, 2 vols (London, 1789)

Adam, William, *Progress of an Estate in Scotland* (Blair Adam, 1836)

Adam, Robert, *The Ruins of Spalatro* (London, 1764)

—, and James, *The Works in Architecture by Robert and James Adam*, ed. H.H. Reed (New York, 1980)

An inventory of the Ancient and Historical Monuments of the City of Edinburgh, Royal Commission on the Ancient Monuments of Scotland, HMSO (Edinburgh, 1951)

Arnot, Hugo, *The History of Edinburgh* (Edinburgh, 1788)

Baird, Rosemary, 'The Queen of the Bluestockings', in *Apollo* vol. 158, no. 498

Barker, Felix and Jackson, Peter, *London* (London, 1974)

Beard, Geoffrey, *The Work of Robert Adam* (Edinburgh, 1978)

—, *Georgian Craftsmen and their Work* (London, 1966)

—, *Craftsmen and Interior Decoration in England, 1660–1820* (Edinburgh, 1981)

Bolton, Arthur, T., *The Architecture of Robert and James Adam*, 2 vols, (London, 1984)

Book of the Old Edinburgh Club, vol. XXII

Boswell, James, *Life of Johnson* (Oxford, 1985)

Branston, James, *The Art of Politics* (London, 1729)

Brimley, R., ed., *Mrs Delany at Court and among the Wits*, (London, 1925)

Brown, Iain Gordon, *Scottish Architects at Home and Abroad* (Edinburgh, 1978)

—, *The Clerks of Penicuik, Portraits of Taste and Talent* (Edinburgh, 1987)

—, 'William Adam's Seal', in *Architectural Heritage* I Edinburgh, 1990

—, 'Atavism and Ideas of Architectural progress in Robert Adam's Vitruvian Seal', in *The Georgian Group Journal*, Edinburgh, 1994

—, *Robert Adam and the Emperor's Palace* (Edinburgh, 1992)

—, 'Spalatro Redevivus', in *Apollo*, January, 1998

Brown, John, *Moffat, Past and Present* (Edinburgh, 1873)

Burney, Frances, *The Early Diary*, ed. A.R. Ellis, 2 vols (London, 1907)

Carlyle, Alexander, *Autobiography*, ed. J. Hill Burton (Edinburgh, 1910)

Chambers, Robert, *Traditions of Edinburgh* (Edinburgh, 1980)

Chancellor, E. Beresford, *The XVIIIth Century in London* (London, 1921)

Checkland, S.G., *Scottish Banking, a History* (Glasgow, 1975)

Ching, Francis, C.K., *A Visual Dictionary of Architecture* (New York, 1995)

Clerk, Sir John of Penicuik, *Memoirs*, ed. John M. Gray (Edinburgh, 1892)

Colvin, Howard, *A Biographical Dictionary of British Architects* (London, 1978)

—, 'A Scottish Source for English Palladianism', in *Architectural History*, vol. 17, 1974

Cosh, Mary, 'Building Problems at Inveraray', in *Bulletin of the Scottish Georgian Society*, vol II, 1973

Coventry, Martin, *The Castles of Scotland* (Musselburgh, 2001)

Dalzeil, Andrew, *History of the University of Edinburgh*, 2 vols (Edinburgh, 1862)

Dunbar, J.G., *The Historic Architecture of Scotland* (London, 1978)

Dutens, L. *Mémoires d'un Voyageur qui se repose*, 3 vols, (London, 1806)

Feiling, Keith, *History of England* (London, 1950)

Fenwick, Hubert, *Architect Royal: the Life and Works of William Bruce* (Kineton, 1970)

Fisher, H.A.L., *History of Europe* (London, 1937)

Fitzgerald, Percy, *The Life of Garrick*, 2 vols (London, 1868)

Fleming, John, *Robert Adam and His Circle* (London, 1962)

—, 'Robert Adam, the Grand Tourist', in *Cornhill Magazine*, vol. 168, London, 1955

—, 'Allan Ramsay and Robert Adam in Italy', in *Connoisseur*, March 1956

—, 'The Journey to Spalatro', in *The Architectural Review*, vol. 123, no. 733, February, 1958

—, (ed.) *Penguin Dictionary of Architecture and Landscape Architecture* (London, 1990)

—, 'James Adam and the Houses of Parliament', in *The Architectural Review*, vol. 119, no.743, June 1956

Fraser, Andrew G. *The Building of Old College* (Edinburgh, 1989)

Garrick, David, *Letters*, eds David M. Little and George M. Kahrl (London, 1963)

Gatrell, Vic, *City of Laughter*, (London, 2007)

Gibbon, Edward, *The History of the Decline and Fall of the Roman Empire* (London, 1984)

Gifford, John, McWilliam, Colin, and Walker, David, *The Buildings of Scotland: Edinburgh* (London, 1988)

Gifford, John, *William Adam, 1689–1748* (Edinburgh, 1989)

Gilbert, C., *The Life and Work of Thomas Chippendale*, 2 vols (London, 1978)

Glendinning, Miles, MacInnes, Ranald, and Mackechnie, Aonghus, *A History of Scottish Architecture* (Edinburgh, 1996)

Gomme, Andor, and Walker, David, *Architecture of Glasgow* (London, 1987)

Gotch, C., 'The Missing Years of Robert Mylne', in *The Architectural Review*, vol. 440, no. 657, September 1951

—, 'Mylne and Adam', in *The Architectural Review*, vol. 119, no. 740, February 1956

Gow, Ian, 'Fragmenting Adam's Charlotte Square', in *Fragments, Architecture and the Unfinished*, eds Barry Bergdol and Werner Oechslin (London, 2006)

Graham, Roderick, *The Great Infidel: A Life of David Hume* (Edinburgh, 2004)

Grant, James, *Old and New Edinburgh*, (London, 1883)

Gunther, R.T., (ed.) *The Architecture of Sir Roger Pratt* (Oxford, 1928)

Gwilt, Joseph, *Encyclopaedia of Architecture* (London, 1842)

Hague, William, *William Pitt the Younger* (London, 2004)

Hardy, John, and Andrew, Caroline, 'The Essence of the "Etruscan" Style', in *Connoisseur*, vol. 208, no. 837,1981

Harris, Eileen, *The Furniture of Robert Adam* (London, 1963)

—, *The Genius of Robert Adam – His Interiors* (Yale, 2001)

—, *British Architectural Books and Writers, 1556–1785* (Cambridge, 1990)

Harris, John, 'Legeay, Piranesi and International Neo-Classicism in Rome 1740–1750', in *Essays in the History of Architecture Presented to Rudolf Wittkower* (London, 1967)

—, *Sir William Chambers, Knight of the Polar Star* (London, 1970)

—, 'Sir William Chambers', in *Dictionary of National Biography* (Oxford, 2006)

Herman, Arthur, *How the Scots Invented the Modern World* (New York, 2001)

Hibbert, Christopher, *The Grand Tour* (London, 1987)

Horn, D.B., *A Short History of the University* (Edinburgh, 1967)

Hume David, *A True Account of the Behaviour and Conduct of Archibald Stewart* (London, 1748)

—, *Letters*, ed. J.Y.T. Greig, 2 vols (Oxford, 1960)

Hutchison, Sidney, C., *The History of the Royal Academy* (London, 1968)

Jacks, Philip, *The Antiquarian and the Myth of Antiquity* (Cambridge, 1993)

Kay, William, 'The Real William Adam', in *Architectural Heritage* I (Edinburgh, 1990)

King, David, 'In Search of Adam', in *Architectural Heritage* IV (Edinburgh, 1993)

—, *The Complete Works of Robert and James Adam* (Oxford, 1991)

Lambert, J, ed., *Grand Tour* (London, 1935)

Langford, Paul, *A Polite and Commercial People* (Oxford, 1989)

Lenman, Bruce, *The Jacobite Risings in Britain 1689–1746* (Aberdeen, 1995)

—, *Integration and Enlightenment: Scotland 1746–1832* (Edinburgh, 1997)

Macaulay, James, *The Classical Country House in Scotland 1660–1800* (London, 1987)

MacIvor, Iain, *Fort George* (Edinburgh, 2001)

McCormick, Thomas, J., *Charles-Louis Clérisseau and the Genesis of neo-Classicism* (New York, 1990)

McKean, Charles, and Walker, David M., *A History of the Scottish Architectural Profession* (Edinburgh, 1996)

Montagu, Elizabeth, *'Queen of the Blues'*, ed. Reginald Blunt, 2 vols (London, 1923)

Montagu, Lady Mary Wortley, *Selected Letters*, ed. Robert Halsband (London, 1970)

Morant, Philip, *The History of Essex, Vol. I* (London, 1748)

Namier, Sir Lewis, *The Structure of Politics at the Accession of George III* (London, 1957)

Namier, Sir Lewis, and Brooke, John, *The House of Commons, 1754–1790* (London, 1964)

Nyberg, Dorothea, 'La Sainte Antiquité', in *Essays in the History of Architecture Presented to Rudolf Wittkower* (London 1967)

Pailthorpe, Richard, *Syon* (Derby, 2003)

Percy, Thomas, *Reliques of English Poetry* (London, 1767)

Pevsner, N., *Academies of Art, Past and Present* (London, 1940)

'Philasthenes', *A letter from a gentleman in town to his friend in the country relating to the Royal Infirmary of Edinburgh* (Edinburgh, 1739)

Phillipson, N.T. and Mitchison, Rosalind, *Scotland in the Age of Improvement* (Edinburgh, 1970)

Piranesi, Gianbattista, *Diverse manieri d'adonare i Camini* (Rome, 1749)

Pope, Alexander, *Moral Essays, Epistle IV* (Edinburgh, 1751)

Pryke, Sebastian, 'Revolution in Taste', in *Country Life*, vol. 186, no 16, April 1992

Ramsay, Allan, *A Dialogue on Taste* (London, 1757)

Ramsay of Ochtertyre, John, *Scotland and Scotsmen in the Eighteenth Century*, (Bristol, 1996)

Rasmussen, Steen Eiler, *London, the Unique City* (London, 1984)

Reynolds, Sir Joshua, *Discourses on Art*, ed. Robert R. Wark (London, 1924)

Richardson, George, *A Book of Ceilings* (Edinburgh, 1776)

Rigby, Richard, *Authentic Memoirs* (London, 1788)

Rosenthal, Angela, *Angelica Kauffman, Art and Sensibility* (New Haven, 2006)

Rowan, Alistair, J., 'William Adam's Library', in *Architectural Heritage I*, (Edinburgh, 1990)

—, 'After the Adelphi: Forgotten Years in the Adam Brothers' Practice', in *Journal of the Royal Society of Arts*, September 1974

—, 'Robert Adam in Kinross and Edinburgh', in *The Architecture of Scottish Cities*, ed. Deborah Mays, (East Linton, 1997)

—, 'Robert Adam's Idea for the North Bridge in Edinburgh', in *Architectural Heritage*, no. 15, 2004

Roworth, Wendy Wassyng, *Angelica Kauffman, a Continental Artist in Georgian England* (Brighton, 1992)

Russell, Francis, 'The House that Became a Hostage', in *Country Life*, vol. 182, no. 44, Oct 29, 1998

Rykwert, Joseph and Anne, *The Brothers Adam: the Men and the Style* (London, 1985)

Sanderson, Margaret, *Robert Adam and Scotland* (Edinburgh, 1992)

—, 'Robert Adam's Last Visit to Scotland', in *Architectural History*, vol. 25, 1982

Scott, Jonathan, *Piranesi* (London, 1975)

Shanhagan, Roger, *The Exhibition, or a Second Anticipation, being remarks on the principal works to be exhibited next month at the Royal Academy* (London, 1779)

Shaw, Stebbing, *A Tour in 1787 from London to the Western Highlands of Scotland* (London, 1788)

Sheppard, F.H.W., ed., *Survey of London* vol. xxxv, (London, 1970)

Simpson, James, 'The Practical Architect', in *Architectural Heritage 1*, (Edinburgh, 1990)

Smirke, Robert (writing as Anthony Fisgrave), *Midas, or a serious inquiry concerning Taste and Genius* (London, 1808)

Soane, Sir John, *Royal Academy Lectures* (Cambridge, 2000)

Sitwell, Sacheverell, *British Architects and Craftsmen* (London, 1973)

Small, John, *Biographical Sketch of Adam Ferguson* (Edinburgh, 1864)

Steele, Alan, J., *Principal William Robertson* (Edinburgh, 1994)

Steven, William *History of George Heriot's Hospital* (Edinburgh, 1872)

—, *History of the Royal High School of Edinburgh* (Edinburgh, 1849)

Stillman, Damie, 'Robert Adam and Piranesi', in *Essays in the History of Architecture Presented to Rudolf Wittkower* (London, 1967)

—, *The Decorative Work of Robert Adam* (London, 1966)

Stroud, D., *Capability Brown* (London, 1957)

Stuart, James and Revett, Nicholas, *The Antiquities of Athens* (London, 1762)

Summerson, John, *Architecture in Britain*, 1530–1830 (New Haven, 1993)

—, 'The Adam Style', in the *Listener*, London, August, 1953

Swarbrick, John, *Robert Adam and his Brothers* (London, 1915)

—, The Works in Architecture of Robert and James Adam (London, 1959)

Symonds, R.W., 'Adam and Chippendale', in *Country Life* Annual, 1958

Tait, A.A., *Robert Adam – Drawings and Imagination* (Cambridge, 1996)

Tilley, John, *The Foreign Office* (London, 1933)

Topham, Captain Edward, *The Life of Mr Elwes, the Celebrated Miser* (Glasgow, 1795)

—, *Edinburgh Life in the Eighteenth Century* (Glasgow, 1989)

Unger, R., *Hannann und die Aufklärung*, (Jena, 1911)

Veitch, G.S., *The Genesis of Parliamentary Reform* (London, 1965)

Wainwright, Clive, 'George Keate', in *Apollo*, vol. 143, no. 47, January 1996

Walpole, Horace, *Anecdotes of Painting* (London, 1879)

—, *Letters Vol. VIII*, ed. Mrs P. Toynbee (Oxford, 1903)

Warner, Richard, *A Tour through the Northern Counties of England, Vol. 2* (London, 1802)

Watson, J. Steven, *The Reign of George III* (Oxford, 1960)

Wheatley, Henry, B., *The Adelphi and its Site* (London, 1885)

Wilkes, John, *The North Briton*, 3 vols (Dublin, 1764–5)

William Adam at Hopetoun, exhibition catalogue, (Edinburgh, 2004)

Wilton-Ely, John, *The Mind and Art of Giovanni Battista Piranesi* (London, 1988)

Winkelmann, J.J., *Briefe an Bianconi*, ed. W. Rehm and H. Diepholder (Berlin, 1952/58)

Wraxall, Sir William, *Historical Memoirs of My Own Time*, vol. I (London, 1815)

Yarwood, Doreen, *Robert Adam* (London, 1970)

Youngson, A.J., *The Making of Classical Edinburgh* (Edinburgh, 1975)

Index

Note: Where it occurs in as part of a heading or subheading 'RA' stands for Robert Adam and where a relationship is given it is the subject's relationship to Robert. Topics relating to Robert Adam are in the main index sequence but for convenience some of his main character traits and projects have been placed as subheadings under his name together with a chronological outline.

Index

Index